Mauser Military
Rifles of the World

Robert W. D. Ball

Published by

**krause
publications**

700 E. State Street • Iola, WI 54990-0001
Telephone: 715/445-2214

Please call or write for our free catalog of firearms/knives publications.
Our toll-free number to place an order or obtain a free catalog is 800-258-0929
or please use our regular business telephone 715-445-2214 for editorial comment and further information.

Library of Congress Catalog Number: 95-82422
ISBN: 0-87341-828-X
Printed in the United States of America

This book is dedicated to the millions of men who lost their lives while carrying Mauser rifles in conflicts around the world, both large and small . . . in death may they find the peace for which they fought.

Contents

Preface

The purpose of this book is to examine the significance of the Mauser rifle in the military and political histories of countries around the world. Mauser rifles have been, in all likelihood, the most widely used weapons system the world has ever seen.

This is not a book about the Mauser brothers, but some background is required in order to appreciate their genius. In 1866, Peter Paul Mauser was just one of many unheralded employees of the Württemberg government arsenal at Oberndorf when he developed a self-cocking system for the Dreyse needle-rifle. Due to interests in other directions, the Württemberg Army showed little enthusiasm for his improvements. Unfazed, Mauser returned to the drawing board and came up with a modified rifle utilizing a completely self-contained metallic cartridge. Once more, the fates intervened, and his work was rejected by both Prussia and Württemberg. Hoping to seize some advantage from the Austrians' search for an improved rifle after the disastrous war with Prussia, Mauser called upon the Austrian ambassador, who was knowledgeable enough to realize the potential in Mauser's designs and forwarded the plans to Vienna. Here, however, the Mauser rifle faced stiff competition from the Remington Rolling Block rifle. The committee expressed a preference for a block action over a bolt action, albeit acknowledging the advantages of the Mauser system.

Word of Mauser's system came to the attention of Samuel Norris, the Remington Company's agent in Europe, resulting in an agreement wherein Norris would finance the project while the Mauser brothers saw to the startup of the business. Paul, the research and development genius, had by this time been joined by his brother, Wilhelm, the salesman extraordinaire. In 1867, Norris and the Mauser brothers moved to Liege, Belgium to develop the rifle, but Norris broke the contract after the unexpected failure of a deal with the French. Paul returned to Oberndorf in 1869, followed by Wilhelm in 1870.

Meanwhile, the Royal Prussian Military Shooting School became wildly enthusiastic over the Mauser rifle that had been supplied by Norris. This rifle was improved and accepted on 2 Dec 1871. Further improvements to the safety lock resulted in final acceptance of the Infantry Rifle Model 71 on 14 February 1872. Work on the G 71 Rifle was done in government arsenals and large, well-established firms, such as the Austrian Arms Company, Steyr, Austria.

In 1872, the Mausers were awarded contracts for three thousand sights for the G 71 Rifle; they were also awarded an order for one hundred thousand G 71 Rifle sights from the Bavarian Rifle Company in Amberg. At this time, the brothers purchased a factory site in Oberndorf on the heights overlooking the Neckar River. At the end of 1872, they negotiated a contract with the Württemberg government for one hundred thousand G 71 Rifles, and the Mauser brothers were off and running! In March 1874, they formed a partnership with a local bank, the Württemberg Vereinsbank, to purchase the Württemberg Royal Armory. They were able to complete the Württemberg rifle order in 1878, and the factory continued to produce rifle sights for the Bavarian army, while at the same time manufacturing twenty-six thousand G 71 Rifles and Carbines for China. In 1881, a large contract for the Serbian Model 1878/80 Rifles helped ease financial strains.

On 13 January 1882, Wilhelm, master sales strategist for the company, died. In April of 1884, the Waffenfabrik Mauser (Mauser Arms Company), a stock company, was formed. Work was also started on the production of the G 71/84 Rifle, followed in 1887 by a huge contract with the Turkish government for a modified G 71/84 Rifle in 9.5mm. In December of 1887, the Württemberg Vereinsbank sold all shares of stock in Waffenfabrik Mauser, including those of Paul Mauser, to Ludwig Loewe and Company, Berlin. At this time, Loewe and Company owned over fifty percent of the shares of Fabrique Nationale d'Armes de Guerre (FN), Herstal, Belgium. This company, FN, was formed in 1889 to make military rifles for the Belgian government.

On 22 October 1889, a license to allow Mauser rifles to be manufactured in accredited private factories was obtained by the Belgian Minister of War; in June of 1891, Loewe and Co. proposed to directly license FN's Mauser production, with the offer quickly being accepted and a contract signed on 26 November 1891. It was a different story with FN Contract Pattern rifles, since by the middle of 1894 FN had supplied rifles and cartridges to Spain, Serbia, Brazil, Chile, China, Norway, the Netherlands, and Costa Rica. When Chile asked FN to make sixty thousand Mauser rifles, Mauser objected to non-Belgian orders. The Chileans placed their order with Ludwig Loewe & Company.

In November 1896, the Deutsches Waffen-und-Munitionsfabriken A.-G. (German Arms and Ammunition Co., Inc.), otherwise known as DWM, was formed by the merger of:

1.) Deutsche Metallpatronenfabrik A.-G. (German Metallic Cartridge Co., Inc.), Karlsruhe
2.) Ludwig Loewe & Co., A.-G., Berlin
3.) Rheinisch-Westfaelischen Powder Co., Cologne
4.) Rottweil-Hamburg Powder Co., Rottweil

Because of Loewe & Co.'s control of more than fifty percent of the stock in FN, as well as ownership of the Mauser Company, these firms also became a part of DWM. Also included was Osterreichische Waffenfabriks-Gesellschaft. A cartel was then formed to divide production among the participants, with this effort ceasing in 1914.

On 5 April 1897, the Mauser Company became incorporated, and on 5 April 1898, one of the world's most famous rifles, the G 98, was adopted by Germany. This was the basic design upon which many different model designations and calibers were adopted by countries around the world; purchasers included Turkey, China, Serbia, Mexico, Costa Rica, and numerous others, with much of the production being handled by DWM. The Mauser plant had seven thousand employees during World War I and produced great quantities of G 98 rifles, pistols, and 13mm anti-tank rifles during the latter part of 1918, an operation that ceased with the armistice.

With the collapse of Germany in 1918, the cartel was broken, and of all of the prewar participants, only FN managed to carve a niche for itself in the now flourishing export market. A growing competitor was Ceskoslovenska Zbrojovka (CZ), the main arms manufacturer of the new Czechoslovakian Republic. After World War I, the Mauser Company converted to peacetime production, making precision tooling, calculators, sewing machines, etc. The name of the company was changed on 30 May 1922 to Mauser-Werke A.-G. (Mauser Works, Inc.). By 1929, employment stood at approximately 750, in sharp contrast to World War I years.

In the mid-1930s, Germany rearmed, and the Mauser factory responded with frenzied activity … the DWM arms plant at Berlin-Wittenau was taken over as a branch factory, with between 4000 and 5000 employees. Oberndorf employed 7000 in 1936, and by 1944, there were 12,000 workers, 5000 of whom were slave laborers. In addition to vast quantities of K98k Carbines, MG-34 Machine Guns, MG 81 Aircraft Machine Guns, 2cm Flak 38 AA guns, MG 151 Aircraft Cannons, Lugers, P-38s, and Hsc Pistols were also manufactured.

The Mauser plant was occupied by French troops on 20 April 1945. German historical figures on bolt action rifle production were destroyed or lost, however one German estimate puts the figure at approximately 102 million rifles produced!

All of the companies referred to in the preceding pages have contributed in one manner or another to equipping many of the world's armies, small and large. This book is my effort to show, country by country, how the Mauser system, in its vast array of different models and calibers, became a worldwide phenomenon.

Acknowledgments for the First Edition

I have, of necessity, turned to many collectors, curators, dealers, and friends in compiling the information in this book. I have also had the pleasure of contacting military personnel from almost every country represented here. Without exception, everyone has been most helpful and considerate. It would not be possible to name everyone who has helped me in ways both large and small, but know that I thank each and every one of you for helping me to accomplish my goal.

My old friends and companions, Hank Wichmann and Lothar Frank, have patiently read and reread this manuscript, as well as supplied rifles and accessories from their collections to be photographed; you guys have always been there for me! Bob Bennett and Cliff Baumann opened up their Mauser collections and allowed me full access to their material; that's what comes of thirty-plus years of friendship! I want to express my deep appreciation to Bruce Stern for the Sundays he spent with me photographing his fantastic collection, when he could have been spending the time with his family. Thanks to Bruce, I met Noel Schott, now a good friend, who most willingly shipped many of the gems from his collection to me for photographing, putting a lot of faith in the powers of UPS! Craig Brown, curator, cheerfully pulled rare items from his personal collection and carted them into downtown Boston on a really hot summer day for a Sunday photographic session … deeply appreciated, Craig!

John McCabe of the Springfield Armory Museum and I really hit it off, with John spending more time than he could probably spare carefully carrying individual rifles out of storage so I could photograph them one at a time. You really made me feel welcome, John, and you have my thanks!

Thanks to Steve Kehaya and a host of other great people at Century International Arms, Inc. of St. Albans, Vermont. I spent four wonderful days climbing and crawling around warehouse areas searching for the elusive, rare rifle, and with the help of some great fellows in the warehouses, found many a gem to include in the book. Val Forgett, Jr. of Navy Arms Co., and Val Forgett III of Gibbs Rifle Co. most graciously offered me the use of their facilities and stock. I would be remiss if I did not mention Paul Reed of Navy Arms Co. and Larry Trial of Gibbs Rifle Co., who added their considerable knowledge and expertise to the search.

Others who have been most helpful include Steve Fjestad of Blue Book Publications, along with John Allen of the same organization, Chris Cox of the Karabiner Collector's Network (KCN), and John Deeks, collector.

My special thanks go to Col. Guillermo Escobar F., Defense Attache and Chief of the Delegation of Paraguay to the Inter-American Defense Board. Col. Escobar's enthusiasm, knowledge, and helpfulness have been of great importance in compiling the section of the book related to Paraguay. I have come away from this experience feeling that I now have a good friend in the nation of Paraguay.

Major General Cyro Leonardo de Albuquerque, Military Attache of the Embassy of Brazil has devoted much time and effort to make certain that the military history section concerning Brazil is correct, and I owe him my deep thanks. Thanks also to the General, the section on the Mauser military rifles of Brazil was reviewed and corrected by Mr. Walter Merling, Jr. of Rio de Janeiro, a noted Brazilian collector and authority.

Lt. Colonel Milos Rydval, Military Attache of the Embassy of the Czech Republic, extended himself more than any author has the right to expect, enlisting the help of the Historical Institute of the Czech Armed Forces in Prague to assist in clarifying even the smallest question. Your help was invaluable, Colonel!

Express Photo of Avon, Connecticut has gone the extra mile in working with me closely to obtain the best possible results in the developing and printing of pictures used in this book. Thanks to everyone there—you're a great bunch of people!

It has been a joy to work with all of the people at Krause Publications. What could have been extremely difficult has been made a pleasure, and where the chance existed for discord, there has been only cooperation. In effect, I have a sweetheart for an editor!

Hardly the least, my deep thanks and my heart go out to my wife, an excellent editor in her own right. God bless her, after reading and correcting these pages countless times, I don't think she ever wants to see or hear about a Mauser rifle again! Thanks, Joanne!

Since so many, many people went out of their way to help make this book a reality, if I have neglected to thank anyone by name, my apologies … you know who you are, and you know I am indebted to you.

Robert W. D. Ball

Acknowledgments for the Second Edition

If you already have the First Edition of this book, I trust you will find the new photos and previously unavailable specimens and information to be of further help in identifying and classifying unknown pieces. I hope it sparks even more interest in the Mauser rifle, provides answers to other questions you might have had . . . and gives you as much pleasure in perusing its pages as I had in putting it together.

After its initial publication, I received numerous letters asking why this or that model wasn't shown (although, by necessity, only a few were omitted!). In most instances, these particular models or variations were, and remain, so scarce as to be virtually unobtainable for photographing.

However, if you have a Mauser bolt action rifle that you believe is authentic and not in the book, please contact me through the publisher, and perhaps it can be included in the Third Edition.

Friends and contributors Bob Jensen, John Wall, and John Sheehan must be added to my acknowledgments list, for without their assistance many of the new photos and information in this edition would not have been possible. Thanks, guys, for giving so generously of your time. Your efforts on my behalf were "above and beyond" . . . but indicative of dedicated Mauser collectors who appreciate not only the variations of the weapon but its place in military history throughout the world.

ARGENTINA

The Argentine army traces its roots to the colonial period when regular forces were recruited from throughout the region, amounting to a single regiment each of infantry and dragoons, totaling 2,509 men. This strength was increased to 14,141 by 1800. The British invasions of Argentina in 1806 and 1807 were repulsed by a force of infantry, grenadiers, and hussars, as well as a battalion each of coast and field artillery. This force became the new national army when independence from Spain was declared in 1816. In 1817, Argentina helped Chilean forces expel the Spanish from Chile and Peru during a grueling four-year war.

In 1825, the breakaway of Uruguay from Brazil fomented a three-year-long war involving Argentina against Brazil. During the ensuing twenty-three years, there were times of great political confusion and turmoil, with the army fighting against the Patagonian Indians in 1832, warring with the Bolivians from 1837 to 1839, and entering into the affairs of Uruguay in 1844. In 1852, Buenos Aires seceded from the Republic, followed by an attempted overthrow of the national government in 1859, which proved unsuccessful. In 1865, Paraguayan dictator Francisco Solano López, while at war with Brazil, attacked the Argentine city of Corrientes, precipitating the war of the Triple Alliance, in which Argentina, Uruguay and Brazil were allied against Paraguay. This war lasted for five long years, ending in the defeat of the Paraguayan forces and the almost complete decimation of the Paraguayan nation.

1870 saw the transformation of the Argentine army into a truly professional force, occupied for the next ten years with subjugation and pacification of the Indians of the state of Patagonia, as well as controlling internal strife.

The late 1800s saw the reorganization and professional upgrading of the army. In 1879, the army adopted the .43 caliber Remington Rolling Block Rifle as standard, the Remington being supplanted by the Mauser Modelo 1891 magazine rifle and carbine in caliber 7.65mm. The Modelo 1891 weapons served faithfully, but were replaced by the more modern Modelo 1909 Rifle and Cavalry Carbine, also in 7.65mm. The Modelo 1909 was a faithful copy of the German Gew. 98 with slight modifications. These rifles and carbines were produced both in Germany, mainly by DWM, and in Argentine government plants, namely Fabrica Militar de Armas Portatiles (FMAP) "Domingo Mathieu" at Rosario and Santa Fe. Not often found is the Modelpo 1909 Mountain/Engineers Carbine, closely resembling the FN Model 30 Carbine. It has been said that these were cut-down Modelo 1909 Rifles; however the author has not been able to determine that this is accurate. Also not seen frequently on the secondary market are the large numbers of FN Model 24 and Model 30 Short Rifles purchased by the Argentine army during the years between World War I and World War II.

In turn, the Modelo 1909 Rifle was replaced by the FN "FAL" Rifle in 7.62mm NATO, later used in the ill-fated invasion and occupation of the Falkland Islands.

MODEL 1891 RIFLE: Made in Germany, the Argentine Modelo 1891 Rifle is a Mauser magazine rifle, with the protruding, in-line box magazine that was first developed for the Model 1889 Belgian Rifle, and used in the Turkish Model 1890 as well. These rifles all

The Argentine National crest as shown on the receiver ring

closely resemble one another, with only minor differences, the major one being the lack of a barrel jacket on the Argentinian and Turkish models.

The initial contract from Argentina called for 180,000 rifles and 30,000 carbines. Since Mauser was filling a Turkish order, Ludwig Loewe & Co. of Berlin handled the manufacture of the majority of the Argentinian weapons; the rest were produced by DWM.

This rifle introduced the rotary lock, which engaged a notch on the front of the magazine to prevent the accidental loss of the magazine. Other modifications included a reinforced extractor and bolt, as well as extensions to both sides of the bolt sleeve.

The rifle is fitted with a straight-wristed stock, with a small upper hand guard in front of the rear sight base, wired to the barrel. There is a swivel on the bottom of the lower barrel band, with another at the bottom of the stock. The simple nose cap has a bayonet lug on the bottom for the attachment of the Model 1891 bayonet.

Length: 48.60"; **Weight:** 8.80 lbs.; **Barrel:** 29.13"; **Caliber:** 7.65 x 53mm; **Rifling:** 4-groove, r/hand; **Operation:** Turnbolt action; **Feed:** 5-round, vertical-column, box magazine; **Sights:** Inverted-V front sight, V-notch rear to 2,000 meters on large leaf, 350 meters on small leaf, and 250 meters on standard. **Remarks:** Argentine national crest on receiver ring, model designation and manufacturer's markings on side rail.

MODEL 1891 CARBINE: As can be seen, the Model 1891 Carbine is fully stocked to the muzzle with a straight wrist, and has a forend capped with protectors for the front sight, a turned-down bolt handle, and a carbine sling loop attached to the bottom of the stock. Many of these were imported into the United States in excellent condition.

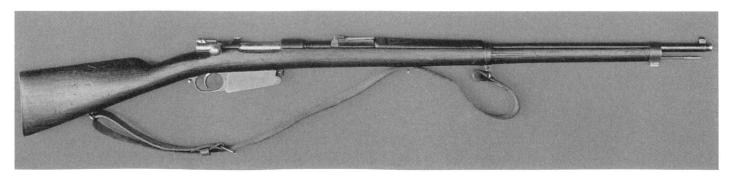

Full-length view of the Modelo 1891 Rifle

Full-length view of the Modelo 1891 Carbine

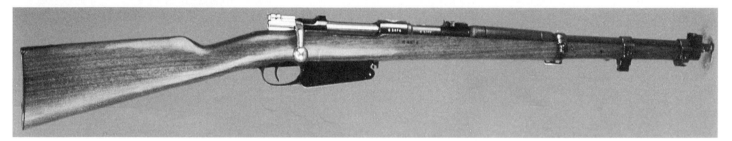

Full-length view of the M1891 Engineer's Carbine; note that these are essentially the M1891 Cavalry Carbine with the addition of an upper band incorporating a half-circle bayonet attachment and a lower band with a bayonet lug. The lowest band now incorporates a sling swivel, with another on the lower left side of the stock. Note that the sling ring bar has been removed and the hole in the stock filled.

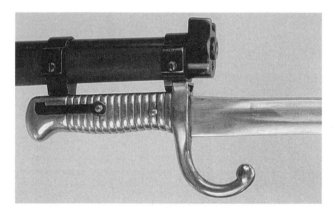

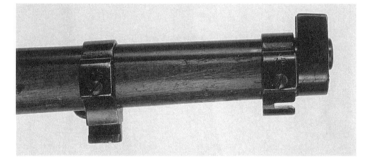

Close-up view of the bayonets lugs permanently attached by screws on the M1891 Engineer carbine.

The M1891 Engineer's Carbine with bayonet attached to illustrate the slot attachment for the half-round bayonet ring on the cut-down M1879 Remington Rolling Block bayonet. This is an altogether ingenious use of an alteration to an out-dated bayonet to utilize existing stocks.

Side rail markings of the Modelo 1891 Carbine (Springfield Armory Museum)

Side rail markings of the Modelo 1891 Rifle and Carbine, indicating that this specimen was produced by DWM

Special presentation plaque attached to the stocks of a Modelo 1891 Rifle and a Modelo 1891 Carbine presented to the United States War Department by the Argentine Ministerio de Guerra in the year 1906 (Springfield Armory Museum)

Crest of the Military Academy above the receiver ring of the Modelo 1891 Rifle

Crest of the Naval Academy above the receiver ring of the Modelo 1891 Rifle

The University Battalion of the Federal District crest above the receiver ring of the Modelo 1891 Rifle

Argentine crest on the receiver of the Modelo 1891 Carbine. Note that this is a slightly different, earlier version of the crest from those shown later. (Springfield Armory Museum)

Argentine crest, or coat of arms, on the receiver ring of the rifle

The Modelo 1891 Rifle with plaque attached to the right side of the buttstock (Springfield Armory Museum)

The Modelo 1891 Carbine with special presentation plaque (Springfield Armory Museum)

Length: 37.0"; **Weight:** 7.20 lbs.; **Barrel:** 17.63"; **Caliber:** 7.65 x 53mm; **Rifling:** 4-groove, r/hand; **Operation:** Turnbolt action; **Feed:** 5-round, vertical-column, box magazine; **Sights:** Inverted-V front, V-notch adjustable from 400 to 1400 meters on large leaf, 350 meters on small leaf, and 250 meters on standard. **Remarks:** Argentine coat of arms on receiver ring, model designation and manufacturer's name.

ARGENTINE MODELO 1909 RIFLE: In 1909, a new model rifle began to replace the 1891 model rifles and carbines; this rifle was based upon the Gew 98 design, modified to Argentinian specifications. The differences included a tangent rear sight rather than the German "Lange Vizier" rear sight, a hinged magazine floorplate with the release in the front of the trigger guard, an upper hand guard extending from the front of the receiver ring to slightly in front of the lower barrel band, and an auxiliary bayonet lug fastened over the original bayonet lug, which enabled the Argentinians to use their large stocks of Modelo 1891 bayonets. It is impossible to determine exactly how many rifles were produced in Germany, but the Argentine production figures are estimated at approximately eighty-five thousand. By Argentinian law, the crest was to be ground off those rifles and carbines sold to foreign buyers, due to embarrassing sales to the Paraguayans during the Chaco War of the 1930s; however, this law was later repealed and many of these weapons came into the United States in untouched, usually excellent condition. These rifles are a collector's dream when found in "as issued" condition, since they never saw combat, and only suffered minor handling dings and bruises.

Length: 49.20"; **Weight:** 9.0 lbs.; **Barrel:** 29.13"; **Caliber:** 7.65 x 53mm; **Rifling:** 4-groove, r/hand; **Operation:** Turnbolt action; **Feed:** 5-round, staggered-column flush box magazine; **Sights:** Inverted-V front sight, V-notch rear sight adjustable from 300 to 2000 meters. **Remarks:** Argentine crest on receiver, Mauser Modelo Argentino 1909, manufacturer's name, with some examples being marked Ejercito Mod. 1909 (Argentine Army Model 1909).

Argentine Air Force Academy cadets on passing out parade, carrying Model 1909 Rifles

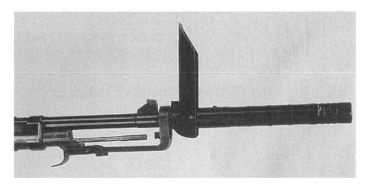

Model 1909 Infantry Rifle with attached Argentine designed and manufactured Grenade Launcher

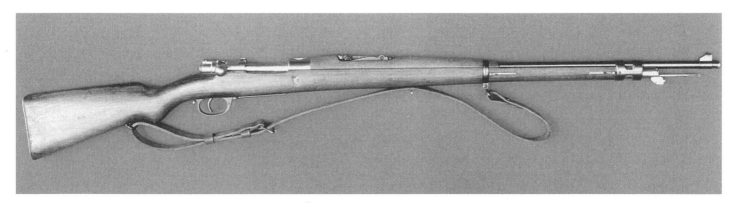

Full-length view of the Argentine Modelo 1909 Rifle

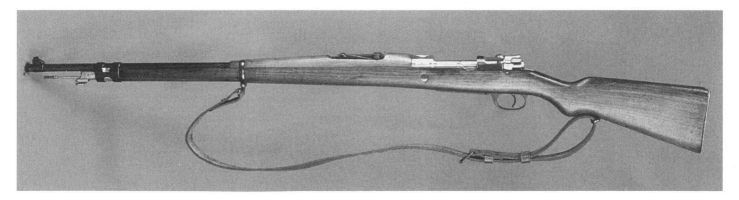

Left full-length view of the Argentine Modelo 1909 Rifle

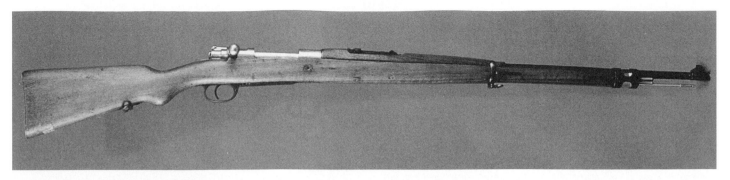

Full-length view of a variation of the Modelo 1909 Rifle. This rifle is unmarked, with the exception of the markings shown in the previous picture. Note that the nose cap does not have the auxiliary bayonet lug.

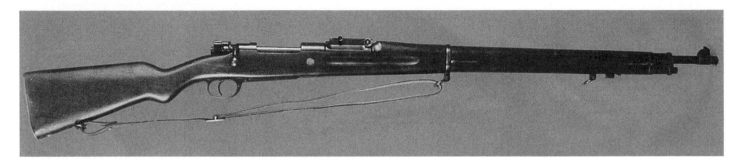

A full-length view of a most unusual variation of the Modelo 1909 Rifle. This rifle has been experimentally restocked in a Springfield Model 1903-style "C" stock with grasping grooves, a Springfield-style rear and front sight, and a most unusual stud-type bayonet lug. The receiver ring is marked in the conventional manner.

The Modelo 1909 side rail, with designation and maker's name

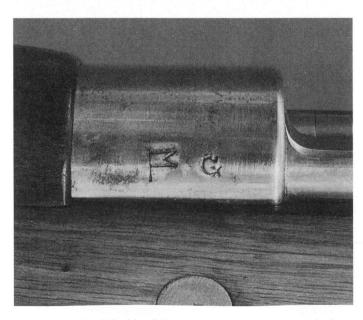

Markings on the left side of the receiver ring of the unmarked Modelo 1909 Rifle pictured above.

Argentine crest, or coat of arms, on the receiver ring of the rifle

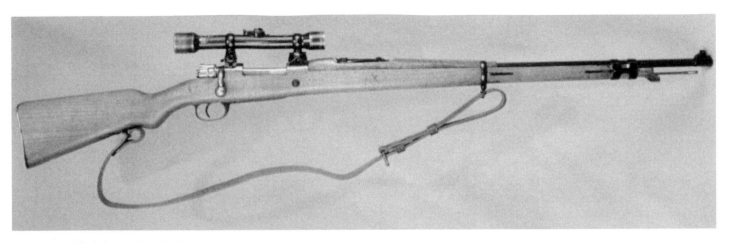

Full-length view of the Argentine Modelo 1909 Sniper Rifle

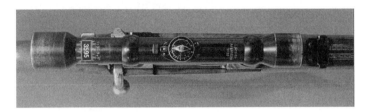

Top view of the Argentine Modelo 1909 Sniper Rifle; note the marking "Ejercito Argentino" over the scope number at the forward end of the barrel. The number visible at the rear of the scope is a collection identification number.

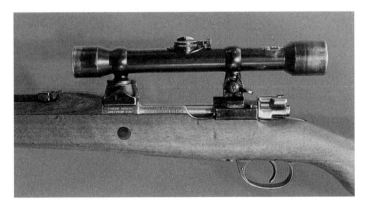

The scope and scope mount from the left hand side of the Argentine Modelo 1909 Sniper Rifle

ARGENTINE MODELO 1909 SNIPER RIFLE: The Argentine Modelo 1909 Sniper Rifle is identical to the standard issue Modelo 1909 Rifle, except the bolt handle has been bent down to prevent the handle from striking the over-the-bore mounted scope. Sniper rifles were picked for their accuracy and smoothness of action. Note that the scope on this rifle is German-made for the Argentine army.

ARGENTINE MODELO 1909 CAVALRY CARBINE: Ordered at the same time as the Modelo 1909 Rifle, the 1909 Cavalry Carbine differed not only in length, but in general configuration. Many of these carbines were produced by DWM; however, the Argentine arms factories also were tooled up to manufacture this carbine, and many will be found with Argentine makers' marks. Equipped with a full Mannlicher-style, straight-wristed stock, the forend is protected by a forecap with sight "ears," and the muzzle extends enough so that it will accept the ring of the model 1891 bayonet, the lug being mounted on the bottom side of the forecap. The upper hand guard extends from the front of the receiver to the lower barrel band. A well-made, handy weapon.

Length: 42.50"; **Weight:** 8.50 lbs.; **Barrel:** 21.50"; **Caliber:** 7.65 x 53mm; **Rifling:** 4-groove, r/hand; **Operation:** Turnbolt action; **Feed:** 5-round, staggered-column, flush, box magazine; **Sights:** Tangent leaf rear sight graduated to 1400 meters.

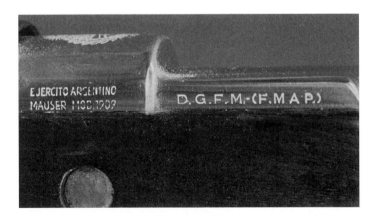

Side rail markings of the Modelo 1909 Cavalry Carbine

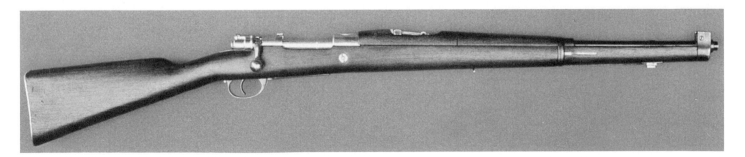

Full-length view of the Modelo 1909 Cavalry Carbine

M1909 Cavalry Carbine with the marking "C.F.S.," which translates into "Commando Federal Seguridad," which is the name of Juan Peron's Secret Police.

M1909 Cavalry Carbine with the markings of the "Gendarmeria Nacional," or National Police

Argentine Marine Corps markings of furled anchor surmounted by crossed cannons on the receiver ring of the FN Model 1930 Short Rifle. (Robert Jensen collection)

Remarks: Argentine crest on the receiver ring, with the maker's name and model designation on the left side rail.

ARGENTINE MODELO 1909 MOUNTAIN CARBINE: There is no definitive history of the Modelo 1909 Mountain Carbine. Some authorities have also referred to it as the "Engineers" model. The few carbines that the author has inspected have all been marked identically to the Modelo 1909 Rifle. It has been speculated that these carbines were cut down from the Modelo 1909 Rifles as a special purpose carbine. Note that the specimen pictured has a short bayonet lug, and incorporates a parade hook on the upper band.

Length: 41.25"; **Weight:** 8.5 lbs.; **Barrel:** 21.25"; **Caliber:** 7.65 x 53mm; **Rifling:** 4-groove, r/hand; **Operation:** Turnbolt; **Feed:** 5-round, staggered-column, flush box magazine; **Sights:** Tangent leaf rear sight graduated to 1400 meters. **Remarks:** Argentine

crest on the receiver ring, maker's name and model designation on the side rail.

AUSTRIA

After the fall of Rome, the territory that was to become Austria was overrun by the Huns, Lombards, Ostrogoths, and Bavarians. In 788 it was incorporated into the empire of Charlemagne, and from the 9th to the 13th century was divided among a number of feudal domains. In the late 13th century, Austria was reunited under Rudolph I of Hapsburg whose dynasty became synonymous with Austrian history for the following seven centuries. By the reign of Charles V (1500-1558), Austria ruled not only the Holy Roman Empire, encompassing most of central Europe, but also Spain, all of Spain's colonies, and the Netherlands.

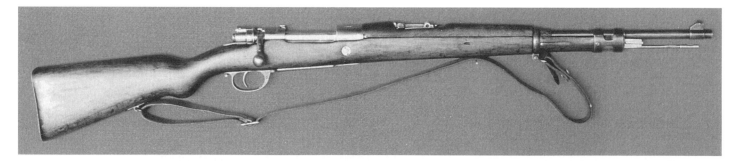

Full-length view of the Modelo 1909 Mountain Carbine

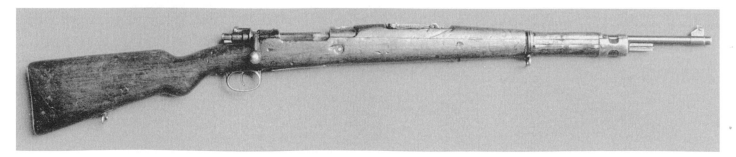

Full-length view of the FN Model 1930 Short Rifle as purchased by Argentina for use by the Argentinian Marine Corps.

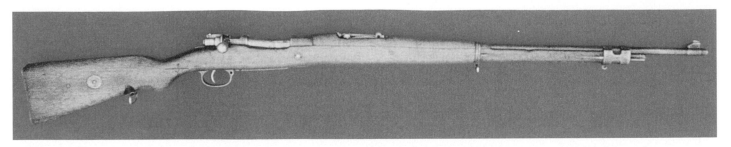

Right side view of the Austrian Model 1914 Mauser Rifle; note the oversize sling swivel on the bottom of the buttstock. (John Sheehan collection)

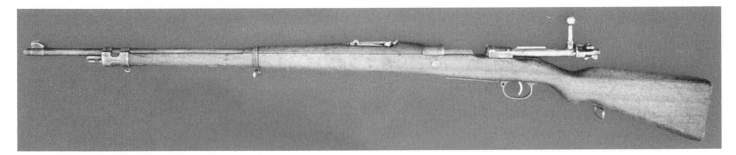

Left side view of the Austrian Model 1914 Mauser Rifle with the bolt in the fully open position. (John Sheehan collection)

After the Thirty Years War (1618-1648), Austria's power declined, but was confirmed in the valley of the Danube after the defeat of the Turkish siege of Vienna in 1683 and the subsequent reconquest of Hungary from the Turks. In 1804, the Austrian empire was founded, and two years later the defunct Holy Roman Empire was abolished. The Ausgleich, or compromise of 1867 transformed the empire into the Dual Monarchy of Austria-Hungary.

In 1914, the assassination of the Archduke Franz Ferdinand, heir to the Austrian throne, led to the outbreak of World War One, with all its resultant tragedy. At the end of the war there was a wholesale redrawing of national boundaries in Central Europe, with Austria emerging as a small Alpine republic retaining about 12 percent of the territory of the old Dual Monarchy. Austria was faced with a terrible political and economic situation following World War One. After the rise of Hitler in 1933, Germany finally forced Austrian unification (the Anschluss) with Greater Germany in 1938. Overrun by American and Russian forces in 1945, Austria was divided into four zones of occupation, American, British, Russian and French, with the occupying forces permitting the formation of a unified national government. The occupation ended in 1955 with the signing of the Austrian State Treaty and the withdrawal of the four power forces.

The Austrian economy, decimated after World War Two, has flourished in the post-war years under a modest form of socialism and with a great boost from the Marshall Plan. Petroleum reserves, tourism, and a highly developed manufacturing sector have greatly contributed to the prosperity of Austria.

AUSTRIAN MODEL 1914 MAUSER RIFLE: In all respects, this rifle is identical to the Model 1912 rifles produced for Mexico, Chile and Columbia, with the exception of the key identifier to Austrian use. Pressed into use because of the ever-increasing need for more rifles at the beginning of the World War One, rifles issued in the Austrian service had their Mauser-style detachable swivel base converted to fit the standard-issue Austrian sling. A very large sling swivel was added to the original base in order to accept the large retaining buckle of the Austrian-pattern sling. Many, but not all rifles were unit marked on either the buttplate, or the buttplate tang.

BELGIUM

From the beginning of the recorded history of gunmaking, Belgium has been in the forefront of firearms development, as well as being an innovator in the design and development of the machinery nec-essary to produce the guns. The ingenuity of the Belgians produced the machinery that enabled the English and the Germans to start up their early gunmaking facilities. Belgian production efforts ran the gamut from the finest, most modern factories, to the poorest garage job-shops that turned out weapons of highly questionable quality for the overseas markets.

The "Manufacture De L'Etat a Liege," a state-run facility, no longer manufactures firearms, but Fabrique Nationale d'Armes de Guerre, more commonly known as "FN," is one of the largest privately-held arms manufacturing plants in the world. This company was formed in 1889 by a syndicate of Liege and Ludwig Loewe & Co. of Berlin, Germany, with the intent of producing Mauser rifles for the armed forces of Belgium. With the defeat of Germany in World War I, FN took over the overseas markets formerly monopolized by Germany, becoming, along with Czechoslovakia, one of the largest suppliers of military weapons in the world.

The Belgian armed forces used the Model 1889 Rifle and Carbine, in all its various models and variations, during the First, as well as the Second World War. Ever a thrifty people, the Belgians modified the 1889 model rifle in 1916, and again in 1936, thus utilizing the vast stocks of Model 1889 weapons on hand and at the same time bringing them into closer conformity with guns produced in more recent years. These weapons have seen service in the jungles of Equatorial Africa, as well as on the battlefields of Europe.

Belgian troops carrying Model 1889 Rifles on route march in a rear area of Belgium, C.1914

Full-length view of the Model 1889 Rifle

The receiver markings on the Model 1889 Rifle

Belgian M1889 Rifle stock cartouche. (Robert Jensen collection)

MODEL 1889 RIFLE: This rifle is the grandfather of all Mauser one-piece bolt designs, with only slight differences between it and those developed at a later date by the Germans. Adopted on 6 February 1892, it was produced at FN, Fabrique d'Armes de L'Etat, Hopkins and Allen in Norwich, Connecticut, as well as in Birmingham, England. Produced for the Belgian armed forces until 1925, total production of this rifle is estimated in excess of 275,000, with approximately 8,000 of those made at the Hopkins and Allen plant. The barrel is covered with a barrel casing for protection of the barrel and the user's hand during operation. The bolt is equipped with only two forward locking lugs, the end of the striker is threaded and has a rib that engages a lengthwise slot in the bolt sleeve to prevent the firing pin from rotating, the cocking piece is held by a notch at the rear of the bolt to keep the sleeve from accidentally turning, there is no safety flange on the bolt sleeve, and the extractor is a short steel claw in the bolt between the two locking lugs. The detachable, single line, vertical column box magazine projects beneath the receiver.

During the invasion of Belgium in World War I, large quantities of this rifle were seized by the Germans, with many issued to support troops without alteration; however it appears that sizable quantities were converted to accept the German 7.92mm cartridge.

Length: 50.0"; **Weight:** 8.1 lbs.; **Barrel:** 30.7"; **Caliber:** 7.65 x 53mm; **Rifling:** 4-groove, r/hand; **Operation:** Turnbolt action; **Feed:** 5-round single line, vertical-column detachable magazine; **Sights:** Ramp-and-leaf sight graduated to 1,900 meters. **Remarks:** Name of manufacturer on receiver ring, serial number on the side, along with proof marks.

Belgian M89 Rifle butt plate markings. (Robert Jensen collection)

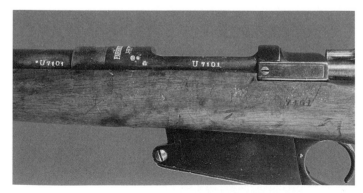

This picture shows the serial number on the left side of the barrel, the side rail, and the stock of the Belgian Model 1889 Rifle.

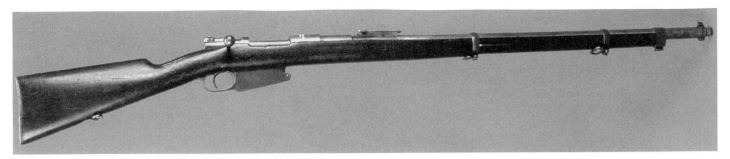

Full-length view of the Belgian Model 1889 Rifle as made by Hopkins and Allen, Norwich, Connecticut (Cliff Baumann collection)

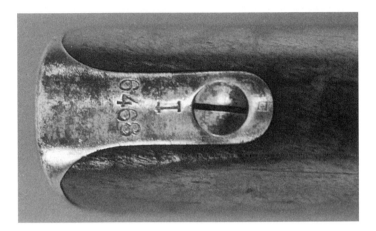

M1889 Rifle butt plate tang numbers

Belgian M1889 Rifle receiver markings indicating that this piece was made in Birmingham, England under the direction of a group of patriotic Belgian refugees.

Receiver markings of the Belgian Model 1889 Rifle produced by Hopkins and Allen of Norwich, Connecticut (Cliff Baumann collection)

MODEL 1889 CARBINE WITH BAYONET: This carbine model of the 1889 rifle differs only in dimensions. It has a shorter barrel and shorter overall length—41.0 inches. Utilizing the standard rifle bayonet, this carbine is commonly referred to as the Carbine M1889 with Bayonet.

MODEL 1889 CARBINE WITH "YATAGHAN": Issued to Foot Gendarmes and fortress Artillery troops, this carbine has the action, stock, and barrel band/nose cap of the Infantry rifle. The barrel band is closer to the nose cap than to the rear sight, and the bolt handle is generally bent downward. The term "with Yataghan" refers to the sword bayonet used with this weapon. These bayonets that were in the hands of the Foot Gendarmerie were replaced with the Mle 16 epee-type bayonet in 1916. Overall length of the carbine is 41.14 inches, with a barrel length of 21.65.

MODEL 1889 CARBINE "LIGHTENED": This carbine is simply a much-shortened form of the infantry rifle; a true cavalry carbine in every sense of the word. With a turned-down bolt, the rear sight mounted on the receiver ring reinforce, and the forend extending only to the barrel band, thus exposing quite a bit of the barrel jacket and cleaning rod, this carbine is readily identifiable. The barrel is 15.75 inches long, sighted to 1900 meters, with the overall length only 34.85 inches. Another identifying feature is the slotted sling bracket screwed to the left side of the buttstock for attachment to the carrying stud worn on the leather harness.

World War One Belgian troops equipped with Model 1889 Rifles, firing at the Germans from a fixed position

Full-length view of the Belgian Model 1889 Carbine (Springfield Armory Museum)

Receiver markings on the Belgian Model 1889 Carbine (Springfield Armory Museum)

Belgian troops armed with the Model 1889 Carbine in a shallow firing position. These troops are obviously not in contact with the enemy.

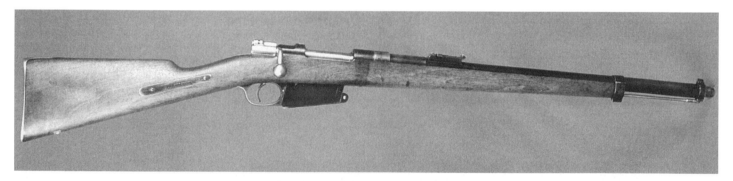

Full-length view of the right hand side of the Belgian Model 1889 Carbine, Lightened version

Full-length view of the left hand side of the Belgian Model 1889 Carbine, Lightened version. Note the slotted sling attachment.

Close-up view of the slotted sling attachment on the left side of the wrist of the stock of the 1889 Carbine, Lightened version

MODEL 1889 CARBINE "LIGHTENED WITH YATAGHAN": This carbine is the same as the Model 1889 Carbine "Lightened," but is equipped with a longer stock, the lower band almost directly behind the upper band, or nose cap. Swivels are mounted on the lower barrel band and on the butt, as with the other carbines; however, this version also a special bracket, different from the preceding carbine. This carbine was also issued with the "yataghan" version bayonet, until replaced by the Mle 16 epee bayonet in 1916.

MODEL 1890 TURKISH MAUSER RIFLE: Captured by the British and supplied to the Belgians. During the Mesopotamia campaign and the ill-advised Gallipoli expedition, the British captured large numbers of Turkish Model 1890 rifles which were the same caliber as those used by the Belgians. These were converted to conform as closely as possible to the Belgian-pattern weapons by replacing the rear sight with the M1889 pattern, eliminating the hand guard, and heavily proofing the barrel and receiver. Other than the proofs, no additional markings were added, and all of the original Turkish markings were allowed to remain.

MODEL 1916 CARBINE: Adopted during the First World War to replace the various types of carbines in use, this carbine is similar to the Model 1889 with "Yataghan" bayonet, but has a new style bracket in the buttstock.

MODEL 1935 SHORT RIFLE: At first, Gew 98s were converted at the Manufacture d'Armes de L'Etat, but between 1935 and 1940, the Model 1935 Short Rifle was manufactured by FN at Liege. This short rifle is a typical standard Model 1898-pattern Mauser action with a non-rotating extractor, a safety lug on the bolt, and most of the improvements to be found on the Gew. 98. The magazine is flush with the bottom of the action, and the barrel jacket is discarded. Interestingly, hinged barrel bands are used, and a stacking swivel is included at the rear of the bayonet lug.

Length: 43.58"; **Weight:** 8.995 lbs.; **Barrel:** 23.43"; **Caliber:** 7.65 x 53mm; **Rifling:** 4-groove, r/hand; **Operation:** Turnbolt action; **Feed:** 5-round staggered-column, flush box magazine; **Sights:** Tangent leaf sight graduated to 2000 meters. **Remarks:** Manufacturer's markings on the receiver ring.

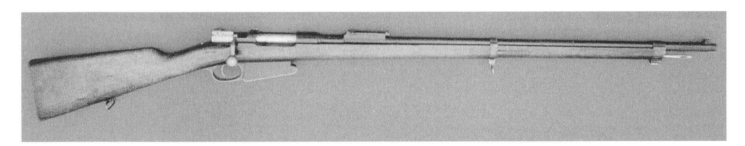

Right side view of the Belgian acquired Turkish Model 1890 Mauser Rifle, converted to conform to Belgian standards; note the bent bold handle. (John Sheehan collection)

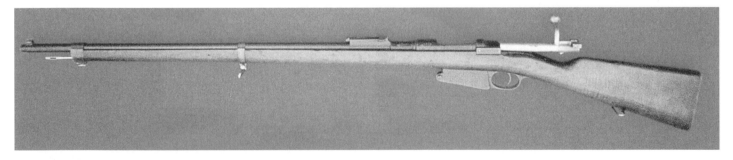

Left side view of the Belgian/Turkish Model 1890 Mauser Rifle with bolt in the fully open position. (John Sheehan collection)

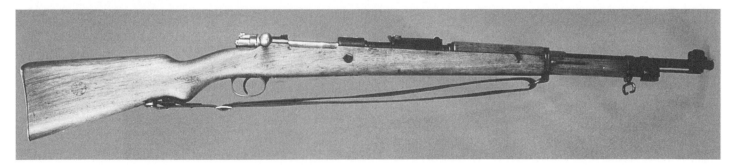

Full-length view of the Belgian Model 1935 Short Rifle

Receiver ring of the Belgian Model 1935 Short Rifle, showing the crown over "L" for Leopold, King of the Belgians

MODEL 1889/36 SHORT RIFLE: In 1936, in order to standardize along the lines of the Model 1935 Short Rifle, conversion of the stocks of Model 1889 Rifles and Carbines commenced in the factory of Pieper and Cie. in Herstal, as well as at the Manufacture d'Armes de L'Etat, and continued until 1940. The resulting rifle combined the action and the shortened stock of the Model 1889 with the barrel, sights, forend, and hinged upper barrel band of the Model 1935 Short Rifle. In order to strengthen the stock, a recoil bolt was also incorporated through the stock beneath the chamber, just forward of the magazine.

Side view of the action of the Belgian Model 89/36 Short Rifle, showing proofs and serial number (Cliff Baumann collection)

Receiver ring markings on the Belgian Model 89/36 Short Rifle (Cliff Baumann collection)

Length: 43.07"; **Weight:** 8.31 lbs.; **Barrel:** 23.62"; **Caliber:** 7.65 x 53mm; **Rifling:** 4-groove, r/hand; **Operation:** Turnbolt; **Feed:** 5-round, vertical column, box magazine; **Sights:** Tangent leaf sight graduated to 2000 meters. **Remarks:** Manufacturer's name on receiver ring.

MODELS 35/46 AND 50 SHORT RIFLES: After World War II, the Belgian armed forces were supplied with tremendous quantities of surplus U.S. weapons and ammunition with which to re-equip. All surviving Model 1935 Rifles were converted to handle the U.S. .30-06 cartridge. These conversions required cutting a notch in the face of the receiver ring to accommodate the longer U.S. cartridge, while the guides on the receiver were recut to accept the U.S. chargers, or clips.

Production of new Mle 1950-type rifles began in the FN factory in Herstal, with the magazine well lengthened to accept the American cartridge, even though the notch in the face of the receiver ring was retained. The track for the left locking lug was milled through the shoulder in the receiver ring, while the receiver was marked with a crowned "B" (for "Baudoin") above "ABL" and the date of manufacture. This rifle is basically the 1924 export model rechambered for .30-06 ammunition.

Length: 43.50"; **Weight:** 8.95 lbs.; **Barrel:** 23.23"; **Caliber:** .30-06; **Rifling:** 4-groove, r/hand; **Operation:** Turnbolt action; **Feed:** 5-round, staggered-column, flush, box magazine; **Sights:** Tangent leaf sight graduated to 2000 meters. **Remarks:** Manufacturer's markings on the receiver ring, or on the 1950 models, a crowned "B" / "ABL" / date. Apparently, "L" marked specimens also exist.

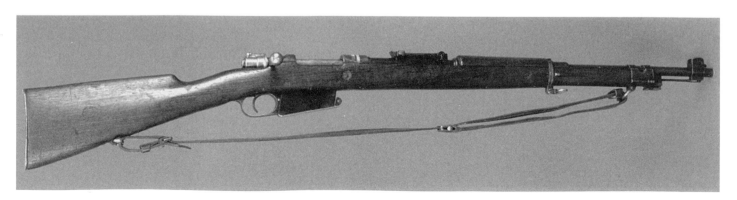

Full-length view of the Belgian Model 89/36 Short Rifle (Cliff Baumann collection)

Composite grouping of Belgian weapons, from top to bottom:
1) M1889 Rifle
2) M1889 Carbine
3) M1935 Short Rifle
4) M89/36 Short Rifle
(Robert Jensen collection)

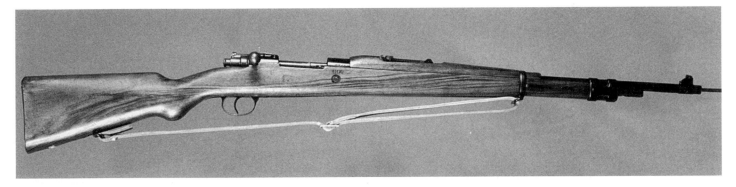

Full-length view of the Belgian Model 24/30 .22 caliber training rifle developed for the Belgian army. The army model has a blue/black finish.

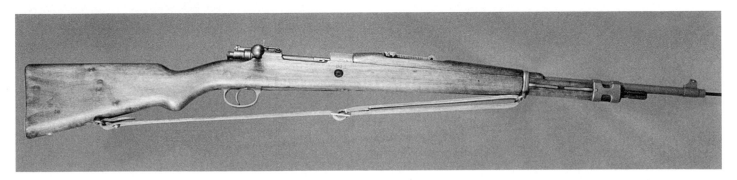

Full-length view of the Belgian Model 24/30 naval .22 caliber training rifle. The naval model is done in a gray-green finish.

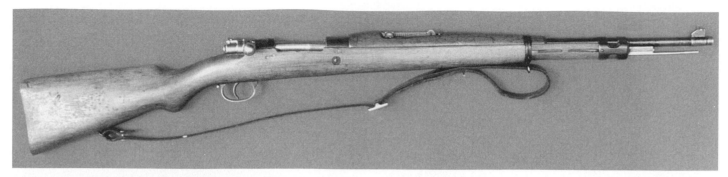

Post-World War II unmarked FN Model 30 style Short Rifle with a straight bolt handle

The receiver ring of the Belgian Model 24/30 army .22 caliber training rifle. Note the crown over "B" (Baudoin), over "ABL" (Armee Belge Leger), over the date of manufacture.

Between the First and Second World War, FN developed contract model Mauser rifles for overseas sales, trying to fill the gaps in the ranks of the suppliers caused by the defeat of Germany. Some of the finest weapons developed were the Models 1924 and 1930, which were almost custom designed to fit the customer's specifica-

tions. There is little difference between the two basic model designations, with customer modifications counting in large part for the differences.

After the Second World War, Model 24/30 .22 caliber training rifles were produced for both the Belgian army and the navy. These rifles were standard in every way with the exception of caliber.

BOLIVIA

While Bolivia was the first of the South American countries to rise in rebellion against Spanish rule (with an uprising in 1661) ironically, in 1825, it became the last country of the southern continent to achieve independence from royalist Spain. From 1835 to 1839, Bolivia formed a confederation with Peru, which, although able to resist attempted invasions by Argentina and Chile, finally collapsed from internal dissension.

The War of the Pacific (1879-1883) was an utter disaster for Bolivia, which was allied with Peru against an invasion by Chile. Chile won the war; Bolivia lost the province of Antofagasta and along with it, their access to the sea. In 1904, after a short and bitter war against Brazil (the Acre War), Bolivia lost even more of her territory.

Unable to gain a seacoast advantage on the Pacific coast, the Bolivians turned eastward, hoping to gain a route to the Atlantic Ocean by establishing a port on the navigable Paraguay River. The territory in question was equally claimed and occupied by Paraguay,

View of the crest of the Belgian Model 24/30 naval .22 caliber training rifle. This shows the crown/"B"/"ABL"/date of manufacture markings common to this rifle.

Bolivian crest as found on the receiver ring of Bolivian rifles (Springfield Armory Museum)

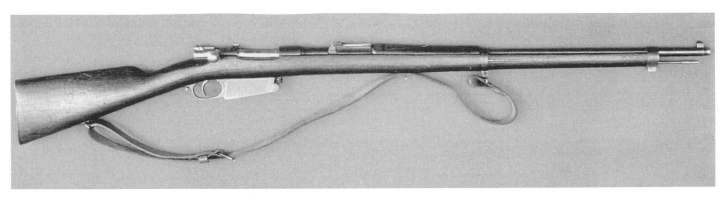

Full-length view of the Bolivian Modelo 1895 version of the Argentine Modelo 1891 Rifle

which was justifiably upset by any Bolivian incursions. Following years of international diplomatic discussions, including arbitration by U.S. President Rutherford B. Hayes, and armed incursions in the areas by both countries, full scale war erupted between Bolivia and Paraguay. The resulting conflict, the Chaco War of 1932-1935, again saw defeat and territorial losses for Bolivia. The Bolivians did, however, obtain access to the sea as a result of the peace negotiations.

The defeats suffered by the Bolivians resulted in extreme and continuing political instability, the final result being the revolution of 1952. In 1967, Che Guevara decided that Bolivia was ripe for communist rebellion, but with full credit to the Bolivian military, Guevara's failing efforts were intercepted, resulting in his capture and eventual death. This provided a necessary boost in morale to the Bolivian armed forces.

Despite international disfavor because of the apparent lack of concerted effort to interdict the drug suppliers of the area, the Bolivian army has been in a position to re-equip during the 1970s and 80s, and are now acknowledged to have made great progress in recent years.

During the late 1890s, Bolivia was able to acquire weapons from Argentina, including fifteen thousand Modelo 1891 (Argentine Pattern) Mauser Rifles. In 1905, realizing that the military establishment needed serious upgrading, a French military mission was engaged. During this period, four thousand Modelo 1907 Mauser Rifles and one thousand Modelo 1907 Short Rifles were purchased from DWM of Berlin, Germany. The First World War cut off the easy access to military equipment that had been previously enjoyed. After the war, there was reorganization and re-equipping on a modest level. In 1926, due to the increased tensions with Paraguay, Bolivia contracted with Vickers Ltd. of Great Britain for huge quantities of war material, including thirty-six thousand Czech-made VZ 24 Short Rifles; this contract was later suspended, but not before at least thirty-nine thousand rifles had been delivered. The great majority of these were VZ 24s, with an undetermined number of German Export Model Standard Modell Rifles making up the balance. During a truce in 1933, an additional forty-five thousand VZ 24s were purchased to compensate for the huge battle losses suffered by the Bo-

livian army. By 12 June 1935, both sides were exhausted and an armistice was signed, with hostilities ceasing two days later. During the armistice, Bolivia continued to purchase Czech VZ 24 Short Rifles, buying a further twenty thousand prior to 1938. The last Mauser rifles to be obtained by Bolivia were the M1950 Czech-made Short Rifle, very similar to the German 98K. These rifles were identified as "Fusil Mauser Boliviano Serie B-50," and were purchased during the period 1950-1952.

MODELO 1895 RIFLE (ARGENTINE MODELO 1891 PATTERN RIFLE): This rifle, purchased from the Argentinian government and presumably made in Argentine Government Arsenals, is identical to the Argentine Modelo 1891 Rifle, with the exception of the Bolivian markings on the receiver ring. All information relative to the rifle will be found under the Argentine section.

MODELO 1907 RIFLE: The Modelo 1907 Rifle and Short Rifle were standard German export model pattern 1904 rifles; these were sold commercially, and were available in calibers 6.5mm, 7mm, 7.65mm and 7.92mm. The rifle is fitted with a pistol grip stock, with the upper hand guard extending from the front of the receiver ring to just beyond the lower barrel band. There is a swivel on the bottom of the lower barrel band, with another on the bottom of the buttstock; there is also a hole in the upper front of the trigger guard

The side rail of the Bolivian Modelo 1907 Rifle, with the DWM markings (Springfield Armory Museum)

Full-length view of the Modelo 1907 Rifle. Note that this rifle is missing the lower sling swivel and cleaning rod. (Springfield Armory Museum)

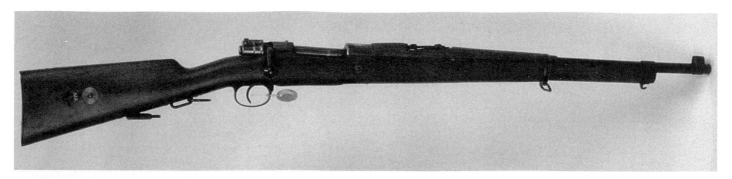

Full-length view of the Bolivian Modelo 1907 Short Rifle (Springfield Armory Museum)

"DWM" marking on the side rail of the Modelo 1907 Short Rifle (Springfield Armory Museum)

to shorten the sling with the use of the sling attachment. Note that the rifle is equipped with the narrow upper band, short bayonet lug, tangent leaf rear sight, and parade hook common to this export version of the Gew 98. Approximately four thousand rifles were purchased from Germany.

Length: 49.0"; Weight: 8.30 lbs.; Barrel: 29.50"; Caliber: 7.65 x 53mm; Rifling: 4-groove, r/hand; Operation: Turnbolt action; Feed: 5-round, staggered-column, flush, box magazine; Sights: Tangent leaf rear sight adjustable to 2000 meters. Remarks: Bolivian crest on the receiver ring, manufacturer's markings on the side rail.

MODELO 1907 SHORT RIFLE: According to records, approximately one thousand Modelo 1907 Short Rifles were purchased from Germany for troop use. These short rifles are identical to the 1907 rifle, except for length, weight, turned-down bolt handle, straight wristed stock, and a carbine-style sling loop at the bottom of the wrist.

Length: 41.50"; Weight: 7.80 lbs; Barrel: 22.25"; Caliber: 7.65 x 53mm; Rifling: 4-groove, r/hand; Operation: Turnbolt action; Feed: 5-round, staggered-column, flush, box magazine; Sights: Tangent leaf rear sight adjustable to 2,000 meters. Remarks: Bolivian national crest on the receiver ring, manufacturer's markings on the side rail.

CZECH MODELO VZ 24 SHORT RIFLE: This short rifle, imported from Czechoslovakia during the 20s and 30s, is covered under the section on Czechoslovakia. The Bolivian model is in caliber 7.65mm.

EXPORT MODEL 1933 "STANDARD MODELL MAUSER BANNER" SHORT RIFLE: This rifle was developed by the Germans after World War I and incorporated design features that had been found desirable from the Germans' experience in the war, resulting in a shortened version of the Gew 98 with the improved tangent leaf rear sight. This short rifle was available in 7mm, 7.65mm, and 7.92mm, and was produced with a straight bolt handle, an upper hand guard extending from in front of the rear sight to just beyond the lower barrel band, an upper band with parade hook, and grasping grooves in the stock. The gun is marked with a Mauser banner trademark on the receiver bridge, while the side rail is marked "Standard Modell."

Bolivian soldier guarding VZ 24 Rifles and German ammunition cases during the Chaco War (Kurt Severin)

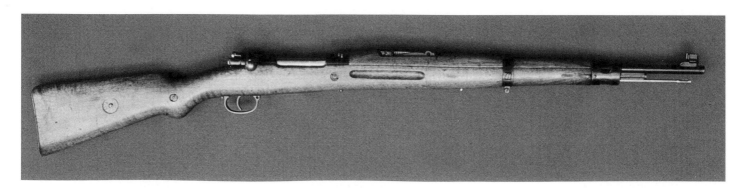

Full-length view of the Bolivian Modelo VZ 24 Short Rifle

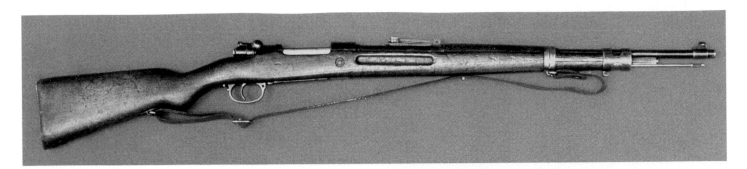

Full-length view of the Export Model Standard Modell Short Rifle

Length: 43.60"; **Weight:** 8.80 lbs.; **Barrel:** 23.62"; **Caliber:** 7.65 x 53mm; **Rifling:** 4-groove, r/hand; **Operation:** Turnbolt action; **Feed:** 5-round, staggered-column, flush, box magazine; **Sights:** Tangent leaf rear sight adjustable to 2000 meters. **Remarks:** Manufacturer's marks on the receiver bridge, with model designation on the left side rail.

BOLIVIAN MODELO 1950 RIFLE (FUSIL MAUSER BOLIVIANO SERIE B-50): The last Mauser rifle to appear in the Bolivian arsenal was the Modelo 1950, made by BRNO of Czechoslovakia from 1950 to 1952. Combining features of the Czech VZ 24 Short Rifle and the German 98K Carbine, the trigger guard assembly, magazine, cupped butt plate, and upper barrel band were stamped steel. The upper and lower barrel bands are held by a single spring on the right side of the stock, and the stock is furnished with a sling swivel on the lower barrel band and the underside of the buttstock.

Length: 43.30"; **Weight:** 8.58 lbs.; **Barrel:** 23.62"; **Caliber:** 7.65 x 53mm; **Rifling:** 4-groove, r/hand; **Operation:** Turnbolt action; **Feed:** 5-round, staggered-column, flush, box magazine; **Sights:** Tangent rear sight graduated to 2000 meters. **Remarks:** Bolivian crest over "Serie B-50" on the receiver ring, Czech manufacturer's markings on the side rail.

A Bolivian foot patrol making its way through the extremely dusty, arid Chaco undergrowth The first and third men on patrol are carrying Czech VZ 24 Short Rifles, while the second man appears to be using a Steyr-Solothurn MP 34 Submachine Gun. (Hist B&W) (Kurt Severin)

BRAZIL

At the end of the eighteenth century, Portugal, allied with Spain, was being ground under the heel of Napoleon as battles were raging over the Portuguese countryside. The Portuguese royal family was forced to flee to Brazil, an overseas possession that had been under Portuguese rule from 1500. Prince Pedro, the son of the King of Portugal, was left in Brazil as Regent upon the return of the royal family to the motherland. In 1822, without the consent or the opposition of the royal family, Pedro was crowned Emperor of Brazil.

Between 1826 and 1828, the recently incorporated Province of Cisplatina rebelled against Brazil and became independent following a disastrous military confrontation conducted by the Brazilian forces. Although Argentina supported the rebels, there was no declaration of war, so no action was taken against the Republic of Argentina during that particular period of time. The conflict resulted in the secession of Uruguay, which became an independent Republic. A military revolt soon occurred, with Emperor Pedro abdicating in favor of his five-year-old son, who became Emperor Pedro II, although he remained under the tutelage of a Regent until he reached his fifteenth birthday. During Pedro II's reign, he proved to be an enlightened, democratically inclined leader of his country, encouraging greatly increased European immigration and improving the lot of his subjects. During his reign, there was a brief war in 1852 against the Argentinian tyrant, Rosas, and in 1865, Brazil headed the Triple Alliance of Argentina, Brazil, and Uruguay in the war against Paraguay, which lasted for five years and resulted in the death of the Paraguayan dictator, Francisco Solano López. The war also caused the utter decimation of the Paraguayan nation, leaving only twenty-three thousand males alive in the entire country.

In his attempt to emancipate the slaves of Brazil, Pedro II evoked the wrath of wealthy landowners and was forced to abdicate; a Republic was declared in 1889, administered by a military govern-

A Bolivian two-man mounted patrol, armed with Czech VZ 24 Short Rifles, checks before leaving heavy cover during the Chaco War (Kurt Severin)

the government until the early 1980s. Since that time, Brazil has enjoyed a more democratically inclined government.

MODEL 1894 RIFLE: After extensive and strenuous testing, the Brazilian government adopted the Model 1894 Mauser Rifle, known as the Fusil Mo. 1894. This rifle is identical to the Spanish Model 1893 Rifle, with the exception of a cylindrical bolt head, rather than a flat-bottomed bolt head, allowing the bolt to close on an empty chamber. These rifles were produced by Ludwig Loewe & Co. (1894-1896), DWM (1897-189?), and FN (1894-1899); the au-

Side rail of the Model 1894 Rifle, showing manufacturer's markings, with the Portuguese spelling of "Berlin" (Century International Arms, Inc.)

Brazilian soldiers from various branches of the army in a composite picture.

Early version of the Brazilian national crest on the Model 1894 Rifle. (Century International Arms, Inc.)

ment until 1894. For the forty years following, Brazil enjoyed peace and prosperity, aside from some occasional internal dissension. In 1917 the Brazilian government entered World War I on the side of the Allies, providing naval assistance for the balance of the war. A revolution by Governor Getulio Vargas of Rio Grande do Sul ended Brazilian democracy in 1930. Assuming the presidency, in 1937 Vargas proclaimed a corporate state, "O Estado Novo," fashioned along the lines of Mussolini's Italy. Despite this political leaning, Brazil came into World War II on the side of the Allies in 1942, sending a well-trained Expeditionary Force to the Italian theatre of operations in 1943, as well as providing naval assistance. Vargas was forced to resign in 1945, and from 1945 through 1964, Brazil enjoyed a broad democracy, while facing significant internal political problems. After a decided turn to the left by then President Goulart, in 1964 the armed forces attained power, retaining control of

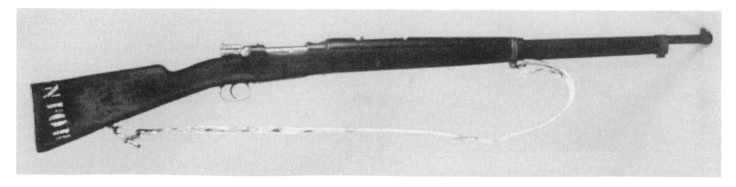

Full-length view of the Brazilian Model 1894 Rifle. (Century International Arms, Inc.)

Full-length view of the Brazilian Model 1894 Carbine (Century International Arms, Inc.)

thor has been unable to determine the number of these rifles purchased by the Brazilian government. These rifles, as well as the carbines, were used by Brazilian forces sent to quell the Jagunco Rebellion of 1897, where regular troops were drawn into a merciless guerrilla war with locals around the town of Canudos.

Length: 48.50"; **Weight:** 8.30 lbs.; **Barrel:** 29.1875"; **Caliber:** 7 x 57mm; **Rifling:** 4-groove, r/hand; **Operation:** Turnbolt action; **Feed:** 5-round, staggered-column, flush, box magazine; **Sights:** V-notch rear sight adjustable from 400 to 2000 meters on large leaf, 300 meters on standard. **Remarks:** Brazilian national crest, early version, on the receiver ring, with manufacturer's markings on the left side rail. Note the Portuguese spelling (Berlim) of "Berlin."

Side rail markings on the Brazilian Model 1894 Carbine (Century International Arms, Inc.)

MODEL 1894 CARBINE: Made strictly as a cavalry carbine, this handy little weapon was adopted at the same time as the Model 1894 Rifle, and with certain exceptions, it is patterned after the rifle. Note that there is no bayonet lug, and the straight wrist stock is equipped with a carbine sling loop on the underside. The upper hand guard extends from in front of the rear sight to just beyond the upper barrel band, the band held in place by means of a tightened screw assembly on the right side. Once common, these carbines are becoming rather scarce. This particular carbine was produced by FN.

Length: 37.38"; **Weight:** 6.85 lbs.; **Barrel:** 18.0"; **Caliber:** 7 x 57mm; **Rifling:** 4-groove, r/hand; **Operation:** Turnbolt action; **Feed:** 5-round, staggered column, flush, box magazine; **Sights:** V-notch rear sight adjustable to 1400 meters. **Remarks:** Early Brazilian national crest on receiver ring, with manufacturer's markings on the left side rail.

MODEL 1904 MAUSER-VERGUEIRO RIFLE: The Model 1904 Mauser-Vergueiro Rifle in caliber 7mm was purchased in small quantities from DWM for use by the Brazilian military police. With the exception of caliber and markings, this version is identical to the Portuguese Model 1904, which is covered under the section on Portugal. The receiver ring has the Brazilian crest, under which are the letters "F.P.D.F.," which stand for Forca Publica Distrito Federal (Military Police of the National Capitol).

Early version of the Brazilian national crest on the Model 1894 Rifle. (Century International Arms, Inc.)

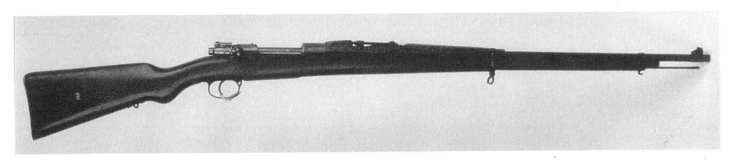

Full-length view of the Model 1907 Rifle as used by Brazil (Springfield Armory Museum)

Left side rail of the Model 1907 Rifle as used by Brazil, showing the model designation (Springfield Armory Museum)

barrel band. The upper band, or nose cap, incorporates a Model 1893-style bayonet lug on the bottom of the band. The barrel band also has a swivel on the left side, while the other swivel is on a short bar attached to the bottom of the stock. The carbine has a tangent leaf rear sight to 2000 meters.

MODEL 1908 RIFLE: Produced by DWM, the Model 1908 Rifle was purchased by Brazil in large quantities between 1908 and 1914. According to some European sources, the rifle was said to have been produced by the Polish Radom plant between 1935-1938. The rifle is quite similar to the Gew 98, with a Gew 98-style action and a pistol grip stock, the hand guard running from the front of the receiver ring to the single barrel band. Swivels are attached un-

Top view of the receiver ring of the Model 1907 Rifle as used by Brazil, showing the manufacturer's markings (Springfield Armory Museum)

MODEL 1907 RIFLE: During the period 1904-1906, an undetermined quantity of Model 1904 rifles, designated the Model 1907, were purchased from DWM in caliber 7mm. This particular model rifle was sold commercially by DWM to many South American countries. The 98-style action rifle has a pistol grip stock, with the upper hand guard running from the front of the receiver ring to just beyond the lower barrel band. This model also incorporates the longer cocking piece and does not have lock screws.

Length: 48.3"; **Weight:** 7.70 lbs.; **Barrel:** 28.98"; **Caliber:** 7 x 57mm; **Rifling:** 4-groove, r/hand; **Operation:** Turnbolt action; **Feed:** 5-round, staggered column, flush, box magazine; **Sights:** Tangent leaf rear sight, graduated to 2000 meters. **Remarks:** Brazilian national crest on receiver ring, manufacturer's markings on the left side rail.

MODEL 1907 CARBINE: This little-known carbine was purchased from DWM during the period 1907-1912 for issuance to cavalry of the military police. This carbine is built with a Model 98 action, with a short, pistol grip stock, the upper hand guard running from in front of the receiver ring to just above the single, narrow, screw-clamping

The markings on the receiver ring of the Model 1907 Carbine; note the "F.P. do D.F." markings and the model number. (Steve Kehaya)

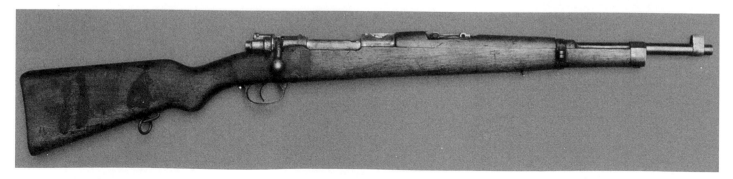

Full-length view of the Model 1907 Carbine supplied to the Forca Publica of the Federal District; note the turned-down bolt. (Steve Kehaya)

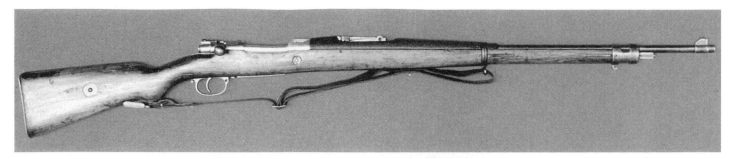

Full-length view the Brazilian Model 1908 Rifle

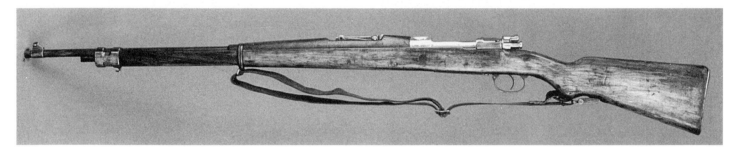

Left full-length view of the Brazilian Model 1908 Rifle

der the barrel band and the bottom of the buttstock. The typical short German "H" bayonet lug (1.1875 inches long) requires a bayonet with muzzle ring; the standard German "H" type bayonet lug is 1.75 inches long. Note that the buttstock has a washer held by a slotted-head screw. This rifle and the short rifle version were Brazilian standard equipment for many years, and served the country well.

Length: 49.13"; **Weight:** 8.38 lbs.; **Barrel:** 29.25"; **Caliber:** 7 x 57mm; **Rifling:** 4-groove, r/hand; **Operation:** Turnbolt action; **Feed:** 5-round, staggered column, flush, box magazine; **Sights:** Tangent leaf rear sight graduated to 2000 meters. **Remarks:** Brazilian national crest on receiver ring, manufacturer's markings on left side rail. Note: DWM contracted some of the work out to Mauser, and in this case the "DWM" over the Oberndorf address is seen instead of "Berlin."

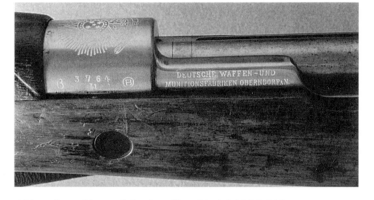

Side rail markings of the Brazilian Model 1908 Rifle

Close-up view of the leather action cover on the Brazilian Model 1908 Rifle

Buttstock markings on the Brazilian Model 1908 Rifle

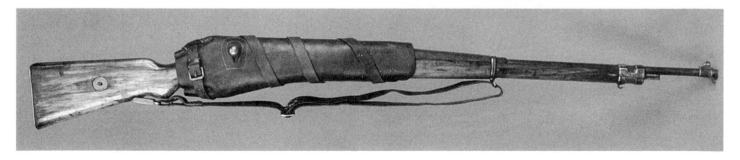

Full-length view of the Brazilian Model 1908 Rifle with leather action cover

Unusual markings on the right side of the receiver ring of the M1908 Rifle. (Robert Jensen collection)

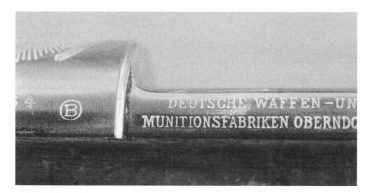

Manufacturer's markings on the side rail of the Brazilian Model 1908 Short Rifle

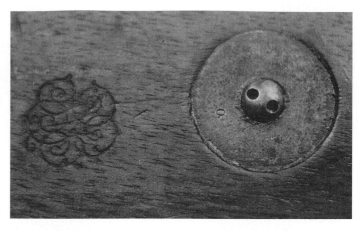

M1908 Brazilian Rifle stock cartouche. (Robert Jensen collection)

MODEL 1908 SHORT RIFLE: Apart from dimensions, the Brazilian Model 1908 Short Rifle is virtually identical to the Model 1908 Rifle. The short rifle has the bolt handle bent down, but like the rifle, it has a pistol grip stock, and the upper hand guard runs from in front of the receiver ring to just beyond the barrel band. Swivels are attached to the barrel band and the bottom of the stock.

Length: 41.875"; **Weight:** 7.95 lbs.; **Barrel:** 22.0"; **Caliber:** 7 x 57mm; **Rifling:** 4-groove, r/hand; **Operation:** Turnbolt action; **Feed:** 5-round, staggered column, flush, box magazine; **Sights:** Tangent leaf rear sight graduated to 2000 meters. **Remarks:** Brazilian national crest on the receiver, manufacturer's markings on the left side rail.

MODEL 1922 CARBINE: During the period 1922-1924, Brazil imported considerable quantities of Model 1922 Carbines for cavalry and artillery troop use from FN; records available to the author do not give the exact numbers purchased. Based on the Model 98 action, the carbines featured a turned-down bolt handle, and a short, straight-wristed stock. The upper hand guard runs from just ahead of the receiver ring to just beyond the spring-held barrel band. The upper band, or nose cap, features a parade hook and short German

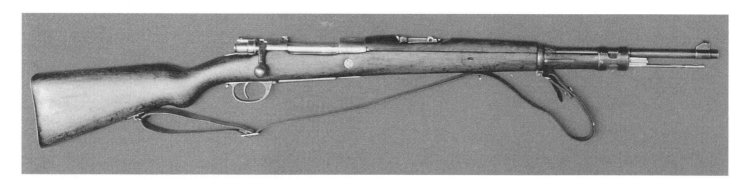

Full-length view of the Model 1908 Brazilian Short Rifle

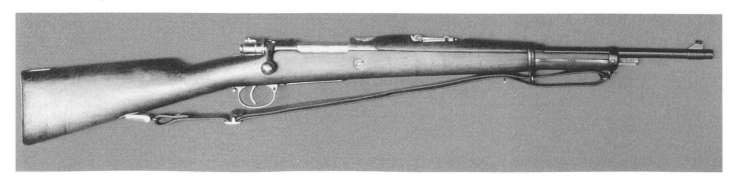

Full-length view the Brazilian Model 1922 Carbine

Manufacturer's markings on the side rail of the Brazilian Model 1922 Carbine

Manufacturer's markings on the receiver ring of the Czech VZ 24 Short Rifle used by Brazilian revolutionaries

"H" type bayonet lug; note that the barrel band and nose cap are quite close together. There is a swivel attached to the lower barrel band and the bottom of the buttstock has a plate with loop for attachment of the detachable sling mount.

Length: 39.1875"; **Weight:** 6.60 lbs.; **Barrel:** 19.63"; **Caliber:** 7 x 57mm; **Rifling:** 4-groove, r/hand; **Operation:** Turnbolt action; **Feed:** 5-round, staggered column, flush, box magazine; **Sights:** Tangent leaf rear sight graduated to 1400 meters. **Remarks:** Brazilian national crest on the receiver ring, manufacturer's markings on the left side rail.

CZECH MODEL VZ 24 SHORT RIFLE: In 1932, revolutionaries from Sao Paulo, Brazil ordered fifteen thousand VZ 24 Short Rifles from Czechoslovakia; these are the standard export Model VZ 24 as covered in the Czechoslovakian section of the book, with the exception that the bolt handle has been bent and the bolt knob flattened and knurled on the underside. The stock has been cut for the bolt knob. The safety operates in the standard manner. Czech side rail markings and Czech manufacturer's markings are found on the receiver ring.

MODEL 1935 MAUSER BANNER RIFLE: Among the last weapons purchased from Germany were the Model 1935 Mauser Banner Long Rifle and the Model 1935 Mauser Banner Short Rifle; unfortunately, the quantities purchased in each case are not available to the researcher. The Model 1935 Rifle is almost identical to the Gew 98, except that it has a tangent leaf rear sight, and an upper hand guard that extends from in front of the receiver ring to just beyond the lower barrel band. The stock has grasping grooves, and the lower barrel band has a swivel on the bottom, while the underside of the buttstock is equipped with a plate that has a loop for the attachment of a detachable sling mount. The upper band is also equipped with a parade hook.

Length: 49.25"; **Weight:** 10.0 lbs.; **Barrel:** 28.75"; **Caliber:** 7 x 57mm; **Rifling:** 4-groove, r/hand; **Operation:** Turnbolt action; **Feed:** 5-round, staggered column, flush, box magazine; **Sights:** Tangent leaf rear sight graduated to 2000 meters. **Remarks:** Brazilian national crest on the receiver ring, Mauser Banner logo on the receiver bridge, manufacturer's markings on the left side rail.

The left side rail of the Czech VZ 24 Short Rifle showing the model designation

Full-length view of the Czech Model VZ 24 Short Rifle specially ordered by Brazilian revolutionarie

Brazilian national crest on the receiver ring of the Model 1935 Rifle

MODEL 1935 MAUSER BANNER SHORT RIFLE: Purchased from Germany at the same time as the Model 1935 Rifle, the Model 1935 Short Rifle was also issued in an unknown quantity to Brazilian troops. The short rifle differed from the rifle in that it had a bent bolt handle, with the stock cut out to accommodate the handle and bolt knob; otherwise it is only a case of smaller dimension.

Length: 42.0"; **Weight:** 9.0 lbs.; **Barrel:** 21.5"; **Caliber:** 7 x 57mm; **Rifling:** 4-groove, r/hand; **Operation:** Turnbolt action; **Feed:** 5-round, staggered column, flush, box magazine; **Sights:** Tangent leaf rear sight graduated to 1400 meters. **Remarks:** Brazilian national crest on the receiver ring, Mauser Banner logo on the receiver bridge, manufacturer's markings on the side rail.

Manufacturer's markings on the side rail of the Model 1935 Mauser Banner Rifle

The Brazilian national crest on the receiver ring of the Model 1935 Mauser Banner Short Rifle

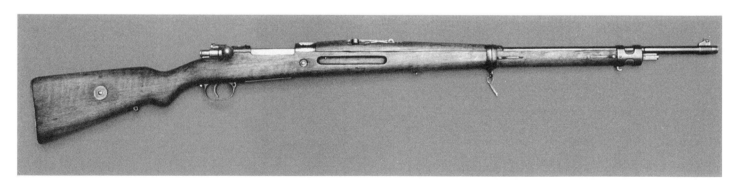

Full-length view of the Brazilian Model 1935 Mauser Banner Rifle

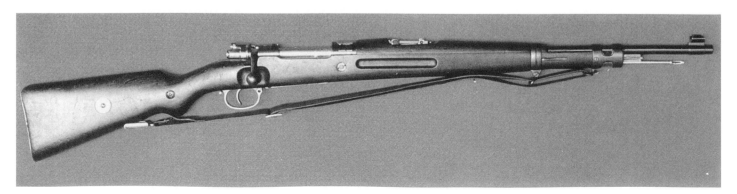

Full-length view of the Brazilian Model 1935 Mauser Banner Short Rifle

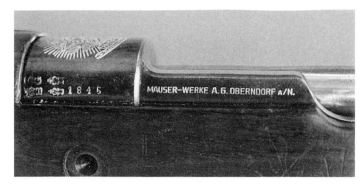

Manufacturer's markings on the left side rail of the Model 1935 Mauser Banner Short Rifle

Manufacturer's markings on the left side rail of the Brazilian Model 1908/34 Short Rifle

MODEL 1908/34 SHORT RIFLE: In order to decrease the country's dependency on foreign arms suppliers, production of the Model 1908/34 Short Rifle was undertaken by the Brazilian government at the arms plant at Itajuba. This is an updated and modernized version (for that time) of the Model 1908 Short Rifle, employing local wood for the stocks as opposed to European walnut. The caliber is also a change in thinking, as the rifle was produced in U.S. .30-06.

Length: 43.75"; **Weight:** 9.75 lbs.; **Barrel:** 23.50"; **Caliber:** .30-06; **Rifling:** 4-groove, r/hand; **Operation:** Turnbolt action; **Feed:** 5-round, staggered column, flush, box magazine; **Sights:** Tangent leaf rear sight graduated to 2000 meters. **Remarks:** Brazilian national crest on the receiver ring, with the manufacturer's markings on the side rail.

M954 CALIBER .30-06 SHORT RIFLE: Last in the series of Mauser rifles employed by the Brazilian armed forces is the M954 .30-06 Short Rifle, which has the unusual feature of a threaded muzzle, allowing for the attachment of a grenade launcher, or a flash suppresser. This is a rifle produced in Brazil in their arms factory at Itajuba. The rifle is fitted with a pistol grip stock with grasping grooves, and the upper hand guard extends from the front of the receiver ring to beyond the lower barrel band. The upper band has a parade hook on the bottom. The nose cap incorporates a short bayonet lug. There

Model designation on the right side of the receiver of the Brazilian Model 1908/34 Short Rifle

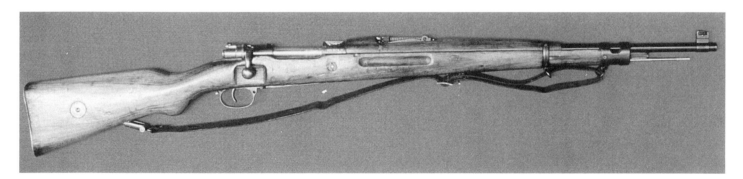

Full-length view of the Brazilian Model 1908/34 Short Rifle

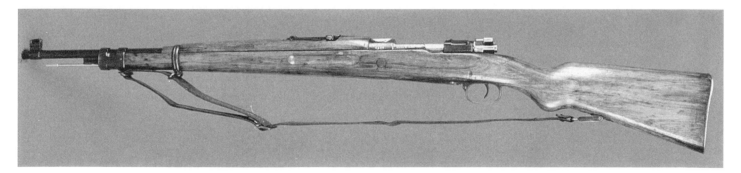

Left full-length view of the Brazilian Model 1908/34 Short Rifle

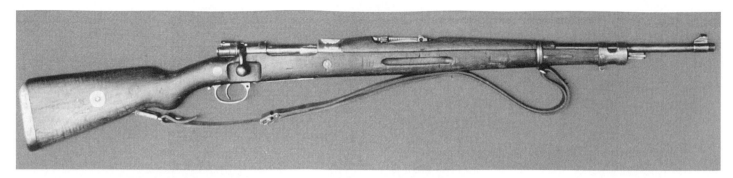

Full-length view of the Brazilian M954 Short Rifle

Markings on the right side of the receiver ring of the Brazilian M954 Short Rifle

is a swivel on the bottom of the lower barrel band, and the bottom of the buttstock has a fitting for a quick-release sling attachment. The stock is cut out for the bolt handle and bolt knob, and the butt plate is cupped.

Length: 43.50"; **Weight:** 8.85 lbs.; **Barrel:** 23.25"; **Caliber:** .30-06; **Rifling:** 4-groove, r/hand; **Operation:** Turnbolt action; **Feed:** 5-round, staggered column, flush, box magazine; **Sights:** Tangent leaf rear sight graduated to 2000 meters. **Remarks:** Brazilian national crest and model designation on the receiver ring, manufacturer's markings on the left side rail.

CHILE

The military and political history of Chile is a tempestuous one. Colonized by the Spaniards in 1541, and forming part of the Viceroyalty of Peru under the colonial empire of Spain, Chile moved towards independence in the year 1810. The Chilean War of Independence lasted eight years, and was aided by an expeditionary force from Argentina, as well a powerful fleet under the command of British Admiral Thomas Cochrane. This fleet was largely manned by American, British, and Irish mercenaries, all eager to fight to help a country free itself.

The first President of the Chilean Republic was General Bernardo O'Higgins. In 1821 he led a force to the aid of the Peruvians, who achieved liberty in 1823. Not so fortunate, O'Higgins' policies led to his own overthrow in the same year, which ushered in almost a decade of anarchy, finally ending in 1830 with a conservative victory led by Diego Portales.

Chile was victorious in a war against the confederation of Bolivia and Peru in the years 1836 to 1839. Allied with Peru, Chile waged a victorious war against Spain in 1865 and 1866, but thirteen years later saw another turnaround when Chile went to war against Bolivia and Peru in the famous War of the Pacific. At the end of this war, the army turned its attention to subduing the Araucanian Indians, who had been a thorn in the side of the country since colonial times.

Considering the many wars involving other countries, a relatively stable government had enabled Chile to enjoy peaceful domestic progress, but this was broken by a short, but bitter, civil war in 1891. It was during this war that the Winchester Model 1886 Lever Action Rifle, as well as the Austrian Mannlicher Model 1888 Straight-pull Rifle, played an active part. The Constitutionalists, backed by the army, were the victors.

The Chilean army much admired the German military machine, which proved successful in the Franco-Prussian War, and this led to the engagement of Captain Emil Koerner, a much-decorated veteran of the war, to revamp the Chilean Military College. When he had completed his initial assignment, it included the addition of thirty-six German military instructors. The German military mission remained in place until the start of the First World War. This heritage is seen in the spike-top "pickelhauben" parade dress helmets and German-style steel helmets that were, until recently, to be found in the TO & E of the Chilean army. Koerner's influence remained evident in the Chilean army Prussian traditions, including the armaments purchased by the Chilean government.

The standard small arm in the army of Chile was the Mauser rifle, short rifle and carbine, Modelo 1895. Friction between Argentina and Chile caused a small arms race in 1896, and by 1898, the Chilean armory included eighty thousand Model 1895 Rifles and thirty thousand carbines of the same model.

The armed forces had to intervene in the governing of the country in 1924, when they supported President Alessandri; sometime later, Colonel Carlos Ibañez del Campo took over as President, ruling until 1931. Anarchy prevailed for one year during the depression, with elections in 1932 returning the country to a succession of democratically-minded administrations until the somewhat inconclusive election of Salvador Allende in 1970. Allende's attempts to turn Chile into a Marxist State resulted in complete and total disorganization and economic collapse, and in 1973 this caused the armed forces to reluctantly assume control of the government. Under the regime of General Pinochet, stability was returned to the country and social and economic growth resumed. Chile is now proud of its full democratic representation, and the country is on the road to a sound political future.

MODEL 1893 RIFLE: Among the many Model 1895 Mauser Rifles supplied to Chile were some "true" Model 1893 Rifles—true in the respect that they were manufactured and delivered with a bent bolt

Manufacturer's markings on the side rail of the Chilean Model 1893 Rifle (Lothar Frank collection)

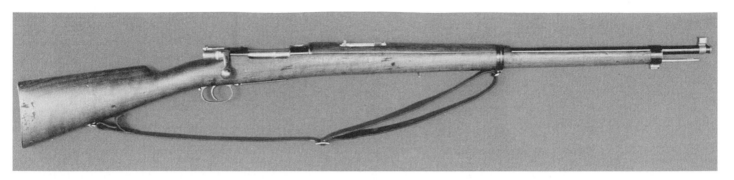

Full-length view of the Chilean Model 1893 Rifle (Lothar Frank collection)

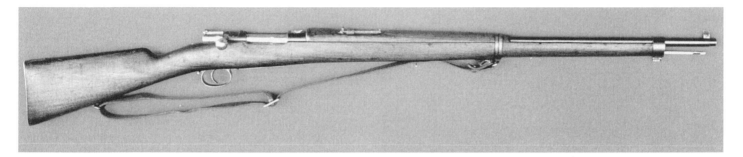

Full-length view of the Chilean Model 1895 Rifle

handle and no auxiliary shoulder behind the bolt handle as a safety; otherwise they were identical with the Model 1895 Rifle. All of the facts listed for the Model 1895 Rifle will apply in the case of the Model 1893 Rifle.

MODEL 1895 RIFLE: Initially supplied by Ludwig Loewe & Co. during the period 1897-1900, some later stands of arms were delivered by DWM. Many of the Model 1893 "OVS" Mauser rifles originally bound for the Boers during the war against the British in South Africa were diverted by DWM to fulfill the Chilean contract. The receivers were overstruck with the crest of Chile, but retained their "OVS" markings.

Almost identical with the Spanish Model 1893 Rifle, the Chilean model differed only in having a cylindrical bolt head and the rear of the follower rounded off so that the bolt would close on an empty

Manufacturer's markings on the side rail of the Chilean Model 1895 Rifle. Note that the manufacturer is Ludwig Loewe & Co., Berlin.

The Chilean national crest on the receiver of the Model 1893 Rifle (Lothar Frank collection)

Chilean national crest on the receiver ring of the Model 1895 Rifle

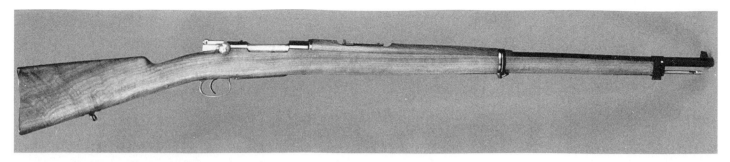

Full-length view of the Chilean Model 1895 Rifle. This particular specimen was never issued, and was kept in the collection of Paul Mauser. (John Deeks collection)

Chilean acceptance marking in the stock of the Chilean Model 1895 Rifle

chamber. An auxiliary shoulder on the receiver behind the bolt handle was intended to serve as a safety in the event the locking lugs gave way. The rifle has a straight-wristed stock, with the upper hand guard extending from in front of the receiver ring to the barrel band. The upper band has a bayonet lug on the bottom of the band to accept the Model 1895-style bayonet. Swivels are on the bottom of the lower barrel band and the buttstock.

Length: 48.60"; **Weight:** 8.80 lbs.; **Barrel:** 29.60"; **Caliber:** 7 x 57mm; **Rifling:** 4-groove, r/hand; **Operation:** Turnbolt action; **Feed:** 5-round, staggered column, flush, box magazine; **Sights:** V-notch leaf rear sight graduated to 2000 meters. **Remarks:** The national crest of Chile on the receiver ring, with the manufacturer's markings on the side rail. In many cases, buttstocks will also be marked with the national crest on the right side, while rifles issued to naval units will carry a fouled anchor in place of the national crest.

MODEL 1895 SHORT RIFLE: The Model 1895 Short Rifle, or "mosqueton," is identical to the Model 1895 Rifle except for the length, the turned-down bolt handle, and the sling swivels on the left side of the stock and the barrel band.

Length: 41.25"; **Weight:** 7.90 lbs.; **Barrel:** 21.25"; **Caliber:** 7 x 57mm; **Rifling:** 4-groove, r/hand; **Operation:** Turnbolt action; **Feed:** 5-round, staggered column, flush, box magazine; **Sights:** V-notch leaf rear sight graduated to 1400 meters. **Remarks:** Chilean national crest on the receiver ring, manufacturer's markings on the side rail.

MODEL 1895 CARBINE: Made to Chilean specifications, the Carabina Mauser Chilena Modelo 1895 was made to accept the Model 1895 Chilean bayonet. The carbine retains the features of the short

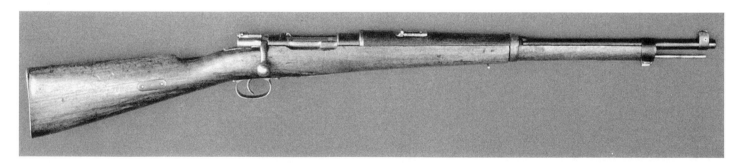

Full-length view of the Model 1895 Short Rifle

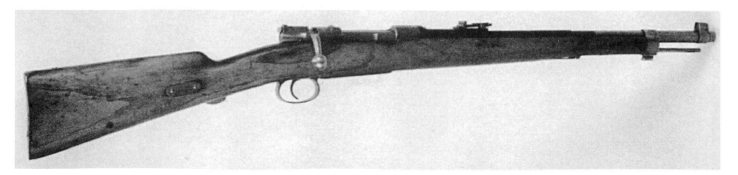

Full-length view of the Chilean Model 1895 Carbine (Springfield Armory Museum)

Side rail of the Chilean Model 1895 Carbine, showing the manufacturer's markings. (Springfield Armory Museum)

Manufacturer's markings on the left side rail of the Chilean Model 1912 Steyr Rifle

rifle, including the bent bolt handle, but in modified form. The sling swivels are on the left side of the barrel band, and on the stock behind the wrist.

Length: 37.25"; **Weight:** 7.50 lbs.; **Barrel:** 18.25"; **Caliber:** 7 x 57mm; **Operation:** Turnbolt action; **Feed:** 5-round, staggered column, flush, box magazine; **Sights:** V-notch leaf rear sight graduated to 1400 meters. **Remarks:** Chilean national crest on the receiver ring, with manufacturer's markings on the side rail.

MODEL 1912 STEYR RIFLE: As part of the effort to modernize and update standard equipment, purchases of the Model 1912 Rifle and Short Rifle were made from Osterrereichische Waffensfabriks-Gesellschaft of Austria just prior to the start of World War I. These rifles are identical to the Mexican and Colombian Model 1912 Pattern Rifles, which are close copies of the Gew 98. The rifle has a pistol grip stock, tangent leaf rear sight, and large receiver ring. The upper hand guard extends from in front of the receiver ring to just beyond the lower barrel band. The upper band has a parade hook and the nose cap incorporates an "H" type, short, flush bayonet lug that requires a bayonet with the muzzle ring flush to the back of the hilt. A swivel is attached to the bottom of the lower band, with a quick-release attachment on the bottom of the buttstock. The total quantity delivered is undetermined.

Length: 49.0"; **Weight:** 9.06 lbs.; **Barrel:** 28.75"; **Caliber:** 7 x 57mm; **Rifling:** 4-groove, r/hand; **Operation:** Turnbolt action;

The Chilean national crest and model designation on the receiver ring of the Chilean Steyr Model 1912 Rifle

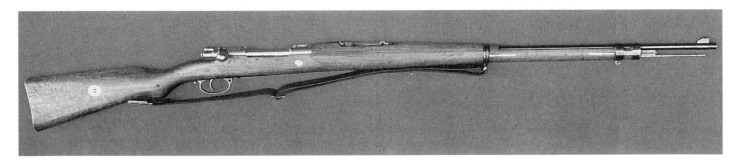

Full-length view of the Chilean Model 1912 Steyr Rifle. Note the identification disk on the right of the buttstock.

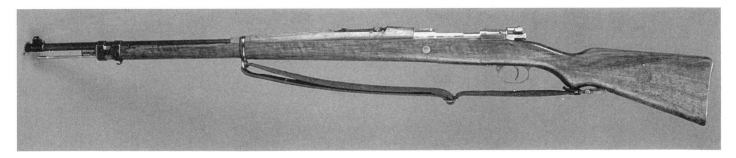

Left full-length view of the Chilean Model 1912 Steyr Rifle

Chilean acceptance marking in the stock of the Chilean Steyr Model 1912 Rifle

Feed: 5-round, staggered column, flush box magazine; **Sights:** Tangent leaf rear sight graduated to 2000 meters. **Remarks:** The Chilean national crest over the markings "MODELO 1912" is on the receiver ring, while the side rail bears the marking, "WAFFENFABRIK STEYR/AUSTRIA."

MODEL 1912 STEYR SHORT RIFLE: With the exception of a bent bolt handle and overall dimensions, the Chilean Model 1912 Short Rifle is identical to the Model 1912 Rifle.

Length: 41.75"; **Weight:** 9.0 lbs; **Barrel:** 21.50"; **Caliber:** 7 x 57mm; **Rifling:** 4-groove, r/hand; **Operation:** Turnbolt action; **Feed:** 5-round, staggered column, flush, box magazine; **Sights:** Tangent leaf rear sight graduated to 1400 meters. **Remarks:** The Chilean national crest and "MODELO 1912" on the receiver ring, with manufacturer's markings on the side rail.

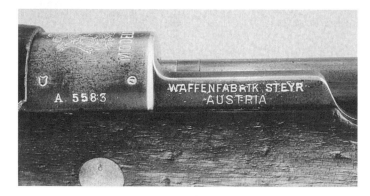

Manufacturer's markings on the side rail of the Chilean Steyr Model 1912 Short Rifle

MODEL 1935 "CARABINEROS" CARBINE: Purchased from Mauser during the mid-1930s, this carbine was evidently intended for use by the elite corps of "Carabineros." The carbine has a pistol grip stock, with the upper hand guard extending from the receiver ring to just beyond the wide lower band. The nose cap incorporates an "H" type short, flush, bayonet lug. Sling swivels are on the left side of the stock at the wrist and on the left side of the lower barrel band. The bottom of the buttstock is also equipped with a quick-release attachment for the sling. The right side of the buttstock has an identification disk, while the left side of the stock has the national crest over the date "1935" in a rectangular block, which is above acceptance marks in a circle.

Length: 42.0; **Weight:** 9.25; **Barrel:** 21.50"; **Caliber:** 7 x 57mm; **Rifling:** 4-groove, r/hand; **Operation:** Turnbolt action; **Feed:** 5-round, staggered column, flush, box magazine; **Sights:** Tangent leaf rear sight graduated to 1400 meters. **Remarks:** On the receiver ring are the following: the word "CHILE" above crossed rifles, over the words "ORDEN Y PATRIA," which is over the date "1935." The side of the receiver ring has the series designation and number, while the side rail shows the manufacturer's markings. On the receiver bridge is the Mauser Banner logo.

Stock markings on the left side of the buttstock of the Chilean Model 1935 Carbine

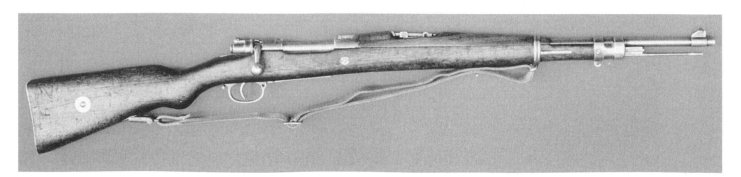

Full-length view of the Chilean Steyr Model 1912 Short Rifle

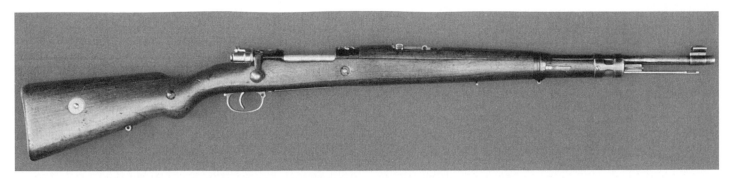

Full-length view of the Chilean Model 1935 "Carabineros" Carbine

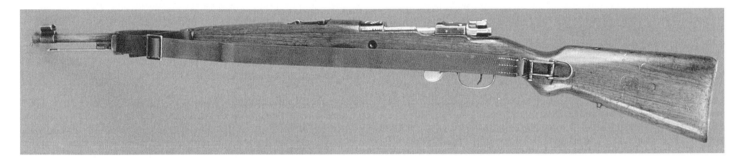

Left full-length view of the Chilean Model 1935 Carbine

The receiver ring markings of the Chilean Model 1935 Carbine

The Mauser Banner logo on the receiver bridge of the Chilean Model 1935 Carbine

Side rail markings of the Chilean Model 1935 Carbine. Note the series indication, which is special in this case, showing "Carabina Chileana" and the serial number.

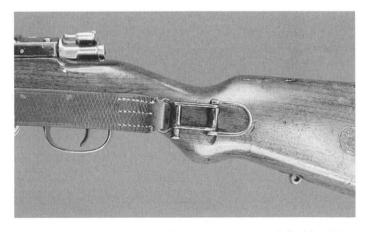

Close up of the "quick release" attachment on the left side of the buttstock of the Chilean Model 1935 Carbine

CHINA

The awakening giant that is China has, in all likelihood, been the most prolific user of Mauser military rifles in the world. Although there is no specific confirmation of this, from the Gew 71 on, China has probably employed every model and variant of the Mauser rifle ever produced. From the time that China first sent arms purchasing commissions to the West during the late 1800s, to the freelance arms merchants of the Far East, the armies of China, including the warlords of the 1920s, have had the most advantageous opportunities to acquire all manner of Mauser rifles. German military missions led by German General von Faulkenhausen in the 1930s helped to provide a further "Prussianization" of the Nationalist army of General Chiang Kai-Shek. The author had the good fortune to become friends with the daughter of General von Faulkenhausen in Heidelberg at the end of World War II. We had some wonderful conversations concerning her father's history, both prior to and during World War II. At the time, he was a prisoner of the Russians.

To attempt to trace the bewildering paths of the weapons used by Chinese forces would be a gigantic endeavor, if not an impossible task. Not only were Mausers plentiful, but there was also an abundance of every other firearm that had ever appeared on the surplus market; these included Mannlicher straight-pull rifles from the 1880s, French Gras and Chassepot single shot rifles, early Carcano and Vetterli models, as well as some U.S. Civil War cap-and-ball relics. China also contracted to produce their own version of the Mauser and Commission Model 1888 Rifle, called the "Hanyang" model; which was used throughout the first half of the twentieth century, and only appeared on the U.S. surplus market in the last five to ten years.

The Chinese army was initially equipped with a selection of Gew 71 Rifles and Carbines, which were replaced at a later date with the Hanyang model rifle, as well as an unknown quantity of Model 1895 Mauser Rifles. China experimented with a version of the Model 1904 Mauser Rifle, designated the Chinese Model 1907 in both 6.8mm and 7mm. The rifle was referred to as the Model 1904/07, while the carbine was officially called the Model 1907 Carbine. Production facilities must also have been set up in China, as the author has a Chinese-produced and marked Model 1907 in his collection. The Chinese revolution of 1911 interfered with testing and troop use of the Model 1907, and the further production of this model was cut short by the advent of the First World War, with the weapons in German factories being converted to 7.92mm and issued to German troops.

During the 1920s and the early 1930s, Chinese forces imported an unknown quantity of Model 98/22 Rifles from Czechoslovakia, as well as approximately 24,000 FN Model 1924 and 1930 Rifles between 1930 and 1934; from 1937 to 1939, it is believed that 165,000 more FN Model 1930 Rifles were purchased from FN. Copied from the FN Model 1930, the Chinese-produced "Model 21" Rifle was a reliable, albeit crude rifle manufactured at the Kwantung Arsenal between 1932 and 1937 for use by the Kuomintang, or North China Army. In 1937, China also purchased 100,000 VZ 24 Short Rifles from Czechoslovakia. These rifles are readily identifiable, as the receiver dates are always "1937," and the serial number is preceded by a "P" prefix. Most of these VZ 24s were captured by the Japanese, who used them to arm approximately five divisions operating in China.

Also used to arm the Chinese were the Mauser Standard Modell Short Rifles, purchased from Germany during the mid-1930s. These rifles will bear the Mauser Banner logo, and will all presumably have a "B" prefix to the serial number.

Cantonese soldier with a Chinese Model 1907 Rifle, ammunition, and Chinese-made "potato masher" grenades, C. 1935 (Edgar Snow collection)

Chinese infantryman with rifle, ammunition, grenades, and a German-style Model 1935 helmet (Edgar Snow collection)

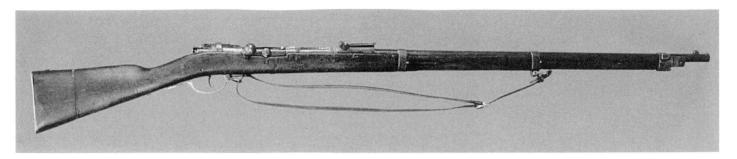

Full-length view of the Gew. Model 71 Rifle as supplied to China

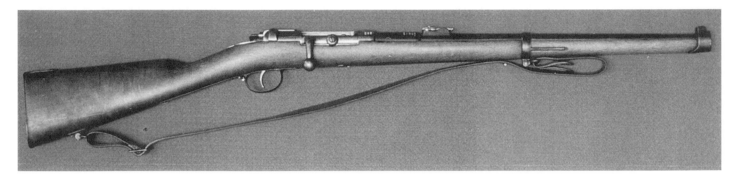

Full-length view of the German Model 71 Carbine

GEW. 71 RIFLE: While the bulk of the production of Model 71 Rifles was by German government arsenals and the Austrian Arms Co. of Steyr, Austria, the Austrian Arms Co. also supplied a total of 70,000 Model 71 rifles to China, Japan, the Transvaal, Honduras, and Uruguay. In addition, in 1876, the Mauser Co. received a contract from China for 26,000 rifles and an undetermined number of carbines were purchased from Spangenberg & Sauer of Suhl, Germany. The Model 71 Rifle supplied to China is identical to that supplied to the German armed forces in caliber 11mm, and technical information on the rifle will be found in the section on Germany.

KAR. 71 CARBINE: The quantity of Model 71 Carbines supplied to China from the stocks of Spangenberg and Sauer, of Suhl, Germany, is lost in the mists of time and records long destroyed by war. The author has been unable to determine the markings, if any, that are peculiar to the Chinese contract weapons. All pertinent data regarding the Model 71 Carbine will be found in the section on Germany.

MODEL 1895 RIFLE: In the year 1896, an unknown quantity of Chilean-style Model 1895 Rifles in caliber 7 x 57mm were ordered from Waffenfabrik Mauser A-G, with the delivery date also unknown. These rifles may bear ideographs on either the receiver or on the buttstock, but this cannot be positively determined. All data relative to this rifle will be found in the section on the Chilean Model 1895 Rifle. These rifles were apparently equipped with a version of the Spanish Model 1893 sword bayonet.

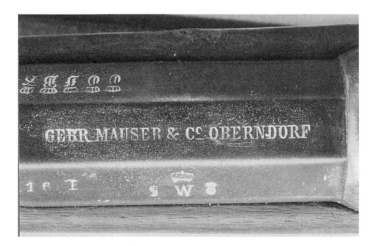

Typical manufacturer's markings on Model 71 Rifles supplied to China

Receiver markings on the German Model 71 Carbine, showing the Spangenberg & Sauer markings

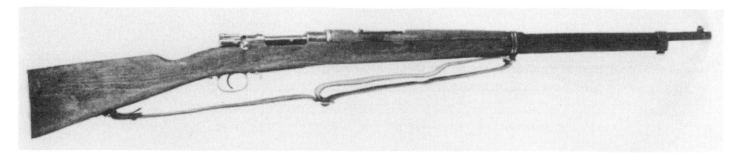

Full-length view of the Chinese Model 1895 Rifle

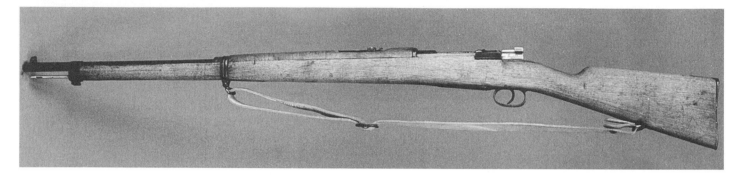

Left full-length view of the Chinese Model 1895 Rifle

CHINESE MODEL 1907 RIFLE: Based on the German Model 1904 Rifle that was produced for commercial sale, the Chinese Model 1907 was originally chambered for the experimental Chinese 6.8mm round. As this rifle was in production when World War I started, it was an easy matter for the rifle to be rebarreled for the 7.92mm cartridge and issued to German troops. As a matter of course, the Chinese also rebarreled the rifle in 7.92mm when it was produced in China. Made with a pistol grip-style stock and an upper hand guard that extends from in front of the receiver to just beyond the lower barrel band, the rifle is identified by the narrow lower band. There are swivels on the bottom of the barrel band and the buttstock. The short bayonet lug requires a bayonet with a muzzle ring.

Length: 49.2"; **Weight:** 8.30 lbs.; **Barrel:** 29.13"; **Caliber:** Originally 6.8mm, later produced in 7.92 x 57mm; **Rifling:** 4-groove, r/hand; **Operation:** Turnbolt action; **Feed:** 5-round, staggered column, flush, box magazine; **Sights:** Tangent leaf rear sight graduated to 2000 meters. **Remarks:** Those rifles that were manufactured in Germany will have the name of the manufacturer (Mauser or DWM) and the year produced. Those rifles manufactured in China will usually have two diamond shapes with one end superimposed on the other, over the Chinese date, which commences from 1911, the date of the Chinese revolution. Ideographs will also be prominently displayed on the buttstock.

Chinese markings on the receiver of the Chinese Model 1907 Rifle

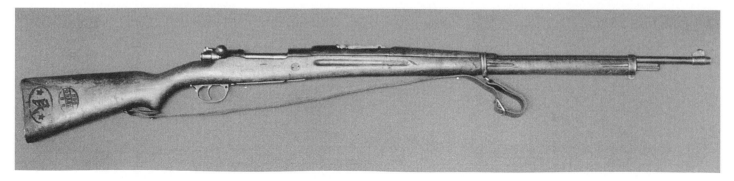

Full-length view of the Chinese Model 1907 Rifle. Note the well-displayed ideographs on the right side of the buttstock.

Ideographs on the buttstock of the Chinese Model 1907 Rifle

The left-hand side of the action of the Chinese Model 1907 Carbine (Noel P. Schott)

CHINESE MODEL 1907 CARBINE: The Chinese Model 1907 Carbine was adopted at the same time as the Model 1907 Rifle. With the exception of the turned-down bolt handle, the shorter rear sight, and the full stock to the muzzle with sight protectors, the carbine is identical to the rifle. The carbine is fitted with a pistol grip stock without grasping grooves, with the upper hand guard running from the front of the receiver ring to just beyond the lower barrel band. There is a swivel on the bottom of the lower barrel band and another on the bottom of the buttstock. The simple nose cap incorporates sight protectors, and there is no provision for the attachment of a bayonet.

Length: 41.25"; **Weight:** 8.1 lbs.; **Barrel:** 21.75"; **Caliber:** Originally 6.8 x 57mm; later rebarreled to 7.92 x 57mm; **Rifling:** 4-groove, r/hand; **Operation:** Turnbolt action; **Feed:** 5-round, staggered column, flush, box magazine; **Sights:** Tangent leaf rear sight graduated to 1400 meters. **Remarks:** Manufacturer's markings on the top of the receiver; in this case, "Waffenfabrik/Mauser/Oberndorf a/n," with serial number on the left side of the receiver and the model designation on the left side rail.

CHINESE STEYR MODEL 1912 RIFLE: Due to the destruction of war, the author has been unable to ascertain the number of Model 1912 Rifles in caliber 7 x 57mm ordered from the Austrian Arms Co. of Steyr, Austria. All of the pertinent data relative to this rifle will be found under the section on Chile.

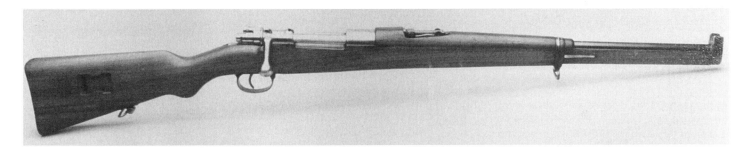

Full-length view of the Chinese Model 1907 Carbine (Noel P. Schott)

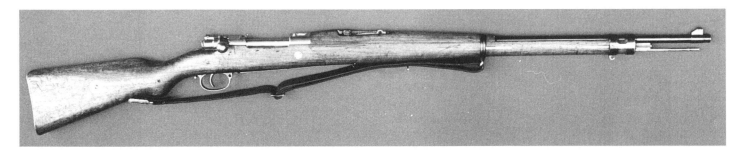

Full-length view of the Chinese Steyr Model 1912 Rifle

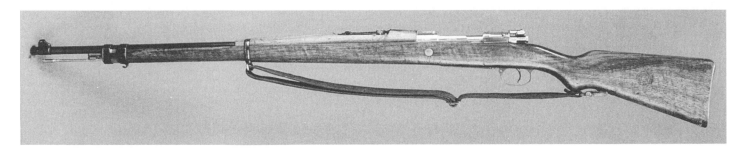

Left full-length view of the Chinese Model 1912 Rifle

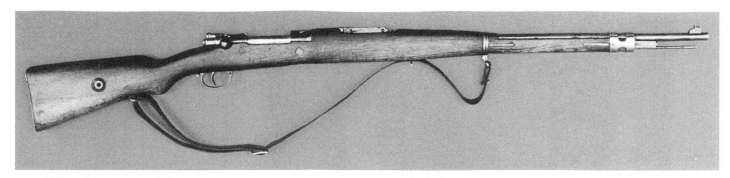

Full-length view of the Czech Model 98/22 as used in China. These will often be found with ideographs at some point on the stock.

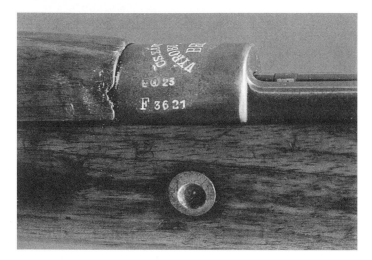

Side view of the Czech Model 98/22 Rifle, showing location of the serial number

Czech markings on the receiver of the Model 98/22 Rifle as used by China

CZECH MODEL 98/22 RIFLE: During the 1920s, China contracted for approximately seventy thousand Model 98/22 Rifles in caliber 7.92 x 57mm from Czechoslovakia. These were delivered over a period of years, and were used in the struggles between the Kuomintang, the Chinese Nationalist forces, and the Red Chinese Army, as well as the various Generals who reigned as warlords. Basically a modified copy of the Gew 98, the Model 98/22 Rifle is equipped with a modified tangent leaf rear sight, and has a pistol grip stock and an upper hand guard that runs from in front of the receiver ring to just beyond the narrow lower band. The lower band has a sling swivel on the bottom, as does the bottom of the buttstock at the rear of the wrist. The nose cap has the German "H" style bayonet lug, and the stock has the washer and rod combination for disassembly of the striker mechanism.

FN MODEL 24 AND 30 SHORT RIFLES: During the period 1930-1934, FN supplied approximately 24,000 Mle 24 and Mle 30 Short Rifles in 7.92mm to China, while a further 165,000 Mle 30 Short Rifles were delivered from 1937 to 1939. These short rifles

proved popular with the Chinese forces (as any of us who served in Korea will attest!), and facilities at the Kwantung Arsenal soon provided a native copy labeled the Model 21 Short Rifle.

As the Mle 24 and the Mle 30 Short Rifles are almost identical, and were produced in the same calibers, available information states that the only really distinctive difference is that the Mle 24 generally has an upper hand guard running from in front of the receiver ring to just beyond the lower barrel band, while the Mle 30 generally has an upper hand guard that runs from in front of the re-

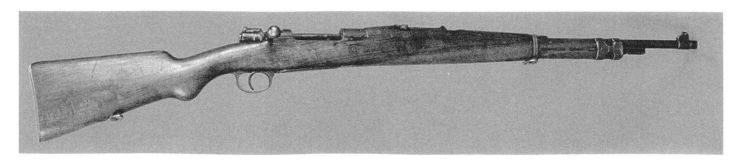

Full-length view of the FN Mle 24 Short Rifle as supplied to the Chinese armed forces

General officer and troops of the Northern Army, C. 1930 (Hist B&W) (Edgar Snow collection)

Chinese troops armed with FN Model 24 Short Rifles and Standard Modell Short Rifles preparing for action, C. 1933 (Edgar Snow collection)

ceiver ring to the upper barrel band. According to FN records, the Mle 30 also had a narrower upper band than the Mle 24, and often the front sight had special protective "ears."

A typical short rifle has a pistol grip stock, with the upper hand guard running from just before the receiver ring to just beyond the lower barrel band, or to the upper barrel band, as the case may be. Sling swivels will be found on the bottom of the lower barrel band, with another on the bottom of the buttstock. The nose cap incorporates the typical German "H" style bayonet lug. The bolt handle is straight, and the rear sights are tangent, graduated to 2000 meters.

MODEL 21 SHORT RIFLE: The Model 21 Short Rifle was a "knock-off" of the FN Mle 30 Short Rifle, produced by the Kwantung arsenal in the early 1930s for the Chinese Nationalist army. There are no real records available for any historical analysis of this weapon, and there are differences in manufacture, i.e., dimensions, quality, and fittings. The typical Model 21 Short Rifle is equipped with a pistol grip stock, an upper hand guard running from the front of the receiver ring to the upper band, and a tangent rear sight. The lower band has a sling swivel, with another inlet into the bottom of the buttstock behind the pistol grip. The bolt handle is straight, and some specimens have been seen without bayonet lugs.

Length: 43.62"; **Weight:** 8.64 lbs; **Barrel:** 23.62"; **Caliber:** 7.92 x 57mm; **Rifling:** 4-groove, r/hand; **Operation:** Turnbolt action;

Markings on the receiver ring of the Chinese Model 21 Short Rifle (Noel Schott collection)

Full-length view of the FN Mle 24 Short Rifle as supplied to the Chinese armed forces

Full-length view of the Chinese Model 21 Short Rifle (Noel Schott collection)

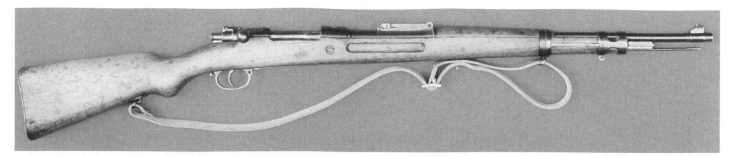

Full-length view of the Chinese "Chiang Kai-Shek" Model Short Rifle

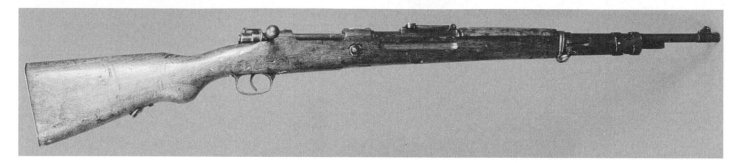

A full-length view of a similar, though shorter version of the "Chiang Kai-Shek" Model Short Rifle (Bob Bennett collection)

Feed: 5-round, staggered column, flush, box magazine; **Sights:** Tangent rear sight graduated to 2000 meters. **Remarks:** Unknown markings on the receiver ring and on the side rail.

"CHIANG KAI-SHEK" MODEL SHORT RIFLE: State arsenals in China made several million copies of the Mauser Standard Modell Short Rifle during the period from November 1936 to 1949, with this weapon becoming standard issue for Chinese troops. Manufacturing quality ranged from the very good (not up to German standards, by any means!) to the very crude, with little attention paid to the bedding of the action or the barrel, and very minimal standards of finish.

Length: 43.60"; **Weight:** 8.8 lbs.; **Barrel:** 23.62"; **Caliber:** 7.92 x 57mm; **Rifling:** 4-groove, r/hand; **Operation:** Turnbolt action; **Feed:** 5-round, staggered column, flush, box magazine; **Sights:** Tangent leaf rear sight graduated to 2000 meters. **Remarks:** Receiver ring will show various markings of Chinese provenance.

Chinese ideographs on the receiver ring of the shorter version of the "Chiang Kai-Shek" Model Short Rifle. These markings have been seen on rifles of the North China Army, probably the Northwestern Army of General Feng Yu-Hsiang. (Bob Bennett collection)

View of the Chinese markings on the receiver ring of the "Chiang Kai-Shek" Model Short Rifle

Variant marking on the receiver ring of a "Chang kai-Shek" Model Rifle. (Robert Jensen collection)

Variant ideograph on the receiver ring of the Chang kai-Shek Model Rifle. (Robert Jensen collection)

Another variant ideograph marking on the receiver ring of the Chang kai-Shek Model Rifle. (Robert Jensen collection)

Chinese troops, armed with Chiang Kai-Shek Model short rifles, receiving training from U.S. officers during World War II (U.S. Signal Corps photo)

Receiver markings on the Chinese contract Czech VZ 24 Short Rifle (Lothar Frank collection)

CZECH MODEL VZ 24 CHINESE CONTRACT SHORT RIFLE: In the mid-1930s, China purchased one hundred thousand Model VZ 24 Short Rifles from Czechoslovakia. These rifles are the standard issue VZ 24s, and all pertinent data regarding these rifles will be found in the section on Czechoslovakia. Those rifles delivered under this contract all bear the date "1937" on the receiver, and have a "P" prefix to the serial number. Most of these rifles were captured by the Japanese and were used to arm their own troops; the rifles were subsequently recovered from Japan at the end of the Second World War and were reissued to Chinese forces.

STANDARD MODELL MODEL 1933 SHORT RIFLE: During the 1930s, in violation of the treaty of Versailles, the Mauser Co. produced a modified, short rifle version of the Gew 98 for commercial sale, called the "Standard Modell." This short rifle was offered in many calibers, but China ordered the weapon in caliber 7.92mm. Developed in the mid-1920s, production of the Standard Modell did not commence until 1933, at which time an alternative version in carbine form, identical to the German 98k with minor exceptions, also became available.

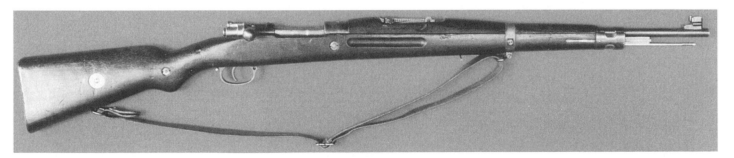

Full-length view of the Chinese contract Czech VZ 24 Short Rifle (Lothar Frank collection)

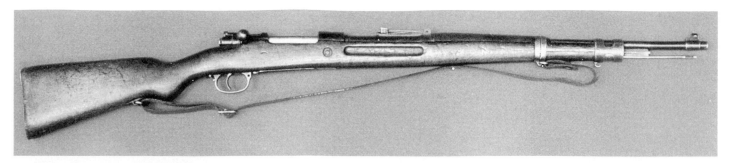

Full-length view of the Standard Modell Model 1933 Short Rifle

Full-length view of the alternate version of the Standard Modell Short Rifle. Note the side mounted sling, and lack of grasping grooves.

The receiver ring of the Standard Modell Model 1933 Carbine, showing the Mauser Banner legend

This rifle was made with a pistol grip stock and an upper hand guard that runs from in front of the rear sight to just beyond the lower barrel band. The upper barrel band incorporates a parade hook and the nose cap has the typical German-style "H" bayonet lug. Swivels are on the bottom of the lower band and the stock. The bolt handle is straight.

Length: 43.60"; **Weight:** 8.8 lbs.; **Barrel:** 23.62"; **Caliber:** 7.92 x 57mm; **Rifling:** 4-groove, r/hand; **Operation:** Turnbolt action; **Feed:** 5-round, staggered column, flush, box magazine; **Sights:** Tangent leaf rear sight graduated to 2000 meters. **Remarks:** Mauser Banner trademark on the receiver ring, with "Standard Modell" on the side rail. Mauser Banner logo on the receiver bridge.

STANDARD MODELL MODEL 1933 CARBINE: Identical to the German Model 98k, with a sling mounted on the left side and a turned-down bolt handle. The lower band is held by a short band retaining spring and the upper band is held by a pin. The stock will often be found with grasping grooves. This is the forerunner of Germany's standardized weapon of World War II.

Length: 43.60"; **Weight:** 8.60 lbs.; **Barrel:** 23.62"; **Caliber:** 7.92 x 57mm (available in 7.65 x 53mm and 7 x 57mm); **Rifling:** 4-groove, r/hand; **Operation:** Turnbolt action; **Feed:** 5-round, staggered column, flush, box magazine; **Sights:** Tangent leaf rear sight adjustable to 2000 meters. **Remarks:** Mauser Banner trademark on the receiver ring, with "Standard Modell" on the side rail, Mauser Banner logo on the receiver bridge.

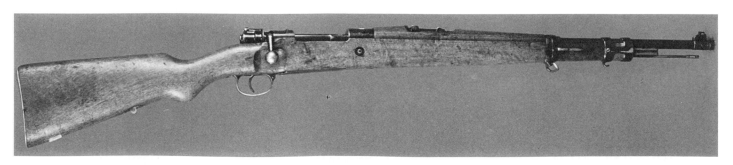

Full-length view of a slightly different version of the Chinese Standard Modell Model 1933 Carbine. Note the bottom mounted swivel on the lower band, and the quick release sling attachment behind the pistol grip.

Side rail of the Standard Modell Model 1933 Carbine. Note the commercial markings and commercial proofs.

The left side of the barrel and receiver of the Chinese Standard Modell Model 1933 Carbine, showing the Nationalist Chinese insignia on the side of the barrel and the receiver. Note the Mauser Banner logo on the top of the receiver ring.

Right side of the stock of the Chinese Standard Modell Model 1933 Carbine, showing the Nationalist Chinese insignias stamped into the wood

CHINESE COPY OF THE VZ 24 WITH FOLDING BAYONET: Obviously manufactured in a Chinese state arsenal, in all probability at the end of World War II, this copy of the Czech VZ 24 Short Rifle also incorporates the added feature of the Japanese Model 44 fold-

Chinese Nationalist troops fighting in the defense of Shanghai against the Japanese, C. 1937 (Frederich Dahlmann)

The Nationalist insignia stamped into the stock behind the rear guard screw of the Chinese Standard Modell Model 1933 Carbine

ing bayonet. It seems logical to assume that stockpiles of Japanese parts were cannibalized to aid in the manufacture of Chinese weapons.

Of typical, less-than-perfect Chinese manufacture of the period, the short rifle incorporates a pronounced pistol grip stock, straight bolt handle, and a shorter than usual barrel. The sling swivels are mounted on the left of the stock. It is absolutely unknown as to how many short rifles of this nature were produced.

Length: 43.25"; **Weight:** 8.90 lbs.; **Barrel:** 23.25"; **Caliber:** 7.92 x 57mm; **Rifling:** 4-groove, r/hand; **Operation:** Turnbolt action; **Feed:** 5-round, staggered column, flush, box magazine; **Sights:** Tangent leaf rear sight graduated to 2000 meters. **Remarks:** Chinese marking (crest or arsenal stamp) on the receiver, star on the left side of stock below sling swivel.

Full-length view of the modified Chinese copy of the Czech VZ 24 Short Rifle with folding bayonet (Springfield Armory Museum)

Chinese crest, or arsenal markings, on the receiver ring of the Chinese modified copy of the Czech VZ 24 Short Rifle with folding bayonet (Springfield Armory Museum)

Star impression on the left side of the buttstock of the Chinese modified copy of the Czech VZ 24 Short Rifle with folding bayonet (Springfield Armory Museum)

COLOMBIA

Permanent settlement of the country now known as Colombia did not take place until 1525, although the Spanish had visited in 1500. This territory was subject to the Viceroyalty of Peru until 1718, when the Viceroyalty of Bogotá was established. In 1794 the movement for freedom began, leading to an abortive rebellion in 1796, which was squashed, but was followed by other attempts until the year 1810, when an independent junta was set up in Bogotá. Led by Simón Bolívar, the Republican forces defeated the Royalist forces in a number of battles and held sway over the western section of present-day Venezuela.

With the defeat of Napoleon, the Spanish were able to reorganize and concentrate superior forces in the country, which gradually led to the Spanish recovering most of the territory previously lost. Under the command of Santander of Colombia and Simón Bolívar of Venezuela, the nationalist forces, aided by American and Irish mercenaries, were able to turn the tide during four years of merciless conflict, culminating in the battle of Boyaca on 7 August 1819. This defeat of the Spanish secured the independence of Colombia, Ecuador, and Venezuela. A Republic of Gran Colombia was formed on 17 December 1819, consisting of the three independent countries. This experiment lasted for only ten years.

Colombia was a federal republic from 1858 to 1885, but following a revolution in 1886, a new constitution proclaimed the country a unitary presidential republic. The country was torn by internal strife between the Conservatives and the Liberals for the rest of the century, culminating in a violent civil war between 1899 and 1902 that cost the lives of one hundred thousand people. In 1903, supported and manipulated by the United States, the people of the province of Panama revolted and declared the Republic of Panama. United States commercial interests, as well as the construction of the Panama Canal, guaranteed that the new Republic would not be overthrown.

In 1932, Peruvian nationalists, without government support, attacked and occupied the Colombian colony of Leticia, located in a remote corner of the Amazon region of Colombia. This incursion was later backed by Peruvian troops and Peruvian naval river units. These moves provoked and united the Colombians, resulting in a small frontier war known as the "Leticia Conflict." Although ill-equipped and fewer in number, the Colombians Armed Forces were victorious in the many small battles that led to the conclusion of the affair.

An interesting sidenote to this border war is that the Colombian forces had to rely upon German Lufthansa pilots and flight crews, as well as American mercenaries, to help fly their newly purchased fleet of Curtiss Hawk II fighters with interchangeable floats and wheels, followed by a large number of Curtiss Falcon F8C reconnaissance bombers. German medal groups have been found on the market with Colombian awards amongst the German decorations.

Rivalry continued throughout the twentieth century between the Conservatives and the Liberals, erupting into one long period of prolonged strife, 1946 through 1958, known as "La Violencia," during which two hundred thousand people lost their lives.

Colombia made a token declaration of war against the Axis powers, but was too preoccupied with internal strife to do more. During the Korean War, in spite of the internal struggles, the Colombian Armed Forces sent four successive infantry battalions, as well as naval units, overseas to serve and gain experience in the Korean conflict. All of these highly trained units served with distinction and honor, proving themselves the equal of any troops then operating in the Korean theatre.

In 1953, the army under General Gustavo Rojas Pinilla took over control of the country and brought a halt to the civil war within four years. In 1957, the Army prevented an attempt by General Rojas Pinilla to extend his term in office, and after a brief period under a military junta, the control of the government was returned to civilian politicians. While striving to maintain a balance of power between Conservatives and Liberals, Colombia has remained one of the few Latin American countries to live under democratic conditions. Beset with internal problems created by the trafficking of drugs, Colombia strives to maintain its democratic principles while seeking to find ways to eradicate the drug trade from within its borders.

MODEL 1891 RIFLE (ARGENTINE PATTERN): As with many Latin American countries, one of the first Mauser rifles with which Co-

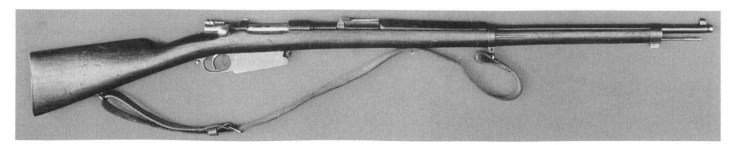

Full-length view of the Model 1891 Rifle (Argentine Pattern)

Full-length view of the Model 1904 Rifle

lombia equipped itself was the venerable Model 1891 Argentine Pattern Rifle, produced by Loewe in caliber 7.65 x 53mm. The data on this rifle will be found under the section on Argentina.

MODEL 1904 RIFLE: Prior to 1914, Colombia was able to acquire small numbers of the Model 1904 Rifle, sold commercially by DWM. These rifles were identical to the Brazilian Model 1907, having a pistol grip stock, an upper hand guard that runs from in front of the receiver ring to just beyond the extremely narrow lower barrel band, a parade hook on the bottom of the upper band, the short German "H" style bayonet lug, sling swivel on the bottom of the lower band, and a quick-release sling attachment on the bottom of the buttstock. The rifle also has a long heavy cocking piece and no guard lock screws.

Length: 49.20"; **Weight:** 8.30 lbs.; **Barrel:** 29.13"; **Caliber:** 7 x 57mm; **Rifling:** 4-groove, r/hand; **Operation:** Turnbolt action; **Feed:** 5-round, staggered column, flush, box magazine; **Sights:** Tangent leaf rear sight graduated to 2000 meters. **Remarks:** National crest on receiver ring, manufacturer's markings on the side rail.

MODEL 1912 STEYR RIFLE: Shortly before the outbreak of the First World War, Colombia ordered an unknown quantity of Model 1912 Rifles from Osterreichische Waffenfabrik-Gesellschaft, Austria. These rifles are identical to those ordered by Mexico, and the order, in both cases, was not completed before hostilities broke out, with the balance of the order being pressed into service by the German army.

The rifle is a faithful copy of the Gew 98, with certain exceptions. The rifle is fitted with a pistol grip stock and the upper hand guard extends from in front of the receiver ring to just beyond the lower

Colombian national crest on the receiver ring of the Model 1904 Rifle

barrel band. The lower band is equipped with a sling swivel, with another on the bottom of the buttstock. The upper barrel band has a parade hook on the bottom, and the nose cap incorporates the short German "H" style bayonet lug that requires a bayonet with muzzle ring. A screw-held washer is countersunk into the right side of the buttstock.

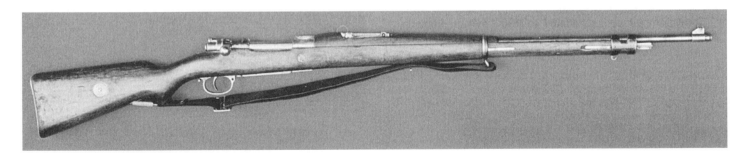

Full-length view of the Colombian Model 1912 Rifle

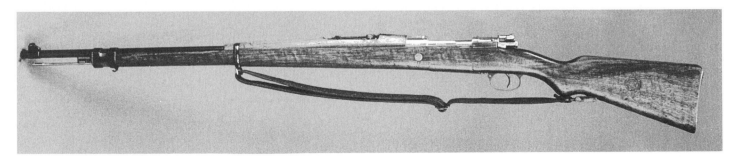

Left full-length view of the Colombian Model 1912 Rifle

Colombian national crest on the receiver ring of the Colombian Model 1912 Rifle

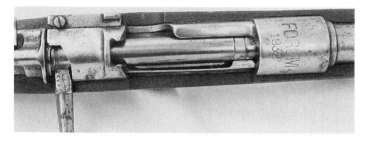

View of the action and receiver ring of an FN made Model 1912 Rifle; note the markings "FORUM/1932." (Michael Gaddini collection)

Length: 49.10"; **Weight:** 9.0 lbs.; **Barrel:** 29.13"; **Caliber:** 7 x 57mm; **Rifling:** 4-groove, r/hand; **Operation:** Turnbolt action; **Feed:** 5-round, staggered column, flush, box magazine; **Sights:** Tangent leaf rear sight graduated to 2000 meters. **Remarks:** Colombian national crest on the receiver ring, with manufacturer's markings on the side rail.

CZECH VZ 23 SHORT RIFLE: In 1929, Colombia acquired approximately five thousand Czech VZ 23 Rifles in caliber 7 x 57mm from Czechoslovakia. This was the first of the Czechoslovakian Short Rifle designs, and was based on the Kar 98AZ, but stocked in the manner of the Gew 98. The VZ 23 was essentially a VZ 24 Short Rifle, but slightly shortened and lightened for use by Latin American

Manufacturer's markings on the side rail of the Colombian Model 1912 Rifle

Stock cartouche on the left side of the FN made Model 1912 Long Rifle. (Michael Gaddini collection)

Czech markings on the receiver ring of the Colombian VZ 23 Short Rifle

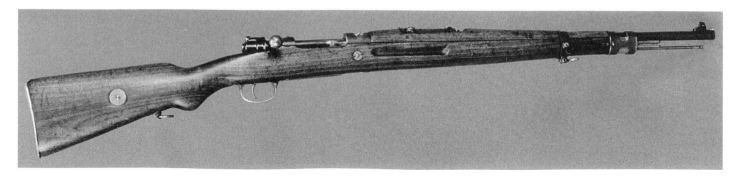

Full-length view of the Czech VZ 23 Short Rifle as used by Colombia

Manufacturer's markings in Spanish on the side rail of the Colombian VZ 23 Short Rifle

Manufacturer's markings on the left side rail, including the serial number on the receiver ring of the Colombian Steyr Model 1929 Short Rifle

countries—it proved a highly popular weapon. Equipped with a pistol grip stock, the lower band of the VZ 23 is located only 2.75 inches from the upper band, with the upper hand guard running from in front of the receiver ring to the upper band. The lower band has an integral sling swivel machined into the left side of the band, while the sling swivel on the bottom of the buttstock is pivoted on the bottom of the buttstock, allowing for lateral movement as well as movement to the front and the rear. Further information on this short rifle will be found under the section on Czechoslovakia.

Colombian national crest on the receiver ring of the Colombian Steyr Model 1929 Short Rifle

STEYR-SOLOTHURN A-G MODEL 1929 SHORT RIFLE: This Colombian contract short rifle was produced and purchased in limited quantities. It was the forerunner of the Model 29/40 Short Rifle that was produced by Steyr-Daimler Puch, A-G of Steyr, Austria for the German Luftwaffe prior to and during World War II. This short rifle shows marked Austrian influences, especially in the barrel bands used.

Equipped with a pistol grip stock, the upper hand guard extends from in front of the receiver ring to the upper band, which is secured by a screw through the stock. The lower band is clamped by a screw attached to the right side. The nose cap is fitted with the short German style "H" bayonet lug, requiring the use of a bayonet equipped with a muzzle ring. The lower band is fitted with a swivel on the bottom, and a swivel attachment on the left side; the buttstock is fitted with a quick release fitting on both the bottom and the left side at the wrist. Note the grasping grooves and the flat, countersunk screw-held washer in the right side of the buttstock.

Length: 43.25"; Weight: 9.0 lbs.; Barrel: 22.50"; Caliber: 7 x 57mm; Rifling: 4-groove, r/hand; Operation: Turnbolt action; Feed: 5-round, staggered column, flush, box magazine; Sights: Tangent leaf rear sight graduated to 2000 meters. Remarks: Colombian national crest on the receiver ring, with manufacturer's markings on the left side rail.

COLOMBIAN FN MODEL 24 AND MODEL 30 SHORT RIFLES: The FN Model 24 and Model 30 supplied to Colombia in the early 1930s were almost identical, and will be discussed together in this section. Presumably at the request of the Colombian government, both models were equipped with the upper hand guard running from in front of the receiver ring to approximately one inch beyond the lower barrel band. Both models have pistol grip style stocks with grasping grooves, and bands that are retained by separate springs. The lower barrel band is fitted with an integral swivel on the left side and another swivel on the bottom of the band. There is a swivel on the bottom of the buttstock, and a quick release attachment on the left side of the stock at the wrist. On the FN Model 24, there is an inset, screw-retained, flat washer on the right side

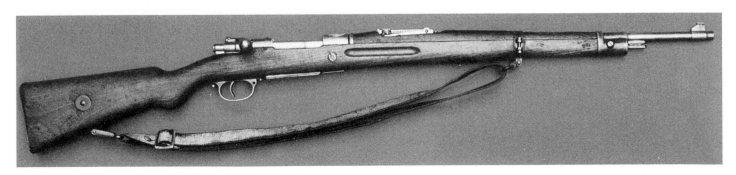

Full-length view of the Colombian Steyr Model 1929 Short Rifle

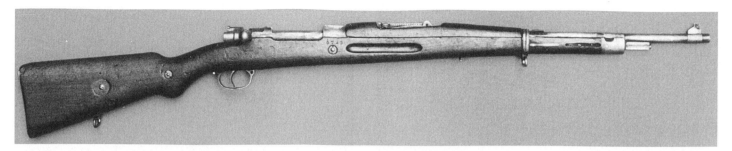

Full-length view of the Colombian FN Model 24 Short Rifle

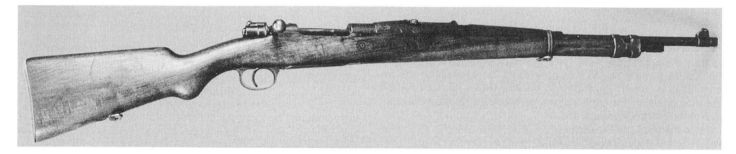

Full-length view of the Colombian FN Model 30 Short Rifle (Cliff Baumann)

Crest of Colombia on the receiver of the Colombian FN Model 24 Short Rifle

Side rail and receiver markings on the Colombian FN Model 24 Short Rifle

of the stock, as well as a recoil crossbolt at the wrist, with another under the receiver.

Length: 43.25"; **Weight:** 10.0 lbs.; **Barrel:** 22.50"; **Caliber:** 7 x 57mm; **Rifling:** 4-groove, r/hand; **Operation:** Turnbolt action; **Feed:** 5-round, staggered column, flush, box magazine; **Sights:** Tangent leaf rear sight graduated to 2000 meters. **Remarks:** Colombian national crest on the receiver ring, with date of manufacture on the left side of the ring. Manufacturer's markings on the left side rail.

COLOMBIAN CZECH VZ 12/33 CARBINE: During the 1930s, Colombia ordered a small number of Czech VZ 12/33 Carbines, a lightened version of the VZ 24 Short Rifle, especially popular in Latin American countries.

The Colombian VZ 12/33 is fitted with a pistol grip stock, without grasping grooves. The upper handguard runs from the front of the receiver ring to just beyond the lower band. The lower and upper

Colombian crest on the receiver ring of the Colombian Czech VZ 12/33 Carbine (Bob Bennett collection)

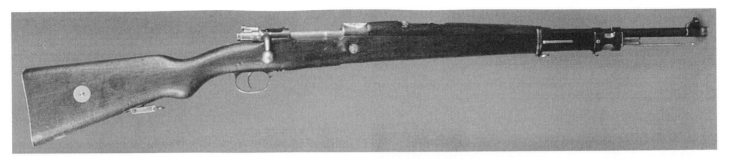

Full-length view of the Colombian Czech Model VZ 12/33 Carbine (Bob Bennett collection)

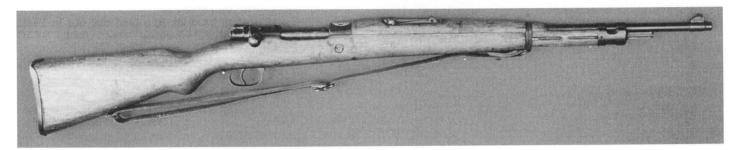

Full-length view of the Colombian FN Model 1950 Short Rifle

Manufacturer's markings in Spanish on the left side rail of the Colombian Czech VZ 12/33 Carbine (Bob Bennett collection)

bands are only a few inches apart, with the lower band retained by a spring, and the upper band held in place by a screw through the stock. The front sight is not protected by "sight ears." There is a swivel on the bottom of the lower band, and a quick release sling attachment behind the pistol grip of the stock. The bolt handle is bent down, but the stock has not been recessed for ease of grasping.

Length: 41.75"; **Weight:** 8.0 lbs.; **Barrel:** 21.50"; **Caliber:** 7 x 57mm (some remaining stocks are believed to have been altered

to .30-06 after the Second World War); **Rifling:** 4-groove, r/hand; **Operation:** Turnbolt action; **Feed:** 5-round, staggered column, flush, box magazine; **Sights:** Tangent leaf rear sight graduated to 1400 meters. **Remarks:** Colombian national crest on the receiver ring, with "EJERCITO DE COLOMBIA" in an arch above. Manufacturer's markings in Spanish stamped on the left side rail.

COLOMBIAN FN MODEL 1950 SHORT RIFLE: In the early 1950s, FN delivered an unknown number of new rifles chambered for the U.S. cartridge .30-06, at which time many of the early FN weapons were converted at Colombian government arsenals to the same caliber cartridge. The Model 1950 Short Rifle is a robust rifle, with a pistol grip stock, and an upper hand guard running from the receiver ring to approximately one inch beyond the lower barrel band. The upper and lower bands are retained by separate springs, with a swivel on the bottom of the lower band and another on the bottom of the buttstock. One further identifying feature of this rifle is the butt plate, which is cupped and overlapping along the sides of the stock rather than being flush. The bottom of the butt plate is also corrugated to provide better contact with the shoulder.

Length: 43.0"; **Weight:** 9.50 lbs.; **Barrel:** 22.75"; **Caliber:** .30-06; **Rifling:** 4-groove, r/hand; **Operation:** Turnbolt action; **Feed:** 5-round, staggered column, flush, box magazine; **Sights:** Tangent leaf rear sight graduated to 2000 meters. **Remarks:** Colombian national crest (alternate version), with "Colombian Armed Forces " in Spanish in an oval.

Manufacturer's markings on the left side rail of the Colombian FN Model 1950 Short Rifle

Caliber marking on the receiver bridge of the Colombian Model 1950 Short Rifle

Colombian crest on the receiver ring of the Colombian Model 1950 Short Rifle

Colombian "Lanceros" being inspected, C. 1988

COSTA RICA

Discovered and named by Columbus in 1502, the region known now as Costa Rica was administered as a Spanish province under the Spanish colonial viceroyalty of Guatemala. The group of provinces that made up the viceroyalty broke with Spain in 1821, and for a period of two years, the former province was absorbed into the Mexican Empire of Agustín de Iturbide. With the collapse of the United Provinces of Central America, Costa Rica became an independent republic in 1838, with the first democratic elections held in 1889.

With the exception of the military dictatorship of Tomás Guardia from 1870 to 1882, Costa Rica has enjoyed one of the most democratic governments in Latin America.

An attempt at election fraud led to a brief civil war in 1948, which was won by the National Liberation forces under the leadership of "Don Pepe" José Figueres Ferrer. As a result of this change in government, the Costa Rican army was abolished. Subsequent governments have directed their efforts towards economic matters, with the result that the country has made great progress in solving its economic problems, while at the same time promoting peace among its Latin American neighbors.

MODEL 1895 RIFLE: As is the case with many Latin American countries, one of the first Mauser rifles that was adopted was the Model 1895 Rifle, which saw long and dependable service in Costa Rica. The total number of rifles purchased is estimated at less than ten thousand, with some being bought from Ludwig Loewe & Co (1895-1896), and the balance from DWM (1897-1900). This rifle is virtually a duplicate of the Chilean Model 1895 and is fully covered under the section on Chile.

COSTA RICAN MODEL 1910 RIFLE: Made by Waffenrabrik Mauser A-G of Oberndorf am Neckar from 1911 to 1914, the Model 1910 Rifle is a close copy of the Gew 98, fitted with a pistol grip stock and an upper hand guard that runs from the receiver ring to just beyond the lower band. The upper band has a bayonet lug on the bottom for use with the Model 1895 bayonet. The lower band has a swivel at the bottom, and another on the bottom of the buttstock.

The major, and most outstanding difference, is the shrouded bolt face enclosing the cartridge case rim. This was patented in Germany in 1898, but rarely used on military weapons. Only the rim of the cartridge protrudes beyond the rear face of the barrel, with the cartridge head enclosed by the barrel, bolt, and extractor. The face of

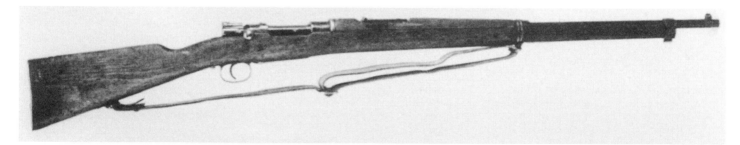

Full-length view of the Costa Rican Model 1895 Rifle

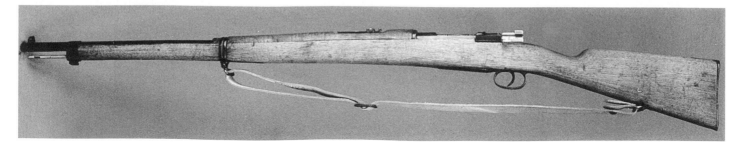

Full-length view of the Costa Rican Model 1895 Rifle

Full-length view of the Costa Rican Model 1910 Rifle

Side rail of the Costa Rican Model 1910 Rifle, showing the model designation

The receiver ring of the Costa Rican Model 1910 Rifle. This particular specimen has the Waffenfabrik Mauser/Oberndorf markings instead of the Costa Rican national crest.

the chamber has a machined recess for the extractor, making barrel alignment and any repairs extremely critical. This also requires that the projection on the bolt head that supports and guides the cartridge during feeding and ejection be removed. Once common on the surplus weapons market, the Costa Rican Model 1910 Rifle is rarely, if ever, seen today.

Length: 48.80"; **Weight:** 8.8 lbs.; **Barrel:** 29.13"; **Caliber:** 7 x 57mm; **Rifling:** 4-grooves, r/hand; **Operation:** Turnbolt action; **Feed:** 5-round, staggered column, flush, box magazine; **Sights:** Tangent leaf rear sight graduated to 2000 meters. **Remarks:** Costa Rican national crest on the receiver ring, manufacturer's markings and "Model 1910" on the left side rail.

FN MODEL 24 SHORT RIFLE: As supplied to Costa Rica by FN in the mid-1930s, the export model short rifle differs little from those supplied to other Latin American countries. Fitted with a pistol grip stock with grasping grooves, the rifle has an upper hand guard that extends from in front of the receiver ring to the upper band. The lower band has an integral sling loop on the left hand side, with another sling swivel on the bottom of the band. The buttstock has a sling swivel on the bottom of the stock and a quick release attachment on the left side of the stock at the wrist. The nose cap has the German "H" type bayonet lug for acceptance of bayonets without a muzzle ring. Note the flat, inset washer held by a screw on the right side of the stock.

Length: 43.25; **Weight:** 10.0 lbs.; **Barrel:** 22.50; **Caliber:** 7 x 57mm; **Rifling:** 4-groove r/hand; **Operation:** Turnbolt action; **Feed:** 5-round, staggered column, flush, box magazine; **Sights:** Tangent leaf rear sight graduated to 2000 meters. **Remarks:** It is unknown as to whether or not the FN Model 24 Short Rifles were marked with the Costa Rican national crest, or simply with the FN logo. Manufacturer's markings are found on the left side rail.

Mauser Banner logo on the right side of the buttstock of the Costa Rican Model 1910 Rifle

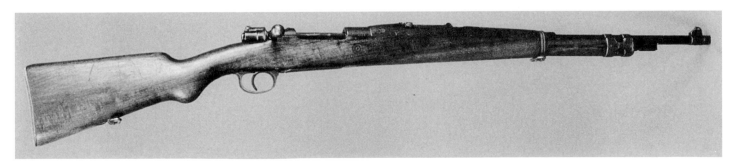

Full-length view of the Costa Rican FN Model 1924 Short Rifle

CZECHOSLOVAKIA

With the collapse of the Hapsburg monarchy at the end of World War I, the new multinational state of Czechoslovakia, founded by Thomas Masaryk and Eduard Benes, emerged from the ashes. This was the most democratic state in central Europe between the wars.

The creation of the new state also established the nucleus of a soon-to-be effective arms industry, based on acquiring the Skoda factory. November 1918 was the month the Brno Arms Works was established by Czech officials, assuming control over the former Austro-Hungarian arms factories at Brno. Known in the beginning as the State Armament and Engineering Works, on 1 February 1919, the plant was reorganized and renamed Czechoslovak State Armament Works, Brno. On 12 June 1924, the name of the works was changed to the Ceskoslovenska Zbrojovka, A. S., or the Czechoslovakian Arms Factory Ltd.

With the disbanding of the Austro-Hungarian armies, the Czechs were supplied, by the order of the Armistice Commission, with one hundred thousand Mauser and Mannlicher rifles, all of which were reconditioned at the factory at Brno. In 1921, five thousand Mannlicher short rifles were manufactured at the plant, and as war reparations, blueprints were supplied by the Mauser Works for the manufacture of Gew 98 military rifles. Parts were received from Mauser that enabled the Czechs to assemble forty-two thousand Gew 98 Rifles.

In 1919, the factory at Brno produced the first Mauser-Jelen short rifles (Puska Mauser-Jelena) in caliber 7 x 57mm. These were standard Model 1898-type short rifles with a distinctive pistol grip stock, and an upper hand guard running from in front of the receiver

Czechoslovakian guard drawn up in the courtyard of the Hradcany Castle (Signal)

Czechoslovakian cavalry unit on patrol in a wooded area, C. 1938 (UPI)

ring to the upper band. It was also fitted with a nose cap similar to that of the British Short Lee Enfield, which runs under the forestock to an intermediate band. As on the SMLE, the nose cap incorporates a special boss for the muzzle ring of the bayonet. Sling swivels are fitted to the underside of the true barrel band and the bottom of the buttstock. These rifles were often fitted with a magazine floorplate quick release button inside the trigger guard. After troop testing by the Czechoslovakian army (some short rifles had also been sent to Yugoslavia), the Mauser-Jelen was abandoned in 1922 in favor of a rifle based upon the Mexican Model 1912.

The Model 1898/22 was the result of the updating of the Mexican Model 1912 Rifle. This rifle was produced from 1924 to 1930 and adopted for troop use by the Czechoslovakian army. Initially popular with foreign purchasers, the Model 98/22 was supplanted by the VZ 24 Short Rifle. 1923 saw the first of the new series of short rifles based on the overall design of the 98/22, but with lesser overall dimensions. The first weapons made were from cannibalized parts and were designated the Model 23, while the Model 23A was produced from completely new parts. The perfected short rifle, called the VZ 24, was produced in 1924, differing in a number of ways from the Model 1923. By 1925, sufficient quantities of the new short rifle had been produced to equip the Czech army infantry, cavalry, and armoured divisions. At this time, the first large orders for export were received, and continued until the time of the German occupation.

The military version of the Model 16/33 Carbine, essentially a shortened, lightened form of the VZ 24 Short Rifle, was exported in 1933. This same carbine was used by Czech gendarmerie and treasury guards, and upon the occupation of Czechoslovakia, became the basis for the German Gew 33/40 Mountain Carbine. The Model 12/33 Carbine was another lightened version of the VZ 24, intended primarily for export to Central and South American purchasers. This model is derived from the Mexican Model 1912 pattern as supplied to Mexico in the 1920s.

Other Czech-made rifles that might be encountered by the collector are the "JC" series of Short Rifles, patterned again after a lightened version of the VZ 24. Lithuania ordered a number of "L" pattern rifles and carbines, easily identified by the oversize magazine that extends below the level of the stock in order to accommodate the British .303 rimmed cartridge for which they were chambered. These weapons also incorporate a bayonet lug on the bottom of the nose cap to accept the Austrian Model 1895 bayonet.

Other Czech-made weapons found with model numbers, such as "VZ 35," "VZ 32," etc. will usually be slight variations of the basic VZ 24.

CZECH MODEL 1898/22 RIFLE: This rifle, based on the design of the Mexican Model 1912 Rifle, was the first rifle adopted for service with the Czechoslovakian army. The rifle is fitted with a pistol grip stock, and the upper hand guard runs from in front of the receiver ring to just beyond the lower barrel band. Both the upper and lower

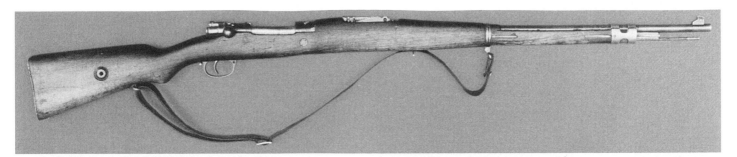

Full-length view of the Czech Model 1898/22 Rifle

The later markings, used from 1922-1923, on the receiver ring of the Czech Model 98/22 Rifle

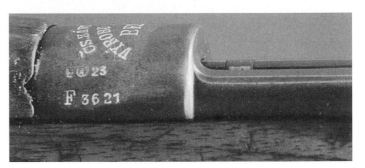

Side view of the Czech Model 98/22 Rifle, showing placement of the serial number

Tangent leaf rear sight graduated to 2000 meters. Note that the sight may be found with Turkish or Farsi numerals. **Remarks:** The receiver ring is liable to show either the early Czech State Armament Works, or the later Czechoslovakian Arms Factory Ltd. markings.

CZECH MODEL VZ 23 SHORT RIFLE: Used mostly by Czech army units, the VZ 23 was the first attempt at producing a short rifle along the lines of the Kar 98AZ, but using the action of the Model 98/22. This rifle has a pistol grip stock, and the upper hand guard extends from the front of the receiver ring to the upper band. Note the very short distance between the upper and the lower band; this was later

bands are held in place by springs. There is a sling swivel on the bottom of the lower barrel band and another on the bottom of the buttstock. Note the domed washers and hollow rod for bolt disassembly in the stock. This rifle was used by many countries and saw service in many of the world's smaller wars and skirmishes; Kurdistan rebels, for example, use and swear by their old 98/22 rifles even to this day! After the 1920-1922 Turkish War of Independence, the Turkish government bought the Model 98/22 by the thousands. Chinese armies were well equipped with the Model 98/22, with some even being used in the Korean War.

Length: 48.90"; **Weight:** 8.55 lbs.; **Barrel:** 29.13"; **Caliber:** 7.92 x 57mm rimless; also available in 7 x 57mm, and 7.65 x 53mm; **Rifling:** 4-groove, r/hand; **Operation:** Turnbolt action; **Feed:** 5-round, staggered column, flush, box magazine; **Sights:**

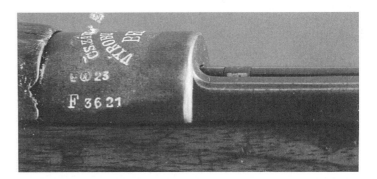

Left side view of the receiver ring showing Czech acceptance marks and the rifle serial number of the Czech VZ23 Short Rifle (Bob Bennett collection)

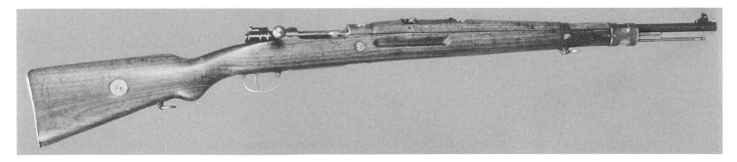

Full-length view of the Czech VZ 23 Short Rifle (Bob Bennett collection)

"Czechoslovakian Factory for Arms Manufacture, BRNO" marking on the receiver ring of the Czech Model VZ 23 Short Rifle (Bob Bennett collection)

Markings on the receiver ring of the Czech VZ 24 Short Rifle

changed in the VZ 24 by moving the lower band further back. The lower band is secured by a screw through the forestock, and a swivel is located on the left side, as well as the bottom of the band. There are also swivels on the side and the bottom of the buttstock. The bolt handle is straight.

Length: 41.50"; **Weight:** 8.90 lbs.; **Barrel:** 21.50"; **Caliber:** As used by Czechoslovakia, the caliber is 7.92 x 57mm; 7 x 57mm and 7.65 x 53mm were available on order; **Rifling:** 4-groove, r/hand; **Operation:** Turnbolt action; **Feed:** 5-round, staggered column, flush, box magazine; **Sights:** Tangent leaf rear sight graduated to 2000 meters. Note that two elevation side locks are provided, and that both sides of the leaf have locking notches. Elevation is in 50 meter increments. **Remarks:** Most VZ 23 Short Rifles will be marked "Czechoslovakian Factory for Arms

Manufacture, Brno" on the receiver ring. Acceptance markings and serial number will be found on the left side of the receiver ring.

CZECH VZ 24 SHORT RIFLE: This is the most famous of the Czech Mauser rifles produced, the standard rifle for the Czech armed forces prior to World War II. Resembling the German Kar 98k to some degree, the VZ 24, unlike the 98K, has an upper hand guard extending from in front of the receiver ring to the upper band; the bolt handle is straight, the lower band, which is secured through the forestock by a screw, has a swivel mounted on the left side and on the bottom of the band. There is another set of swivels on the bottom of the buttstock and left side of the stock. Many VZ 24 short rifles will be found with a front sight protector, which is secured by a screw clamp.

The VZ 24 Short Rifle was employed by many countries and served not only during World War II, but in many smaller, earlier, but nonetheless deadly wars. Chinese armies were equipped with

Full-length view of the Czech VZ 24 Short Rifle

Czech VZ24 Sniper Rifle, with turned down bolt handle for clearance of the claw-mounted Czech Sniper Scope. (Robert Jensen Collection)

the VZ 24 (all marked "1937" and having a "P" serial number prefix), which eventually were captured by the Japanese, who then equipped five of their divisions with captured weapons. The Roumanian army standardized on the VZ 24 in the late 1930s, with the rifles serving them well on the Eastern front. Yugoslavia had purchased VZ 24 Short Rifles and produced their own version, and these dependable weapons served the Yugoslav partisans well in the mountains of Serbia, Bosnia, and Croatia.

Bolivian armies were equipped mail order-style with VZ 24 Short Rifles in their struggles with Paraguayan forces during the epic battles of the Chaco during the Gran Chaco War of 1932-1935; unfortunately for Bolivia, most of these VZ 24 Short Rifles ended up in the hands of the Paraguayans, who used them to good effect. Brazil, Colombia, Guatemala, Peru, and Venezuela were also satisfied users of the VZ 24 Short Rifle. The small army of Lithuania was also equipped with VZ 24 Short Rifles. Many of these were captured by the German forces, and then by the Russians, who later supplied them from storage to the Viet Cong, from whom they were captured by the Americans!

Length: 43.30"; **Weight:** 9.2 lbs.; **Barrel:** 23.23"; **Caliber:** 7.92 x 57mm; also available in 7x 57mm, and 7.65 x 53mm; **Rifling:** 4-groove, r/hand; **Operation:** Turnbolt action; **Feed:** 5-round, staggered column, flush, box magazine; **Sights:** Tangent leaf rear sight graduated in 50 meter increments to 2000 meters. **Remarks:** VZ 24 Short Rifles used by Czech forces will have either the rampant lion crest, or the markings "Ceskoslovenska/Zbrojovka/BRNO" on the receiver ring.

CZECH VZ 12/33 CARBINE: Developed for the export market, and purportedly derived from the Mexican contract Model VZ 12 Mex.,

the VZ 12/33 Carbine closely resembles a shortened and lighter Czech VZ 24 Short Rifle.

The carbine is fitted with a pistol grip stock, and the upper hand guard extends from the front of the receiver ring to just beyond the lower barrel band. The upper and lower barrel bands are quite close together, with the lower band secured by a retaining spring and the upper band by a screw through the stock. The bolt handle is bent down, but the stock is not cut out to facilitate grasping of the bolt knob. There is a swivel on the bottom of the lower band and a quick release attachment on the bottom of the stock behind the pistol grip.

Length: 41.75"; **Weight:** 8.0 lbs.; **Barrel:** 21.50"; **Caliber:** 7.92 x 57mm; **Rifling:** 4-groove, r/hand; **Operation:** Turnbolt action; **Feed:** 5-round, staggered column, flush, box magazine; **Sights:** Tangent leaf rear sight graduated to 1400 meters. **Remarks:** Normally stamped with the national crest of the country purchasing the weapon. The side rail will have the manufacturer's markings in either Spanish or Czechoslovakian on the left side rail.

CZECH VZ 16/33 CARBINE: The Czech Model VZ 16/33 Carbine is a lightweight carbine specifically designed for use by police and similar paramilitary organizations. The carbine is compact, with the bolt handle turned down and the bolt knob hollowed out on the underside. The stock is cut to facilitate handling of the bolt knob. The pistol grip stock has grasping grooves, and the upper hand guard extends from in front of the receiver to the upper band. The lower barrel band has an integral sling swivel on the left side, with another on the bottom of the band. There is a swivel at the bottom of the buttstock, but no corresponding side mount swivel on the left of the stock. On the sides of the small-diameter receiver, this carbine has

Full-length view of the Czech VZ 12/33 Carbine

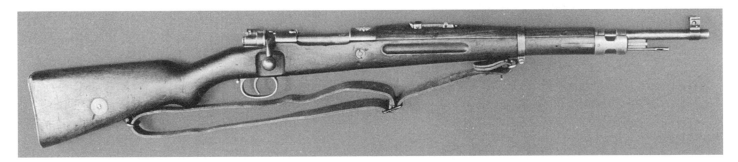

Full-length view of the Czech Model VZ 16/33 Carbine

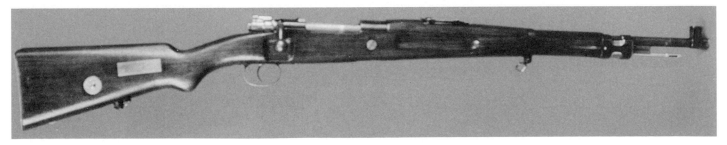

Full-length view of a presentation model of the Czech VZ 16/33 Carbine. Note the presentation plaque on the buttstock.

The Czech national crest on the receiver ring of the Czech Model VZ 16/33 Carbine

Close-up view of the presentation plaque on the buttstock of the Czech VZ 16/33 Carbine

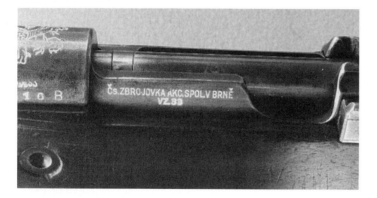

The side rail of the Czech Model VZ 16/33 Carbine, showing the manufacturer and the model number

lightening cuts that are concealed by the stock. The side walls of the receiver are also appreciably thinner. The Czech rampant lion coat of arms will always be found on the receiver ring. A special bayonet was made for this carbine, due to the shortened bayonet lug.

Length: 39.20"; **Weight:** 7.7 lbs.; **Barrel:** 19.29"; **Caliber:** 7.92 x 57mm as used in Czechoslovakia; also available in 7 x 57mm and 7.65 x 53mm; **Rifling:** 4-groove, r/hand; **Operation:** Turnbolt action; **Feed:** 5-round, staggered column, flush, box magazine; **Sights:** Tangent leaf rear sight graduated to 1000 meters in increments of 100 meters. **Remarks:** The Czech national crest of the rampant Czech lion on the receiver ring, with manufacturer's markings and model designation on the side rail.

DENMARK

After the Second World War, Denmark made use of the captured and abandoned equipment left behind by the Germans. One of these uses was the conversion of weapons into military target rifles made from the actions of both World War I and World War II German rifles.

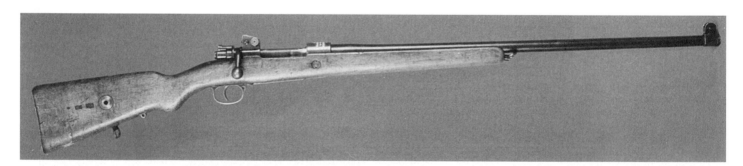

Full-length view of a Danish Military Target Rifle utilizing the action of a German G 98 Rifle. Note the bending of the bolt handle.

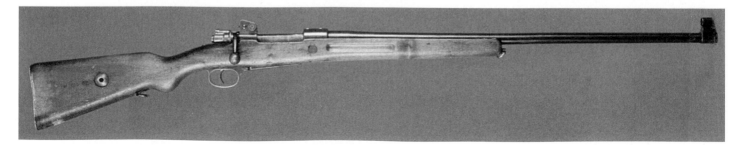

Full-length view of the Danish Military Target Rifle made with the action of a German Model 98k Carbine

Receiver ring of the Danish Military Target Rifle made with a Model G 98 action, showing the original German markings

Receiver ring markings on the Danish Military Target Rifle made with a Model 98k Carbine action

The Danish stampings, "Gevaerfabriken, Otterup," on the barrel of the Danish Military Target Rifle made with a World War I Model G 98 action

Barrel markings on the Danish Military Target Rifle at bottom, indicating that the action had been rebarreled by "Schutz & Larsen, Otterup"

zilian markings and restamping the weapons with Dominican markings. These rifles were also rechambered and rebarreled to .30-06, and began to appear on the U.S. surplus market in the 1960s. Presumably, they could have been in use by the Dominican forces during the political strife that occurred prior to the U.S. intervention in 1965 and 1966. All data relative to these rifles will be found under the section on Brazil.

DOMINICAN REPUBLIC

The Dominican Republic, the oldest continuously inhabited European settlement in the Americas, occupies two-thirds of the island of Hispaniola, sharing the island with Haiti. The country has had a tumultuous history, suffering occupation by various powers, including the forces of the United States, during its past. Under the reign of General Rafael Trujillo (1930-1961), a very efficient arms industry was established with the help of emigree Hungarian engineers and designers.

During the early 1950s, the national arsenal reconditioned surplus Brazilian Model 1908 Rifles and Short Rifles, removing all Bra-

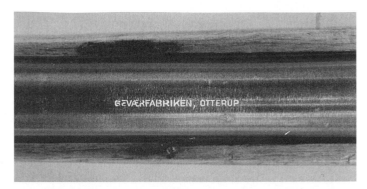

Stampings on the left side of the receiver ring of the Dominican Republic Model 1953 Rifle

Full-length view of the Dominican Republic Model 1953 Rifle (Ex-Brazilian Model 1908)

Full-length view of the Dominican Republic Model 1953 Short Rifle (Ex-Brazilian Model 1908 Short Rifle)

The receiver ring of the Dominican Republic Model 1953 Short Rifle (Ex-Brazilian Model 1908 Short Rifle), showing the markings and caliber applied by the Dominican arsenal

ECUADOR

Although Spanish exploration from Peru pushed into southern Ecuador in 1527, Spanish rule over the territory was not firmly established until 1533. During the early period of the Spanish colonization, the country was constantly in turmoil from civil wars between opposing conquistadore factions. Administered consecutively through the viceroyalty of Peru and New Grenada (Bogata), Spanish control of Quito, the capital, was terminated by a local junta in 1809, with full independence achieved in 1821 with the defeat of the royalists by a combined Colombian and Venezuelan army under José Antonio de Sucre at Pinchincha.

As part of the Republic of Gran Colombia, Ecuador joined politically with Venezuela and Colombia from 1822 to 1830. General Juan José Flores, leader of the forces of independence, removed Ecuador from the confederation in 1830 and ruled as a military dictator until ousted in 1845.

A brief war with Colombia firmly established the present day border between Colombia and Ecuador; however the border with Peru has been in contention to the present day (Peru/Ecuador incursions of January and February, 1995).

The first seventy years of liberty were beset with strife, insurrection, and continuous internal disturbances. The country was ruled as a theocracy by the religious fanatic Garcia Moreno from 1860 until his overthrow and assassination in 1875. However, it was during this period that the basis for the modern state of Ecuador was laid. Following the fall of Garcia Moreno, the country was torn apart by almost total anarchy for the next twenty years, followed by twenty years of enlightened secular rule by the Liberal party.

Boundary problems with Peru persisted, and in July 1941, Peru invaded at two separate points in southern Ecuador. Using paratroops for the first time on the America continent, as well as massive air, artillery, and naval support, fifteen thousand Peruvian troops, equipped with a battalion of new Czech tanks, pushed deep into the area of the Zarumilla River. This invasion was resisted by only 1,724 Ecuadoran troops from a total army strength of 5,610 men. Ecuadoran forces were mainly equipped with VZ 24 Short Rifles and VZ 12/33 Carbines. Ecuadoran resistance was finally broken by the capture of Puerto Bolivar by airborne troops. All fighting ceased after a campaign that lasted less than three weeks, with most of the territory in question being ceded to Peru by the Protocol of Rio de Janeiro. This protocol was never ratified by the Ecuadoran Congress, thus nothing changed.

After a period of economic instability following the brief war, Ecuador, which had been one of the poorest countries in South America, discovered oil fields that revolutionized the economy, boosting Ecuador into the position of being one of the continent's greatest oil export-

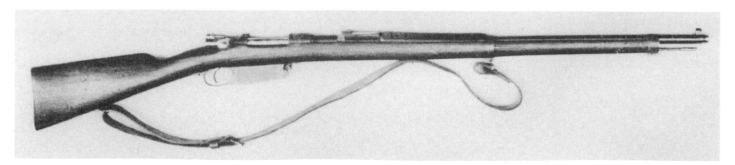

Ecuadoran army officers in the area of the Zarumilla River during the period of hostilities with Peru. (Col. Luis A. Rodriguez)

Full-length view of the Model 1891 Rifle (Argentine Pattern)

ers. Unfortunately, the majority of the fields of oil are found in the territory adjacent to the disputed boundary with Peru, thus ensuring a further bone of contention between the two countries, as evidenced by full-scale battles during January and February of 1981.

The frontier situation with Peru remains the major national problem for Ecuador, which keeps the bulk of its armed forces deployed in the southern area of the country. The Ecuadoran armed forces, while numerically smaller than the forces of Peru, are in a much more effective state of readiness than at any time since 1941, thanks to the infusion of oil money into the national economy.

In the late 1800s, Ecuador's arsenal resembled the late Bannerman's Army/Navy Store, with the army acquiring approximately 12,000 obsolete German Model 71/84 rifles, 11,000 Model 1888 Mauser and Commission rifles, as well as a like number of mixed model (M1885, M1886 and M1888/90) Austrian Mannlicher straight-pull rifles; an ordnance officer's nightmare, to say the least!

MODEL 1891 RIFLE (ARGENTINE PATTERN): The earliest Mauser rifle adopted by the Ecuadoran armed forces was the venerable Model 1891 Rifle (Argentine Pattern) in caliber 7.65 x 53mm, produced by Ludwig Loewe & Co. The data for this rifle will be found under the section of the book on Argentina.

MODEL 1907 RIFLE: The Ecuadoran Model 1907 Rifle is the export model of the German Model 1904 Rifle, patterned after the Gew 98 Rifle. The quantity purchased by Ecuador is unknown. This rifle has a pistol grip stock, and the upper hand guard runs from in front of the receiver ring to just beyond the lower barrel band. Swivels are on the bottom on the lower barrel band and the bottom of the buttstock. The upper barrel band has a lug on the bottom to accommodate the Model 1895-style bayonet. This rifle uses the longer cocking piece and does not have guard locking screws.

Length: 49.20"; **Weight:** 8.30 lbs.; **Barrel:** 29.13"; **Caliber:** 7.65 x 53mm; **Rifling:** 4-groove, r/hand; **Operation:** Turnbolt action; **Feed:** 5-round, staggered column, flush, box magazine; **Sights:** Tangent leaf rear sight graduated to 2000 meters. **Remarks:** Ecuadoran national crest on the receiver ring, with either "EJERCITO DEL EQUATOR," or "EJERCITO EQUATORIANO" marked on the side rail, with manufacturer's markings.

MODEL 1910 RIFLE: Ecuador purchased an unknown quantity of Model 1910 Export Model Rifles from Waffenfabrik Mauser A-G. This model is a close copy of the Gew 98 Rifle, fitted with a pistol grip stock, with the upper hand guard running from in front the receiver ring to just beyond the lower band. The upper band is fitted with a bottom lug to accommodate the Model 1895 bayonet. There

Receiver ring markings on the Model 1910 Rifle as used by Ecuador

Model designation on the side rail of the Model 1910 Rifle as used by Ecuador

is a sling swivel on the lower barrel band, and another on the bottom of the buttstock.

Length: 48.80"; **Weight:** 8.8 lbs.; **Barrel:** 29.13"; **Caliber:** 7 x 57mm; **Rifling:** 4-groove, r/hand; **Operation:** Turnbolt action; **Feed:** 5-round, staggered column, flush, box magazine; **Sights:** Tangent leaf rear sight graduated to 2000 meters. **Remarks:** Found with either the Ecuadoran crest, or the Waffenfabrik

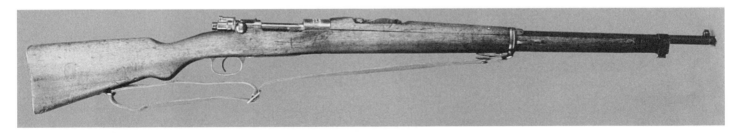

Full-length right hand view of the M1910 Mauser Rifle as used by Ecuador

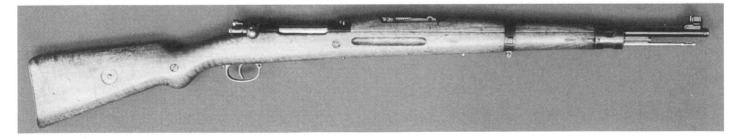

Full-length view of the Czech VZ 24 Short Rifle

Full-length view of the Czech VZ 12/33 Carbine

Full-length view of the Ecuadoran FN Model 30 Short Rifle (Cliff Baumann collection)

Mauser markings on the receiver ring, with the model designation on the side rail.

CZECH MODEL VZ 24 SHORT RIFLE: Substantial quantities of the Czech Model VZ 24 Short Rifle were introduced into the Ecuadoran army during the 1930s. These short rifles were supplied in caliber 7.65 x 53mm, and all pertinent data relative to the Model VZ 24 Short Rifle will be found under the section on Czechoslovakia. This short rifle was used to good effect in the War of 1941 with Peru.

CZECH MODEL VZ 12/33 CARBINE: In conjunction with the orders for the Czech VZ 24 Short Rifles, an unknown quantity of Czech VZ 12/33 Carbines were also purchased by the Ecuadoran army during the 1930s. It is understood that this carbine was ordered in caliber 7.65 x 53mm. This carbine would have been used during the 1941 War with Peru. All relative data on this carbine will be found in the section on Czechoslovakia.

FN MODEL 1930 SHORT RIFLE: This FN Model 1930 Short rifle is the standard FN export market short rifle as supplied to many Central and South American countries. Fitted with a pistol grip stock without grasping grooves, the rifle has an upper hand guard that extends from the receiver ring to just beyond the lower barrel band. The lower band has a swivel at the bottom, while a further swivel is on the bottom of the buttstock.

Length: 43.25"; **Weight:** 10.0 lbs.; **Barrel:** 22.50"; **Caliber:** 7.65 x 53mm; **Rifling:** 4-groove, r/hand; **Operation:** Turnbolt action; **Feed:** 5-round, staggered column, flush, box magazine; **Sights:** Tangent leaf rear sight graduated to 2000 meters. **Remarks:** "FN" logo on the receiver ring, manufacturer's markings on the side rail.

EL SALVADOR

Colonized by the Spanish in 1524, El Salvador gained its independence from Spain in 1821, first under the aegis of the Mexican Empire, and then, two years later, as a member of the United Provinces of Central America. This confederation fell apart in 1838, and in 1840 El Salvador emerged from a bloody two-year war as an independent republic.

The country of El Salvador has been dominated by an economy based on coffee production, with the means of production, land ownership, and political power resting in the hands of a small oligarchy. A reform president won election in 1931, but was dismissed by the army; this action was followed by a revolution in 1932, during which approximately fifteen thousand Salvadoran peasants were killed. The result of these tribulations was a period of relative peace that lasted into the 1970s.

In 1969, El Salvador was involved in a brief, but vicious war with Honduras. This war evolved from the massacre of Salvadoran natives in the border zone with Honduras. The outrages perpetuated upon the Salvadoran natives finally exploded during the qualifying rounds of the World Cup Championship: El Salvador won two of the three games, riots against Salvadorans living in the border area with Honduras immediately erupted, and what was labeled in the United States as "The Football War" was on! On 12 and 13 July 1969, Salvadoran forces pushed across the border of Honduras, immediately becoming engaged with the numerically inferior and less well-equipped Honduran forces. The Salvadoran Air Force achieved air superiority, and the army pushed twenty-five kilometers into Honduran territory, capturing several towns in the north and east before a cease-fire was imposed by the Organization of American States.

In 1979, President General Carlos Humberto Romero was overthrown by a group of junior military officers. After the resignation of two civilian-military juntas, a third government including Christian Democrat José Napolean Duarte assumed office on 5 March 1980, based on the army carrying out a policy of agrarian reform. Twelve long years of civil war followed, culminating in a peace treaty between the government and the armed opposition on 16 January

The side rail of the Czech VZ 12/33 Carbine, showing the manufacturer's markings in Spanish

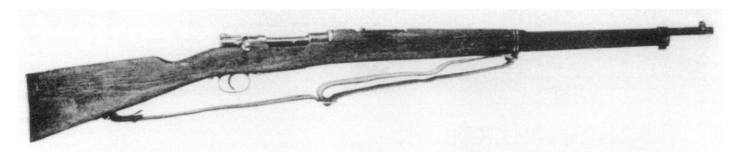

Full-length view of the Chilean-style Model 1895 Rifle

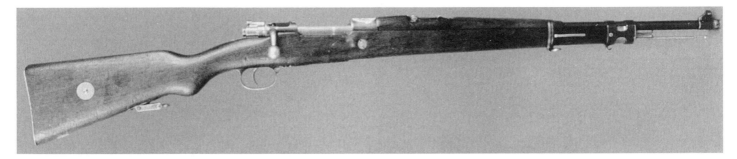

Full-length view of the Model VZ 12/33 Carbine

1992, at a cost of seventy-five thousand lives. This treaty also called for the reduction of the Salvadoran army by more than fifty percent.

The opportunity now exists for the country to bind up its wounds, and unite the people to work for the common good.

MODEL 1895 RIFLE: The government of El Salvador purchased unknown quantities of the Chilean-style Model 1895 Rifle directly from DWM. Other quantities of the Model 1895 rifle were ordered from Oviedo in Spain. These weapons were the mainstay of the Salvadoran army for many years, and were doubtless used throughout the many years of strife that were inflicted on the country during the first half of the twentieth century. Specific data on this rifle will be found under the section on Chile.

CZECH MODEL VZ 12/33 CARBINE: During the early 1930s, the Salvadoran army contracted with Czech authorities to purchase an unknown quantity of Czech Model VZ 12/33 Carbines. Whether or not these arrived in the country in time to be used in "La Matanza," which was the revolt of 1932, cannot be determined. In any event, these weapons were continually in use by the Salvadoran armed forces until the end of the Second World War, when the Salvadoran army was reequipped with U.S. weapons.

Specific information relative to this carbine may be found in the section on Czechoslovakia.

In the early part of the 20th century, Sweden, in an attempt to create a foreign market for their locally produced weapons, sent a selection of Swedish Mauser carbines, Model 94/17 in 7mm for

The side rail of the Czech VZ 12/33 Carbine showing the manufacturer's markings in Spanish

troop testing by the Salvadorans; results were not encouraging, and orders were never placed. Prior to the rearming of the Salvadoran army with surplus U.S. equipment, several thousand Model K98k carbines converted to 7.62 NATO were purchased overseas. Whether the conversion was done prior to acquisition, or after, is unknown at this time.

ESTONIA

Ethnic "cousins" of the Finns, it was not until the twentieth century that the Estonians acquired their own country. Throughout recorded history, the country had been ruled in turn by the Danes, who first colonized the area, the Teutonic Knights, and the Swedes, with the German element predominant during this entire period of time. "Baltic Barons" ruled the towns, while the Ests were regarded as little more than serfs.

In the 1800s, serfdom was abolished, and a cultural revival began. This revival became politicized with the treaty of Brest-Litovsk in 1918 when the independence of the new state of Estonia was recognized by the Soviet Union. In 1939 independence was terminated, with Russian forces occupying the country and amalgamating the Estonian armed forces in the Soviet army. During World War II, the Estonians suffered terrible losses, not only in battle, but in deportations, murders, and flights to safety.

Independence returned to Estonia on 30 March 1990, with a freely elected government notifying the Soviet Union of its intent to secede and form a separate country. Russia recognized the independence of Estonia in September 1991, with free elections being held in 1992. As with other eastern nations, Estonia has been plagued with economic and political problems since independence.

ESTONIAN CZECH MODEL "L" SHORT RIFLE: Purchased from the Czechs in the early 1920s, the Estonian Model "L" Short Rifle was chambered for the British caliber .303 cartridge, which required the magazine well and floor plate to slightly project at an angle from the bottom of the stock in order to accept the rimmed cartridges. This rifle is fitted with a pistol grip stock without grasping grooves, and the upper hand guard runs from in front of the receiver ring to the upper barrel band. The upper band is fitted with a bayonet lug on the bottom to accept the Model 1895 Austrian bayonet. A sling swivel is attached to the bottom of the buttstock, with an integral swivel on the left side of the lower barrel band. The bolt handle is bent, but the stock is not recessed to accept the bolt knob. There are protecting sideguards on the front sight. There is little in the way of data on this short rifle, and there is no way at the present time to determine if, and exactly how, the weapons were marked, other than Czech export markings. These short rifles would have been used during World War II, presumably by support troops because of ammunition problems, but with capture by German forces, and recapture by the Russians, there is no way of knowing where these weapons finally came to rest, unless on the junk piles of war.

ETHIOPIA

Ethiopian history begins in the mists of early time, founded, according to legend, by Menelik I, son of King Solomon and the Queen of Sheba. After successfully repulsing two Italian attempts at invasion in the 1880s, Ethiopia began to enter the modern world under the tutelage of Menelik II (r. 1889-1913). Following his death, the country went through a period of instability until the accession to the throne in 1930 of Haile Selassie.

Haile Selassie was burdened with the task of trying to bring into the twentieth century a country that was living in the middle ages. He attempted to formalize the system of levies that had previously

Ethiopian Imperial Guard on review prior to the invasion of Ethiopia by Italy

Ethiopian army officers on review. Note the lion mane fringe around the tops of their hats, testimony to their bravery.

supplied the manpower to resist invaders. Hiring a Belgian military mission to train his soldiers, Haile Selassie built the basis of a new Ethiopian army, albeit an army that refused to wear shoes! At the same time, contracts were concluded with both Mauser and FN for the supply of short rifles and carbines, as well as other vital military equipment with which to arm and equip his troops.

In 1936, Italy invaded on several fronts, and the Ethiopians resisted with everything in their arsenal (one arms expert of the day was totally incapable of cataloging the variety of weapons that were recovered at the end of the Italian occupation!); however, the Italian armies prevailed, overrunning the country. The Italians were driven out during World War II by the British and Ethiopians, with Haile Selassie being returned to the throne.

Unrest erupted in 1974, and Haile Selassie was deposed on 13 September 1974. He was replaced by a coalition of elitists and the

Mounted Ethiopian soldier with shield, seen at the beginning of the Italian invasion of Ethiopia, C. 1935

One of the few organized formations in the Ethiopian army at the time of the Italian invasion, the Imperial cavalry was held in reserve until near the end of the war.

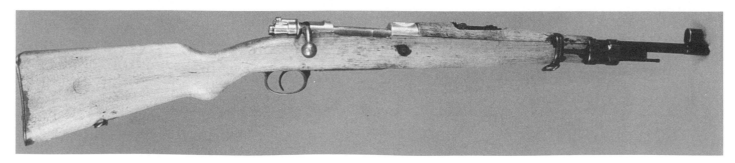

Full-length view of the Ethiopian FN Model 1924 Carbine (Springfield Armory Museum)

Ethiopian national crest on the receiver ring of the FN Model 1924 Carbine. This crest incorporates the stylized head of a lion at the bottom of the crest. (Springfield Armory Museum)

Side rail of the Ethiopian FN Model 1924 Carbine, showing the Lion of Judah acceptance mark on the left of the receiver ring, and the manufacturer's markings on the side rail. (Springfield Armory Museum)

army, with the monarchy abolished in 1975. From that time, Ethiopia has been wracked by internal and external strife, including civil war, which has left the country desolated and in a political shambles. What the future of this ill-fated country will be is anyone's guess.

ETHIOPIAN FN MODEL 24 CARBINE: Ethiopia ordered both short rifles and carbines from FN during the period 1933-1935; the total quantity of both models is given as twenty-five thousand. Both the short rifle and the carbine have a pistol grip stock, and the upper hand guard runs from in front of the receiver to the upper band. The nose cap is fitted with the longer style German "H" bayonet lug. The lower band has a swivel on the bottom, with another swivel at the bottom of the buttstock. On the carbine model, the bolt handle is bent down, but the stock is not recessed for the bolt knob. Note the comparatively short distance between the lower and the upper barrel bands.

Length: 43.25"; **Weight:** 10.0 lbs.; **Barrel:** 22.50"; **Caliber:** 7.92 x 57mm; **Rifling:** 4-groove, r/hand; **Operation:** Turnbolt action; **Feed:** 5-round, staggered column, flush, box magazine; **Sights:** Tangent leaf rear sight graduated to 1400 meters (carbine). **Remarks:** The Ethiopian national crest on the receiver ring (Note that this crest by FN is different than that used on the Mauser Standard Modell Short Rifle), the Lion of Judah acceptance mark on the left side of the receiver ring, and the manufacturer's markings on the side rail.

ETHIOPIAN M1933 MAUSER STANDARD MODELL SHORT RIFLE: Three different contracts for approximately twenty-five thousand short rifles and carbines were placed with Mauser Werkes in 1933, 1934, and 1935. Some of the early models were identified by an "A" prefix and full receiver crest. The numbers for the 1934 order are unknown; however the 1935 order is from the "B"-prefix

Close-up view of the receiver bridge and bolt handle of the Ehtiopian FN24 Rifle; note the matching number, a novelty for weapons from this country and this era! (Robert Jensen collection)

Close-up view of the stock cartouche on the side of the Ehtiopian FN Model 24 Rifle. (Robert Jensen collection)

Full-length view of the Ethiopian FN Model 24 Rifle with turned down bolt handle (Robert Jensen collection)

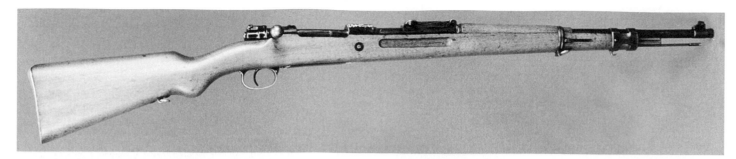

Full-length view of the Ethiopian Model 1933 Mauser Standard Modell Short Rifle (Bob Bennett collection)

Receiver ring markings on the Ethiopian Model 1933 Mauser Standard Modell Short Rifle. This short rifle is unusual, not only for its fine condition, but for the markings on the receiver ring that indicate that this particular weapon was used by the Emperor's guard. (Bob Bennett collection)

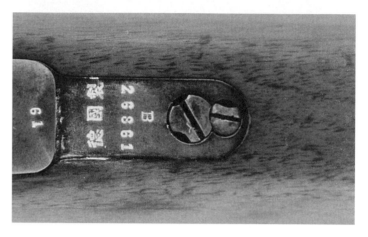

An interesting point to consider is that this Ethiopian Model 1933 Mauser Standard Modell Short Rifle was part of the commercial series being produced at that time, which included different contract rifles. Observe that while the serial number matches all of the others on this short rifle, there are Chinese characters marked just in front of the floorplate! (Bob Bennett collection)

Side rail of the Ethiopian Model 1933 Mauser Standard Modell Short Rifle. Note the Lion of Judah acceptance marking on the left side of the barrel, as well as the 5-digit serial number preceded by a "B"-prefix. It is interesting to note that the year following the Standard Modell designation is "1924." (Bob Bennett collection)

Members of the Ethiopian Imperial Guard in an overrun position. The rifle on the right appears to be an Ethiopian Standard Modell Short Rifle.

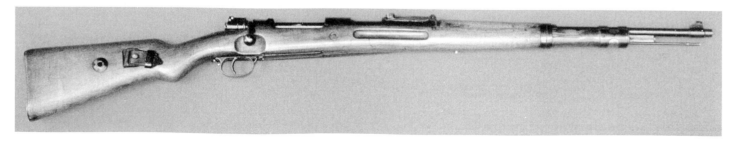

Full-length view of the Ethiopian Model 1933 Mauser Standard Modell Carbine

series, with five serial numbers and the "Mauser Banner" logo with date on the receiver ring. The short rifle is fitted with a pistol grip stock with grasping grooves, and the short-style upper hand guard runs from in front of the sight base to the lower band. The lower band is fitted with a swivel on the bottom, with a further swivel on the bottom of the buttstock, just behind the wrist of the stock. The upper band is equipped with a parade hook for shortening of the sling, while the nose cap incorporates a longer version of the German "H"-style bayonet lug.

Length: 43.60"; **Weight:** 8.8 lbs.; **Barrel:** 23.62"; **Caliber:** 7.92 x 57mm; **Rifling:** 4-groove, r/hand; **Operation:** Turnbolt action; **Feed:** 5-round, staggered column, flush, box magazine; **Sights:** Tangent leaf rear sight graduated to 2000 meters. **Remarks:** "Mauser Banner" logo on the receiver ring over the date of manufacture. Serial numbers and manufacturer's markings on the side rail.

ETHIOPIAN MODEL 1933 MAUSER STANDARD MODELL CARBINE: Almost identical to the K98k, the 1933 carbine is fitted with a pistol grip style stock with grasping grooves, the bolt handle is bent down, and the stock is recessed to accommodate the bolt knob. The upper hand guard is the typical short version running from in front of the sight base to the lower barrel band. The lower barrel band is held by a spring, while the upper barrel band is pinned to the stock. This carbine was the predecessor of the Wehrmacht's K98k, the standard German weapon of World War II.

Length: 43.60; **Weight:** 8.60 lbs.; **Barrel:** 23.62"; **Caliber:** 7.92 x 57mm; **Rifling:** 4-groove, r/hand; **Operation:** Turnbolt action; **Feed:** 5-round, staggered column, flush, box magazine; **Sights:** Tangent leaf rear sight graduated to 2000 meters. **Remarks:** "Mauser Banner" trademark over the date on receiver ring, "Standard Modell" on the side rail, and the "Mauser Banner" logo on the receiver bridge. The Lion of Judah acceptance mark is on the left side of the barrel between the front of the receiver and the rear sight base.

FRANCE

During the period July through December, 1939, 6,500 Belgian 24/30 Short Rifles in caliber 8mm were purchased from FN by the French. In the French Occupation Zone of Germany, production of a slightly modified version of the German K98k continued for a short period after the war. It is possible that some wartime carbines were

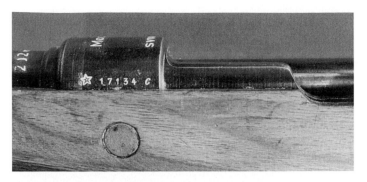

The left side of the receiver ring with serial number of the French-modified German 98k Carbine (Bob Bennett collection)

The left side of the receiver ring with serial number and "star" French proof mark for an arm of foreign origin of the French-modified German 98k Carbine. (Bob Bennett collection)

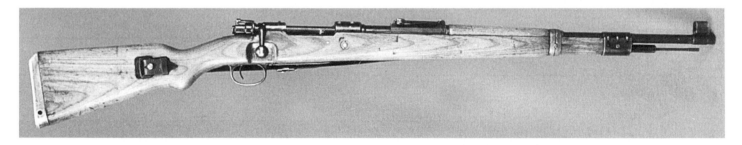

Full-length view the French-modified, post-World War II version of the German 98k Carbine (Bob Bennett collection)

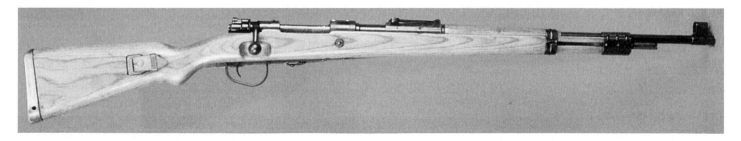

Full-length view of the French-used German 98k carbine, with the large "winter" trigger guard. Note that this particular rifle does not have the hexagonal stacking rod found in most other French Model 98k Rifles.

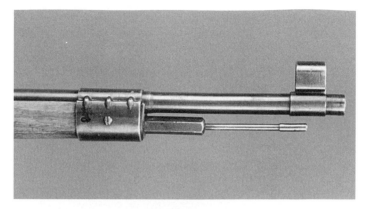

Upper barrel bands, and hexagonal stacking rod on the French-modified German 98k Carbine (Bob Bennett collection)

The left side of the buttstock of the French Model 98k Carbine, showing the crude bar-and-screws sling attachment. Note the hole in the butt plate for dismounting of the firing pin.

The receiver ring markings of the French-used Model 98k Carbine

Receiver ring of a French Model 98k Carbine, illustrating another version of the markings to be found on the receiver of those rifles issued to French forces

also altered and reconditioned at the same time. These carbines were used to arm some French units, especially units of the French Foreign Legion, who carried them in French Indo-China for a brief period. West German border guards were also equipped with these modified Mauser carbines.

Basically, the carbine is almost identical to the wartime German K98k, with the exception that the carbine does not have a bayonet lug; in its place is a threaded hexagonal base that is screwed into the stock, with a thinner, rod-like, upper segment used for stacking arms. Both barrel bands, which are the late-war welded style, are held by a screw through the stock. The lower barrel band has an integral swivel on the left side, while a crude sling attaching bar is held on the lower left side of the stock by two screws. The stock is also cut for the German-style sling. The cupped butt plate has the late-war hole for the disassembly of the firing mechanism.

All other data relative to this modified French version of the German 98k Carbine will be found under the section on Germany.

GERMANY

Beginning with the Mauser-Norris Model 67/69 Rifle, followed by the interim forerunner of the Mauser Model 71 Rifle, the Mauser rifle made its impact upon the world—an impact that only became greater with time. The strongest, most successful bolt action rifle ever developed, it could hardly be improved upon today.

The Model 71 Rifle became the standard rifle of Prussia, and was subsequently adopted by the other German states, thus holding the honor of being the first rifle used by the new German Empire. In 1876, foreign orders for the Model 71 opened up the export market, helping to make the Mauser rifle the most important weapon in the world.

Magazine rifles were the way of the future, with many inventions vying for the easiest method of providing additional cartridge capacity. The Model 71/84, with its tubular, under barrel magazine, was Mauser's answer. However, this was developed as the black powder era was coming to an end, and when France developed and adopted a rifle in 1886 using a small caliber, metal-jacketed bullet, propelled by smokeless powder, it caused other nations to follow in this direction.

Recognizing the superiority of this French development, Germany hurriedly devised a rifle designed by a commission, incorporating Mauser and Mannlicher design features, as well as some of the commission's own misguided ideas. Known as the Commission Rifle Model 1888, it was a victim of the old adage, "Too many cooks spoil the soup," and was fraught with design weaknesses and shortcomings. This was adopted in 7.92 x 57mm on 12 November 1888, which later led to the Model 1889 rifle, adopted by Belgium as standard for its armed forces. This was followed by the Turkish Model 1890 Rifle. The start of trade with South America in 1891 introduced the Model 1891 rifle, which ultimately saw usage throughout the South American continent. In 1892, Mauser made many improvements to the Model 1891 design, and a major step in the development of the Mauser rifle occurred with the introduction of the Spanish Model 1893 Rifle one year later. Slight variations of this basic model were created over the years for individual nations wishing to incorporate their own ideas into the design.

Swedish Mauser rifles were developed in 1894, with the weapons being produced under contract in Sweden. In 1896, Mauser began experimenting with various designs meant to replace the Model 1888 Rifle system. One experimental weapon manufactured for troop testing was the Model 1896 Rifle in 6 x 58mm. After variations of many designs were tested, the German Rifle Testing Commission decided to adopt a new, improved Mauser rifle in caliber 7.92 x 57mm. This was the historic Model 98 Rifle.

The Model 98 Rifle was officially adopted by Germany on 5 April 1898. This rifle was to become the most widely used and one of the most famous rifles in the world. The Model 98 Rifle was subjected to many and varied design alterations over the years, while still retaining the basic system that is integral to the rifle. The first Model 98 Carbines were introduced at about the same time as the Model 98 Rifle; they were used to some extent in the Herero rebellion in German South-West Africa, and to a lesser extent in World War I, but due to the shortness of the carbine barrel and its inherent violent muzzle blast, the weapon never gained favor with the troops. In 1908, a carbine with a 23.62-inch barrel was introduced as the Carbine 98AZ, but it was redesignated the Carbine 98a (Kar98a) following World War I. This also helped to differentiate it from the Model 98b Carbine introduced during the time of the Weimar Republic.

Experiences gained from use of the Gew 98 during the First World War were later incorporated in design changes during the years leading up to World War II. One of these changes was the use of a tangent leaf rear sight, graduated to 2000 meters, to replace the old-style "Lange Vizier" sight of the Model 98. Many of the original Model 98 Rifles were remodeled into the Model 98b. This was done by bending the bolt handle and cutting a recess in the stock to accommodate the bolt knob, removing the parade hook on the upper band, adding the tangent leaf rear sight, and cutting a sling slot in the buttstock to receive a side mounted sling. Many Kar 98b Carbines were also manufactured from new parts, and are so stamped on the side rail. Another improved version was the Model 98k, a short rifle that was the standard weapon for the German armed forces during the Second World War. Development commenced in 1924; however, full production was started in 1935 when Hitler ignored the Armistice Commission and put German industries on a path to war.

The 98k proved a rugged weapon for war, sustaining the German soldier through many a battle. In the hands of the Yugoslavs, Czechs, Israelis, Norwegians, Danes, and Chinese, the 98k soldiered on after the defeat of Germany. To this day, 98k carbines are to be found in many small brush wars and skirmishes as second line weapons. Many different Mauser rifles have been based on the Model 98 Rifle, and these are covered under the sections on the various countries in this book.

MAUSER-NORRIS MODEL 67/69: While employed at the Wuerttemberg Royal Armory, Paul Mauser developed a rifle based upon

Top view of the receiver area of the Model 67/69 Mauser-Norris Rifle; note the mainspring incorporated as part of the bolt handle. (Springifled Armory Museum)

Close-up view of the markings "BREVET DE W. & P. MAUSER" on the extractor of the Model G7/G9 Mauser-Norris Rifle. (Springfield Armory Museum)

the principles of the Dreyse needle gun. With his improvements incorporating a self-cocking mechanism that included primary extraction, and eventually a firing pin instead of a firing needle. This turn-bolt operation became the key-stone of all future Mauser bolt-action rifles. Tested by the Austrian War Ministry, the rifle was favorably received, but not accepted as the Austrians had just adopted the Waenzl system of conversion of muzzleloaders to breechloaders.

Shown to Samuel Norris, the European agent for Remington Firearms, Norris felt that the turn-bolt action of the rifle would be ideal

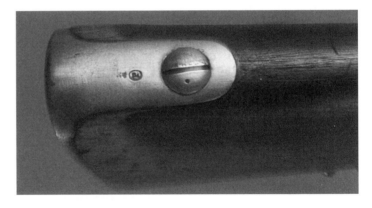

Belgian proof marks os the tang of the buttplate of the Mauser-Norris Rifle. (Springfield Armory Museum)

Full-length view of the Model 67/69 Mauser-Norris Rifle. This is the original Patent Model. (Sprinfield Armory Museum)

for the conversion of the French Chassepot needle gun to a metallic cartridge rifle. He immediately went to Oberndorf and formed a partnership with the Mauser brothers, wherein he, Norris, would provide the financing and the Mauser brothers would provide the technical know-how. In 1867, the partnership moved to Liege, Belgium, where the brothers continued to develop their rifle, while Norris failed in his attempts to convince the French that this was the perfect system to convert their Chassepots to a metallic-cartridge rifle, whereupon, Norris broke his contract with Mauser brothers, causing them much financial distress. The brothers returned to Oberndorf, Paul in 1869 and Wilhelm in 1870, where they continued developmental work on their rifle.

Although only experimental, this rifle used a non-rotary bolt head, which protected the heads of paper cartridges from friction and damage while locking the bolt, and also allowed for a non-rotary seat for the extractor when metallic cartridges were introduced.

After much work, and another interim model, the design evolved into the Model 71 Rifle which was officially adopted by Prussia.

GERMAN MODEL 71 RIFLE: Officially adopted by Prussia on 14 February 1872, the Model 71 Rifle was also accepted by the other German states, making the Model 71 the standard rifle for the German Empire. Bavaria clung to the Werder rifle until 1877, at which time standardization became complete. The Model 71 had a long and illustrious history, serving as a robust and dependable rifle for

Left rear flat of the receiver showing the model designation of the German Model 71 Rifle

the German soldier. In the German army, First World War service of the Model 71 Rifle was limited to reserve troop use on the continent.

China purchased large quantities of the Model 71 Rifle, which, along with the Chinese version of the German Model 1888 Rifle, was the rifle of choice by the fanatical Chinese "Boxers" during the

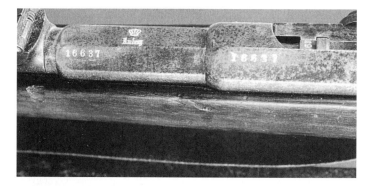

Marking of the royal arsenal at Amberg on the top flat of the chamber, with the serial numbers on the left flats of the chamber and the receiver of the German Model 71 Rifle

Proof markings on the right side of the chamber of the German Model 71 Rifle

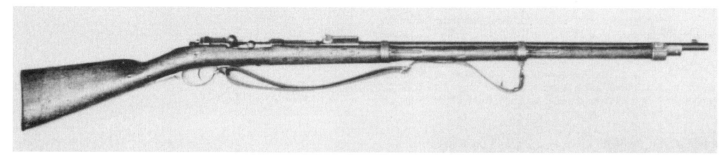

Full-length view of the German Model 71 Rifle

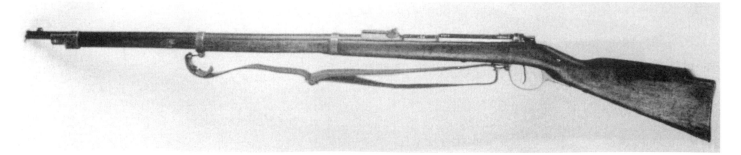

Left full-length view of the German Model 71 Rifle

Year of manufacture on the right rear receiver flat of the German Model 71 Rifle

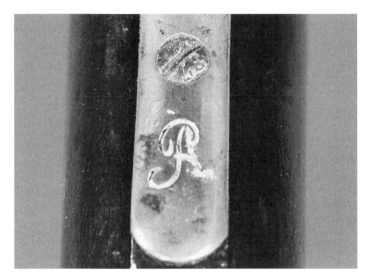

Script "A" on the rear of the brass trigger guard of the German Model 71 Rifle

Boxer Rebellion in 1900. Sold to the Transvaal State in South Africa, the Model 71 Rifle was in the hands of the Boers at the time of the Jameson raid. The poet Erskine Childers, with his wife and others, secretly transported fifteen hundred Model 71 Rifles and forty-nine thousand cartridges from Germany to Ireland aboard his yacht, The "Asgard." This cargo was landed at Howth Harbor, Ireland, 26 July 1914, and from that time on, the weapons, which were used in the Easter Rebellion of 1916, were called "Howth Mausers" by the Irish.

The Model 71 also saw service with Honduras, Japan (used for troop testing), and Uruguay. After the Model 71 Rifle was declared obsolete, large quantities were sold to surplus military equipment dealers, such as Adolph Frank Export Gesellschaft of Hamburg, Germany and Francis Bannerman & Co., 505 Broadway, New York.

Stocked almost to the muzzle with a straight-wristed stock, the Model 71 Rifle does not have an upper hand guard. The barrel is held to the stock with three barrel bands, the lower two secured by springs, while the upper band, held by a screw, incorporates a bayonet lug on the right side for the Model 71 bayonet. The middle barrel band has a swivel at the bottom, with another mounted on the front of the trigger guard. The Model 71 Rifle is profusely proofed, with practically every small component being serially numbered to the weapon.

Length: 52.90"; **Weight:** 10.1 lbs.; **Barrel:** 33.56"; **Caliber:** 11 x 60mm; **Rifling:** 4-groove, r/hand; **Operation:** Turnbolt action; **Feed:** Single shot; **Sights:** V-notch rear sight adjustable to 1600 meters on large leaf, 350 meters on the small leaf, and 250 meters on standard. **Remarks:** Name of manufacturer over the

German East African askaris on parade with German Model 71 Jaeger Rifles, C. 1914

chamber, serial numbers, as well as the model designation, on the left flat of the chamber and the receiver. Proof marks will be found on the right flats, while year of manufacture will be found on the right rear of the receiver.

GERMAN MODEL 71 JAEGER RIFLE: The Model 71 Jaeger intended for use by Light Infantry Troops (Jaegers), who were picked for their superior marksmanship abilities; the rifle was designed to meet the specifications of the Jaegers, and was also issued to Engineers, Fortress Troops and the Navy. Serving long and well with the troops, these rifles were eventually declared obsolete and consigned to arsenal storage for second-line use. Eventually, they were withdrawn from storage, and, in a slightly modified form, were issued to Schutztruppen in the German colonies.

The Model 71 Jaeger Rifle was the standard weapon of the German Askari Troops in German East Africa, Togo, the Cameroons, and New Guinea. Eight of the fourteen field companies of German Askaris in German East Africa were armed with the Jaeger Model 71 Rifle, which had been found to be quite adequate for use in controlling restless natives. With the advent of World War I, the black smoke thrown out by the Model 71 Rifle was a dead giveaway in the jungles. In 1915, the German blockade runner "Rubens," renamed "Kronberg," was sunk close to the East African shore by the British. German troops were successful in salvaging eighteen hundred Model 98 Rifles and three million 7.92 x 57mm cartridges. Later, ammunition shortages forced the Model 71 Jaeger Rifle into service once again. It wasn't until July 1918 that the Model 71 Jaeger Rifle was completely replaced.

German East African askaris firing from behind a post shelter, C. 1914. Note the relatively complete field equipment for each man. (Die Deutschen Kolonien)

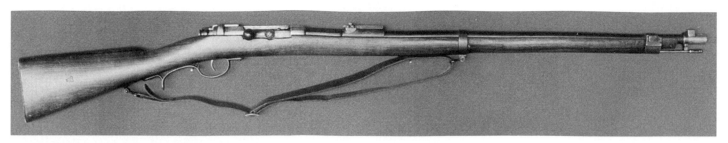

Full-length view of the Model 71 Jaeger Rifle (Henry Wichmann collection)

It is an interesting note that during World War I, the German Model 71 Jaeger Rifle was bored out to accept incendiary ammunition, carried aboard aircraft, and fired at observation balloons on the Western front.

The Model 71 Jaeger Rifle differs from the Model 71 Rifle in that it is shorter, making it handier to use, as well as resulting in the need for only a lower and upper barrel band. A swivel is attached to the bottom of the lower barrel band, and there is another swivel at the bottom of the buttstock. The trigger guard is extended at the rear and so shaped as to provide a pistol-style grip. The Jaeger Model 71 is also 1.10 pounds lighter than the Model 71 Rifle. The muzzle is stepped in order to accept the wide variety of bayonets available.

The chamber and receiver flats of the Model 71 Jaeger Rifle. This specimen is unusual in that, while the German markings are still visible, it appears to have been refurbished in Belgium (post WW I?) and Belgian proof marks applied. (Henry Wichmann collection)

German East African askari from the 11th Field Company on parade, equipped with the Model 71 Jaeger Rifle. (Die Deutschen Kolonien)

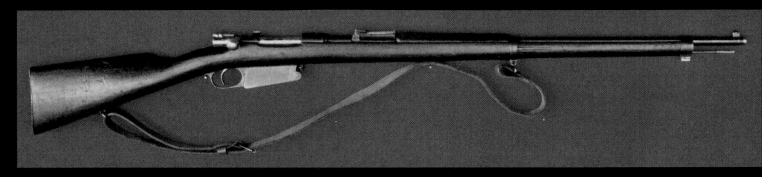

Modelo 1891 Rifle

The University Battalion of the Federal District crest above the receiver ring of the Modelo 1891 Rifle

Crest of the Military Academy above the receiver ring of the Modelo 1891 Rifle

Crest of the Naval Academy above the receiver ring of the Modelo 1891 Rifle

Argentina

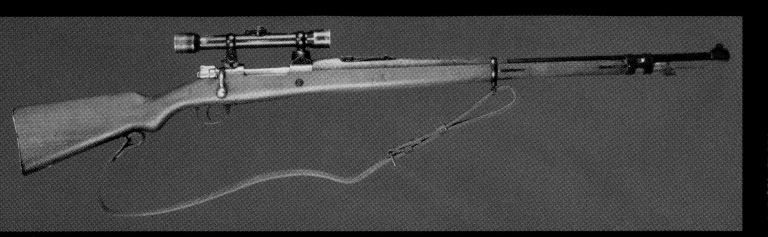

Argentine Modelo 1909 Sniper Rifle

Top view of the Argentine Modelo 1909 Sniper Rifle; note the marking "Ejercito Argentino" over the scope number at the forward end of the barrel. The number visible at the rear of the scope is a collection identification number.

Full length view of the M1891 Engineerís Carbine; note that these are essentially the M1891 Cavalry Carbine with the addition of an upper band incorporating a half-circle bayonet attachment and a lower band with a bayonet lug. The lowest band now incorporates a sling swivel, with another on the lower left side of the stock. Note that the sling ring bar has been removed and the hole in the stock filled.

Close-up view of the bayonet lugs permanently attached by screws on the M1891 Engineerís Carbine.

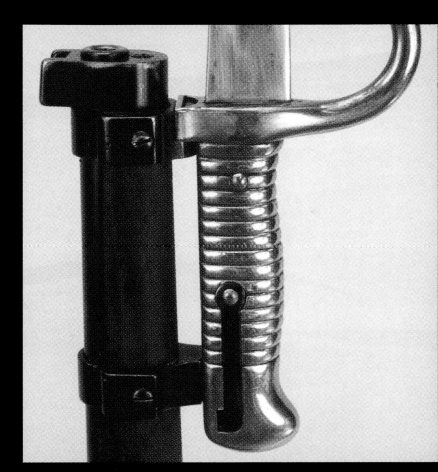

The M1891 Engineerís Carbine with bayonet attached to illustrate the slot attachment for the half-round bayonet ring on the cut-down M1879 Remington Rolling Block bayonet. This is an altogether ingenious use of an alteration to an out-dated bayonet to utilize existing stocks.

M1909 Cavalry Carbine with the markings of the ìGendarmeria Nacional,î or National Police.

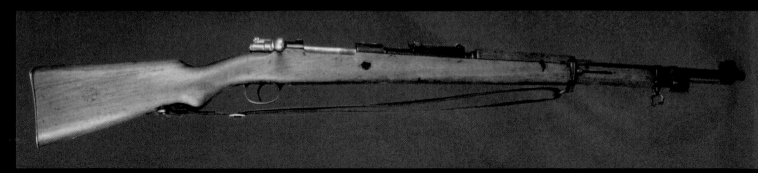

Belgian Model 1935 Short Rifle

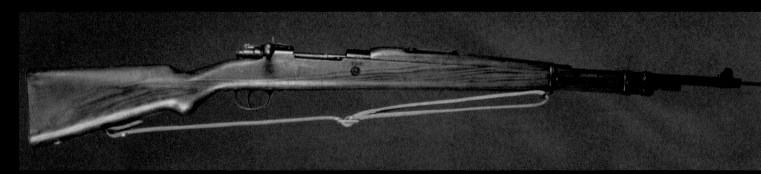

Belgian Model 24/30 .22 caliber training rifle developed for the Belgian army. The army model has a blue/black finish.

Bolivia

Bolivian Modelo 1907 Short Rifle
(Springfield Armory Museum)

Chile

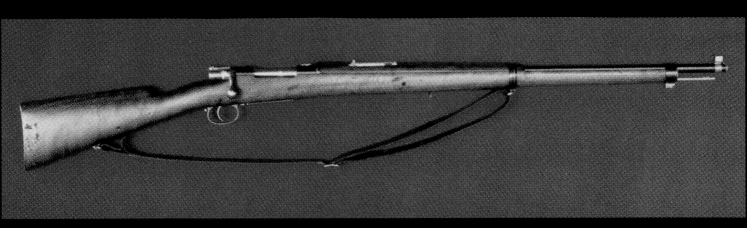

Chilean Model 1893 Rifle
(Lothar Frank collection)

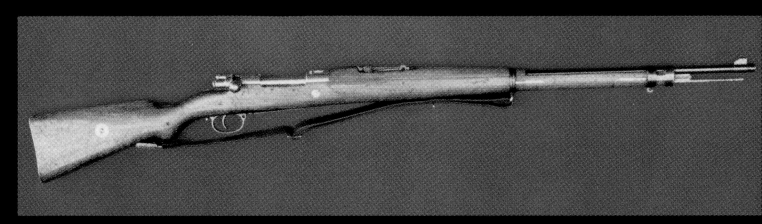

Chilean Model 1912 Steyr Rifle. Note the identification disk on the right of the buttstock.

Chilean Model 1935 "Carabineros" Carbine

Manufacturer's markings on the left side rail of the Chilean Model 1912 Steyr Rifle

China

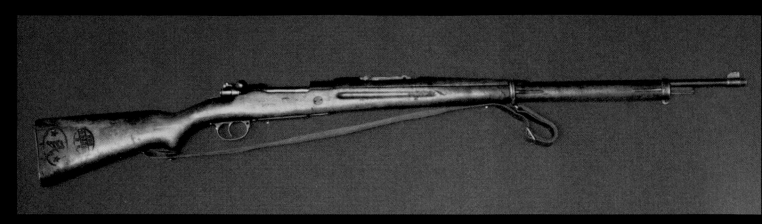

Chinese Model 1907 Rifle. Note the well-displayed ideographs on the right side of the buttstock.

Chinese Model 1907 Carbine
(Noel Schott collection)

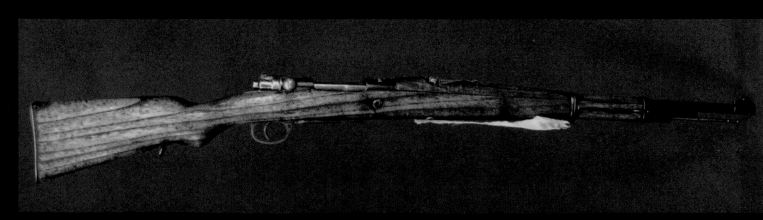

Chinese Model 21 Short Rifle

China

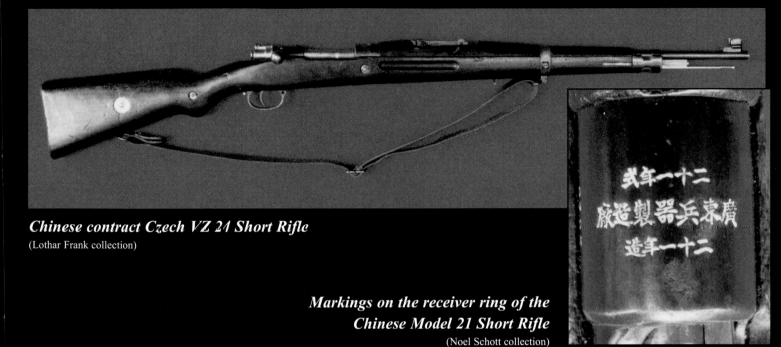

Chinese contract Czech VZ 24 Short Rifle
(Lothar Frank collection)

Markings on the receiver ring of the
Chinese Model 21 Short Rifle
(Noel Schott collection)

貳年一十二
厰造製器兵東廣
造年一十二

Columbia

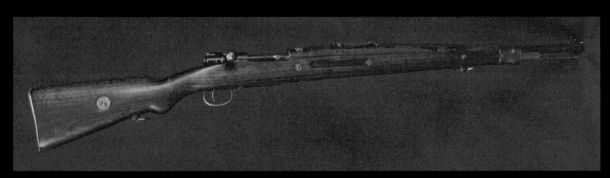

Czech VZ 23 Short
Rifle as used by
Colombia

Colombian Steyr
Model 1929 Short
Rifle

Czechoslovakia

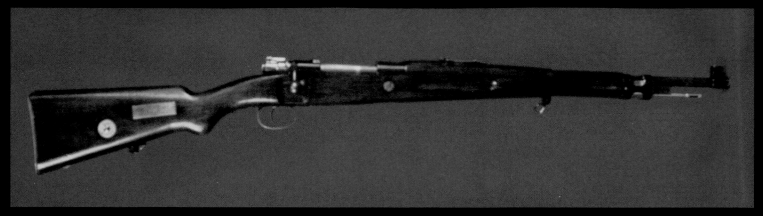

Presentation model of the Czech VZ 16/33 Carbine. Note the presentation plaque on the buttstock.

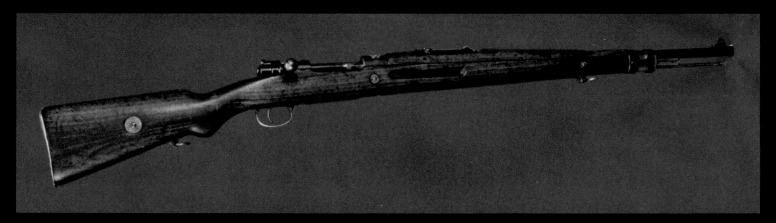

Czech VZ 23 Short Rifle
(Bob Bennett collection)

The Czech national crest on the receiver ring of the Czech Model VZ 16/33 Carbine

Dominican Republic

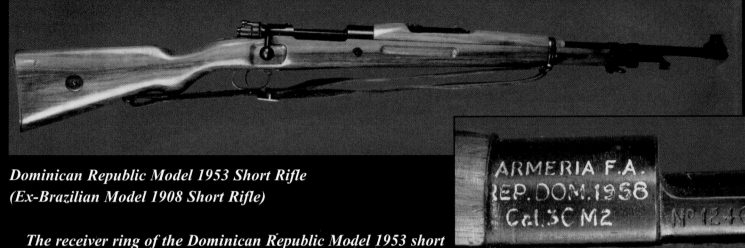

Dominican Republic Model 1953 Short Rifle (Ex-Brazilian Model 1908 Short Rifle)

The receiver ring of the Dominican Republic Model 1953 short Rifle (Ex-Brazilian Model 1908 Short Rifle), showing the markings and caliber applied by the Dominican arsenal.

Ethiopia

Ethiopian Model 1933 Mauser Standard Modell Short Rifle
(Bob Bennett collection)

Side rail of the Ethiopian Model 1933 Mauser Standard Modell Short Rifle. Note the Lion of Judah acceptance marking on the left side of the barrel, as well as the five-digit serial number preceded by a "B"-prefix. It is interesting to note that the year following the Standard Modell designation is "1924."

Receiver ring markings on the Ethiopian Model 1933 Mauser Standard Modell Short Rifle. This short rifle is unusual for the markings on the receiver ring that indicate that this particular weapon was used by the Emperors guard.
(Bob Bennett collection)

France

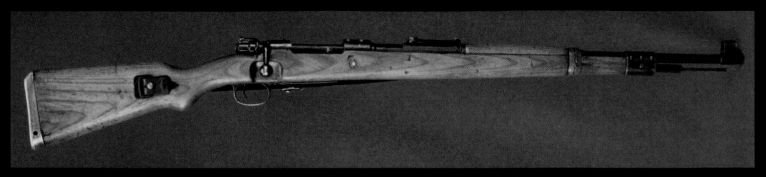

French-modified, post-World War II version of the German 98k Carbine
(Bob Bennett collection)

Germany

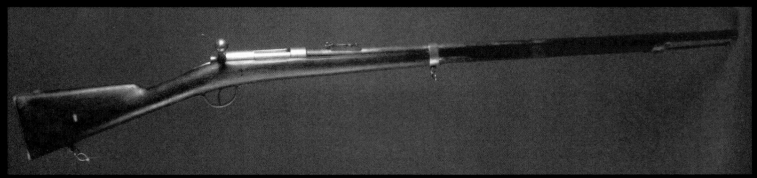

Full-length view of the Model 67/69 Mauser-Norris Rifle. This is the original Patent Model.
(Springfield Armory Museum)

Top view of the receiver area of the Model 67/69 Mauser-Norris Rifle; note the mainspring incorporated as part of the bolt handle.
(Springfield Armory Museum)

Close-up view of the markings "BREVET DE W. & P. MAUSER" on the extractor of the Model 67/69 Mauser-Norris Rifle.
(Springfield Armory Museum)

Germany

German Model 98 Rifle

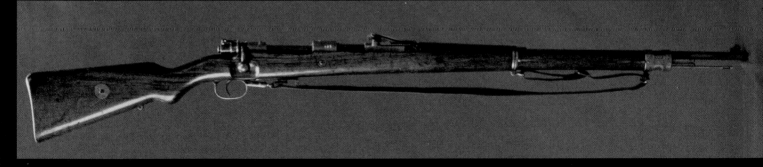

German Model 98 Rifle, marked for Colonial Service, and believed to have been modified locally in German Southwest Africa. The bolt handle has been bent down, and the stock recessed for handling, while the "Lange Vizier" sight is registering on 200 meters. This lower sight setting is presumably due to close-in fighting in the bush country. The washer in the stock is marked "K.S." for Colonial Service, while the reverse of the washer is

Germany

"K.S." marked washer in the right side of the buttstock of the modified German Model 98 Rifle used in German Southwest Africa

The Professionally bent bolt handle and recessed stock of the Colonial Service marked, modified German Model 98 Rifle

Rear sight of the Colonial Service marked, modified German Model 98 Rifle, showing it registering on 200 meters. This was probably a necessity due to the brush war nature of engagement with the Hereros during the uprisings.

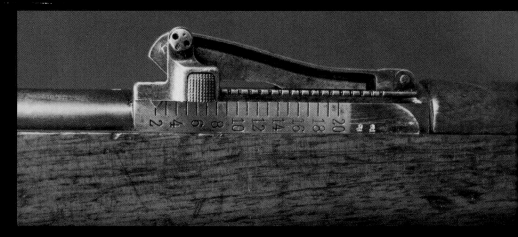

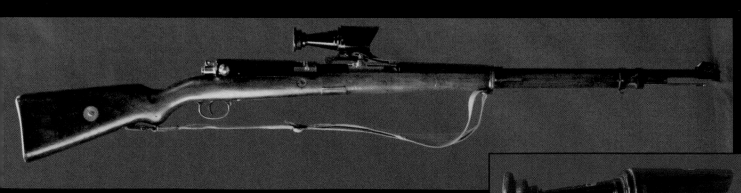

German Model 98 Sniper Rifle fitted with a sliding bolt cover and a Low Light optics, Bifocal sniper scope and front sight.

The Low Light Bifocal sniper scope mounted on the "Lange Vizier" rear sight. Note how the base of the scope conforms to the curvature of the rear sight ramp, while the spring-loaded mounting arms lock into the recessed bottom portion of the rear sight ramp. The eyepiece is molded leather.

Germany

German Model 71
Carbine

*German Model 98A
Carbine. Unfortunately,
this specimen is lacking
the rear sight and the
barrel band.*
(Springfield Armory Museum)

*German Model 98 Rifle
equipped with a sliding bolt
cover designed to keep mud
and debris out of the action
of the rifle. The rifle is also
fitted with a non-detachable
large-capacity magazine,
which increased the rifle
capacity to 25 cartridges.*

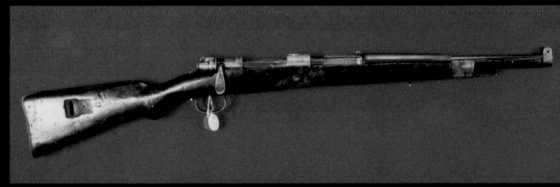

*German Model G 98
Rifle with a most
unusual pressed steel
action cover, held in
place by a buckle and
strap arrangement at
the front of the cover*

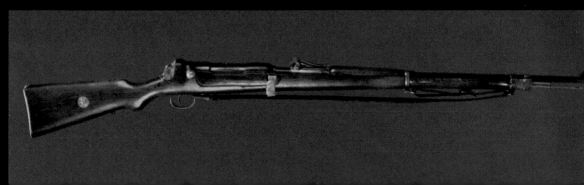

Germany

German 13mm T-Gewehr, bolt action, single shot, anti-tank rifle

The massive T-Gewehr action open, with a round ready to be fed into the chamber

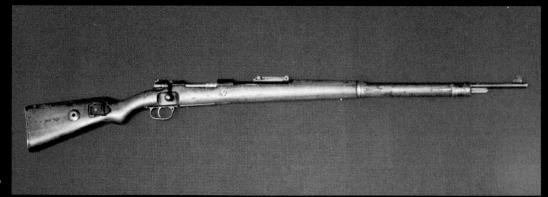

German Model Kar 98b Rifle, as originally manufactured

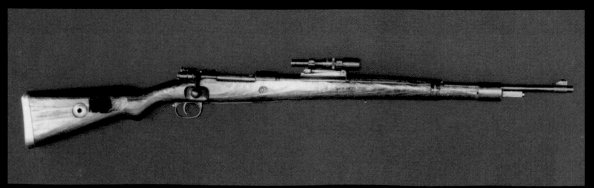

Sniper model German Model 98k Carbine with side rail mount and ZF-41 scope

Full-length view of the German Model 71 Carbine

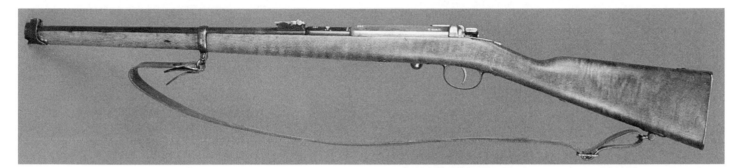

Left full-length view of the German Model 71 Carbine

Length: 48.70"; **Weight:** 9.0 lbs.; **Barrel:** 29.44"; **Caliber:** 11 x 60mm; **Rifling:** 4-groove, r/hand; **Operation:** Turnbolt action; **Feed:** Single shot; **Sights:** V-notch rear sight adjustable to 1600 meters on large leaf, 300 meters on small leaf, 200 meters on standard. **Remarks:** Name of manufacturer over the chamber, serial numbers, as well as the model designation, on the left flat of the chamber and the receiver. Proof marks are on the right flats, with the year of manufacture on the right rear flat of the receiver.

GERMAN MODEL 71 CARBINE: The Model 71 Carbine, adopted on 31 August 1876, was developed for issue to dragoons, hussars, and lancers to replace the captured and converted French Chassepot Carbines with which they had been armed. Specialized troops, such as line-of-communication and supply troops, were also equipped with the Model 71 Carbine. Fully stocked to the muzzle and lacking an attachment for bayonet, the carbine has a bolt handle that is bent down almost flat to the stock. The stock is straight wristed as in the Model 71 Rifle. The barrel is retained by a single spring-retained barrel band with a swivel attached at the bottom. Another swivel is at the foot of the buttstock. The upper end of the barrel is held by a nose cap with front sight protectors. Those car-

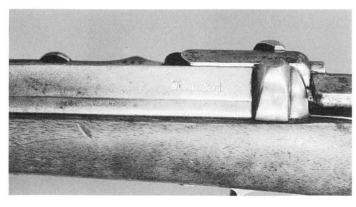

Model designation on the left receiver side rail of the German Model 71 Carbine

Butt plate markings on the German Model 71 Carbine

bines produced for Prussia were made by Spangenberg and Sons, Suhl, and at Steyr, Austria. Mauser Works manufactured the carbines for the state of Wurttemburg.

Length: 39.30"; **Weight:** 7.30 lbs.; **Barrel:** 20.0"; **Caliber:** 11 x 60mm; **Rifling:** 4-groove, r/hand; **Operation:** Turnbolt action; **Feed:** Single shot; **Sights:** V-notch rear sight adjustable to 1300 meters on the large leaf, 300 meters on the small leaf, 200 meters on standard. **Remarks:** Model designation on the left rear receiver wall, proofing, caliber designation, serial number, and manufacturer's markings on the receiver and chamber flats.

GERMAN MODEL 71 SHORT RIFLE: The German Model 71 Short Rifle is somewhat of a minor mystery. It is believed that the rifle was never manufactured to this configuration, but was arsenal refurbished as a short rifle. There are no special markings signifying that this is a special model weapon. The bolt handle, as with the Model 71 Carbine, is turned down. The short rifle is fitted with a lower and upper band, with a bayonet lug on the right side of the upper band.

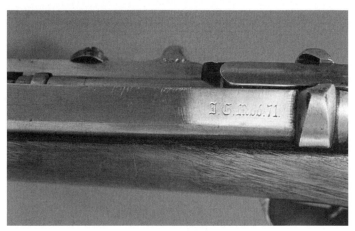

Chamber and receiver markings on the German Model 71 Carbine. Note that this carbine was produced for Prussia by the firm of Spangenberg and Son, Suhl.

Regular G 71 markings on the left receiver side wall of the German Model 71 Short Rifle

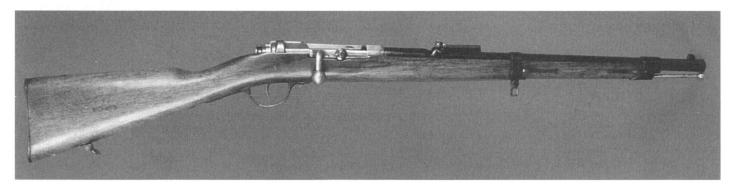

Full-length view of the German Model 71 Short Rifle

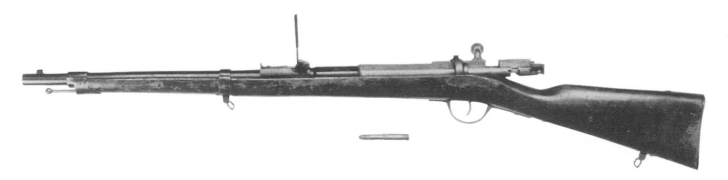

Full-length view of the left side of the German Model 71 Short Rifle, showing the bolt in the open position and the rear sight in the extended position; note the cartridge below. (John Wall collection)

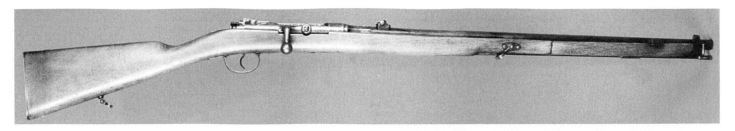

Full-length view of the German Model 79 Rifle

The chamber markings on the German Model 79 Rifle, showing the Prussian line Eagle over the initials of C.G. Haenel, Suhl

Left side wall stampings on the German Model 79 Rifle, indicating "G.A.G." and "Mod:79"

Right side wall stamping indicating date of manufacture of the German Model 79 Rifle. Note the serial number 19.

German army recruits at drill in the Kaserne, using Model 71/84 Rifles, C. 1900 (Deutsche Soldaten Jahrbuch, 1966)

GERMAN MODEL 79 GRENZ-AUFSICHTS-GEWEHR (G.A.G.) RIFLE: This weapon is longer than the Model 71 Short Rifle and somewhat shorter than the J 71 Jaeger Rifle. Manufactured by Haenel, Suhl, the rifle is marked "G.A.G." and "Mod: 79" on the left receiver side wall. These rifles were issued to the Customs Service, who acted as Border Guards. Full stocked almost to the muzzle, there is a short stud on the upper band that extends to the end of the muzzle. The upper swivel is fitted midway between the rear and front sights through the stock in the manner of Dreyse stock fittings, with the lower swivel approximately six inches from the toe of the butt.

Length: 44.635"; **Weight:** 7.0 lbs.; **Barrel:** 24.75"; **Caliber:** 11x37.5mm, about half the length of the regular issue 11x60mm cartridge; **Rifling:** 4-groove, r/hand; **Operation:** Turnbolt action; **Feed:** Single shot; **Sights:** Double folding leaf rear sight. **Remarks:** Prussian line eagle over the initials "C.G.H./SUHL" over the chamber, with the initials "G.A.G. Mod:79." on the left side rail, with the date of manufacture on the right side rail.

GERMAN MODEL 71/84 RIFLE: With many nations adopting magazine rifles in the 1880s, the Germans were catapulted into the race. Paul Mauser had been working on the development of a magazine-fed rifle since 1880, arriving at two different versions of a tubular feed magazine rifle that were demonstrated for the Kaiser at Stuttgart, with one of the models being chosen for troop testing. The tests were highly successful, and the rifle was officially adopted on

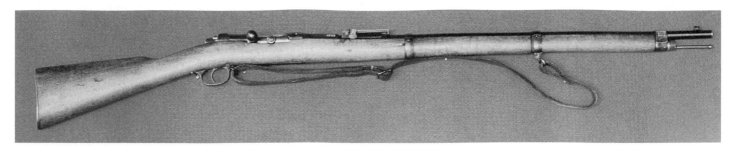

Full-length view of the German Model 71/84 Rifle

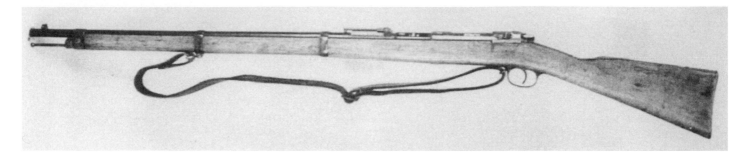

Left full-length view of the German Model 71/84 Rifle

31 January 1884, with the designation of Infantry Rifle Model 71/84.

While of completely new construction, the Model 71/84 Rifle was basically similar to the Model 71 Rifle with the addition of an 8-round tubular magazine. The bolt is similar to that of the Model 71, but also incorporates an ejector as well as an extractor. A carrier pivoted in the receiver accepts cartridges from the tubular magazine, moving them to the proper level for feeding into the chamber. A cutoff is built into the left side of the receiver wall in order that the rifle may be used as a single shot, holding the contents of the magazine in reserve. The stock of the rifle is straight wristed, as in the basic Model 71 Rifle, with the barrel retained by three bands. Identical to the Model 71 Rifle, the upper band has a bayonet lug on the right side for attachment of the Model 71 bayonet. The middle band has a swivel attached at the bottom, while a second swivel is attached to the front of the trigger guard. The German Jaeger Model 71/84 Rifle was the same as the regular issue Model 71/84, but with the swivel on the trigger guard relocated to the butt of the rifle.

Markings on the chamber flats of the German Model 71/84 Rifle. This rifle was produced at Erfurt.

Regimental markings on the butt plate tang of the German Model 71/84 Rifle

Model designation, "I. G.Mod 71/84" on the left side rail of the German Model 71/84 Rifle

Length: 50.90"; **Weight:** 10.2 lbs.; **Barrel:** 31.56"; **Caliber:** 11 x 60mm; **Rifling:** 4-groove, r/hand; **Operation:** Turnbolt action; **Feed:** 8-round tubular magazine in forestock; **Sights:** V-notch rear sight adjustable to 1600 meters on the large leaf, 350 meters on the small leaf, and 250 meters on standard. **Remarks:** Arsenal markings on the top chamber flat, serial number and proof marks on the left chamber flat, proofs on the right chamber flat. Model designation on the left rear receiver side rail.

Never defeated! German East African askaris after several years of fighting the British in East Africa under Von Lettow-Vorbeck (Die Deutschen Kolonien)

Possibly posed propaganda shot of German troops fighting from a ruined farmhouse in Belgium

Spike-top helmeted infantrymen firing their G 98 Rifles in the forests of eastern Poland

GERMAN MODEL 98 RIFLE: The German Rifle Testing Commission adopted the Model 98 Rifle on 5 April 1898. This rifle was the result of much experimentation on the part of the Mauser Company, and the action was in great part derived from the experimental Model 1896 Rifle. The Model 98 incorporates a third (safety) lug, shrouded bolt face, guide rib, under-cut extractor, full-depth thumb cut in the left receiver side rail, extra large gas escape holes in the bolt, and a gas shield on the bolt sleeve. The bolt sleeve lock was introduced for the first time, the firing pin travel was reduced to accelerate lock time, and the receiver ring was a larger diameter, greatly increasing strength. The action cocks on opening, and when the bolt is fully drawn to the rear, considerable sidewards bolt action is noticeable. This is due to generous clearance between the bolt and the receiver, as well as the short bolt bearing when the bolt is fully retracted.

The rifle is fitted with a pistol grip stock, incorporating a recoil bolt across the full width of the rifle to help absorb shock. The upper hand guard extends from in front of the rear sight base to just beyond the lower barrel band. The upper barrel band is fitted with a parade hook for sling shortening, and the nose cap has the long "H" style bayonet lug. The lower barrel band has a swivel on the bottom, and there is another swivel to the rear of the pistol grip stock wrist. An inset, screw-mounted marking disk is on the right side of the lower stock.

In 1901, the first troop issues of the Model 98 Rifles were made to the East Asian Expeditionary Force, the Navy, and the three premier Prussian army corps. In 1904, contracts were placed with Waffenfabrik Mauser for 290,000 rifles and DWM for 210,000 ri-

German "Schutztruppen" in German Southwest Africa mounted on camels for ease of movement through the desert. Note the special boot for the butt of the G 98 Rifle.

German "Schutztruppen" in German Southwest Africa armed with G 98 Rifles are seen blowing up the rail lines to Windhuk, the capitol (Die Deutschen Kolonien)

Full-length view of the German Model 98 Rifle

Full-length view of the right side of an experimental version of the German Model 98 Rifle with a fluted cooling jacket and shortened forestock. (John Wall collection)

fles. In 1905, the change to the S-Patrone bullet required modification of the sights, with the modified "Lange Vizier" much taller than its predecessor. All rifles converted at this time were marked with a small (2.5mm) "s" above the chamber and on the barrel at the back of the rear sight base. During the First World War, slight changes were made to the Model 98 Rifle: the marking disk on the right side was replaced by two domed washers connected by a short, hollow metal tube, used for dismounting the firing pin, and grasping grooves were incorporated on the forestock. The Model 98 Rifle received its baptism in battle during the Boxer Rebellion, as well as during the long-running (1904-1907) war against the Hereros in

German Southwest Africa. Total production of the Model 98 Rifle, the standard German rifle of World War I, is estimated at more than five million weapons.

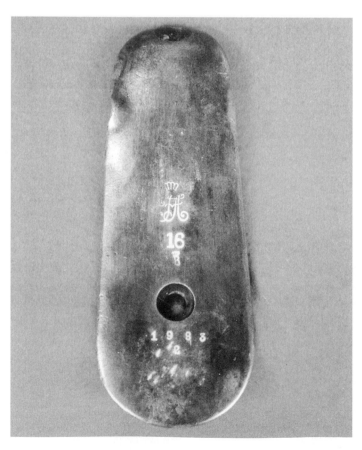

Rare G 98 Saxon-marked rifle butt plate

Two German servicemen, early in the 20th century, the one on the left in tropical field order, while the one on the right is in Naval Infantry dress, both carrying Gew 98s.

German Jaeger troops moving through a rear area in France. German troops would often sling their rifles across the front of the body.

Markings on the G 98 Rifle receiver ring on a Naval issued weapon, dated 1903

Receiver markings on the German Model 98 Rifle, indicating manufacture at the royal arsenal at Danzig in 1905

The left side of a naval issue G 98 Rifle, showing the naval acceptance mark on the side of the receiver

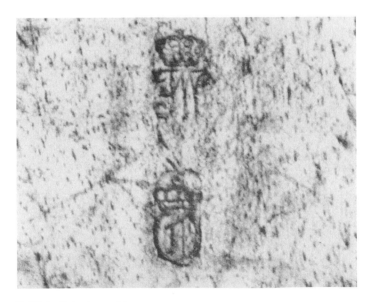

G 98 buttstock markings

G 98 buttstock markings

Receiver of a naval issue G 98, showing date of manufacture as 1899, by DWM...a real early one!

The receiver of this DWM-made G 98 Rifle is marked with a star. Note the dating at the bottom of the receiver, 1915/16.

Various representative World War I and Weimar Republic German Manufacturer's receiver markings (Robert Jensen collection)

WAFFENWERKE/OBERSPREE/KORNBUSCH & Co./1916

CROWN/ERFURT/1916

DWM/BERLIN/190-

J.P.SAUER & SOHN/SUHL/1917

SIMSON & Co./SUHL/1917

V.CHR.SCHILLING/SUHL/1916

C.G.HAENEL/SUHL/1917

CROWN/AMBERG/1915

DANZIG 1915/CROWN/SPANDAU/1900

CROWN/SPANDAU/1916

WAFFENBRIK/MAUSER A.-G./OBERNDORF A/N./1916

CROWN/DANZIG/1916

CROWN/DANZIG/1899/15

BS/WAFFENWERKE/OBERSPREE/1918

DANZIG 1915/CROWN/SPANDAU/1900

Naval acceptance stamping in the bolt root underside. This is the only sign of naval acceptance on this weapon, other than the marking disk.

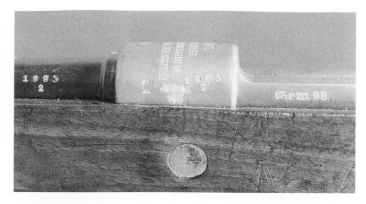

Side view of the receiver ring of the star-marked G 98 Rifle shown left. Another interesting fact is that these rifles had a numeral suffix, as opposed to alpha suffix. Note how the former serial number is canceled.

Marking disk in the right side of the buttstock of the naval-issue G 98 Rifle, showing Danzig

This receiver ring shows the alternate variation of the star marking on the receiver ring of a "Stern" marked G 98 rifle

Length: 49.20"; **Weight:** 9.0 lbs.; **Barrel:** 29.13"; **Caliber:** 7.92 x 57mm; **Rifling:** 4-groove, r/hand; **Operation:** Turnbolt action; **Feed:** 5-round, staggered column, flush, box magazine; **Sights:** V-notch rear sight graduated to 2000 meters. Post war production models, as well as renovated Model 98 Rifles have a tangent leaf rear sight graduated to 2000 meters. **Remarks:** Marked over the chamber with a crown/place of manufacture/date. The side rail is marked with the model designation. The serial number will be found on the left side of the receiver ring.

Stern, or "Star" marked G 98 Rifles: These rifles were marked with a star on the upper front portion of the receiver ring to indicate that one or more parts used in the manufacture of the rifle were manufactured by small firms other than state armories and the large private rifle factories that were not up to handling the demand for the millions of rifles required. There were two different types of star markings used according to sources.

GERMAN MODEL 98 CARBINE (KAR 98), FIRST AND SECOND PATTERN: Produced in 1898 for troop testing, the official Model Kar.98 Carbine was manufactured in Erfurt from 1903 to 1905. The first pattern carbine, in caliber 7.92 x 57mm, of which approximately three thousand were produced, was a miniature of the standard infantry Model 98, with a pistol grip stock that ran to the muzzle, and a nose cap from which only the crown of the muzzle appeared. The upper hand guard ran from the front of the rear sight

to the muzzle. The bolt handle was spoon-shaped and turned down; there was no provision for a bayonet. This model was soon abandoned, and the second pattern Model 98 Carbine, or Model 1898A, was adopted in 1902 to replace the first pattern.

German infantryman with G 98 Rifle in action in France, C. 1917

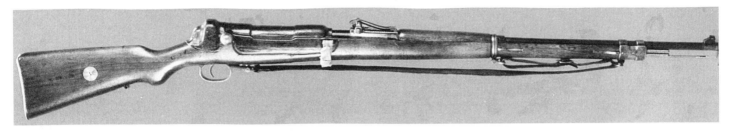

Right side view of a German Model G 98 Rifle with a most unusual pressed steel action cover, held in place by a buckle and strap arrangement at the front of the cover

Right side view of the German Model G 98 Rifle action cover, showing the slot for the bolt handle and the cloth strap and buckle

This close-up shows the attachment of the nonadjustable aircraft rear sight on the German Model G 98 Rifle

Left side view of the German Model G 98 Rifle action cover. This piece represents the prewar workmanship that went into designing and producing an accessory such as this.

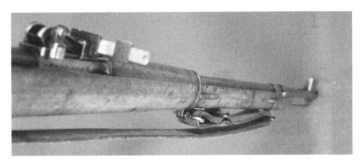

This close-up shows the attachment of the adjustable aircraft rear sight on the German Model G 98 Rifle

Aircraft sights were produced for attachment to the regular sights of the German Model G 98 Rifle, both front and rear. These sights were manufactured so that they could also be used on the G 88 Rifle. The picture shows the two types of rear sights produced, adjustable on the left and nonadjustable to the right. To the right of the rear sights is the front sight, which has two sets of notches in the base; the upper set of notches fit the G 98 Rifle, while the lower set fit the G 88 Rifle.

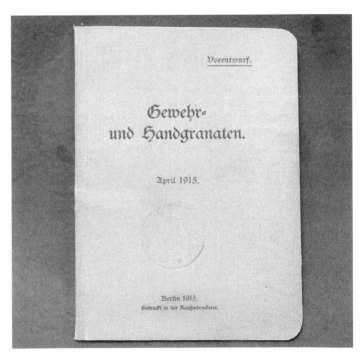

The cover of the German field manual for rifles and hand grenades, April 1915

The second pattern, or Model 1898A, was almost identical to the first pattern carbine, but provision was made for mounting a bayonet, with a short lug set well back from the muzzle. The front sight has sight protectors. The bolt handle is spatulate. Spatulate bolt handles normally match the serial number of the weapon, while the round-head bolts do not match. There were seven variations of sights that are to be found on the Kar.98. One official model was accepted on 16 June 1902, by Kaiser Wilhelm. This official model (Einheitskarabiner) was made at the Erfurt Arsenal from 1903 to 1905. All other Kar.98 Carbines must be considered as troop-test weapons.

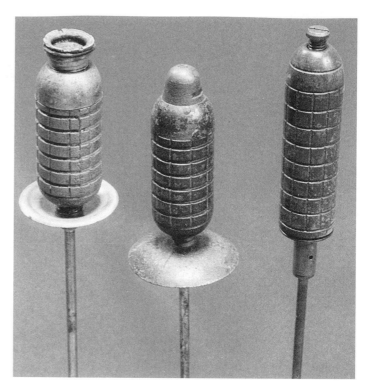

These World War I rifle grenades are for use with the G 98 Rifle, the rod being inserted down the muzzle of the rifle, and, by use of a special propellant cartridge, fired at the enemy. The serrated body is of cast iron, weighing approximately 2 lbs., with a 2-3/4 oz. charge contained in a thin cardboard cylinder. The nose is screw threaded to take the percussion fuse, and the base to take a nipple for a tin disk and tail rod with gas check. Until fused, the grenade is protected by a plug and leather washer. From the left, the Model 1914 Rifle grenade, with plug; next, the Model 1914 Rifle grenade, with fuse, and on the right, the Model 1913 Rifle grenade, fused.

This picture shows two German rifle grenade variant launchers available for use with the German Model Gew 98 Rifle; after being fitted to the muzzle of the rifle; these launchers are then locked in place. In front is the rifle grenade; derived from the French V-B grenade.

Close-up view of the "K.S." marked washer in the right side of the buttstock of the modified German Model 98 Rifle used in German Southwest Africa

Full-length view of the German Model 98 Rifle, marked for Colonial Service, and believed to have been modified locally in German Southwest Africa. The bolt handle has been bent down, and the stock recessed for handling, while the "Lange Vizier" sight is registering on 200 meters. This lower sight setting is presumably due to close-in fighting in the bush country. The washer in the stock is marked "K.S." for Colonial Service, while the reverse of the washer is marked "F.K." for Field Company, a term used earlier.

Left full-length view of the Colonial Service marked, modified German Model 98 Rifle. The washer in the stock is marked "K.S." for "Kaiserliches Schutztruppen," or Imperial Defense Force. The reverse of this particular washer is marked "F.K." which was the expeditionary force sent against the Hereros during their rebellion in German South-West Africa from 1904-1907.

The receiver ring of the Colonial Service marked, modified German Model 98 Rifle, marked "S" on the barrel, and "Crown/SPANDAU/1900" on the ring

Close-up view of the professionally bent bolt handle and recessed stock of the Colonial Service marked, modified German Model 98 Rifle

Rear sight of the Colonial Service marked, modified German Model 98 Rifle, showing it registering on 200 meters. This was probably a necessity due to the brush war nature of engagement with the Hereros during the uprisings.

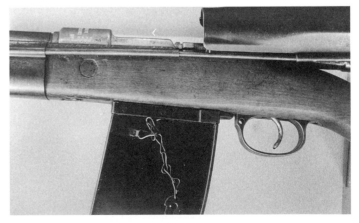

Left side view of the action of the German Model 98 Rifle with extended magazine and sliding bolt cover (see next page, top). This picture clearly shows the clip and rod that allows the bolt cover to slide back and forth with the action of the bolt, as well as rotating into position with the closing of the bolt. Also shown is the chain and key attachment used to hold the spring and follower in position during installation and removal of the extended magazine.

German Model 98 Rifle equipped with a sliding bolt cover designed to keep mud and debris out of the action of the rifle. The rifle is also fitted with a non-detachable large-capacity magazine, which increased the rifle capacity to 25 cartridges.

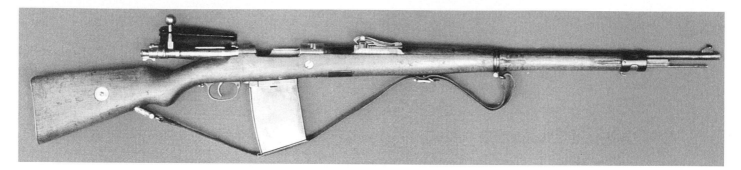

The German Model 98 Rifle with bolt cover and large capacity magazine, showing the action open, illustrating how the sliding bolt cover is attached to the bolt handle

The German Model 98 Rifle modified in 1915 for use as a sniper rifle. The receiver and the receiver bridge have claw mounts for a 4 x Goerz or Zeiss telescopic sight. The scope mount would be offset to the left in order that the rifle could be used as a clip loader. The bolt handle is bent down, and there is a recess cut in the stock to accommodate the bolt knob. The rifle is otherwise identical to the standard issue Model 98 Rifle. (Springfield Armory Museum)

The German Model 98 Sniper Rifle as viewed from above, showing the location of the claw mounts (Springfield Armory Museum)

The left side of the German Model 98 Sniper Rifle, showing the model designation on the side rail, and the proof marks and serial number on the left of the receiver ring (Springfield Armory Museum)

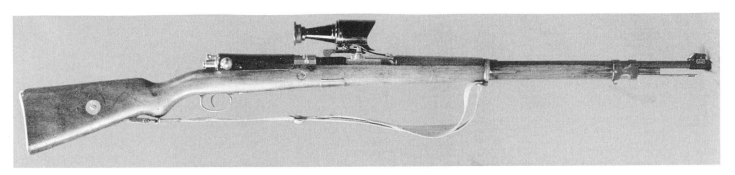

Full-length view of the German Model 98 Marksman Rifle fitted with a sliding bolt cover and a low light optics, bifocal marksman scope and front sight

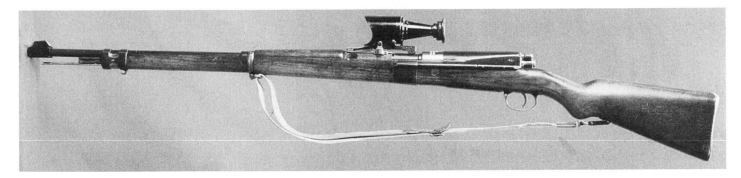

Left side view of the German Model 98 Marksman Rifle fitted with the low light bifocal marksman scope and front sight, as well as with a sliding bolt cover

The receiver of the German Model 98 Rifle with sliding bolt cover (shown on previous page), showing how the forend of the bolt cover fits snugly up against the face of the receiver. This also illustrates how the bolt cover rides on a rod that is attached by a steel clip fitting just in front of the receiver.

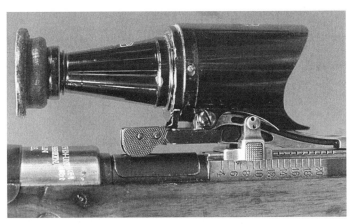

Right side view of the low light bifocal marksman scope mounted on the "Lange Vizier" rear sight. Note how the base of the scope conforms to the curvature of the rear sight ramp, while the spring-loaded mounting arms lock into the recessed bottom portion of the rear sight ramp. The eyepiece is molded leather.

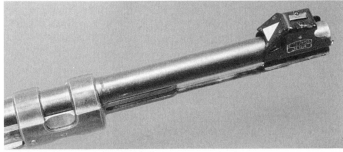

Close-up view of the auxiliary front sight used in conjunction with the low light bifocal marksman scope. This auxiliary sight with white diamond aiming point fits over the regular front sight and appears in the sight picture in the lower portion of the bifocal sight, with the target aligned with the top point of the triangle.

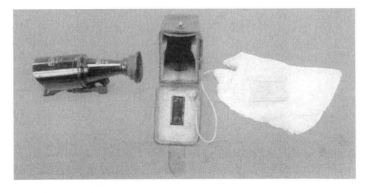

Complete low light bifocal marksman scope, with carrying case, white cotton bag secured to the lid, and instructions for use of the scope. A complete set like this is rarely seen.

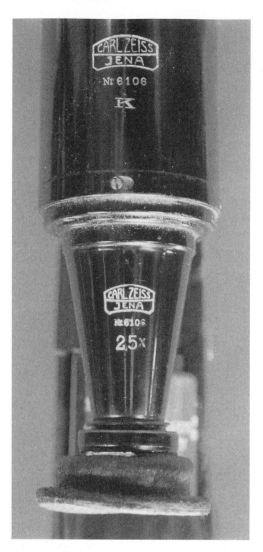

A sniper from the 9th Bavarian Infantry Regiment; this soldier managed to survive World War I, and with this same rifle, fought in the ranks of the Freikorps Wurzburg during the postwar revolutionary period. The rifle was confiscated by American Occupation troops, however the sniper scope and other memorabilia were retained and are in the collection of a German collector at this time.

Top view of the low light bifocal marksman scope, showing manufacturer's markings and specifications

Full-length view of the Radfahrer Gewehr, or Bicycle Troops Rifle, after which the Kar 98b is patterned. These rifles were issued to the Bicycle Troop companies that were active at the beginning of the First World War. The main differences between the Radfahrer Gewehr and the Kar 98b are the use of the Lange Vizier rear sight, the marking disc in the stock of the Radfahrer Gewehr, and that the lower band is held with a screw in the case of the Radfahrer and by a spring in the Kar 98b..

Left full-length view of the Bicycle Troops Rifle

Close-up view of the rear sight of the Bicycle Troops Rifle with the auxiliary pressed steel night sights attached

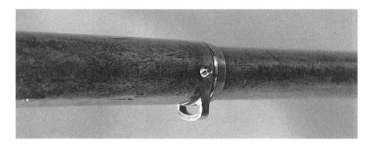

The lower barrel band on the Radfahrer Cewehr is held on by a screw through the bottom

A comparison of the pressed steel auxiliary night sights on the left, as opposed to the machined steel auxiliary night sights at the right. Both sights were phosphorous coated in the two inset to either side of the sight notch.

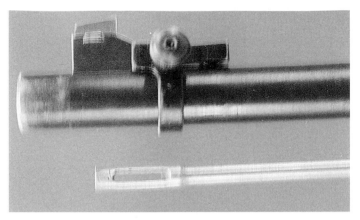

The auxiliary night front sight in a lowered position

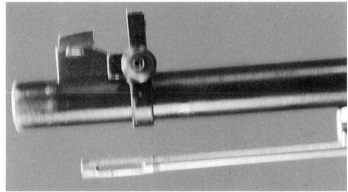

The auxiliary night front sight seen in an upright position mounted just behind the front sight

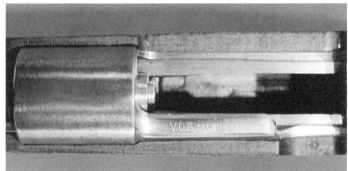

The chamber area of the German Model 98 .22 caliber Training Rifle. This view shows to advantage the spring-loaded chamber that extends into the magazine well area when the bolt is opened, allowing the single .22 caliber round to be loaded by hand. The only markings on the rifle are those seen on the top of the left side rail, in this case, "V.C.S." for Schilling, and "D.R.G.M."

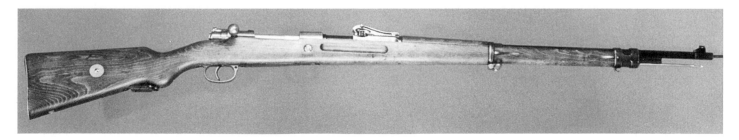

Full-length view of a German Model 98 .22 caliber purpose-built rifle

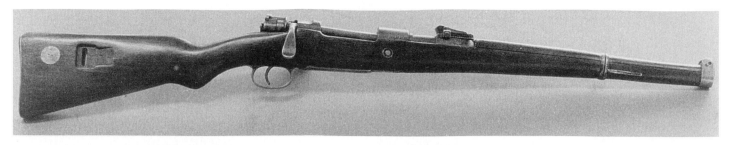

Full-length view of the First Pattern Model 98 Carbine, (Kar 98), fully stocked to the muzzle and without a bayonet lug. Note the end cap, with only the muzzle appearing, and note as well the placement of the marking disc. (Ben Musgrave collection)

Full-length view of the German Model 98 Carbine, Second Pattern; note the bayonet lug and cleaning rod, as well as the lack of a marking disc. (Robert Jensen collection)

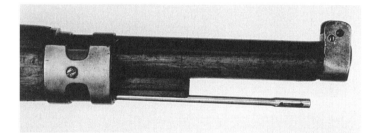

Close-up view of the muzzle area of the Model 98 Carbine, Second Pattern, showing the bayonet lug and cleaning rod. (Robert Jensen collection)

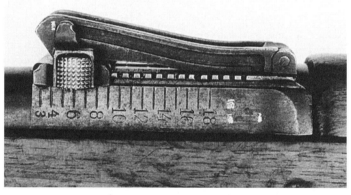

Close-up view of the rear sight of the Model 98 Carbine, Second Pattern, marked from 300 to 1800 meters. (Robert Jensen collection)

Crown/ERFURT/1904 markings on the receiver ring of the Model 98 Carbine, Second Pattern. (Robert Jensen collection)

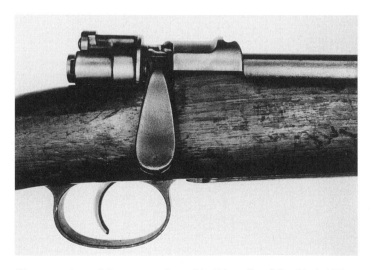

Close-up view of the spoon-shaped bolt handle of the Model 98 Carbine, Second Pattern. (Robert Jensen collection)

The receiver ring of the German Model 1898 Carbine (Kar 98A), showing the crown, the Erfurt arsenal marking, and the date "1904" (Springfield Armory Museum)

A pre-war photo of three Bavarian Policemen standing, with another policeman kneeling, with the rare pre-1907 Kar98 Carbine.

The Kar.98 was designed to use the same cartridge as the Kar.88, the Patrone 88. In 1903, the new "S" cartridge was introduced, which meant that all the Gew. 98 and Kar. 98s had to be modified to accept the new cartridge, with the letter "S" stamped on the top of the receiver to show that the change had been made. The new S-Patrone caused excessive recoil, as well as a foot-long muzzle blast, proving much too strong for the short carbine. Production was terminated in 1905, with those weapons produced limited to using the Patrone 88. It is believed that total production was approximately twenty thousand pieces. Most of the production went to

the Schutztruppe in Africa and to the Deutches Ostasiatische Expeditionskorps. Interestingly enough, pictures exist showing small numbers of Mexican troops in the early days of the Mexican revolution equipped with Kar.98s!

Length: 37.40"; **Weight:** 7.7 lbs.; **Barrel:** 17.32"; **Caliber:** 7.92 x 57mm; **Rifling:** 4-groove, r/hand; **Operation:** Turnbolt action; **Feed:** 5-round, staggered column, flush box magazine; **Sights:** Miniature "Lange Vizier" style rear sight graduated to 1800 meters. **Remarks:** Crown/Arsenal (Erfurt)/date on the receiver ring, model designation on the side rail.

GERMAN MODEL 1898AZ AND MODEL 1898a CARBINES: Germany adopted the Model 98AZ Carbine in 1908 after extensive testing for a replacement for the Model 1898 (98A) Carbine. It was found that a longer-barreled version of the Model 98A Carbine reduced recoil and muzzle blast to an acceptable level. The Model 98AZ Carbine, while labeled thus by the Germans, is actually a short rifle. The action of the new carbine is similar to the Model 98 Rifle, but the external diameter of the receiver ring is considerably smaller. When war broke out in 1914, the Model 98AZ Carbine was carried by the cavalry, the foot artillery, bicyclists, riflemen, sharpshooters, pioneers, telegraphists, telephonists, and air, ship and motor transport units.

The stock is the familiar pistol grip style, with the upper hand guard running from the front of the receiver ring to the upper barrel band. The upper band is also a combination nose cap, employing a unique hinged action that opens from left to right. There is a bayonet lug under the extremely short muzzle and prominent front sight protectors. A stacking hook protrudes from the bottom of the forestock, the lower barrel band incorporates an integral swivel on the left side, and a slot is cut through the buttstock to accommodate the German-style sling with keeper. The bolt handle is turned down, the back of the bolt knob is flattened and checkered, and the stock is cut out at this point to allow the bolt knob to be more easily grasped.

German East African askaris armed with Model 98AZ Carbines in firing positions on the side of a brush-covered hillside (Die Deutschen Kolonien)

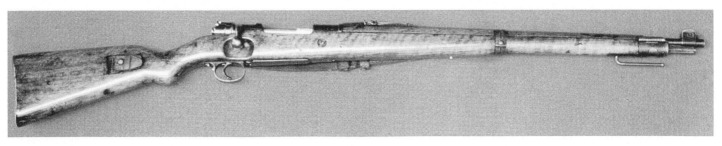

Full-length view of the German Model 98AZ (98a) Carbine. Note that this specimen was produced prior to the date in 1915 when grasping grooves were cut in the forestock.

World War I German troops in spike-top helmets armed with Model 98AZ Carbines are seen firing across a river, C. 1914

German troops in a shallow trench, armed with Model 98AZ Carbines, awaiting the order to advance

World War I German Mountain Troops armed with Model 98AZ Carbines engaging the enemy

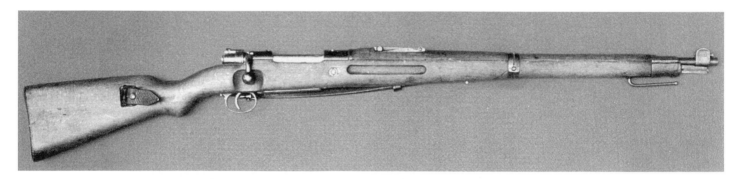

Full-length view of the post-1915 German Model 98AZ (98a) Carbine, with grasping grooves

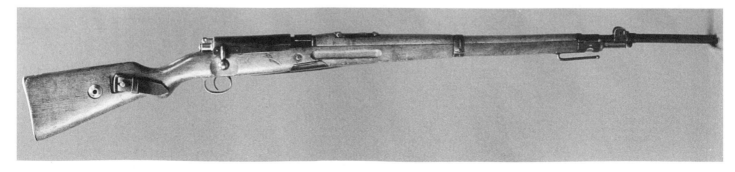

Full-length illustration of a German Model 98A Carbine with a sliding bolt cover and a flash hider

Interesting picture of World War I German troops in Macedonia, going through inspection of their Model 98AZ Carbines. Note the Macedonian-issue spike top helmets.

The receiver ring of the German Model 98AZ (98a) Carbine, showing the crown/"Erfurt"/1915

The left side rail of the German Model 98AZ Carbine, showing the model designation

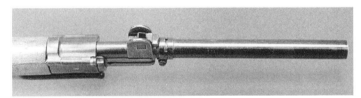

Close-up view of the flash hider attached to the muzzle of the German Model 98A Carbine

A youthful German soldier armed with a Model 98AZ Carbine hears of Germany's surrender during World War I.

The receiver ring of the German Model 98AZ (98a) Carbine, showing post-1915 production. Note the true caliber stamped at the front of the receiver ring, in this case "7.93".

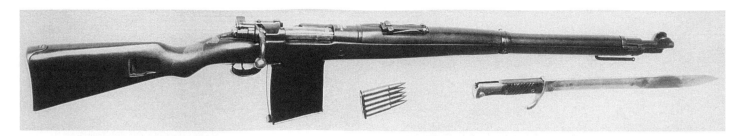

Full-length view of the right side of a German Model 98A Carbine fitted with an extended 20 round magazine, also showing a clip of cartridges and the customary bayonet. (John Wall collection)

Top view of a KAR 98A Carbine, double-dated, with a side rail scope mount; note the date "1920" at the front of the receiver ring, while at the rear of the receiver ring is "CROWN/DANZIG/ 1916." This is probably Post-WWI Police issue. (Robert Jensen collection)

Left side of the KAR 98A Carbine, showing the side mounted sniper scope. (Robert Jensen collection)

With the advent of British tanks, the Germans quickly devised a 13mm, bolt action, single-shot, anti-tank rifle to combat this new threat. Based upon the G 98 action, the anti-tank action is enormously strong and capable of withstanding considerable pressure. The rifle can only be used from a prone position, and is supported by a bipod. The bipod shown on this rifle is purpose-made, while the bipod from the German 08/15 Light Machine Gun will often be encountered.

German Model 98AZ Carbines made prior to 1915 did not have grasping grooves, while those produced after 1915 were made with them. After the First World War, the stocks of German Model 98AZ Carbines were renamed the "Model 98a." This also differentiated them from the "Model 98b" carbines then being produced.

Length: 43.30"; **Weight:** 8.0 lbs.; **Barrel:** 23.62"; **Caliber:** 7.92 x 57mm; **Rifling:** 4-groove, r/hand; **Operation:** Turnbolt action; **Feed:** 5-round, staggered column, flush, box magazine; **Sights:** Tangent leaf rear sight adjustable to 2000 meters. **Remarks:** Crown/arsenal/date on the receiver ring, with model designation of the left side rail.

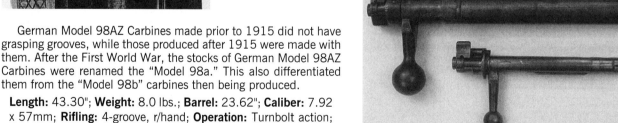

Comparison of the 13mm anti-rifle bolt to that of the standard 8mm Gew 98. (Robert Jensen collection)

Full-length view of the German 13mm T-Gewehr, bolt action, single shot, anti-tank rifle

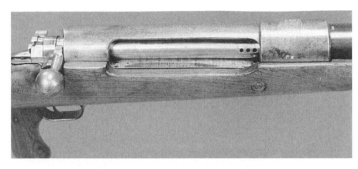

Right close-up view of the action of the German 13mm anti-tank rifle. Note the three holes near the front of the bolt for gas bleed-off.

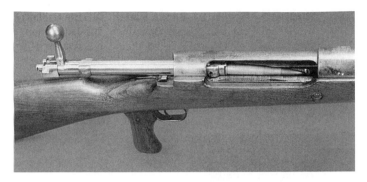

Close-up view of the massive action open, with a round ready to be fed into the chamber

Mauser banner logo over date on the receiver ring of the German 13mm anti-tank rifle. (Robert Jensen collection)

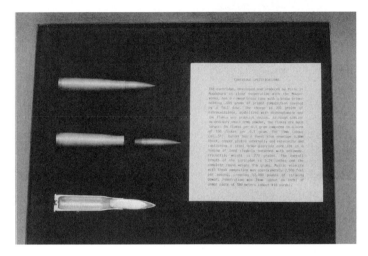

Display and specifications of the 13mm German anti-tank rifle cartridge

Comparison of the 13mm anti-rifle bullet to the standard 8mm rifle bullet. (Robert Jensen collection)

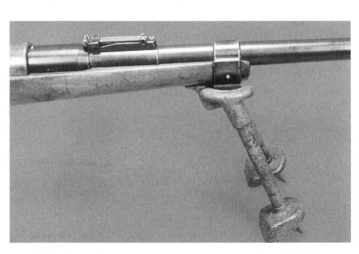

Close-up view of the right side of the purpose-made bipod of the German 13mm anti-tank rifle. Note that there is no supporting horizontal bracing bar between the legs as is found on the German 08/15 bipod.

Close-up view of the date-only on the receiver ring of the M1918 13mm anti-tank rifle.

Length: 66.60"; **Weight:** 37.0 lbs.; **Barrel:** 38.75"; **Caliber:** 13mm; **Rifling:** 8-groove, r/hand; **Operation:** Turnbolt action; **Feed:** Single shot (while never used during the war, a few specimens were made with a magazine); **Sights:** V-notch adjustable rear sight graduated from 100 to 500 meters. **Remarks:** Mauser Banner trademark stamped on the upper receiver over the date, 1918.

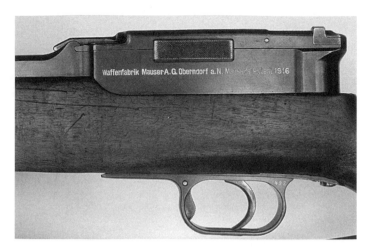

Left side view of the receiver area, showing the Mauser markings

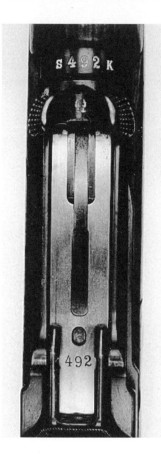

Top view of the Flier's Rifle's action area; note serial number on receiver. (Robert Jensen collection)

Left side view of the rear sight of the Flier's Rifle. (Robert Jensen collection)

Right side full-length view of the Flier's Rifle (Robert Jensen collection)

Left side full-length view of the Flier's Rifle (Robert Jensen collection)

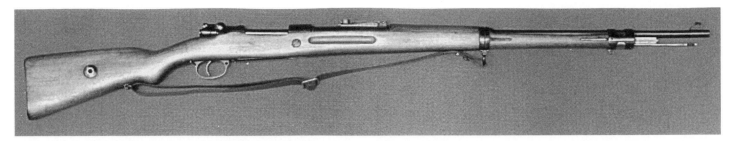

Full-length view of the German Model 98 Transitional Model Rifle (Weimar Republic)

Full-length view of the German G 98 Transitional Model Rifle with the narrow lower barrel band

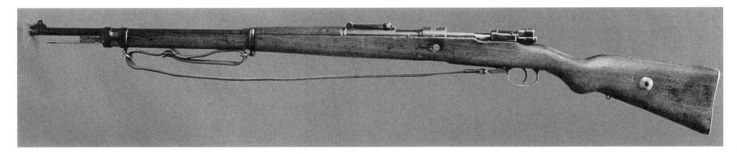

Left full-length view of the German G 98 Transitional Model Rifle with narrow lower barrel band

GERMAN MODEL 98 TRANSITIONAL MODEL RIFLE (WEIMAR REPUBLIC): Those Model 98 Rifles retained in 1920 by the Reichswehr, the postwar army allowed under the terms of the armistice, in most cases were modified by the replacement of the "Lange Vizier" sight with a simple tangent rear sight. The markings on the receiver ring of many of these rifles were ground off and the weapons were arsenal refinished. Other than the sights, the rifles are identical to the German Model 98 Rifle.

Close-up view of the broad lower band found on many of the G 98 Transitional Model Rifles

Reichswehr soldiers armed with Transition Model Rifles during maneuvers , C. 1920s

Close-up view of the narrow lower barrel band on the German G 98 Transitional Model Rifle

A scene of revolution in Post-World War I Berlin. Note the old-timer atop the armored car with a G 71 Rifle, while the first soldier on the ground uses a captured Belgian 89/16 carbine. The rest of the soldiers are using G 98 Rifles and 98AZ Carbines. (Anon.)

1920/Crown/DANZIG/1917 markings on the receiver of a GEW 98 Rifle, reissued by the Reichswehr after WWI. (Robert Jensen collection)

Date "1920" stamped into the left side of the stock of the GEW 98 Rifle reissued after WWI. (Robert Jensen collection)

Weimar Eagle inspector's markings on the bottom of the stock of the DANZIG 1920/1917 reissued GEW 98 Rifle. (Robert Jensen collection)

GERMAN MODEL KAR 98b RIFLE: Included in the armory allowed the Reichswehr by the terms of the armistice were the Model 98 Rifles altered or manufactured to Model Kar 98b specifications. According to German nomenclature, this prefix "Kar" indicates a "Carbine," but in actuality, the weapon is a rifle. While retaining the overall dimensions of the Model 98 Rifle, the rear sight was replaced by a flat tangent leaf sight graduated to 2000 meters, the parade hook was removed from the upper band, the lower barrel band with attached swivel was replaced by a barrel band with integral swivel on the left side, and a slot was cut for the sling in the buttstock. The quick-release attachment on the bottom of the buttstock was removed.

Many of the Kar 98b specimens found are converted Model 98 Rifles, with the original markings. Recently, some manufactured Kar 98b Rifles have appeared on the market, and these are marked

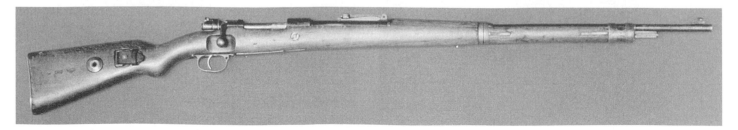

Full-length view of the German Model Kar 98b Rifle, as originally manufactured

on the side rail with the model designation. Aside from the minor differences noted, the Kar 98b is identical to the Model 98 Rifle, and much resembles the rifle produced for the bicycle troops (Rad-fahrer-Gewehr 98) of the First World War.

Interesting scene of street fighting in Postwar Berlin. Note the use of Kar 98b Rifles, including those piled on the front of the carriage.

Rare SIMSON & Co/SUHL/1926 dated receiver ring (Robert Jensen collection)

Receiver ring markings on the converted German Model Kar 98b Rifle shown below

Side rail of the German Model Kar 98b Rifle, showing the model designation

The side rail markings on the converted German Model Kar 98b Rifle. Note that this is marked "Gew. 98"

Full-length view of the German Model Kar 98b Rifle, as originally manufactured

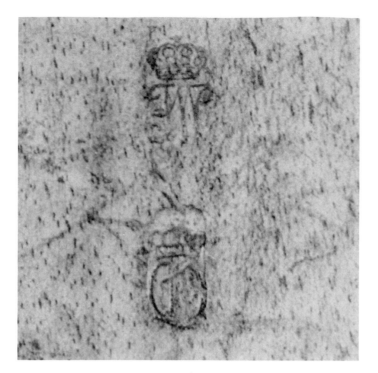

Acceptance markings on the stock of the converted German Model Kar 98b Rifle

German naval ratings armed with Standard Modell Mauser rifles on parade, 1936 (Deutche Soldaten Jahrbuch, 1966)

German sniper armed with the scope-mounted Kar 98b in action on the Russian front during World War II. (Signal)

Side rail model designation on the German Standard Modell Short Rifle

GERMAN STANDARD MODELL MODEL 1933 SHORT RIFLE:
The Standard Modell Short Rifle was conceived and developed in 1924. However, production did not commence until 1933, at which time an alternate model with turned-down bolt and side mounted sling was also offered. The alternate carbine was identical to, and the precursor of the Kar 98k, with the exception that the upper band was retained by a pin and the lower barrel band was held by a short band retaining spring holding only the lower band.

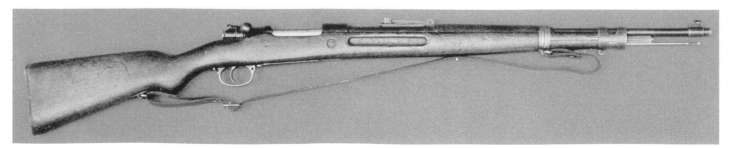

Full-length view of the German Standard Modell Short Rifle

Early picture of SS troops wearing World War I-style helmets while on parade with Standard Modell Short Rifles (Bundesarchiv)

"Mauser Banner" logo on the receiver ring of the German Standard Modell Short Rifle

Rare "Mauser Banner" rifle with military acceptance stamp "Eagle/655." (Robert Jensen collection)

SS recruits armed with Standard Modell Short Rifles at training. Note that each rifle has a muzzle cover. (Bundesarchiv)

Full-length view of the German Mauser Standard Modell Carbine

The Standard Modell is a handy size short rifle, allowing it to be standard for infantry and cavalry. This short rifle was offered commercially for police and security guard duty, as well as being sold worldwide. The men of the German Condor Legion that fought in Spain during the Spanish Civil War (1936-1939) were armed with the Standard Modell Short Rifle. At the same time, it was being used by both sides in the Chaco War between Bolivia and Paraguay (1932-1935), as well as in China by the Chinese Nationalist army.

The short rifle is fitted with a pistol grip stock with grasping grooves, with the short style upper handguard running from in front of the rear sight base to the lower band; the lower band is fitted with a swivel on the bottom, with another on the bottom of the buttstock just behind the wrist of the stock. The upper band is equipped with

Manufacturer's address marking on the side rail of the German Mauser Standard Modell Carbine

"Mauser Banner" logo over date of manufacture on the receiver ring of the German Mauser Standard Modell Carbine

a parade hook for shortening the sling, while the nose cap incorporates the long German "H" style bayonet lug.

Length: 43.60"; **Weight:** 8.8 lbs.; **Barrel:** 23.62"; **Caliber:** 7.92 x 57mm; **Rifling:** 4-groove, r/hand; **Operation:** Turnbolt action; **Feed:** 5-round, staggered column, flush, box magazine; **Sights:** Tangent leaf rear sight graduated to 2000 meters. **Remarks:** "Mauser Banner" logo on the receiver ring over the date of manufacture. Serial numbers and manufacturer's markings on the side rail.

GERMAN MODEL 1933 MAUSER STANDARD MODELL CARBINE: Almost identical to the Kar 98k, the Standard Modell Carbine is fitted with a pistol grip stock with grasping grooves, the bolt handle is bent down, and the stock is recessed to accommodate the bolt knob. The upper hand guard runs from in front of the rear sight base to the lower barrel band, which is held by a spring, while the upper

German soldier of the "Grossdeutschland" regiment in parade tunic at the "present" (Brian L. Davis)

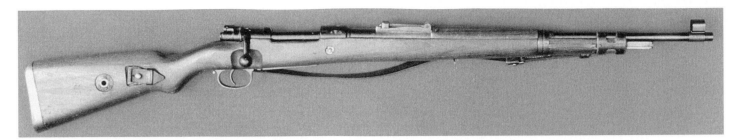

Full-length view of the German Model 98k Carbine

band is pinned to the stock. The sling is side mounted, with the stock slotted for the typical German-style sling and keeper.

Length: 43.60; **Weight:** 8.60 lbs.; **Barrel:** 23.62"; **Caliber:** 7.92 x 57mm; also available in 7 x 57mm and 7.65 x 53mm; **Rifling:** 4-groove, r/hand; **Operation:** Turnbolt action; **Feed:** 5-round, staggered column, flush, box magazine; **Sights:** Tangent leaf rear sight graduated to 2000 meters. **Remarks:** "Mauser Banner" logo on the receiver ring over the date of manufacture, with the manufacturer's address on the side rail.

GERMAN MODEL 98k CARBINE: This carbine, in actuality a short rifle, was the standard shoulder arm of the German armed forces in World War II, and, with approximately 11.5 million carbines made, was the most produced of all of the Mauser rifles. It was manufactured at the following locations:

Mauser-Werke AG, Oberndorf am Neckar, Wurttemberg (code "S/42K," "S/42G," "S/42," "42," "BYF," or "SVW")

Mauser-Werke AG, Berlin-Borsigwalde (code "S/243G," "S/243," "243," or "ar")

Sauer & Sohn, Suhl (code "S/147," "S/147K," "S/147G," "147," or "ce")

The Waffen-SS in action, using their Model 98k Carbines with bayonet attached (Signal magazine)

A good illustration of the markings on a KAR 98k Carbine receiver when work was done on one weapon by two different manufacturers, in this case Eagle/bcd/ar over "42." (Robert Jensen collection)

Review of the Bosnian-Croatian Moslem troops of the Waffen-SS Legion "Handschar," equipped with the Model 98k Carbine (Bundesarchiv)

An example of a Navy marked washer in the stock of a KAR 98k carbine. (Robert Jensen collection)

Side view of the German Model 98k Carbine, showing the Russian crossed rifle marking over the serial number, and the model designation on the left side rail

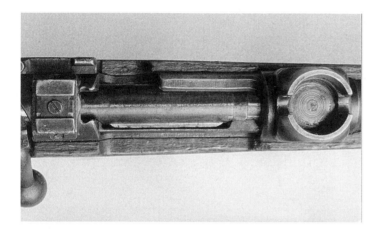

Close-up view of the turret mount on the German Model 98k Carbine (Century International Arms, Inc.)

An example of the markings of a WWI DWM/BERLIN/1918 receiver reworked into a KAR 98k Carbine configuration; in this case ', BNZ marked with a single Rune, indicating work done by Steyr at a concentration camp under SS supervision. (Robert Jensen collection)

Full-length view of a late-war turret mount sniper model of the German Model 98k Carbine (Century International Arms, Inc.)

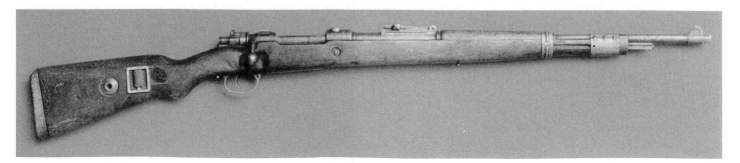

Full-length view of the claw mount sniper model of the German Model 98k Carbine (Century International Arms, Inc.)

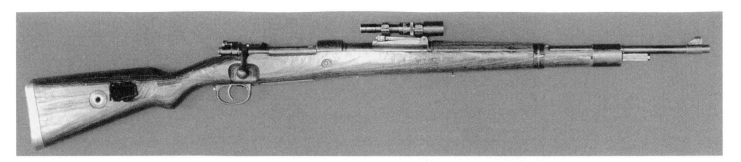

Full-length view of the marksman model German Model 98k Carbine with side rail mount and ZF-41 scope

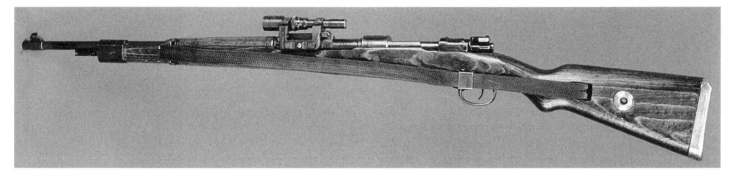

Left full-length view of the German Model 98k Carbine with side rail mount and ZF-41 scope

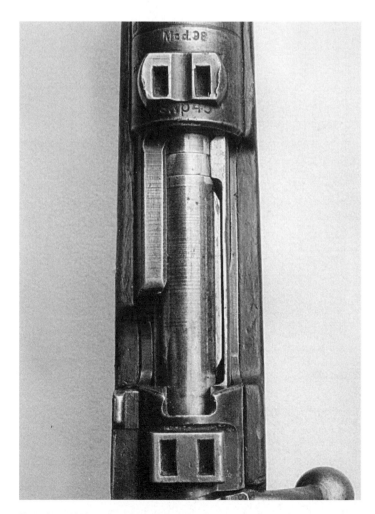

Top view of the claw mounts on the sniper model German Model 98k Carbine (bottom of previous page). Note the markings on the receiver both in front of and behind the front mount. (Century International Arms, Inc.)

German sniper with scope-mounted Model 98k Carbine, somewhere on the Russian front (Signal magazine)

Receiver markings on the sniper model German 98k Carbine, produced at Brno, Czechoslovakia in 1944

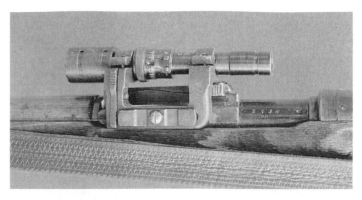

Close up view of the left side of the mount and ZF-41 scope on the German Model 98k Carbine

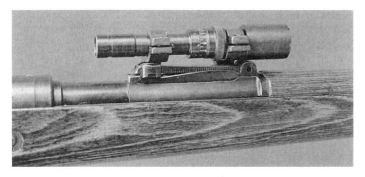

Right side view of the ZF-41 scope mounted on the German Model 98k Carbine

Side view of the German Model 98k Carbine with extended integral magazine, showing the crossed Russian rifles signifying Russian capture and reissue

Full-length view of a German Model 98k Carbine equipped with an integral box magazine giving a 25-round capacity to the weapon. This carbine was captured on the Russian front, arsenal refinished, put into arsenal storage, and later shipped to Vietnam where it was used by the Viet Cong. This was its condition when captured, so one assumption is that the magazine, which is permanently attached to the trigger guard, was affixed experimentally by the Germans. It is also possible that this was done post WWII by the Czechs.

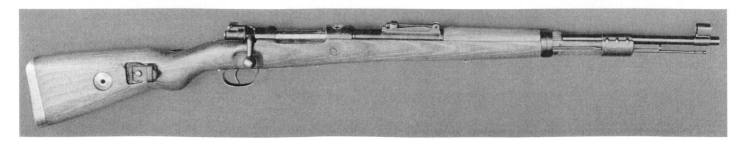

Full-length view of a late-war German Model 98k Carbine, FN manufacture. Note the laminated stock, the crude bands, and cupped butt plate.

A Waffen-SS sniper team, armed with a turret-mounted scope on a Model 98k Carbine in action on the Russian front (Signal magazine)

Left side view of the rear claw mount engaging. (Robert Jensen collection)

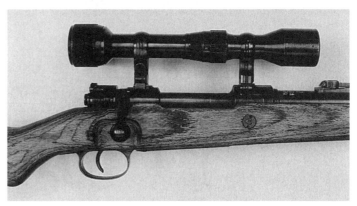

Right side view of a KAR 98k Carbine, showing the action and a high claw mounted sniper scope. (Robert Jensen collection)

Left side view of the same KAR 98k Carbine illustrating the method of attachment of the front claw of the sniper scope. (Robert Jensen collection)

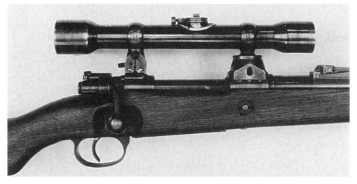

Right side view of a KAR 98k Carbine Sniper with high turret mounts and a 4x scope. (Robert Jensen collection)

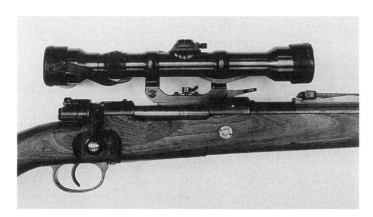

Right side view of a KAR 98k Carbine with a side rail mount with 4x scope. (Robert Jensen collection)

Right side view of a KAR 98k Carbine with a variant side rail mount incorporating a 4x scope. (Robert Jensen collection)

A visual record of the production and simplification of the KAR 98k Carbine, from the pre-war period to late-war manufacture:

Full-length view of the right side of a pre-war manufacture KAR 98k Carbine. (Robert Jensen collection)

Full-length view of the right side of a mid-war production KAR 98k Carbine. (Robert Jensen collection)

Right side view of the full-length of a late-war production KAR 98k Carbine, illustrating the gradual simplification and short cuts, i.e. lack of bayonet lug, take-down hole in the butt plate, omission of the stock washer, poorly finished laminated stock, etc. taken at the end of WWII in order to keep production as high as possible.

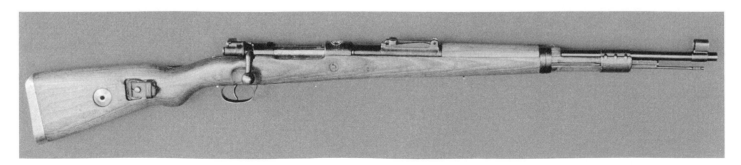

Full-length view of a late-war German Model 98k Carbine, FN manufacture. Note the laminated stock, the crude bands, and cupped butt plate.

View of the FN-produced German Model 98k Carbine receiver ring, showing the FN logo. This most likely resulted from using receivers and other parts from the old stocks on hand at the FN factory.

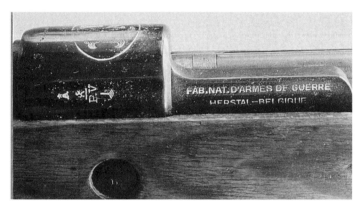

Side view of the receiver area of the FN-made German Model 98k Carbine, showing the original FN markings on the side rail and the Belgian proofing on the side of the receiver ring.

Waffen SS soldier, eating with his German Model 98k Carbine slung across the front of his body (Signal)

Full-length view of the German Model 98k Carbine with an Erma Model EL .22 caliber insert for training purposes. These Erma models were produced in either a single-shot version, or a 5-round magazine version. Shown is the 5-round magazine version with detachable clip. The insert barrel in this version goes to the muzzle.

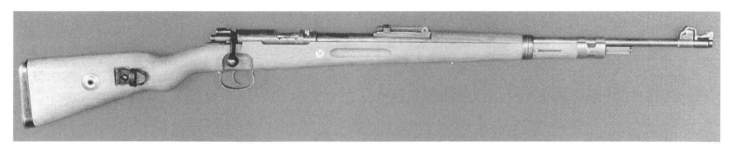

Purpose-made German Model 98k-style KK Wehrsportsgewehr single-shot, .22 caliber training rifle. All specifications are the same as for the Model 98k Carbine. At some time, this particular specimen was arsenal restocked.

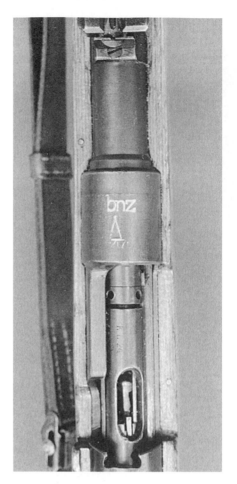

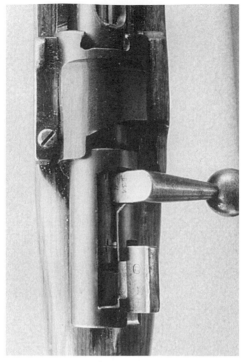

The action of the German Model 98k Carbine with the Erma Model EL .22 caliber insert. Note the collar with holes for locking the insert into place with the aid of a short rod. Note also the port for ejection of the spent cartridge casing.

Another view of the German Model 98k Carbine with Erma Model EL .22 caliber insert, giving a better impression of the bolt and the action itself. This was an inexpensive, as well as practical, method of training unskilled recruits in the handling of military weapons. The Erma unit would normally be kept in a lidded wooden chest that had been machined to accept the various components of the insert.

The receiver ring area of the KK Wehrsportsgewehr .22 caliber training rifle, showing the manufacturer's logo, name and address. This training rifle was produced by Gustloff-werke of Suhl.

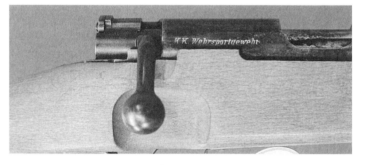

The right side of the receiver of the KK Wehrsportsgewehr .22 caliber training rifle, showing the model designation

Marking on the receiver ring of a German Model 98k Carbine, indicating that this particular weapon was made under the auspices of Steyr-Daimler-Puch at a concentration camp under SS supervision. This is indicated by the single rune between the "BNZ" marking and the date below. (Century International Arms, Inc.)

Barrel and receiver markings on a German Model 98k Carbine, showing an SS "Death's Head" on the barrel, indicating issuance to an SS unit. Note that the left side of the receiver ring bears commercial nitro proofs under the serial number. (Century International Arms, Inc.)

Left side view of an "SS" marked barrel and receiver group of a KAR 98k Carbine. (Robert Jensen collection)

"SS" Runes in the side of the KAR 98k Carbine stock. (Robert Jensen collection)

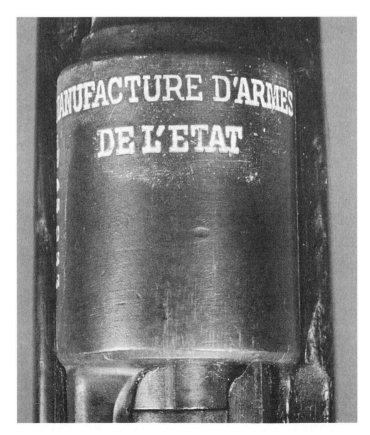

Markings on the receiver ring of the FN Model 30 Short Rifle issued to the German Postal Service. (Cliff Baumann collection)

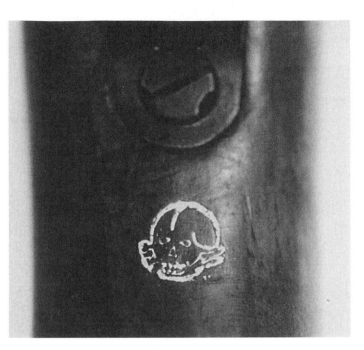

"SS" death's head cartouche on the underside of the KAR 98k Carbine. (Robert Jensen collection)

Markings on the bottom side of the KAR 98k Carbine barrel. (Robert Jensen collection)

Stock marking on an FN-made Model 30 Short Rifle, indicating issue to a unit of the German Postal Service. Guards on mail trains, as well as at main post offices were equipped with rifles, usually German-made weapons. This case is an exception. (Cliff Baumann collection)

Receiver ring of the German Model 98k Carbine, showing the code "S/42" over the barely-discernible date "1938." What is interesting is that this carbine bears the crossed Russian rifle mark on the left rear of the receiver ring, indicating capture and later reissue by the Russians. This particular specimen was captured from the Viet Cong in 1968!

Berlin-Lubecker Maschinenfabrik, Lubeck (code "S/237," or "237")

Waffenfabrik Brunn AG, Brno (code "945," "dot," "dou," and "swp")

Feinmechanische Werke GmbH, Erfurt (code "S/27," "27," and "ax")

Gustloff-Werke, Weimar (code "bcd," or "337")

Steyr-Daimler-Puch, Steyr/Oberdonau (code "660," or "bnz")

Berlin-Suhler Waffenwerke (code "bsw")

A direct descendant of the Model 98 Rifle, which it superficially resembles except for size, the Kar 98k incorporates those changes that were deemed necessary after the lessons learned during the First World War. The intervening years also played a hand in the development of the K98k, with quantity production going into full operation in 1935 when Hitler undertook the complete rearmament of Germany.

Made under strict quality control, the K98k has a stepped barrel like the Model 98 Rifle, a side positioned sling, a compact turned-down bolt handle, a wide lower barrel band, and a tangent leaf rear sight. As the war progressed, manufacturing standards were modified and simplified to save production time and material, but quality control never declined, with the "Kreigsmodell" introduced in 1942. This rifle was distinguished from early production models by a stamped nose cap, barrel bands, and butt plates. Trigger guards were crudely finished, and most of the stocks used were of laminated woods, which had been shown to withstand warping much better than the conventional walnut one-piece stocks used initially. As the war ground on to its inexorable end, production methods declined rapidly, with shortcuts taken in many of the manufacturing steps. By 1945, bayonet lugs were done away with and barrel bands were held on the stocks by means of wooden screws!

The grenade launcher for use with the German Model 98k Carbine, shown here with two propelling cartridges of differing strength, as well as the shaped-charge, armor piercing rifle grenade shown mated to the barrel of the launcher.
(Henry Wichmann collection)

German soldier with German Model 98k Carbine with grenade launcher attached. The soldier is shown matching the grooves of the rifle grenade to the lands of the grenade launcher. (Signal)

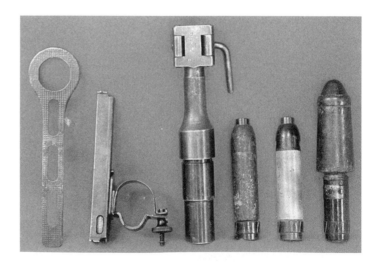

Grenade launcher and equipment used by the Germans with German Model 98k Carbine. From left to right: the launcher wrench, used to tighten or loosen the removable barrel; the inclinometer that attaches to the rifle to provide the proper level; two different style high explosive rifle grenades; lastly, an armor-piercing, shaped charge rifle grenade. (Henry Wichmann collection)

Length: 43.60"; **Weight:** 8.6 lbs.; **Barrel:** 23.62"; **Caliber:** 7.92 x 57mm; **Rifling:** 4-groove, r/hand; **Operation:** Turnbolt action; **Feed:** 5-round, staggered column, flush, box magazine; **Sights:** Tangent leaf rear sight graduated to 2000 meters. **Remarks:** Letter or number code of manufacture over the date manufactured on the receiver ring, with various proof marks on the left and right side of the receiver ring. The model designation is on the left side rail.

A rare piece of equipment for the German Model 98k Carbine that is seldom found today is the canvas webbing and leather action cover. This was an important item, especially when the carbine was transported in an area where dirt and debris could foul the action.

One other item of equipment for the German Model 98k Carbine that is considered a rarity is the leather rear sight cover, used to protect the rear sight when the weapon is being transported.

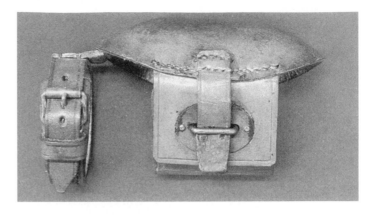

Right side view of the leather rear sight cover for the German Model 98k Carbine. Note that the cover is held in place by a strap attachment that goes between the front of the receiver ring and the rear of the sight base. The rounded portion of the cover is held by a simple strap and metal closure. (Henry Wichmann collection)

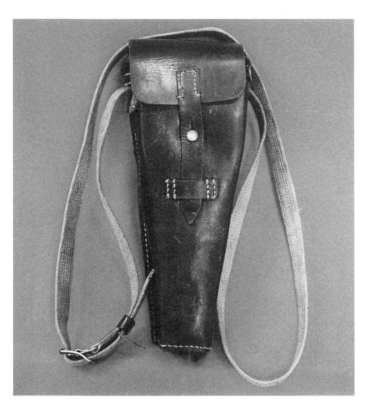

Model 98K Carbine grenade launcher case with carrying straps

Top view of the opened leather rear sight cover for the German Model 98k Carbine (Henry Wichmann collection)

German soldier in action, carrying his German Model 98k Carbine with grenade launcher attached (Signal)

Markings on the heavy strap portion of the leather rear sight cover for the German Model 98k Carbine. (Henry Wichmann collection)

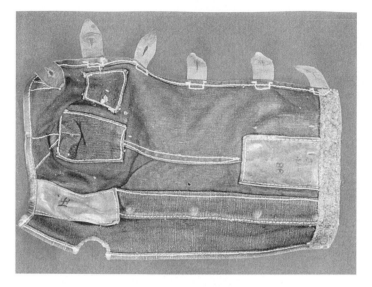

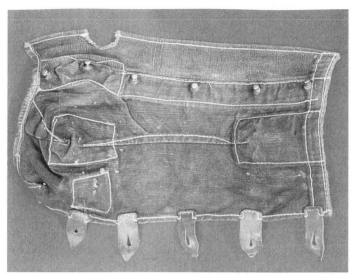

Inside view of the German World War II canvas webbing and leather Model 98k action cover (Henry Wichmann collection)

Outer view of the German World War II canvas webbing and leather Model 98k action cover (Henry Wichmann collection)

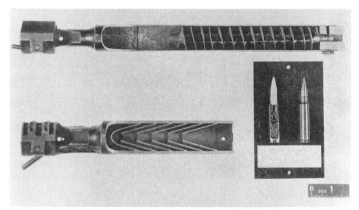

Markings on the German Model 98k action cover. (Henry Wichmann collection)

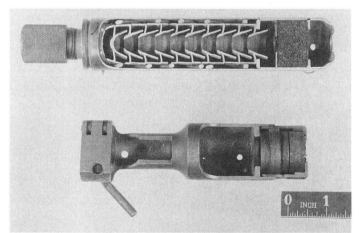

Sectionalized views of four different silencers utilized by the Germans during WWII; note the low velocity cartridges developed for use with the silencers. (John Wall collection)

GERMAN MODEL G33/40 CARBINE: After the conquest of Czechoslovakia, German industry assumed control of the arms industry at Brno. In 1940, after testing and evaluating the Czech Model VZ 33, the German Model G33/40 Carbine was introduced. The prefix to the model number would indicate that, in German nomenclature, this is a rifle, while actually it is a carbine. The German Model 33/40 Carbine differed from the Model VZ 33 Carbine by having a laminated stock and hand guard, as well as a sheet steel protector plate on the left side of the buttstock, curving to the bottom. The German 33/40 Carbine does not have grasping grooves, and the front sight protectors of the VZ 33 are replaced by a steel sight hood, or cover. An extremely rare variant of the German Model 33/40, in a single prototype form only, was the folding stock version for paratroop use. Many of the Model 33/40 Carbines were issued to the German "Gebirgstruppen," or Mountain Infantry, where the buttstock protecting plate helped keep the stock from harm when it was used for assistance in climbing. The German Model 33/40 Carbine has always been a highly prized addition to any Mauser collection.

Length: 39.10"; **Weight:** 7.9 lbs.; **Barrel:** 19.29"; **Caliber:** 7.92 x 57mm; **Rifling:** 4-groove, r/hand; **Operation:** Turnbolt action; **Feed:** 5-round, staggered column, flush box magazine; **Sights:** Tangent leaf rear sight graduated to 1000 meters. **Remarks:** All German Model 33/40 Carbines produced after 1940 are marked on the receiver ring with the same code, "dot" for Brno, or Brunn as it was called in German. Code "945" was used for the first production pieces made in 1940 with a walnut stock, rather than a laminate stock. This was the only manufacturer of Model 33/40 Carbines. This code will be found over the date of manufacture. The side rail is marked with the model designation.

The left side of the German Model 33/40 buttstock, showing the sheet steel protecting plate adjoining the cupped butt plate

The receiver ring of the German Model 33/40 Carbine, illustrating the "945" code that was used only in 1940. (Henry Wichmann collection)

The receiver ring of the German Model 33/40 Carbine, showing the manufacturer's code over the date of manufacture

The receiver ring of the German Model 33/40 as marked by the Czechs prior to the changeover to the German coding. (Robert Jensen collection)

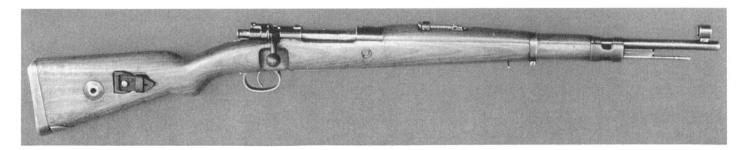

Full-length view of the German Model 33/40 Carbine

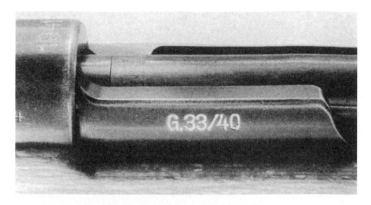

The side rail of the German Model 33/40 Carbine, showing the model designation

GERMAN MODEL 29/40 RIFLE: There are two explanations for the origin of this short rifle, neither of which has been conclusively proven. What is clear about these rifles is that they were all made by Steyr (receiver code 660) in 1938 and 1939, that they were all made for the Luftwaffe (stock marked "L") and that there was no known official German designation for these rifles. German collectors call them "Luftwaffe Karabiner," while other collectors refer to them as G29o, or "Gewehr 29 Osterreich," (Rifle 29 Austrian). To simplify things, they will be referred to as G29o.

There is general agreement that the G29o derives from an export M98 short rifle made by Steyr prior to the Austrian Anschluss with Germany in 1938, but what is unresolved is the question of what version of export rifle it is derived. Two possibilities are the Steyr M29 short rifle made for Columbia which has similar stock fittings, a straight bolt and a 30mm bayonet stud, while the other option is the Steyr M31a short rifle , of which no specimens are currently known; it is similar to the M29, but is in caliber 8mm, and has a sliding bolt cover.

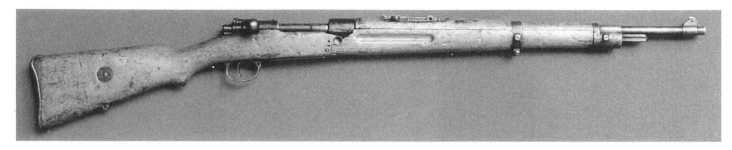

Full-length view of the unaltered Colombian Model 29 rifle, redesignated the Model 29/40 as issued to the Luftwaffe. Note the sharp point to the pistol grip, the Austrian-style lower and upper bands held by screws, and the deeply cupped ends of the recoil crossbolt. This specimen has unfortunately lost a piece of the stock at the right side of the receiver ring. (Century International Arms, Inc.)

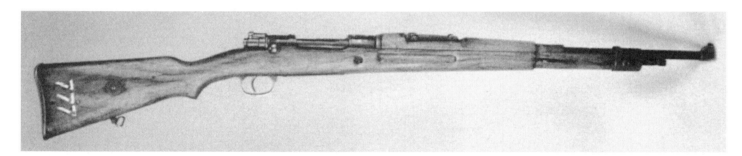

Full-length view of a specimen Model 29/40 Rifle (Gibbs Rifle Company)

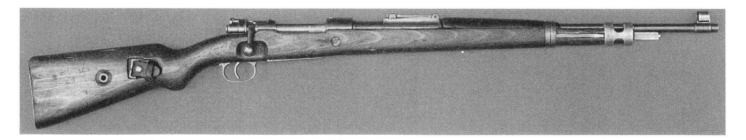

Full-length view of the later version of the German Model 29/40 Rifle, fully comparable to the German K98k Carbine except for the markings

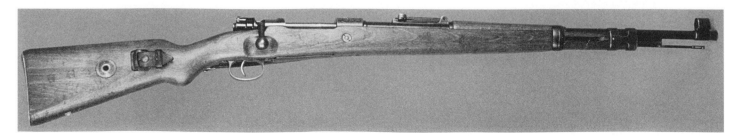

Full-length view of a Polish Wz 29 Short Rifle converted by Steyr to 29/40 configuration

Whatever the origin of the G29o, the rifle made for the Luftwaffe has a bent bolt, but no clearance cut for the bolt knob, a 50mm German bayonet stud, is in caliber 8mm and has a walnut stock with grasping grooves. The G29o uses a sling similar to that for the German Gew98 which can be attached to the underside of the stock, or to the left side of the stock, or a combination of the two. The G29o and the G29/40 are frequently confused by collectors as well as writers; the G29o is always marked 660 over 1938 or 1939 on the receiver, and there are no markings on the left side rail. The Austrian-style pointed pistol grip and four-point sling arrangement are quite distinctive. It is reported the Luftwaffe only used the G29o for training purposes. It may be that the production of the G29o was terminated in favor of the G29/40. No G29o is known dated after 1939, while no G29/40 is known dated prior to 1939.

When the Germans invaded Poland in 1939 and took the Fabryka Broni works in Radom, they found numbers of Polish wz 29 Short Rifles in the process of manufacture. Receivers were shipped to Steyr where the rifles were completed in K98k configuration, using German barrels, stocks and other components, as well as Polish

Steyr code "660" over "1939" on the receiver ring of the German Model 29/40 Rifle. Note the German waffenamt proofing on both sides of the receiver ring.

The receiver ring of the German Model 29/40 Rifle, showing the "660" code for the Steyr-Daimler-Puch factory over the date "1940"

The side rail of the German Model 29/40 Rifle, showing the model designation

The receiver ring of the converted Polish Wz 29 Short Rifle, illustrating the "660" code stamped above the Polish eagle crest

Side rail of the converted Polish Wz 29 Short Rifle. Note the crossed-out model number "wz," and the addition of the "/40" behind the "29."

bolt stops, trigger guards, etc. The original Polish wz 29 is stamped with the Polish Eagle over "F.B." over "RADOM" over the year of manufacture on top of the receiver, while the left side rail is marked "wz 29." The German rebuilds are found in two forms: with the Steyr code 660 over the Polish eagle on the receiver ring, and the wz struck out and the letter "G" added ahead of the wz and the "/40" added after the "29." The other style found is with the normal German-style receiver markings of "660" over the year, and "G29/40 on the left side rail. German sources indicate procurement of 54,500 G29/40s 1940-1942, but this figure may be too low. Most G29/40s went to the Navy ("M" stamp on stock) or the Luftwaffe ("L" stamp on stock). It is known that one (!) Polish K98 has been found converted into a G29/40.

GERMAN MODEL 24(t) RIFLE: After the takeover of Czechoslovakia in 1938, Germany continued the production of the Czech VZ 24 Rifle, but in conformity to prevailing German standards. Some of the rifles encountered have the original Czech-style flat butt plate, while those of a later date, usually beginning sometime in 1941, were fitted with the German-designed cupped butt plate. The stocks were fitted with the domed washers and hollow rod for disassembly of the firing mechanism, and a slot was cut in the stock for the side mounted German-style sling and keeper. Later examples are found with laminated stocks and hand guards.

The receiver ring of the German Model 24(t) Rifle, showing the code "dou," for Waffenwerke Brunn, A-G, Bystrica, over the date of manufacture

Camouflaged Waffen SS trooper on the Russian Front (Signal)

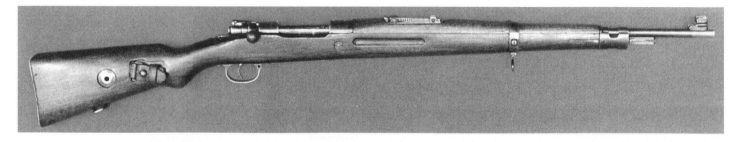

Full-length view of the German Model 24(t) Rifle. Note that this particular rifle is fitted with bottom swivels on the lower band and center of the buttstock, in addition to the side mounted sling arrangement. The stock is walnut.

Full-length view of a German Model 24(T) Rifle fitted with a laminated stock

The side rail of the German Model 24(t) Rifle, showing the model designation. Note the typical deep-dished recoil crossbolt.

Acceptance marks on the stock of the German Model 24(t) Rifle

Property number on the left side of the buttstock of the German Model G 24(T) Rifle

German Waffen SS troops of the SS "Polizei" Division armed with Czech-made German G 24 (T) Rifles, operating in a marshy area on the Eastern Front (Signal)

All data relative to the German Model 24(t) Rifle will be found under the section on Czechoslovakia, with the exception of the details mentioned above.

Right side view of the receiver markings on a Portuguese Model 1940 KAR 98k, which was never shipped to the Portuguese, but was remarked and issued to the Luftwaffe. Notice the Portuguese crest. (Robert Jensen collection)

GERMAN "VOLKSGEWEHR," OR "PEOPLE'S RIFLE": A last-ditch effort to arm the German populace ushered in the VK-98 (Volkssturmkarabiner-98) or the "People's Rifle." Many were produced, but only infrequently put to the purpose for which they were intended. There are several single- shot and five-shot models.

Crudely made at best, there is almost a complete lack of any refined machining; the stock is only roughly contoured to a sporter-style shape, and the trigger guard is often simply a piece of bent strap steel screwed into position.

Length: 40.50"; **Weight:** 6.90 lbs.; **Barrel:** 21.0"; **Caliber:** 7.92 x 57mm; **Rifling:** 4-groove, r/hand, surprisingly well done!; **Operation:** Turnbolt action; **Feed:** 10-round, detachable, box magazine; **Sights:** Elementary fixed V-notch rear sight. **Remarks:** Model designation, date, and manufacturer's code are found on the front of the left side of the receiver.

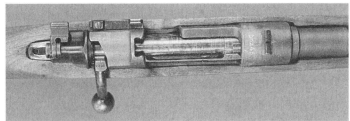

Top view of the German VK-98, showing the action and the receiver ring markings "BNZ 45"

Close-up view of the straight handled bolt of the German VK-98, showing the lack of a stop on the bolt sleeve

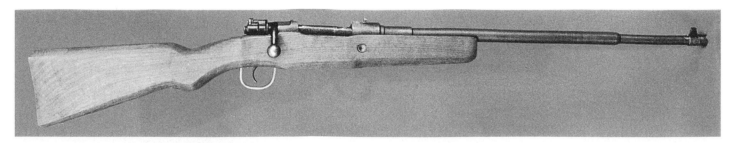

Full-length view of the German VK-98 Rifle. This particular rifle has an integral 5-shot, staggered column, flush, box-style magazine. The trigger guard is a simple piece of bent steel, held in place by two wood screws. Note the use of a machine gun barrel. Note the absence of a butt plate and lack of provision for a sling.

Left full-length view of the German VK-98 Rifle. All versions were counterbored smooth to a depth of 10mm to 25mm for the most part.

Full-length view of the German VK-98 Rifle. Note the fixed rear sight, the 5-shot internal magazine, and the machine gun barrel. This rifle is fitted with a butt plate and provision for a sling, with a swivel on the left front of the stock and a cut through the stock for a sling.

Left full-length view of the preceding German VK-98 Rifle, showing the sling swivel on the front of the stock

Full-length view of a variation of the German VK- 98 Rifle. This weapon has a straight bolt handle, a machine gun barrel, a butt plate, and an internal magazine with floorplate, as well as provision for a sling. The bolt of this rifle was produced without a stop on the bolt sleeve.

Left full-length view of the German VK-98 Rifle with straight bolt handle. Again, note the provision for attachment of a sling.

Full-length view of another variation of the German VK-98 Rifle. This rifle has a machine gun barrel, cupped butt plate, recessed stock for the bolt handle and knob, domed washer and tube for bolt disassembly, and magazine floorplate, as well as provision for a sling.

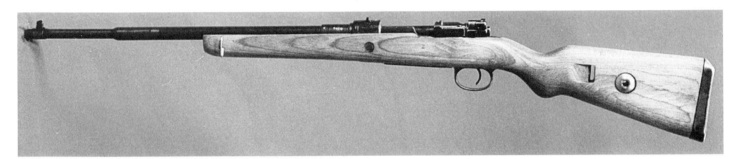

Left full-length view of the previous German VK-98 Rifle

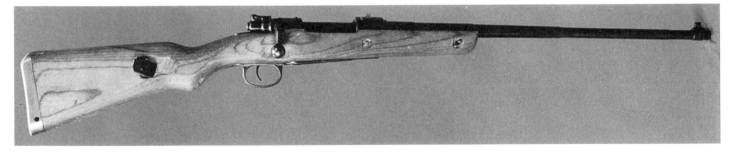

Full-length view of another German VK-98 Rifle. This rifle is fitted with a cupped butt plate with a hole in the side for bolt disassembly, a K98k barrel, a magazine floorplate, and provision for a sling.

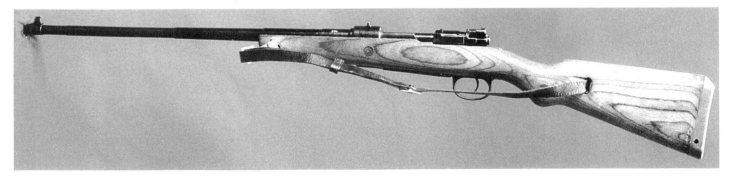

Left full-length view of the German VK-98 Rifle with the K98k barrel, etc.

Bottom view of the stock and trigger guard of the German VK-98 Rifle shown on page 144, showing the simple attachment of the trigger guard

Barrel stampings on the Mauser-style rifle produced by F.W. Heym. Note that this particular rifle is marked "Made in Germany."

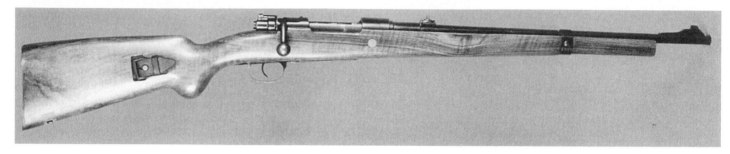

Full-length view of the Mauser-style rifle produced by F.W. Heym

GERMAN VK-98 CARBINE: As the end of the war with Germany approached, the need to turn out weapons that were cheap, easy to produce, and capable of arming the populace was of paramount importance. This rifle is the result of that desperation. Crudely made, with the stock only roughly outlined, machine gun barrels were often adapted to a Mauser receiver. Many of these weapons were single shot, with a fixed rear sight set for one hundred meters.

WEST GERMAN POLICE/BORDER GUARDS HEYM MAUSER RIFLE: F.W. Heym Arms Factory, of Muennerstadt, West Germany commenced production of a modified Model 98 action design rifle in the early 1950s. Some of these rifles were also imported into the U.S. by Imperial Arms, a firm operated by Ed Hoffschmidt during the 1950s. While superficially resembling the K98k, this rifle has a fixed rear sight, no upper hand guard, nose cap, upper band, or bayonet lug. The front sight is a sporter-style sight.

This rifle was known as "The Widowmaker," as the receiver walls are notoriously weak and prone to bursting. It has been recommended that they not be fired.

THE 7.92MM MODEL 41M (GEW41(M)) SEMI-AUTOMATIC RIFLE: As developed by Mauser, the 41M was an unsuccessful design that was abandoned in 1943, with very few rifles being actually produced beyond prototypes and troop test rifles, making them a collector's dream. The 41M operates from the gas at the muzzle rebounding from a muzzle cone and striking the piston under the barrel, which in turn forces back the operating rod which is connected to the rear portion of the two-piece bolt. The rear section of the bolt pulls back the forward section, causing the front-mounted locking lugs to be cammed out of their recesses in the receiver. The 41M has a manually-operated, non-reciprocating bolt handle which has the same appearance as a bolt handle on a manually-operated bolt-

Right side view of the Gew 41M Semi-Automatic Rifle; note the bolt handle knob, as well as the awkward distance from the trigger guard to the fixed magazine. (Robert Jensen collection)

Left side view of the Gew 41M Semi-Automatic Rife; note the muzzle cone by which the gas is trapped to operate the system (Robert Jensen collection)

Left side view comparison of the G 41M Semi-Automatic Rifle to the G 41W Semi-Automatic Rifle. (Robert Jensen collection)

action rifle, and which is operated in the same manner. When the weapon is fired, the bolt does not reciprocate with the action. The weapon has a fixed magazine which is loaded with two five-round clips.

Length: 46.25"; **Weight:** 11.25 lbs; **Barrel:** 21.75"; **Caliber:** 7.92X57mm; **Operation:** Gas semi-automatic only; **Feed:** Fixed 10-round staggered-row box magazine; **Sights:** Tangent leaf w/U notch; **Remarks:** Well-marked on the receiver of the action.

Operating bolt on the G 41M Semi-Automatic Rifle. (Robert Jensen collection)

Receiver markings on the G 41M Semi-Automatic Rifel (Robert Jensen collection)

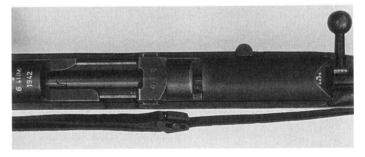

Top view of the receiver area and operating bolt of the G 41M Semi-Automatic Rifle. (Robert Jensen collection)

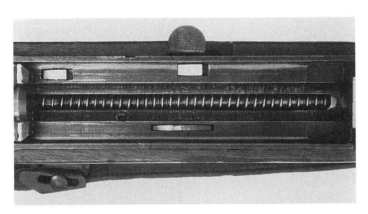

Top view of the G 41M Semi-Automatic Rifle with the cover removed to show the recoil spring and firing pin. (Robert Jensen collection)

G 41M Semi-Automatic Rifle stock cartouche. (Robert Jensen collection)

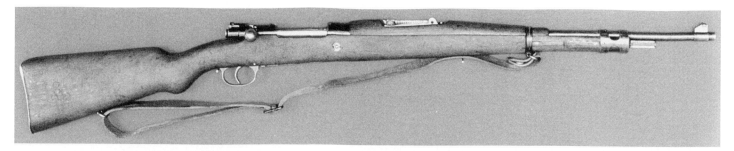

Full-length view of the Greek Model 1930 Short Rifle

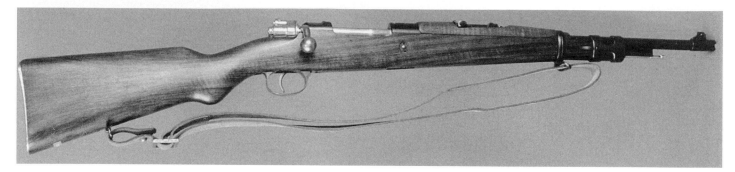

Full-length view of the Greek FN Model 1930 Carbine

GREECE

From the beginning of the twentieth century, the Greek armed forces had relied heavily on the Model 1903 Mannlicher-Schoenauer Rifle and Carbine to equip their troops. Due to the Greek participation in numerous small Balkan wars preceding World War I, the unavoidable loss of weapons and material left the Greek forces in a weakened position at the beginning of the First World War.

With the opening of the Salonika front, French, British, Russian, Serbian, as well as troops from other nations, were shipped to the Macedonian front to probe and attack the soft underbelly of Europe. The Greek army was the recipient of French war material, including French Gras Mle 74 Rifles, Model 1907 3-shot Mannlicher Rifles, Model 1892 3-shot Carbines, French Model 86/93 Rifles, French 07/15 Rifles, and captured Austrian Model 1895 Straight-Pull Rifles and Carbines.

As a result of Greek participation in the First World War, Greece was granted by the treaty of Sevres (1920) the territory of Smyrna (Izmir) in Turkey as spoils of war. Expansionist policies led to Greek attempts to annex as much of Anatolia and Thrace as they could control, waging a protracted, bound-to-fail war against the Turkish forces of Kemal Ataturk. Finally repulsed at the battle of the Sakarya River after a three-week struggle, the Greek army was forced into an agonizing 250-mile retreat to Smyrna, which was captured in September 1921. Thousands upon thousands of Greeks were slain by the Turks, with the Treaty of Lausanne ending the war and forcing the Greeks out of Asia Minor.

Material losses as a result of the Anatolian debacle were enormous, with the Greeks contracting for more of the Model 1903 Mannlicher-Schoenauer Rifles, albeit an updated version made by the Italians at Breda. To supplement these weapons, the Greek authorities also contracted with FN for an unknown quantity of the FN Model 30 Short Rifle, known as the Greek Model 1930. These rifles were used by the Greek armed forces in resisting the Italian and German invasions during the Second World War.

This is a typical FN export model short rifle, fitted with a pistol grip stock, with the upper hand guard running from in front of the

Stock cartouche on the side of the butt stock of the Greek FN 30 Short Rifle. (Robert Jensen collection)

Cartouche of Saint George and the Dragon on the underside of the small of the stock of the Greek FN 30 Short Rifle. (Robert Jensen collection)

The receiver ring of the Greek Model 1930 Short Rifle, showing the Greek crest of a crowned shield with short-armed cross over the model date

receiver ring to approximately one inch in front of the lower barrel band. There are no grasping grooves, the lower barrel band has a bottom swivel, with another on the bottom of the buttstock, and the bolt handle is straight. Both upper and lower barrel bands are held by separate band-retaining springs.

Length: 43.25"; **Weight:** 9.0 lbs.; **Barrel:** 22.50"; **Caliber:** 7.92 x 57mm; **Rifling:** 4-groove, r/hand; **Operation:** Turnbolt action; **Feed:** 5-round, staggered column, flush, box magazine; **Sights:** Tangent leaf rear sight graduated to 2000 meters. **Remarks:** Greek crest over the model date on the receiver ring, manufacturer's markings on the side rail.

GUATEMALA

Colonized by the Spanish in 1524, Guatemala became the military authority for all of Central America under the captaincy general of Guatemala. Gaining independence from Spain in 1821, and later from Mexico in 1823, Guatemala, despite its lack of economic and social progress, became the center for the United Provinces of Central America. Upon the collapse of the United Provinces of Central America, Guatemala became an independent country in 1832.

In power from 1851 to 1944, the Liberal party under Cabrera (1898-1920) and Ubico (1931-1944) promoted economic prosperity and development, despite the repressive nature of their regimes. Arevalo was elected president in 1945, followed in turn by Jacobo Arbenz, a leftist elected with strong Communist support. Plagued by rumors of an impending coup, Arbenz made arrangements for the importation of a shipment of rifles and munitions from Czechoslovakia. The shipment included Czech VZ 24 Short Rifles and VZ 33 Carbines. As these weapons were entering port in 1954, a U.S.-backed coup led by Colonel Carlos Castillo Armas overthrew the government of Arbenz.

Either directly or indirectly, the military has ruled Guatemala since that time, although democracy officially returned to Guatemala in 1986. Beginning in the early 1960s and intensifying in the 1980s, guerrilla activity has plagued the country, resulting in the deaths of at least one hundred thousand people, mostly civilians, at the hands of the Guatemalan right-wing death squads, the Guatemalan National Revolutionary Union (URNG), and the army.

In May of 1993, President Jorge Serrano Elias attempted to suppress student protesters and the unions but, faced with overwhelming opposition from the population, the business community, and the free world, the military replaced Elias with Ramiro de Leon Carpo. In March, 1994, the government and the URNG reached agreement on a treaty that paves the way toward resolving the thirty-year struggle that has rent this poor nation.

MODEL 1910 RIFLE: An undetermined number of ex-Serbian Model 1910 Rifles were purchased by Guatemala, presumably after the First World War. These rifles were marked with the standard Waffenfabrik Mauser export markings on the receiver ring, and did not incorporate any Guatemalan markings. This export Model 1910 Rifle is quite similar to the Gew. 98, fitted with a pistol grip stock, with the upper hand guard extending from in front of the receiver ring to just beyond the lower barrel band. The upper barrel band has the bayonet lug fitted to the bottom for use with the Model 1895 bayonet. The lower barrel band is fitted with a swivel, as is the bottom of the buttstock.

Length: 48.80"; **Weight:** 8.80 lbs; **Barrel:** 29.13"; **Caliber:** 7 x 57mm; **Rifling:** 4-groove, r/hand; **Operation:** Turnbolt action; **Feed:** 5-round, staggered column, flush, box magazine; **Sights:** Tangent leaf rear sight graduated to 2000 meters. **Remarks:** This rifle will be marked on the receiver ring with the Waffenfabrik Mauser Oberndorf a/m stamping, typical of the export model. The model designation will be on the side rail.

Receiver ring markings on the Model 1910 Rifle as used by Guatemala

Full-length view of the Model 1910 Rifle as used by Guatemala

Model designation on the side rail of the Model 1910 Rifle used by Guatemala

GUATEMALAN CZECH VZ 24 SHORT RIFLE: This is your typical Czech export model rifle, fashioned after the VZ 24 Short Rifle. The pistol grip stock is fitted with grasping grooves, and the upper hand guard runs from in front of the receiver ring to the upper barrel band. The upper barrel band is retained by a single band-retaining spring, while the lower band is held by the typical screw fitting through the stock. The front sight is protected by a set of screw-on sight protectors. There is an integral swivel on the left side of the lower band, as well as one on the bottom. A swivel is positioned on the left side of the stock at the pistol grip, and on the bottom of the buttstock at

The side rail of the Guatemalan VZ 24 Short Rifle showing the manufacturer's markings—in this case, in Czechoslovakian. The number on the side of the receiver ring is not the date produced, but the serial number.

the midway point. There is also a screw-held, inset washer on the right side of the buttstock. The bolt handle is straight.

> **Length:** 43.0"; **Weight:** 9.90 lbs.; **Barrel:** 22.50"; **Caliber:** 7 x 57mm; also available in 7.65 x 53mm, and 7.92 x 57mm; **Rifling:** 4-groove, r/hand; **Operation:** Turnbolt action; **Feed:** 5-round, staggered column, flush, box magazine; **Sights:** Tangent leaf rear sight graduated to 2000 meters. **Remarks:** Guatemalan crest on the receiver ring, manufacturer's markings on the side rail.

GUATEMALAN CZECH VZ 33 CARBINE: The exact quantity of Czech VZ 33 Carbines purchased from Czechoslovakia is not known, but they were the standard export model of the VZ 33, fitted with a pistol grip stock without grasping grooves. The upper hand guard extends from the front of the receiver ring to just beyond the lower barrel band. The upper band is secured by a band-retaining

Guatemalan crest on the receiver ring of the Guatemalan Czech VZ 24 Short Rifle. The bird at the top is the famous Guatemalan quetzal bird.

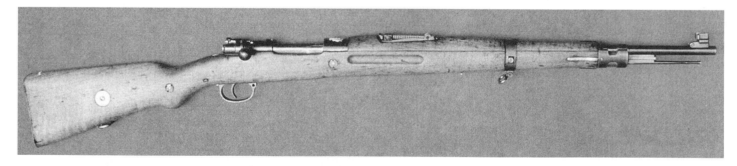

Full-length view of the Guatemalan Czech Model VZ 24 Short Rifle

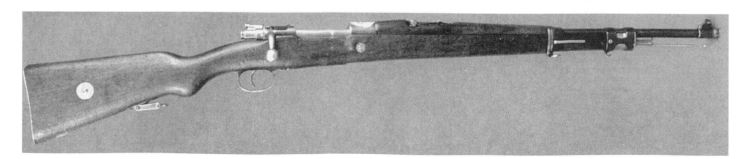

Full-length view of the Guatemalan Czech VZ 33 Carbine

spring. The lower band, which has an integral swivel on the left side, as well as a bottom mounted swivel, is held on by a screw clamp at the bottom. There is a quick-release mount midway on the bottom of the buttstock. Note the inset, screw-retained washer in the center of the buttstock.

Length: 39.25"; **Weight:** 9.0 lbs.; **Barrel:** 18.75"; **Caliber:** 7 x 57mm; also available in 7.65 x 53mm, and 7.92 x 57mm; **Rifling:** 4-groove, r/hand; **Operation:** Turnbolt action; **Feed:** 5-round, staggered column, flush, box magazine; **Sights:** Tangent leaf rear sight graduated to 1000 meters. **Remarks:** Guatemalan crest on the receiver ring, manufacturer's markings on the side rail.

HAITI

Discovered by Christopher Columbus in 1492, he renamed the island of Haiti "Hispaniola." The indigenous population were brutally overworked by the Spanish and decimated by disease over the next one hundred years, resulting in the importation of African slaves to labor in the fields as their unfortunate predecessors had. Harassed by French pirates and freebooters, the western third of the island was ceded to France in 1697. This French colony of Haiti, with its slave-based economy, accounted for two-thirds of France's return on their overseas investments.

A slave revolt in 1791 brought about abolition in 1794, with the whole island, including San Domingo (The Dominican Republic), coming under the control of the French in the same year. An ex-slave, Toussaint L'Overture, became the governor-general of Haiti, but was deposed by the French, who sent vast armies to reconquer and reclaim the island in the name of France. Haiti proved to be the graveyard for some of France's finest veterans, with fever and guerrilla warfare cutting the troops down like weeds. Jean-Jacque Dessalines (Emperor Jacques I, 1804-1806) and Henri Christophe (Henry I, 1806-1820) forged a black army that defeated the French forces in 1803, with independence declared in 1804.

The next 150 years have proven to be the worst that this poor nation could have experienced, marked by complete political and social instability and ever-growing U.S. interference in the financial and political affairs of the country. The U.S. had a military presence in Haiti from 1915 to 1934, and once again in 1994 under the

One of the few pictures in existence to show the Haitian army soldiers in parade uniforms. Note the rather casual attitude of the enlisted men. (H.P. Davis)

guise of UN leadership. Haiti today is the poorest and most illiterate nation in the Western Hemisphere.

In 1986, the military, such as it was, removed the then president from power, an interim president was named, and in 1990, the first free democratic elections ever in the Republic of Haiti were held. The Rev. Jean-Bertrand Aristide was the victor of the election, but after seven months of rule, he was overthrown by the army. UN sponsored intervention, with the U.S. filling the primary role of policeman, returned Aristide to power in 1994, ousting the military leaders and redefining the role of the Haitian military into that of an internal security force with extremely limited military potential.

HAITIAN FN MODEL 24/30 SHORT RIFLE: Due to the presence of the U.S. military from 1915 to 1934, the Haitian army, originally named Gendermerie D'Haiti, was initially equipped with Krag-Jorgensen rifles and Colt machine guns. By 1945, the Garde d'Haiti, as the military had been renamed, was taking on the characteristics of a national army. Re-armed with surplus U.S. weapons, the Garde still remained basically a paramilitary constabulary, with a total force fluctuating between 4500 and 6000 effectives.

Haitian army markings on the side of the receiver ring of the Haitian FN Model 24/30 Short Rifle, also showing the manufacturer's markings on the side rail

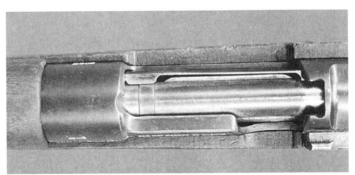

Top view of the action of the Haitian FN Model 24/30 Short Rifle showing the cut in the receiver face to accommodate the longer .30-06 caliber cartridge

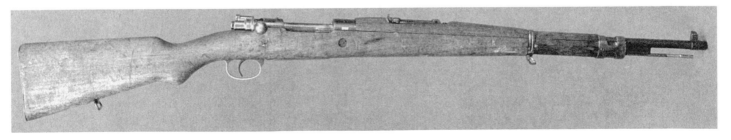

Full-length view of the Haitian FN Model 24/30 Short Rifle

Rifle serial number on the right side of the receiver ring of the Haitian FN Model 24/30 Short Rifle

The "corrugated"-style butt plate used on the Haitian FN Model 24/30 Short Rifle

During the 1930s, as a means of expanding the military's potential, the government contracted for the delivery of an unknown quantity of the standard export FN Model 24/30 Short Rifles in caliber .30-06. These rifles were held in reserve for use by the 15,000-man Volontaires de la Securite National, a partisan militia loyal only to the then president, "Papa Doc" Duvalier. These Model 24/30 Short Rifles are still being confiscated even as this book is written.

The FN Model 24/30 Short Rifle is fitted with a pistol grip stock without grasping grooves, and the upper hand guard runs from in front of the receiver ring to the upper barrel band. The lower band has a swivel affixed to the bottom, with another swivel at the mid-point of the bottom of the buttstock. The bolt handle is straight.

Length: 43.0"; **Weight:** 8.20 lbs.; **Barrel:** 23.375"; **Caliber:** .30-06; **Rifling:** 4-groove, r/hand; **Operation:** Turnbolt action; **Feed:** 5-round, staggered column, flush, box magazine; **Sights:** Tangent leaf rear sight, the slide fitted with peep sight, graduated to 1900 meters. **Remarks:** Serial number on the right hand side of the receiver ring, with "Armee d'Haiti" on the left side of the receiver ring, manufacturer's markings on the left side rail.

HONDURAS

The early history of Honduras parallels that of the remainder of Central America. Honduran General Francisco Morazan was the last president of the United Provinces of Central America, serving from 1830 to its dissolution in 1838. He then became president of El Salvador, but was forced to flee when the remaining Central American states ousted him. Not to be deterred, Morazan returned to Central America in 1842, and became president of Costa Rica, where he attempted to reestablish the Federation of Central American States. This time a bullet stopped him! Disregarded by his own country during his lifetime, Morazan has since become the originator of Central American union and is now considered a great Honduran hero!

Honduran history, for most of the nineteenth century, has been overwhelmed by the confusion of civil strife, rebellions, coups and countercoups, with economic and social progress suffering terribly as a result. From the beginning of the twentieth century, the United Fruit Company has played a large role in the domestic progress of Honduras, both economically and politically. The company operated under the policy of "What is good for the company is good for Honduras!"

Under the iron-fisted reign of General Tiburcio Carias, the most stable period of this century for Honduras was from 1933 to 1949. Since that time, the country has been ruled by a succession of military dictatorships, punctuated by brief periods of civilian control, which in turn were overthrown by the military. There was a short, but disastrous war with El Salvador in 1969—the so-called "Football War"—which ended in favour of the Salvadorans.

The troop level of the Honduran army has remained at approximately ten thousand effectives. In the past, Honduras has shopped the world for military equipment, with purchases from the Germans, Danes, Italians, French, British, and the U.S. The U.S. supplied Honduras with ten thousand Remington Model 30 Rifles in the 1930s, in caliber 7 x 57mm.

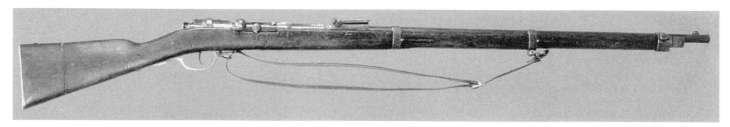

Full-length view of the German Model G 71 Rifle as used by Honduras

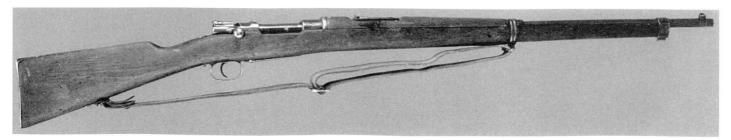

Full-length view of the Model 1895 Rifle (Chilean type), as used by Honduras

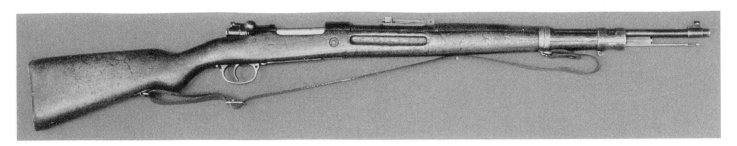

Full-length view of the German Standard Modell Export Model Short Rifle, as used by the Honduran military

HONDURAN GERMAN MODEL G 71 RIFLE: In the late 1880s, Honduras contracted with Germany for an unknown quantity of German Model G 71 Rifles, identical to those issued to the German armed forces; whether these rifles were marked with the Honduran national crest is unknown. Honduran-marked specimens of this rifle have, to the author's knowledge, never been seen on the surplus market. All relative data on this rifle will be found under the section on Germany.

HONDURAN CHILEAN-STYLE MODEL 1895 RIFLE: Prior to 1914, Honduras purchased an unknown quantity of Model 1895 (Chilean style) Rifles in caliber 7 x 57mm. The firm from which these rifles were obtained is not known, however the weapons served as the standard rifle in the Honduran forces until the introduction of the Standard Modell Mauser Short Rifle in the 1930s, along with the purchase of Remington Model 30 Rifles, both in caliber 7 x 57mm. The specifications relating to this Chilean-style Model 1895 Rifle will be found under the section on Chile.

HONDURAN STANDARD MODELL MODEL 1933 MAUSER SHORT RIFLE: As a supplement to their arms acquisitions in the 1930s, the Honduran government contracted for the purchase of an unspecified number of German Standard Modell Mauser Short Rifles in caliber 7 x 57mm. These short rifles are the standard export model of the Standard Modell, and it is unknown as to whether or not they were marked with the Honduran crest. All relative data pertaining to the Honduran Standard Modell Short Rifle will be found in the section on Germany.

IRAQ

Iraq, the site of the world's oldest civilization, has had a dizzying history, especially in the years since World War I, when Great Britain was given a mandate over the country. Independence was gained in 1932, but close ties were maintained with Great Britain, mainly in the area of petroleum production and regional defense. Britain was called upon several times to put down attempted anti-British coups prior to World War II, and in April 1941, was forced to land troops and take over the country when a coup was attempted with German and Italian aid.

In 1948, Iraq allied with the Arab League and joined in the war against the Jews. While British military equipment predominated in the Iraqi armed forces, refurbished German Model 98k Carbines were purchased for the Republican Guard. These rifles are standard in all respects, and specific data will be found under the section on Germany.

Close-up view of the Republican Guard stamping on the Iraqi Model 98k Carbine

Receiver markings showing the Royal Iraqi crest on the receiver ring of the 1948 98k Carbine. (Robert Jensen collection)

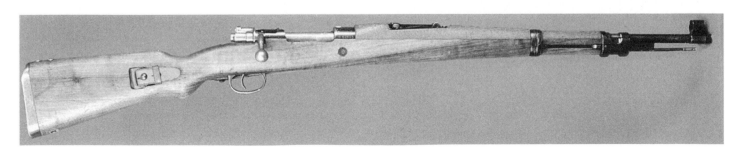

Full-length view of the Iraqi Model 98k Carbine

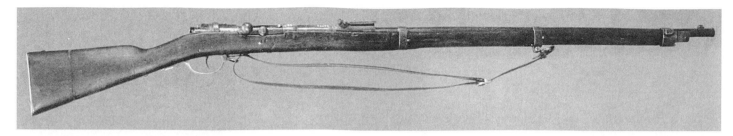

Full-length view of the German Model G 71 Rifle, as used by members of the Irish Citizen Army during the Easter Uprising. All data relative to this rifle will be found under the section on Germany.

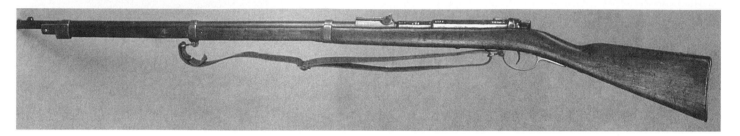

Left full-length view of the G 71 Rifle as used by the Irish

IRELAND

Some may find it strange to see Ireland listed as a country that used Mauser rifles, but in the early years of this century the Irish Republican Brotherhood and the Irish Volunteers were making plans for an

Irish Citizen Army on parade with G 71 Mauser (Howth) Rifles (George Morrison)

Irish Volunteers drilling with German Model G 71 (Howth) Mauser Rifles, C. 1914 (George Morrison collection)

armed uprising against the British, who had controlled Ireland for centuries. A Citizen Army, viewed by the British as little more than men involved in play-acting, was formed, with an embryonic General Staff, tables of Organization and Equipment, and a nucleus of enthusiastic, patriotic men.

With virtually no material to speak of, the Irish were forced to look abroad—to the continent for the arms necessary to carry out a rebellion, and to America for the money to pay for them. Sailing to Germany on his yacht, the "Asgard," for an ostensible yachting vacation among the Frisian Islands, Erskine Childers, a well-known British author of Anglo-Irish descent, was accompanied by his wife and the Hon. Mary Spring Rice. In Hamburg, the yacht was loaded with fifteen hundred German Model G 71 Rifles and forty-nine thousand 11mm cartridges. This cargo was safely returned to Ireland, being landed at Howth Harbor on 26 July 1914. Volunteers, including many Boy Scouts, were on hand to convey the rifles and ammunition openly to Dublin. Irish police, unsuccessfully, attempted to seize the weapons. From that time forward, in Ireland, these rifles have been called "Howth Mausers."

On Easter Monday, 1916, the Irish Rebellion started in Dublin with the seizure of the General Post Office and other strong points scattered throughout the city. Due to political misgivings, counter-orders were received prior to the general mobilization, as a result of which only 1,250 men mustered to start the struggle known as the Easter Week Rising. The German Model G 71 Rifles were used to good effect, potting away from behind the chimney-pots and holding down British troops at the strategic strong points throughout the city of Dublin. At the end of the struggle, the British checked the shoulders of men on the street to see if they were black-and-blue from using the Mauser rifle. Upon examining a captured Model G 71 Mauser Rifle, one British officer was heard to refer to it as "a bally elephant gun!"

ISRAEL

Prior to the founding of the State of Israel, the Jews had formed clandestine skeleton army formations upon which to build an army when, and if, they should achieve nationhood. This shadow army

Haganah soldiers fighting on the outskirts of Jerusalem, 1948. Note the American helmets, the mixture of British and American web equipment, and the Model K98k Carbines. (Robert Capa, Magnum)

required weapons, and the Jews used every means at their disposal to begin stockpiling weapons, ammunition, and military material of all kinds, both in Palestine and abroad.

The last British troops left Palestine on 14 May 1948, and the State of Israel was declared. The overseas purchasing network of arms agents had been in action since the end of World War II, with former German army weapons purchased from Czechoslovakia (one of the few nations willing to deal with the Jews on a cash-only ba-

The Israeli crest and the caliber designation on the receiver ring of the Israeli Model 98k Short Rifle. FN proof marks are on the left side of the receiver ring.

Haganah troops in the battle for Jerusalem, 1948. Note the British helmets and the K98k Carbines. (Robert Capa, Magnum)

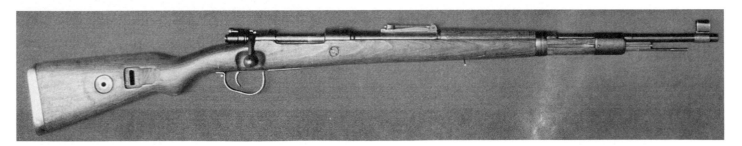

Full-length view of the Czech-manufactured German Model 98k Carbine

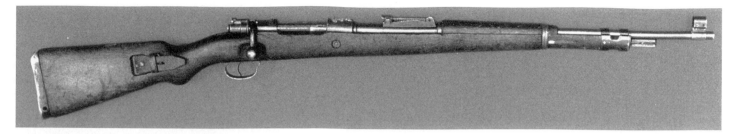

Full-length view of the Israeli Model 98k Short Rifle

sis). These became one of the standard weapons of the Haganah, as the Jewish defense force was named. Most of these weapons had been arsenal refinished by the Czechs, with many still bearing German markings. In the meanwhile, anything that could shoot, and for which ammunition was available, was in the Israeli arsenal, from British SMLE Mo 1 Mk IIIs, to every model of French service rifle, along with German and Turkish battlefield relics from the First World War.

With the first flights of the Israeli Air Transport Command, weapons were arriving from Czechoslovakia on a daily basis into former RAF bases in Israel, where they were immediately cleaned and issued to the raw troops going into the lines. Often, immigrants ("D.P.s", i.e., displaced persons) right off the boats were given as little as five hours of basic training before being sent into battle. Aside from the automatic weapons, the basic infantry rifle was the Czech winter version of the German Model 98k Carbine, with the oversize trigger guard for use with gloves. Early in 1949, Jewish authorities purchased a complete Kar 98k factory production line. Due to the availability of effective semi-automatic weapons, work on completely new rifles terminated after the manufacture of only a few. The plant was then used to rebarrel and refurbish German actions and FN-purchased weapons to the 7.62 x 51mm cartridge.

ISRAELI CZECH MODEL 98k CARBINE: With the exception of the oversize trigger guard developed from the German experience on the Russian front, this rifle is identical in every other respect to the German Model K98k Carbine produced for the German armed forces during World War II. This rifle is in caliber 7.92 x 57mm, (unless converted to 7.62 x 51mm (NATO) and so marked on the receiver ring), and all relative data on the rifle will be found in the section on Germany.

ISRAELI FN SHORT RIFLE: During the early 1950s, the Israelis supplemented their stocks of weapons with purchases of FN short rifles from Belgium. These rifles are identical to the German Model 98k Carbine; however the short rifles bear Israeli markings on the receiver ring and are in caliber 7.62 x 51mm (NATO), which is prominently marked on the receiver ring. Specifications and data on this rifle will be found in the section on Germany.

JAPAN

During the 1880s, Japan was undergoing the transformation from a feudal system, in effect for centuries, to a country awakening to the wonders of the modern world. Sealed off for centuries from outside influences, in the space of a few short decades Japan went from a country of warriors in ancient armor to an army uniformed and equipped to European standards, although still imbued with the spirit of the Samurai.

A French military mission was active in Japan on a small scale until the results of the Franco-Prussian War caused the Japanese to consider the Prussian military caste in the light of their own warrior traditions. A small German military mission was invited to Japan, bringing with it the Prussian love of discipline and order, in which it steeped the fledgling Japanese national army. Uniforms adopted by the Japanese combined French and Prussian characteristics, with the Japanese experimenting with various weapons systems while, at the same time, working on the development and production of an indigenous Japanese rifle, the Murata.

As a result of this trial and experimentation period, the Japanese imported a modest quantity of the German Model G 71 Rifle for troop testing. While never used to a great extent, the German G 71 Rifle did provide a basis for comparison, and was closely examined for any design features that could be incorporated in the Murata rifle.

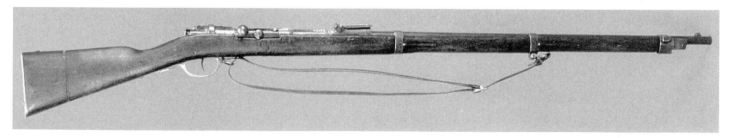

Full-length view of the German Model G 71 Rifle, as used for Japanese troop testing. All specific data on this rifle will be found in the section on Germany.

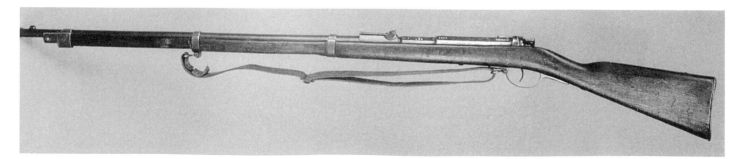

Left full-length view of the Model G 71 Rifle as used in Japan for troop testing

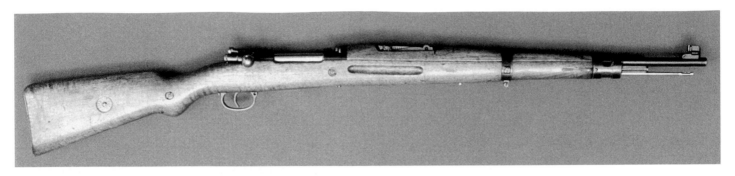

Full-length view of the Czech VZ 24 Short Rifle as used by Latvian forces

The Japanese Navy is said to have used a number of Standard Model 1933 Short Rifles that were possibly captured in China; the Navy was also issued a number of VZ24 Short Rifles, all dated "1937" with a "P" prefix to the serial number.

LATVIA

Latvia's history parallels that of Estonia. German incursions of knights, merchant princes, and religious missionaries all contributed to making Latvia seem a German quasi-religious colony in the thirteenth century. Absorbed first by Sweden in the sixteenth century, Latvia later came under the rule of Lithuania, and became part of the Great Russian Empire under Peter the Great in the eighteenth century. The treaty of Brest-Litovsk between the Soviet Union and Germany in 1918 granted independence to Latvia for the first time in its history.

The Hitler-Stalin pact called for the country of Latvia to come under the control of Russia, and Latvia was incorporated into the USSR as a new union republic in 1940. Fifty years of harsh Russian rule followed, until, following the lead of Lithuania, Latvia declared its intention to secede from the Soviet Union. Since cutting all ties with the former Soviet Union, times have been difficult for the Latvians, politically, economically and socially, as it is with all of the Baltic countries.

LATVIAN CZECH VZ 24 SHORT RIFLE: During the Latvian period of independence between 1918 and 1939, the Latvians formed a small, but highly trained national army, based upon the two divisions that had been fighting alongside the Germans against the Russians in Courland and Livonia during the First World War.

In 1935, Latvia ordered and took delivery of fifteen thousand Czech VZ 24 Short Rifles; whether these rifles were marked with the Latvian crest is unknown. Apparently, these rifles were used to good effect in the partisan war that raged against the Germans during World War II. All data relative to this rifle will be found under the section on Czechoslovakia.

LIBERIA

A West African nation initially explored by the Portuguese in 1461, Liberia remained virtually unexplored and sparsely populated until the nineteenth century. In 1816, the U.S. Congress granted a charter to the American Colonization Society (ACS), a private society dedicated to the resettlement of freed slaves. In 1822, the first settlers arrived at what was to become Monrovia, the capital of the Liberian nation. In 1847, adopting a constitution modeled on that of the United States, Liberia became the first independent republic in Africa.

Backed by the United States, Liberia spent the next one hundred years opposing encroachment by French and British interests trying to wrest territory from the Liberians. In 1980, the then president, William R. Tolbert, was deposed by M/Sgt. Samuel K. Doe in a military takeover of the country. Elections were held in 1986, and Doe was elected president. In 1989, National Patriotic Front of Liberia (NPFL) rebels crossed the border into the country from the Ivory Coast. In September 1990, Doe was captured and killed, and a cease fire was signed in November 1990. In 1992, the West African States helped establish a new government under the leadership of Amos Sawyer. An interim government composed of the three primary factions assumed uneasy power in 1994. Estimates are that 150,000 people perished during the civil war.

The Liberian army has been a self defense force from the time of its inception, without the ability to initiate action other than as a paramilitary constabulary. During the early 1930s, in an effort to update the weapons in the Liberian arsenal, an undetermined number of FN Model 24 Mauser Short Rifles were purchased from Belgium. These rifles were the standard infantry rifle for the Liberian forces until after World War II, when the army was equipped with surplus U.S. weapons.

LIBERIAN FN MODEL 24 SHORT RIFLE: The Liberian FN Model 24 Short Rifle is fitted with a pistol grip stock with grasping grooves, and the upper hand guard runs from in front of the receiver ring to the upper barrel band. The nose cap incorporates a German-style "H" bayonet lug, and the front sight does not have sight protectors. There is a swivel on the bottom of the lower barrel band, and another behind the pistol grip on the buttstock. An inset, screw-retained, flat washer is on the right side of the stock.

Length: 43.25"; **Weight:** 8.54 lbs.; **Barrel:** 22.50"; **Caliber:** Believed to be 7.92 x 57mm; **Rifling:** 4-groove, r/hand; **Operation:** Turnbolt action; **Feed:** 5-round, staggered column,

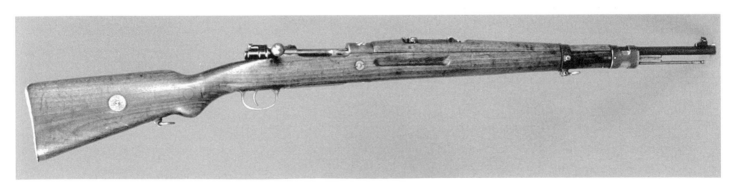

Full-length view of the FN Model 24 Short Rifle as used by the Liberian army

flush, box magazine; **Sights:** Tangent leaf rear sight graduated to 2000 meters. **Remarks:** It is believed that the receiver ring of the Liberian FN Model 24 Short Rifle is marked with the Liberian crest, which is a shield bearing a star above eleven vertical bars.

LITHUANIA

The peoples of Lithuania and Latvia are closely related, for their languages—the only two in the Baltic group of languages—are quite similar. Until 1795, however, the individual histories of the two countries were radically different. The Lithuanians were a fierce, warlike race who defended their lands against the German tide that threatened to envelope them. They retained their own language and religion against tremendous odds. During their epic history, the Lithuanians extended their rule from the Baltic to within miles of the Black Sea.

With the third breakup of Poland in 1795, Lithuania was deeded to Russia, but the upper class and educated people of Lithuania fought to keep alive a national awareness and identity based upon ethnic, religious, and linguistic grounds. In January 1921, the Allies recognized the independence of Lithuania that had come into being with the signing of the Treaty of Brest-Litovsk. A French garrison re-

Lithuanian army unit armed with the Lithuanian Model VZ 24 Short Rifle on parade just prior to World War II (UPI)

mained in Lithuania for another two years, where they were helpful in the formation of the new Lithuanian army.

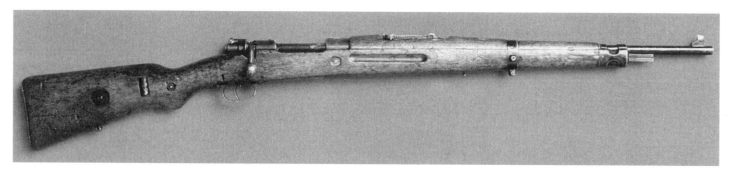

Full-length view of the Lithuanian FN Model 30 Short Rifle. Note that this version has the bent bolt handle. For some unknown reason, this specimen has a quick-release sling attachment on the right side of the stock, instead of on the left, as is usual. (Steve Kehaya collection)

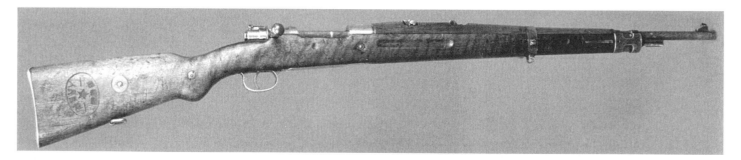

Full-length view of the Lithuanian FN Model 30 Short Rifle. Note the Chinese markings on the right side of the stock. Apparently this rifle had a well-traveled history, presumably captured from the Lithuanians by either the Germans, or the Russians. If captured by the Germans, it was later taken by the Russians, who then supplied it, and others, to the Chinese following World War II. This rifle could possibly have turned up in Korea, as many were in the hands of Chinese troops during that war. Note that this specimen has the straight bolt handle. (Bob Bennett collection)

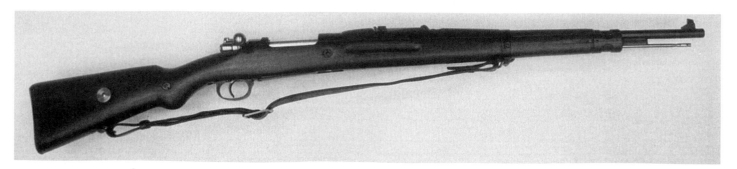

Full-length view of the Lithuanian VZ24 Short Rifle. (Robert Jensen collection)

Receiver marking on the Model 24L Short Rifle, showing the gate motif over the model designation. (Robert Jensen collection)

Due to political upheaval from both the left and the right, the Lithuanian army suspended Parliament in December 1926. An authoritarian regime followed, but was doomed by the secret Hitler-Stalin pact of 1939. In 1940, phony elections were held, with only pro-Soviet choices permitted to run. Thousands fled to the West, or disappeared into Siberia. For those remaining, a high birth rate helped the Lithuanians prevent Russianization of their country.

In the late 1980s, a strong underground nationalist movement began to be heard and felt, culminating in the Lithuanian declaration of independence on 11 March 1990; Soviet reaction included armed attacks on public institutions, but the last Russian troops eventually departed Lithuania on 31 August 1993. Elections held since have seen the former Communist leaders winning election to the presidential and premier's positions. Both members have vowed to pursue a slow path to a freer national economy, as well as promoting better relations with Russia and other former Soviet states.

In the mid-1920s, the Lithuanian army purchased Czech Model VZ 24 Short Rifles from Czechoslovakia in caliber 7.92 x 57mm; in 1931, the government also purchased Czech Model "L" Short Rifles in caliber British .303. Whether these rifles were to be used by the Gendarmerie or were for army issue has not been determined. In

Receiver marking on the Model 24L Short Rifle, showing the variant markings of "GINKLU FONDAS/1937/CREST/24L.". (Robert Jensen collection)

Chinese markings on the right side of the Lithuanian FN Model 30 Short Rifle, as previously described (Bob Bennett collection)

any event, the quantities were modest, and examples are rarely seen in this country. During the period 1935-1938, FN Model 30 Short Rifles were purchased from FN. All of these rifles were used in the Lithuanian arsenal under the designation "Model 24 L."

LITHUANIAN FN MODEL 30 SHORT RIFLE: The Lithuanian FN Model 30 Short Rifle apparently came in a straight-handled bolt version, as well as with a bent bolt handle. The rifle is fitted with a pistol grip stock with grasping grooves, the upper hand guard running from in front of the receiver ring to the upper barrel band. The nose cap incorporates a German-style "H" bayonet lug. There is a swivel on the bottom of the lower barrel band and another on the bottom of the buttstock, halfway between the end of the pistol grip and the toe of the butt. There is a recoil crossbolt under the receiver ring and another at the pistol grip. There is also an inset, screw fastened, washer in the right side of the stock.

Length: 43.25"; **Weight:** 10.0 lbs.; **Barrel:** 22,50"; **Caliber:** 7.92 x 57mm; **Rifling:** 4-groove, r/hand; **Operation:** Turnbolt action; **Feed:** 5-shot, staggered column, flush, box magazine; **Sights:** Tangent leaf rear sight graduated to 2000 meters. **Remarks:** Stylized Lithuanian crown over the model designation on the receiver ring, manufacturer's markings on the side rail.

LUXEMBOURG

During the days of the Holy Roman Empire, Luxembourg was one of hundreds of small principalities of that era. When the Holy Roman Empire was abolished, Luxembourg joined the German League, sharing a monarchy with the Netherlands, but with the two countries separate entities. In 1867, Luxembourg was granted sovereignty by the treaty of London; when King William III passed away in 1890, the dual monarchy was severed, and Whilhelmina became Queen of the Netherlands, while Adolph of Nassau became the Grand Duke of Luxembourg. The independence of Luxembourg dates from that period.

Traditionally neutral, Luxembourg was instantly overrun by Germany during both World Wars, reestablishing itself at the end of each war. Luxembourg was a founding member of the United Nations, and has been a member of NATO since 1949.

With less than 400,000 citizens, and a total land area of less than 1000 square miles, there has never been a large military establishment in the country. The small Luxembourg national army was equipped with a special Model 1900 Mauser Rifle that resembled the Chilean Model 1895 Rifle, as well as the Swedish Model 1896 Rifle. During the 1930s, a small quantity of FN Model 24/30 Short Rifles were obtained to upgrade the weapons available to the small army of Luxembourg.

LUXEMBOURG MODEL 1900 RIFLE: The Luxembourg Model 1900 Rifle is rarely seen, as there were very few produced. Exact

Full-length view of the Luxembourg Model 1900 Rifle (Noel P. Schott collection)

numbers have proven impossible to determine, but the figure is presumed to be less than five thousand in total. The rifle is fitted with a straight wrist stock with grasping grooves, with the upper hand guard running from in front of the receiver ring to just beyond the lower barrel band. The lower barrel band has a swivel on the bottom, with another at the bottom of the buttstock. The nose cap, which is almost identical to the Spanish Model 1893, has a bayonet lug on the bottom for use with the Model 1895 knife-style bayonet.

Length: 48.50"; **Weight:** 9.4 lbs.; **Barrel:** 28.0"; **Caliber:** 6.5 x 53mm; **Rifling:** 4-groove, r/hand; **Operation:** Turnbolt model 1893 action; **Feed:** 5-round, staggered column, flush, box magazine; **Sights:** Tangent leaf rear sight graduated to 2000 meters. **Remarks:** Manufacturer's markings stamped on the top of the receiver ring, with the serial number on the left side.

LUXEMBOURG FN MODEL 24/30 SHORT RIFLE: In order to modernize the arms available to the small army of Luxembourg, a modest number of FN Model 24/30 Short Rifles were obtained during the early 1930s. When overrun by Germany during the Second World War, these arms were no doubt absorbed into the German army reserves. Whether or not these short rifles were marked for Luxembourg is unknown. The rifle is fitted with a pistol grip stock without grasping grooves, with the upper hand guard running from the front of the receiver ring to just beyond the lower barrel band. There is a swivel on the bottom of the lower barrel band, with an-

Close-up view of the manufacturer's markings on the receiver ring of the Luxembourg Model 1900 Rifle. (Noel P. Schott collection)

other on the bottom of the buttstock. The nose cap incorporates a German-style "H" bayonet lug. The bolt handle is straight.

Length: 43.25"; **Weight:** 8.54 lbs.; **Barrel:** 22.50"; **Caliber:** Believed to be 7.92 x 57mm; **Rifling:** 4-groove, r/hand; **Operation:** Turnbolt action; **Feed:** 5-round, staggered column, flush, box magazine; **Sights:** Tangent leaf rear sight graduated to 2000 meters. **Remarks:** Markings, if any, are unknown.

MANCHURIA

During the era of the Japanese-inspired puppet state of Manchukuo (1932-1945), which consisted in great part of the province of Manchuria in the northeast region of China, there was a large arsenal in the city of Mukden. This arsenal was under Japanese management, and during the period 1933-1939, an unusual rifle was produced embodying both Mauser and Arisaka characteristics. This rifle was made for the Manchukuo army; however, it was also used by the Japanese, and later, by the Chinese.

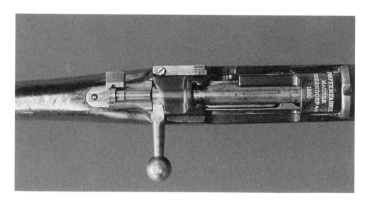

The action of the Luxembourg Model 1900 Rifle. (Noel P. Schott collection)

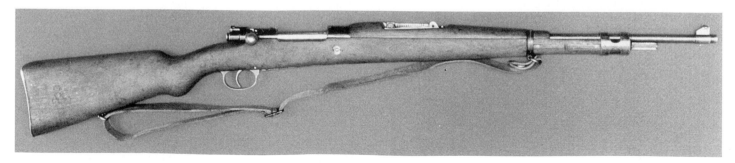

Full-length view of the FN Model 24/30 Short Rifle as used by Luxembourg

Germany

German Model 98k Carbine equipped with an integral box magazine giving a 25-round capacity to the weapon. This carbine was captured on the Russian front, arsenal refinished, put into arsenal storage, and later shipped to Vietnam where it was used by the Viet Cong. This was its condition when captured, so one assumption is that the magazine, which is permanently attached to the trigger guard, was affixed experimentally by the Germans.

German Model 33/40 Carbine

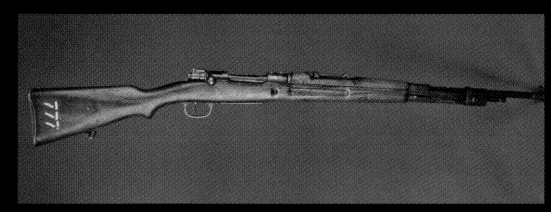

Full-length view of a specimen Model 29/40 Rifle

German Model 24(t) Rifle. Note that this particular rifle is fitted with bottom swivels on the lower band and center of the buttstock, in addition to the side mounted sling arrangement. The stock is walnut.

 Germany

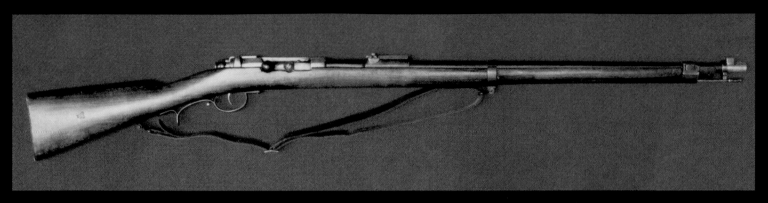

Model 71 Jaeger Rifle
(Henry Wichmann collection)

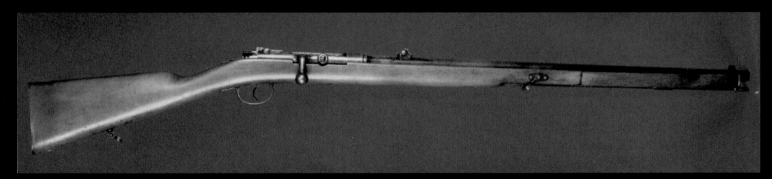

German Model 79 Rifle

The only remaining example of one of 12 rifles made for troop trials. This photo shows the experimental rear sight produced just weeks before the end of World War II. Note the "BYF 45" on the receiver. (Craig Brown collection.)

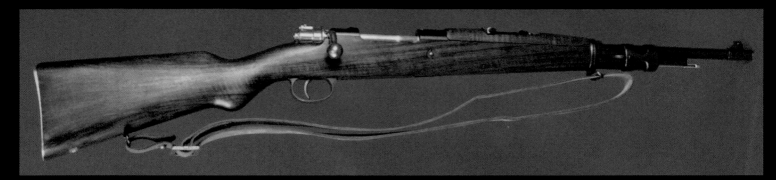

Greek FN Model 1930 Carbine

Guatemala

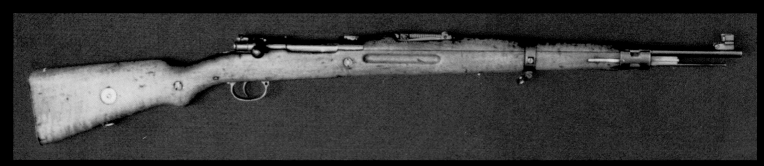

Guatemalan Czech Model VZ 24 Short Rifle

Haiti

Haitian FN Model 24/30 Short Rifle

Haitian army markings on the side of the receiver ring of the Haitian FN Model 24/30 Short Rifle, also showing the manufacturer's markings on the side rail

Israel

The Israeli crest and the caliber designation on the receiver ring of the Israeli Model 98k Short Rifle. FN proof marks are on the left side of the receiver ring.

Lithuania

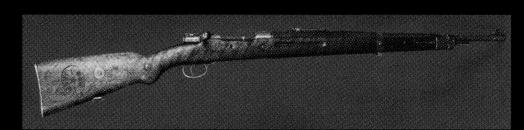

Lithuanian markings on the receiver ring of the Lithuanian FN Model 30 Short Rifle, showing the stylized crown over the model designation (Bob Bennett collection)

Lithuanian FN Model 30 Short Rifle. Note the Chinese markings on the right side of the stock. Apparently this rifle had a well-traveled history, presumably captured from the Lithuanians by the Russians. It was then supplied to the Chinese following World War II. Note that this specimen has the straight bolt handle.

Luxembourg

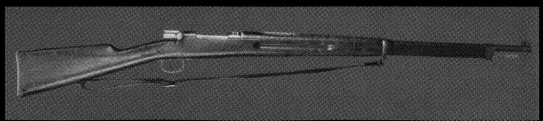

Luxembourg Model 1900 Rifle
(Noel P. Schott collection)

Manufacturer's markings on the receiver ring of the Luxembourg Model 1900 Rifle
(Noel P. Schott collection)

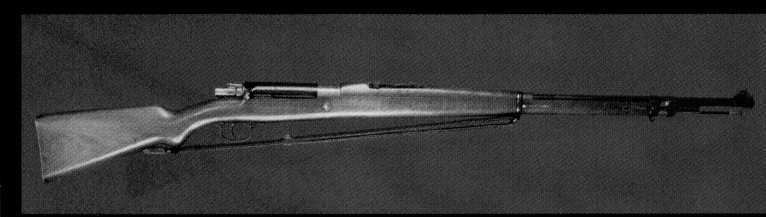

Manchurian Mauser Rifle as manufactured at the Mukden Arsenal

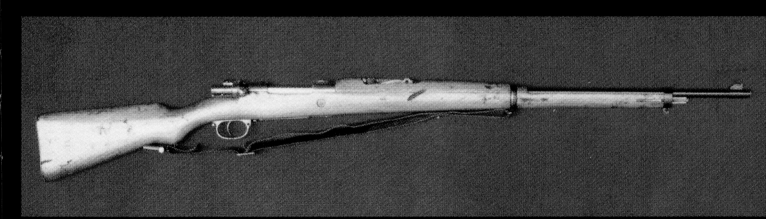

Manchurian Mauser Rifle incorporating the sliding bolt cover that is rarely found with the rifle. Note the difference in the upper barrel band.

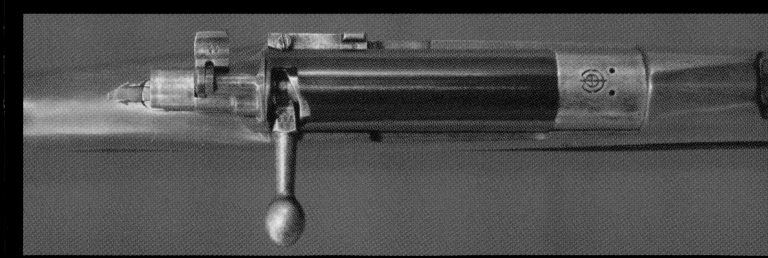

Top view of the Manchurian Mauser Rifle, showing the crest of the Mukden arsenal and the close fit of the bolt cover.

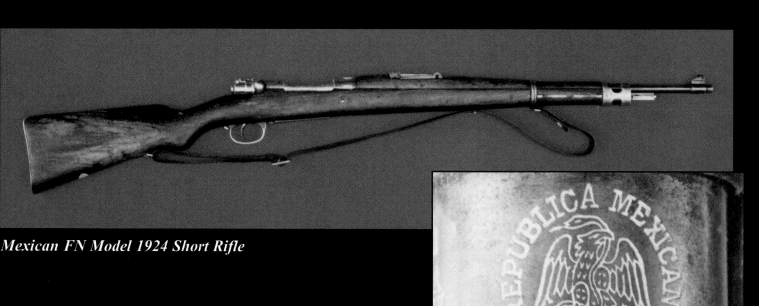

Mexican Model 1910 Carbine

Mexican FN Model 1924 Short Rifle

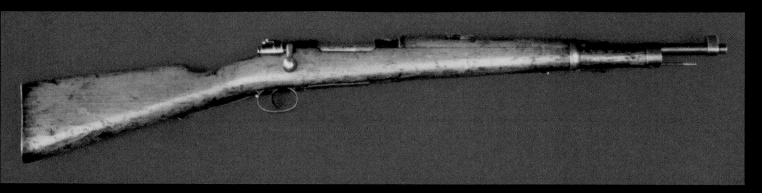

The receiver ring of the Mexican FN Model 1924 Short Rifle, showing the national crest and date of manufacture

Mexican FN Model 1924 Carbine
(Steve Kehaya collection)

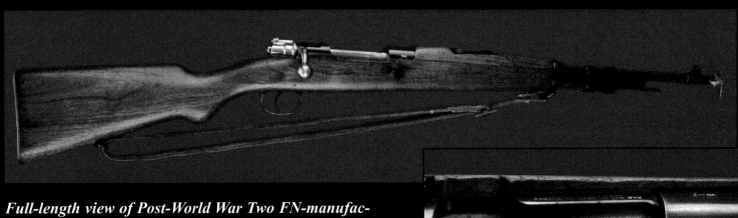

Full-length view of Post-World War Two FN-manufactured carbine, possibly M1950. This carbine was produced in both .30-06 and .308 caliber, with all dimensions identical. It is believed, from what little information the author has been able to glean, that these carbines were used to arm the Moroccan gendarmerie. Information relative to these weapons is almost non-existent.

Top view of the receiver area of the Moroccan FN-made carbine in caliber .30-06; note that the face of the receiver has been notched to accommodate the over-long .30-06 cartridge. Also note the lack of a national crest on the top of the receiver.

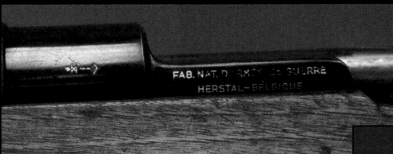

Left side rail markings on the Moroccan FN-made .30-06 carbine. There is nothing unusual in these markings to indicate Moroccan ownership.

Top view of the FN-made Moroccan .308 carbine; the only difference between this and the carbine in .30-06 is that the face of the receiver has not been notched.

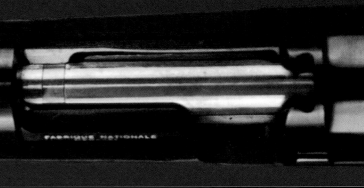

View of the left side rail of the FN-made Moroccan .308 carbine; please note the difference in the marking of the carbine in .30-06.

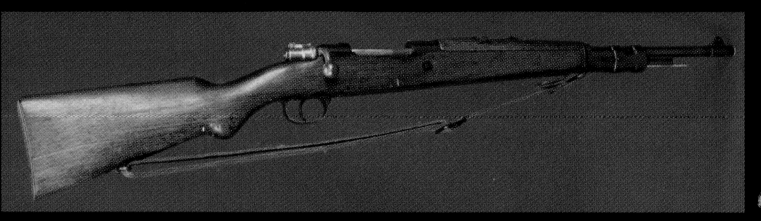

Dutch FN Model 1948 Carbine
(Cliff Baumann collection)

The receiver ring of the Dutch FN Model 1948 Carbine, showing the crest "J" for "Juliana"
(Cliff Bauman collection)

The receiver ring of the Dutch FN Model 1948 Carbine, showing the crest "W" for "Wilhelmina"

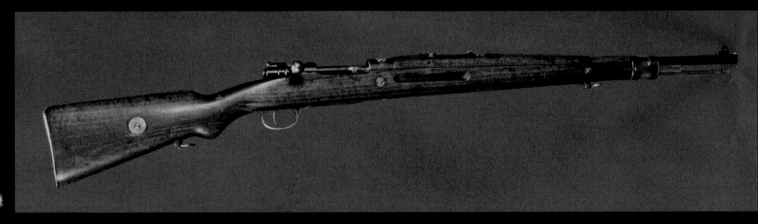

Czech VZ 23 Short Rifle as used by the armed forces of Nicaragua
(Bob Bennett collection)

Nicaraguan cartouche on the left side of the butt-stock of the Nicaraguan VZ24 Short Rifle.

Circle within a circle receiver marking on the Nicaraguan VZ 24 Short Rifle.

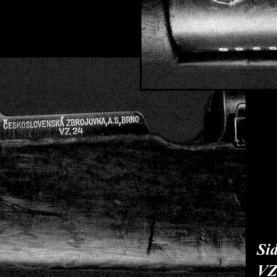

Side rail markings on the Nicaraguan VZ 24 Short Rifle.

Norway

Norwegian Reissue German Model K98k Carbine
(Bob Bennett collection)

Receiver markings on the Norwegian Reissue Model K98k Carbine. Note how the face of the receiver has been milled to accept a different size cartridge.
(Bob Bennett collection)

Orange Free State

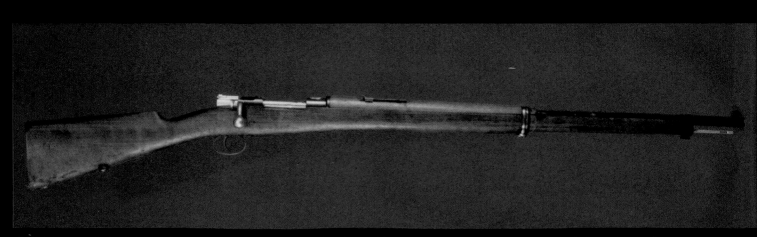

"OVS" Model 1895 Rifle as overstamped for the Republic of Chile. Note that the bolt handle is bent down. These rifles will be found with both a straight and bent bolt handle.

Ludwig Loewe and Co. Model 1896 "OVS" marked Mauser Rifle

The Ludwig Loewe & Co. crest on the receiver ring of the Model 1896 "OVS" marked Mauser Rifle. The finish on this weapon is peppery due to exposure to the elements.

"DWM" script crest on the "OVS" marked Model 1897 Mauser Rifle

Paraguay

Paraguayan Model 1907 Rifle

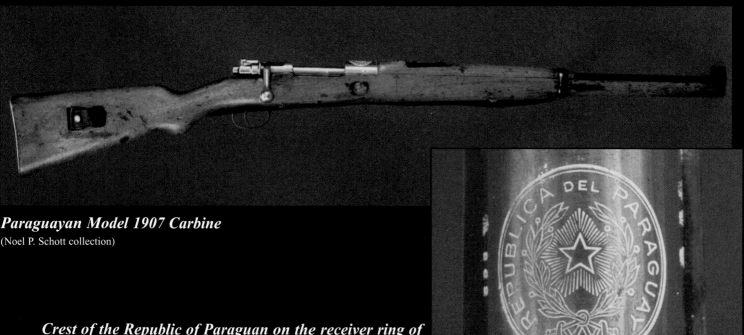

Paraguayan Model 1907 Carbine
(Noel P. Schott collection)

*Crest of the Republic of Paraguan on the receiver ring of
the Paraguayan Model 1907 Carbine*
(Noel P. Schott collection)

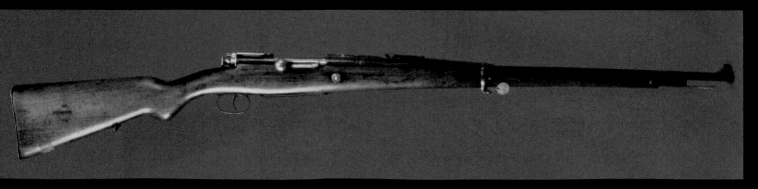

Paraguayan Model 1909 Haenel Export Model Rifle

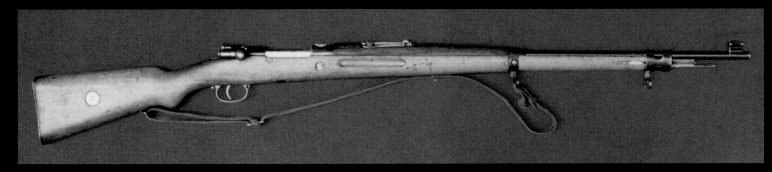

Persian Model 98/29 Long Rifle (Persian Model 1310)

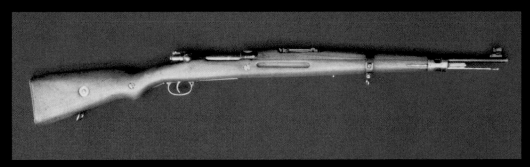

Persian Czech Model VZ 24 Short Rifle

Receiver ring of the Persian Model 98/29 Long Rifle showing the Persian national crest

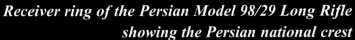

Persian Czech Model 30 Carbine

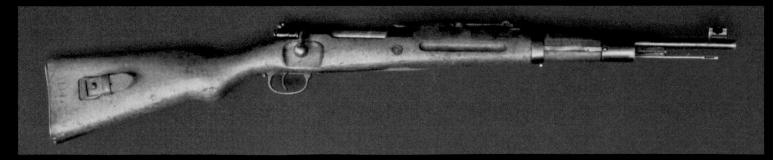

Iranian Model 49 Carbine

Peru

Peruvian Model 1891 Rifle

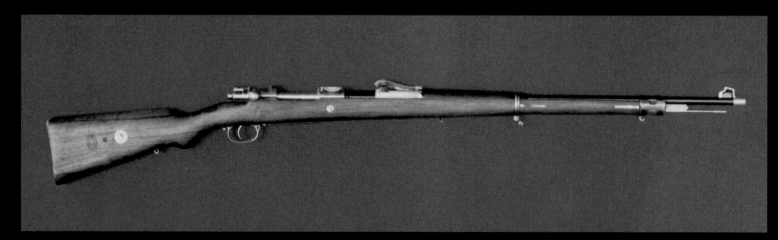

Peruvian Model 1909 Rifle. Note the original Peruvial muzzle cover.
(Lother Frank collection)

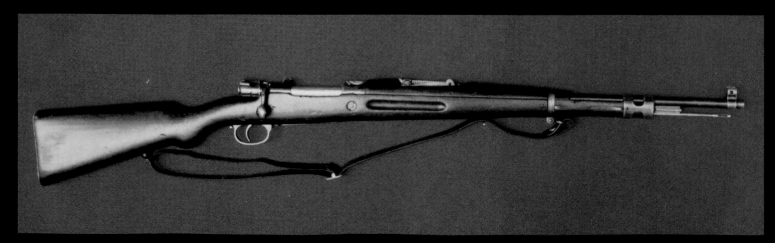

Peruvian Model 1935 Short Rifle

Full length view of the Model 1891 Rifle converted to Carbine configuration. This was originally an Argentin-

Poland

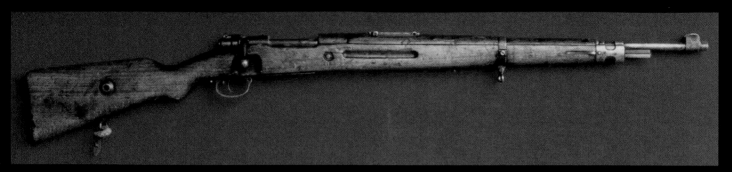

Polish Wz 29 Short Rifle as issued for cavalry. Note the bent bolt handle.

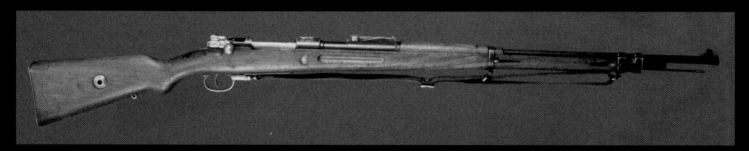

Seldom found is this Polish Model Wz 98a Rifle, which was produced in the middle to late 1930s

Portugal

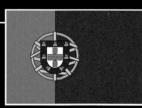

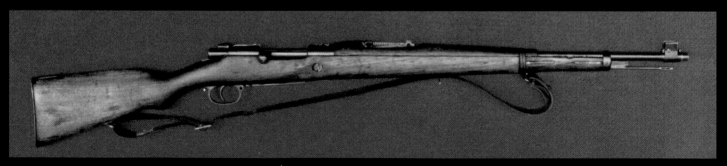

Portuguese Model 937/M39 Rifle

Portuguese Model 937-A Short Rifle

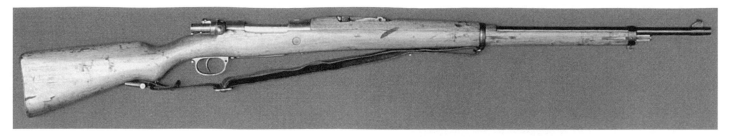

Full-length view of the Manchurian Mauser Rifle as manufactured at the Mukden Arsenal

The rifle incorporates many design features of the Arisaka rifle, including the Japanese-style two-part stock, the ovoid knob on the bolt handle, and the double gas escape ports in the top of the receiver. There is a removable sliding bolt cover that could be attached to the bolt. Like the Arisaka, the bolt was bored out from the rear to accept the mainspring, with a large housing resembling a cocking piece that acts as a fixed guide for the mainspring. The safety is like that of the Model 98, but instead of being threaded, the bolt sleeve is held to the bolt by lugs.

The rifle is fitted with a pistol grip stock without grasping grooves, and the upper hand guard runs from the front of the receiver ring to just beyond the lower band. Both the upper and lower

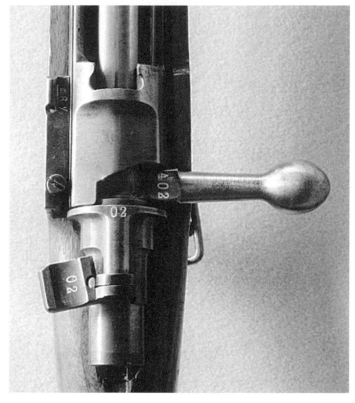

Overhead view of the Mukden Arsenal Mauser Rifle, showing the Japanese-style ovoid bolt knob. Note the safety is slightly bent on this specimen.

Manchurian troops, among the best equipped in Asia, are shown here armed with the Mukden arsenal Mauser rifle. (Edgar Snow collection)

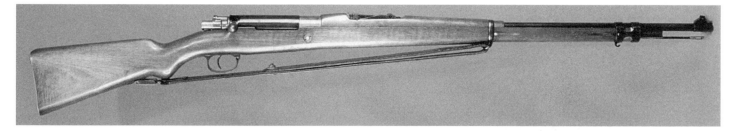

Full-length view of the Manchurian Mauser Rifle incorporating the sliding bolt cover that is rarely found with the rifle. Note the difference in the upper barrel band.

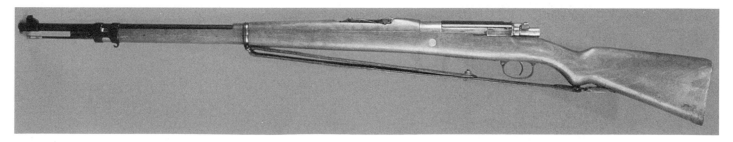

Left full-length view of the Manchurian Mauser Rifle. Note the streamlined appearance when the bolt cover is in place.

bands are thinner than are usually found on Mauser rifles, and the upper band includes a parade hook. The nose cap has the short German-style "H" bayonet lug, requiring a bayonet with a muzzle ring. The lower barrel band has a swivel, while there is a quick release sling fitting just behind the pistol grip of the stock.

These rifles, when found, are liable to be in any condition from excellent to extremely poor. They are normally quite scarce on the U.S. collector's market.

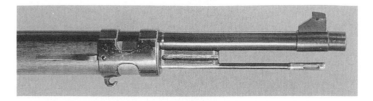

Upper barrel band, nose cap, cleaning rod, and muzzle of the Manchurian Mauser Rifle

Serial number and prefix on the left side of the receiver ring of the Manchurian Mauser Rifle made in the Mukden Arsenal

The receiver ring markings on the Manchurian Mauser Rifle, showing what is believed to be the symbol for the Mukden Arsenal

Top view of the Manchurian Mauser Rifle, showing the crest of the Mukden Arsenal and the close fit of the bolt cover

Length: 48.82"; **Weight:** 9.40 lbs.; **Barrel:** 29.13"; **Caliber:** 7.92 x 57mm (some specimens will be found modified for the Japanese 6.5mm semi-rimless cartridge) ; **Rifling:** 4-groove, r/hand; **Operation:** Turnbolt action; **Feed:** 5-round, staggered column, flush, box magazine; **Sights:** Tangent leaf rear sight graduated to 2000 meters. **Remarks:** Marked on the top of the receiver ring with what is believed to be the symbol of the Mukden Arsenal. Serial number on the left side of the receiver ring.

MEXICO

Led by Hernan Cortez, the first Spaniards arrived in Mexico in 1519 and during the next three centuries extended Spanish rule to the south, over Central America, and north into what eventually became the southwestern United States and Texas.

In 1810, a rural priest named Father Miguel Hidalgo led an unsuccessful uprising against the Spanish American empire. With Hidalgo defeated and executed, another priest, José Maria Morelos, managed to establish an independent republic in the southern portion of Mexico. Morelos was captured and executed in 1815, and the short-lived republic came to an end.

The liberal uprising in Spain in 1820 triggered fears among the conservative elements of a similar liberal insurrection in Mexico. The conservatives made a preemptive strike by staging an uprising of their own, and quickly overcame Spanish resistance. In 1822, unable to agree on a European monarch to sit on the newly-established Mexican throne, Augustín Iturbide, the leader of the revolution, declared himself Emperor Augustín I. This empire lasted less than a year, with Iturbide forced to abdicate in March 1823. The Federation of Central American States declared their independence, and in 1824 Mexico adopted a federal republican constitution.

A Spanish invasion in 1828 was easily repulsed, but the country was sliding into anarchy. The government abolished slavery in 1829, infuriating the American settlers in Texas, and causing a rebellion in 1836. An independent Republic of Texas was declared, with the republic being annexed by the United States in 1845. This annexation provoked the disastrous war between Mexico and the United States, resulting in the complete and utter defeat of Mexican forces and the loss of forty percent of Mexican national territory for the meager sum of fifteen million dollars.

Antonio López de Santa Anna, the general responsible for the defeats suffered by Mexico, was installed as president in name, but a monarch in truth. Economic disintegration resulted in Santa Anna's flight in 1855, precipitating a civil war—1858 to 1860—between conservatives and liberals. The end of the war brought about the installation of Benito Juárez as president. Economic problems continued to plague Mexico, with the country defaulting on its foreign debt payments. This resulted in Britain, France, and Spain landing troops in Vera Cruz during 1861 and 1862. Due to the civil war in the United States, they were able to do so without interference from the enforcement of the Monroe Doctrine by the United States government.

This foreign intervention ushered in the period of the French occupation of Mexico, with the installation of a puppet monarch, Archduke Maximilian of Austria as Emperor Maximilian I, kept in power only by the French bayonets of Emperor Napolean III. Juárez was left with only a small segment of the country until the end of the American Civil War, at which time support for the Mexican republicans, both political and material, eventually resulted in the withdrawal of French forces and the defeat and execution of Maximilian in 1867. Juárez resumed the presidency, but died in office in 1872.

A rebellion against the next president gave General Porfirio Díaz the chance to take over the presidency, ruling Mexico with an iron hand from 1876 to 1911, with only a short four-year period when a hand-picked general served as president in order for Díaz to keep the promise that he would not succeed himself. The thirty-four years of the Díaz reign were the most stable in the history of Mexico, but resulted in the worsening of the miserable condition of the working classes.

During the 1910 election, Díaz was challenged by Francisco Madero, who later fled to the United States where he helped to orga-

A mobilized Mexican Federal soldier takes leave of his family, C. 1913 (Sr. Y.C. de Casasola)

Revolutionary justice! A Mexican rebel firing squad executes a suspected spy. (Sr, Y.C. de Casolas)

nize a rebellion against Díaz in conjunction with the revolts of Emiliano Zapata in the south and Doroteo Arango, otherwise known as Pancho Villa, in the north. The successes of the rebellion set off a series of army revolts, causing Díaz to flee the country on 25 May 1911. Madero was elected president, but proved inept; he was denounced by Zapata and faced with a revolt by Orozco in the north.

The revolt of Orozco was put down by General Victoriano Huerta, who also overthrew Madero, having him shot on 22 February 1913. Huerta assumed the presidency, but was forced to flee in 1914, plunging the country into total anarchy, with four revolutionary factions attempting to form a government. Carranza and Obregon gained the upper hand, rejecting the proposed candidates of Zapata and Villa. Villa then sought to implicate the United States in the ongoing struggles by organizing and conducting raids into United States territory, resulting in the Mexican Border expedition of General "Black Jack" Pershing in 1916. U.S. forces were withdrawn on the eve of America's entry into World War I. Carranza was then president, followed by Obregon, who finally pacified the country. Obregon was followed by Calles, who ruthlessly persecuted the Catholic church, causing a revolt by the fanatical Catholic "Cristeros." Calles was succeeded by Obregon, who was assassinated by a religious fanatic. During the 1920s and the 1930s, the succeeding presidents consolidated the gains of the revolution.

Mexico joined the Allies in 1942 in the war against the Axis, providing naval patrols and an air force fighter squadron that served in the Pacific theatre. Since World War II, the size of the Mexican armed forces has been inconsistent with the size of the country, with the services reduced by spending cutbacks. It would appear the future of the Mexican armed forces will most probably be limited to the internal security of the country.

MEXICAN MODEL 1895 RIFLE: The Mexican government has had extensive experience and involvement with not only arms procurement, but also the manufacture of weapons for their armed forces. In the late 1800s, after careful testing and consideration by their

Federal troops firing on rebels from a rooftop with Model 1895 Rifles. Note the sandals on the soldier nearest the camera.

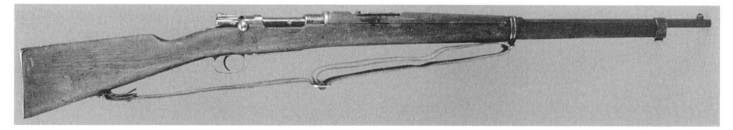

Full-length view of the Mexican Model 1895 Rifle, as made under contract in Oviedo, Spain

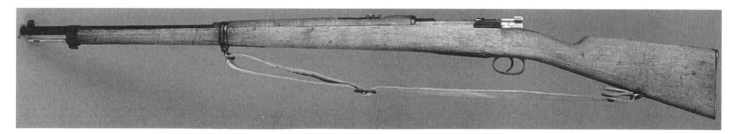

Left full-length view of the Mexican Model 1895 Rifle

Mexican rebels in northern Chihuahua armed with Model 1895 Rifles and Winchester lever-action rifles, C. 1913-1914 (I. Thord-Gray)

arms commission, the Mexican government accepted the Mauser Model 1895 Rifle. This was the standard rifle of the Mexican army under Porfirio Díaz and is almost identical to the Spanish Model 1893. Along with other model Mauser rifles, it served throughout the long period of rebellion and unrest that began with the revolution of 1910.

The Mexican Model 1895 Rifle is fitted with a straight-wristed stock without grasping grooves, the upper hand guard running from the sheet steel ring on the front of the receiver ring to just beyond the lower barrel band. The upper barrel band has a bayonet lug on the bottom for use with the Model 1895 knife bayonet. The lower barrel band has a swivel on the bottom, and there is another approximately six inches from the toe of the buttstock.

Length: 48.50"; **Weight:** 8.75 lbs.; **Barrel:** 29.0"; **Caliber:** 7 x 57mm; **Rifling:** 4-groove, r/hand; **Operation:** Turnbolt action; **Feed:** 5-round, staggered column, flush, box magazine; **Sights:** Adjustable leaf rear graduated to 2000 meters. **Remarks:** Rifles were produced either by DWM or Oviedo. Those made by DWM are stamped with the manufacturer's marks on the left side rail, while those manufactured under contract by Oviedo have the Spanish crest on the receiver ring and the manufacturer's markings stamped on the left side rail.

MEXICAN MODEL 1895 CARBINE: The Mexican army also received large numbers of Model 1895 Carbines from both DWM and Oviedo, Spain. The Model 1895 Carbine is identical to the Model 1895 Rifle with the following exceptions: total length, barrel length, weight, bent bolt handle, side-mounted sling, and graduations on the rear sight. Note that there is no provision for a bayonet, and both the upper and lower band are retained by a flat spring on the bottom of the forestock.

Length: 37.25"; **Weight:** 7.50 lbs.; **Barrel:** 17.25"; **Caliber:** 7 x 57mm; **Rifling:** 4-groove, r/hand; **Operation:** Turnbolt action; **Feed:** 5-round, staggered column, flush, box magazine; **Sights:** Adjustable leaf rear sight graduated to 1400 meters. **Remarks:** Carbines were initially marked with the Republic of Mexico crest on the top of the receiver ring; however, many of these crests have been removed during arsenal renovation at some time in the past. The top of the barrel is usually marked by a stylized cross between the upper and lower band.

MEXICAN MODEL 1902 RIFLE: In 1902, Mexico adopted the Model 1902 Rifle, which resembled the Model 1895 Rifle, but was fitted with the improved Model 98 action; these improvements included a third locking lug and a gas shield on the bolt. Due to the great stocks of Model 1895 bayonets on hand, the bayonet lug is on the bottom of the upper band. The straight wrist stock, similar to the Model 1895, was also retained, with the upper hand guard running from in front of the receiver ring to just beyond the lower barrel band. These rifles were produced by both DWM, Berlin, and the Austrian Arms Company (Steyr). By 1903, Mexico had accepted delivery of approximately thirty-eight thousand rifles made by DWM, while it is believed that a further forty thousand rifles manufactured by Steyr were also delivered.

Manufacturer's markings, in this case DWM, stamped on the side rail of the Mexican Model 1902 Rifle

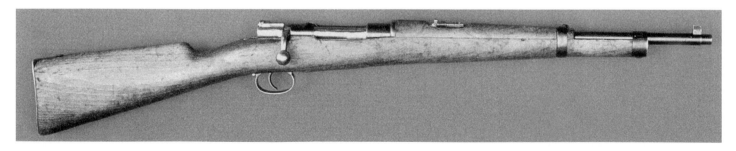

Full-length view of the Mexican Model 1895 Carbine

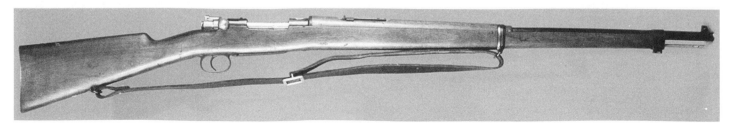

Full-length view of the Mexican Model 1902 Rifle. Note the close similarity to the Model 1895 Rifle

The Mexican national crest on the receiver ring of the Mexican Model 1902 Rifle

Length: 48.50"; **Weight:** 8.75 lbs.; **Barrel:** 29.0"; **Caliber:** 7 x 57mm; **Rifling:** 4-groove, r/hand; **Operation:** Turnbolt action; **Feed:** 5-round, staggered column, flush, box magazine; **Sights:** Adjustable leaf rear sight graduated to 2000 meters. **Remarks:** Arched "REPUBLICA MEXICANA" over Mexican eagle, over date of manufacture. Manufacturer's markings on side rail.

MEXICAN MODEL 1907 STEYR RIFLE: The Mexican Model 1907 Rifle was the first rifle produced for Mexico that incorporated the pistol grip stock and also accepted the Model 98-style bayonet. The upper hand guard extends from the front of the receiver ring to approximately .50 inches beyond the lower barrel band. The upper band has a parade hook, while the lower barrel band has a swivel on the bottom. Just behind the pistol grip portion of the stock, there is a quick release sling attachment.

This rifle was produced for the Mexican goverment by the Austrian Arms Company (Steyr) between 1907 and 1910, and is one in a series of Model 98-style Mauser rifles used by the Mexican army. The quantity of rifles delivered is unknown.

Length: 48.50"; **Weight:** 8.75 lbs.; **Barrel:** 29.0"; **Caliber:** 7 x 57mm; **Rifling:** 4-groove, r/hand; **Operation:** Turnbolt action; **Feed:** 5-round, staggered column, flush box magazine; **Sights:** Tangent leaf rear sight graduated to 2000 meters; these were replaced by the 1800 meter pattern in 1924. **Remarks:** The receiver ring is marked STEYR/Model 1907/date of manufacture.

MEXICAN MODEL 1910 RIFLE: This was the first Mexican Mauser rifle produced in Mexico. During the presidency of Porfirio Díaz, many members of the Mexican armed forces were sent abroad to study firearms manufacture with the intention of providing Mexico with the means to equip themselves. The first small arms ammunition factory, the Fabrica Nacional de Cartuchos, was started in 1906; the national arms factory, Fabrica Nacional de Armas, commenced operation in Mexico City just before the start of the 1910 revolution.

The Model 1910 Mauser Rifle is based upon the Model 1902 Rifle. These rifles are well-made and dependable, and approximately forty thousand weapons were produced prior to the Model 1910 being phased out of production in 1934.

The receiver ring of the Mexican Model 1910 Rifle

Full-length view of the Mexican Model 1907 (Steyr) Rifle (Springfield Armory Museum)

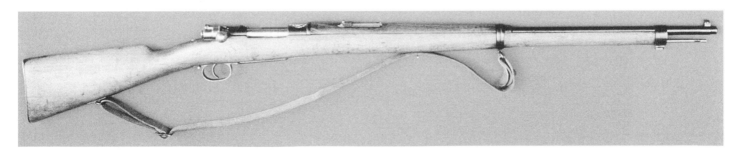

Full-length view of the Mexican Model 1910 Rifle

The rifle is fitted with a straight-wristed stock, and the upper hand guard extends from in front of the receiver ring to just beyond the lower barrel band. The lower barrel band is fitted with a swivel on the bottom, and another is fitted to the bottom of the buttstock. The upper barrel band has a bayonet stud on the bottom for use with the Model 1895 bayonet.

Length: 48.50"; **Weight:** 8.75 lbs.; **Barrel:** 29.0"; **Caliber:** 7 x 57mm; **Rifling:** 4-groove, r/hand; **Operation:** Turnbolt action; **Feed:** 5-round, staggered column, flush, box magazine; **Sights:** Adjustable leaf rear sight graduated to 1800 meters. **Remarks:** On the receiver ring, "FABRICA NACIONAL DE ARMAS-MEXICO D.F." in an oval around the Mexican eagle, over the date of manufacture. Serial number on the left side of the receiver ring.

MEXICAN MODEL 1910 CARBINE: The Mexican Model 1910 Carbine is almost identical to the Model 1895 Carbine, with the exception of the improved Model 98-style action and protecting "ears" for the front sight. There is no provision for a bayonet, and the sling is side mounted.

Length: 37.50"; **Weight:** 8.0 lbs.; **Barrel:** 17.50"; **Caliber:** 7 x 57mm; **Rifling:** 4-groove, r/hand; **Operation:** Turnbolt action; **Feed:** 5-round, staggered column, flush, box magazine; **Sights:** Adjustable leaf rear sight graduated to 1400 meters. **Remarks:** Mexican national crest over date of manufacture on the receiver ring, serial number on the left side.

MEXICAN MODEL 1912 STEYR RIFLE: Due to difficulties in manufacture of the Mexican Model 1910, the Mexican government was forced to purchase Model 1912 Rifles from Steyr. As deliveries began, the First World War started, with the balance of the Mexican order being taken over by the Austrian government. After World War I, some of the undelivered Model 1912 Rifles were converted to 7.92 x 57mm and sold to Yugoslavia, where they were used as the Model 24B.

The national crest and date of manufacture on the receiver ring of the Mexican Model 1910 Carbine

The Mexican Model 1912 Rifle has a large diameter receiver ring, a pistol grip stock similar to the Model 1907, an upper hand guard that runs from in front of the receiver ring to just beyond the lower barrel band, a tangent leaf rear sight, and a German-style "H" bayonet lug. There is a swivel on the bottom of the lower barrel band and a quick release sling attachment behind the pistol grip of the stock. The upper barrel band incorporates a parade hook.

Length: 49.0"; **Weight:** 8.75 lbs.; **Barrel:** 29.0"; **Caliber:** 7 x 57mm; **Rifling:** 4-groove, r/hand; **Operation:** Turnbolt action; **Feed:** 5-round, staggered column, flush, box magazine; **Sights:** Tangent leaf rear sight graduated to 1800 meters. **Remarks:** The receiver ring is marked "Model 1912" over "STEYR," over the date of manufacture.

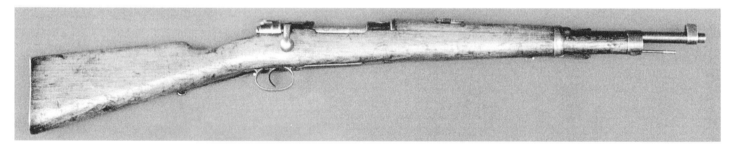

Full-length view of the Mexican Model 1910 Carbine

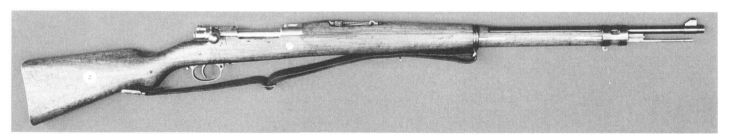

Full-length view of the Model 1912 Steyr Rifle as used by Mexico

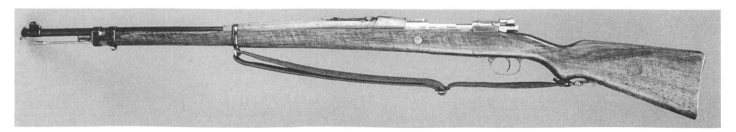

Left full-length view of the Mexican Model 1912 Rifle

MEXICAN MODEL 1912 STEYR SHORT RIFLE: The Mexican Model 1912 Short Rifle is identical to the Model 1912 Rifle, but for length and weight, and a turned down bolt handle. All specific data relative to the short rifle may be found under the section on Chile.

MEXICAN FN MODEL 1924 SHORT RIFLE: During 1926 and 1927, Mexico purchased approximately twenty-five thousand FN-produced short rifles and carbines; this was to be the last Mauser rifle produced on a foreign contract for Mexico.

This is the standard export version of the FN Model 1924 Short Rifle. The short rifle is fitted with a pistol grip stock without grasping grooves, and the upper hand guard extends from in front of the receiver ring to the upper barrel band. The lower barrel band has a swivel on the bottom, with another at the rear of the pistol grip of the stock. The nose cap incorporates a German-style "H" bayonet lug.

Length: 43.0"; **Weight:** 8.50 lbs.; **Barrel:** 23.50"; **Caliber:** 7 x 57mm; **Rifling:** 4-groove, r/hand; **Operation:** Turnbolt action; **Feed:** 5-round, staggered column, flush, box magazine; **Sights:** Tangent leaf rear sight graduated to 2000 meters. **Remarks:** "REPUBLICA MEXICANA" in a curve around the Mexican eagle, over the date of manufacture. Manufacturer's marking on the left side rail. Usually found with a metal tag bearing the property number tacked to the bottom of the buttstock, near the toe.

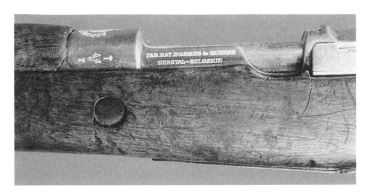

The left side rail of the Mexican FN Model 1924 Short Rifle, showing manufacturer's markings

The receiver ring of the Mexican FN Model 1924 Short Rifle, showing the national crest and date of manufacture

Property number tag on the bottom of the stock of the Mexican FN Model 1924 Short Rifle

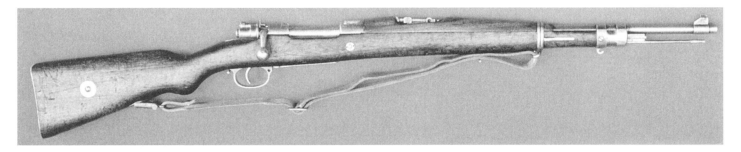

Full-length view of the Mexican Model 1912 Short Rifle

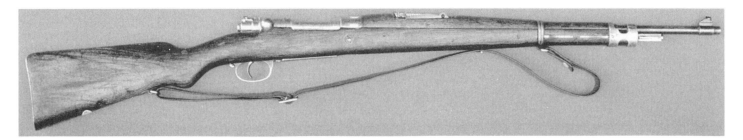

Full-length view of the Mexican FN Model 1924 Short Rifle

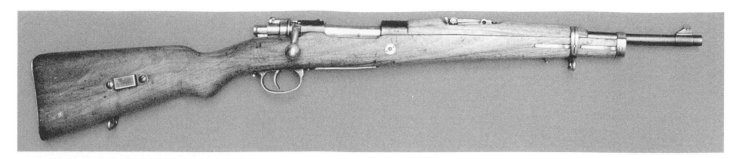

Full-length view of the Mexican FN Model 1924 Carbine (Steve Kehaya collection)

MEXICAN FN MODEL 1924 CARBINE: This is the export version of the standard FN Model 1924 Carbine, as made for Mexico. The pistol grip stock is without grasping grooves, and the upper hand guard extends from in front of the receiver ring to beyond the lower barrel band. The upper and lower barrel band are quite close together, with each held by a separate retaining spring. The carbine is not fitted to accept a bayonet. There is a swivel on the bottom of the lower barrel band, and another on the bottom of the buttstock; also note the carbine attachment on the right side of the stock midway between the wrist and the butt.

Length: 35.75"; **Weight:** 7.50 lbs.; **Barrel:** 15.25"; **Caliber:** 7 x 57mm; **Rifling:** 4-groove, r/hand; **Operation:** Turnbolt action; **Feed:** 5-round, staggered column, flush, box magazine; **Sights:** Tangent leaf rear sight graduated to 1400 meters. **Remarks:** Mexican national crest over the date of manufacture on the receiver ring, manufacturer's markings on the left side rail.

Side rail of the Mexican Czech Model VZ 12/33 Carbine, showing the manufacturer's markings in Spanish

MEXICAN CZECH VZ 12/33 CARBINE: During the early 1930s, Mexico acquired a small number of Czech VZ 12/33 Carbines. This is the standard Czech export Model 12/33 Carbine, from which the later VZ 16/33 Carbine and the German G33/40 Carbine were developed. This carbine has a pistol grip stock, with the upper hand guard extending from the front of the receiver ring to beyond the lower barrel band. The lower barrel band is fitted with a bottom swivel, while there is a quick release sling attachment just behind the pistol grip of the stock. The upper barrel band is fitted with a parade hook. Note that the lower band is secured to the stock by a retaining spring, while the upper band is held in place by a screw.

Length: 41.97"; **Weight:** 8.49 lbs.; **Barrel:** 21.89"; **Caliber:** 7 x 57mm; **Rifling:** 4-groove, r/hand; **Operation:** Turnbolt action; **Feed:** 5-round, staggered column, flush, box magazine; **Sights:** Tangent leaf rear sight. **Remarks:** The national crest of Mexico is on the receiver ring, with the manufacturer's markings on the left side rail in Spanish.

MEXICAN MODEL 1936 SHORT RIFLE: This was the last Mauser rifle adopted in caliber 7 x 57mm. These short rifles were produced by the Government Arms Factory in Mexico City, beginning in 1936 and continuing into the late 1940s. Built on the Mauser 1898 action, the Model 1936 Short Rifle also combines certain features of the United States Model 1903 Springfield Rifle, including a Springfield-type cocking knob, barrel bands and swivels, stacking swivel, and front sight band and mounting.

The rifle is fitted with a pistol grip stock with grasping grooves, and the upper band incorporates a bottom mounted stud for use with the Model 1895 bayonet. The upper hand guard extends from in front of the receiver ring to the upper band.

Full-length view of the Mexican Czech Model VZ 12/33 Carbine

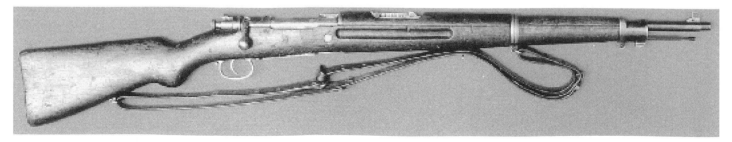

Full-length view of the Mexican Model 1936 Short Rifle

Close-up of the Mexican national crest over the date of manufacture on the receiver ring of the Mexican Model 1936 Short Rifle

Close-up view of the Mexican national crest on the receiver ring of the Mexican Model 1954 Short Rifle

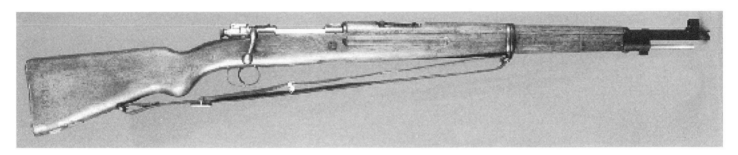

Full-length view of the Mexican Model 1954 Short Rifle

Left side view of the receiver ring of the Mexican Model 1954 Short Rifle, showing caliber and model designation

MEXICAN MODEL 1954 SHORT RIFLE: After World War II, a huge influx of war-surplus weapons, including M-1 Garands, influenced the Mexican authorities to upgrade the Model 1936 Short Rifle. The new Model 1954 Short Rifle was adapted to chamber .30-06 ammunition, and allowances were made for ease of manufacture. The Model 1954 utilized Model 1936 actions, with the trigger guards and magazine floorplates made from a continuous stamping. The pistol grip stock with grasping grooves is laminated, the upper band is fitted with a bayonet lug on the bottom to accept the ever-present Model 1895 bayonet. The lower band has a swivel on the bottom, with another on the bottom of the stock behind the pistol grip.

Many of these Model 1954 Short Rifles were fitted with rear sights on the receiver bridge similar to those on the Springfield Model 03-A3; others still retained the tangent leaf rear sight of the Model 1936 Short Rifle. Due to the availability on the worldwide market of semiautomatic weapons, production of the Model 1954 Short Rifle was discontinued in 1955.

Length: 44.02"; **Weight:** 9.6 lbs.; **Barrel:** 24.0"; **Caliber:** .30-06; **Rifling:** 4-groove, r/hand; **Feed:** 5-round, staggered column, flush, box magazine; **Sights:** Tangent-ramp rear sight graduated to 1000 meters. **Remarks:** Mexican national crest on the receiver ring over the date of manufacture (of the action), "Cal. 7.62mm" over "Mod. 54" on the left side of the receiver ring.

MOROCCO

Following the establishment of Phoenician and Carthaginian settlements along the Mediterranean coast, Morocco came under the Roman rule around 40 A.D.; later, in the 5th century, Morocco was invaded by Germanic Vandals via Spain. During the 7th century, Islamic invaders swept over the country, with Arab rule and the conversion of most of the indigenous population to Islam a result. Ever since, ethnic tension in politics and society has existed between Berber and Arab.

In the 11th century, the Almoravid dynasty from Mauretania conquered Morocco, western Algeria and Spain; they were ousted by another Muslim sect, the Almohads. After approximately 1200, the tide turned and the Moorish expansion was repulsed, with Ferdinand and Isabella expelling the last Moors from Spain in 1492.

In the mid-17th century, Morocco was reunited under the present Alawid dynasty. In the 19th century, American and British forces fought Moroccan piracy in the Mediterranean, while at the same time, Spain established colonies in Tangier in the north, as well as along the Atlantic coast between Morocco and Mauretania. By the early 20th century, France, securely established in Algeria, began to exert influence, pressure and control in Morocco. A special conference confirmed Moroccan independence, but upheld the special rights claimed by both Spain and France. In 1912, the treaty of Fez ended Moroccan independence by granting the country to

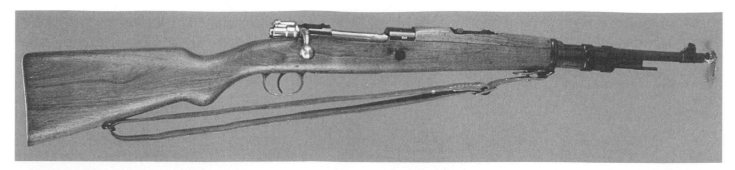

Full-length view of Post WWII FN manufactured carbine, possibly M1950. This carbine was produced in both .30-06 and .308 caliber, with all dimensions identical. It is believed, from what little information the author has been able to glean, that these carbines were used to arm the Moroccan gendarmerie. Information relative to these weapons is almost non-existant.

Left side rail markings on the Moroccan FN made .30-06 carbine. There is nothing unusual in these markings to indicate Moroccan ownership.

View of the left side rail of the FN made Moroccan .308 carbine; please note the difference in the marking of the carbine in .30-06.

France and reaffirming a Spanish sphere of influence in the southwest.

During the entire period of French administration, nationalist unrest and tribal uprisings disrupted all efforts of the French. During World War Two, Morocco became a battleground, and the Istiqlal (Independence) party was formed to fight for independence from foreign rule during the post-war era. In 1947, open warfare began against the French, while the Sultan Mohammad V was allowed to return to Morocco, and the French promised independence by 1955. Morocco became independent on 2 March 1956.

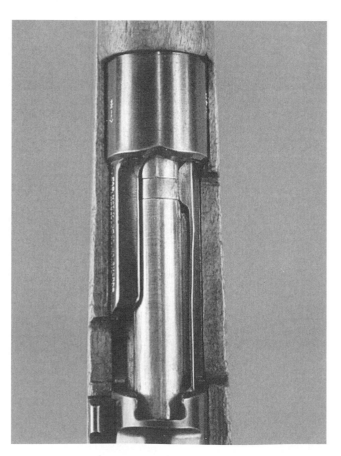

Top view of the receiver area of the Moroccan FN made carbine in caliber .30-06; note that the face of the receiver has been notched to accommodate the over-long .30-06 cartridge. Also note the lack of a national crest on the top of the receiver.

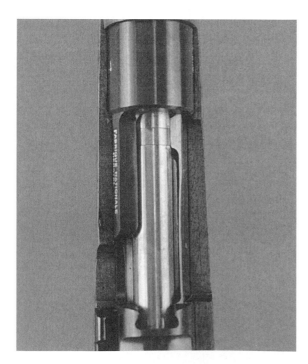

Top view of the FN made Moroccan .308 carbine; the only difference between this and the carbone in .30-06 is the fact taht the face of the receiver has not been notched.

THE NETHERLANDS

The Dutch armed forces replaced their 1871/88 Beaumont Vitali Rifles in 1895 with Model 1895 Mannlicher Rifles. These Mannlicher rifles served the Dutch forces throughout the First and into the Second World War, being replaced by Allied weapons and equipment as the Netherlands' forces-in-exile were formed.

After World War Two, the Dutch adopted the FN Model 1948 Carbine for gendarmerie and police units. This short-barreled weapon is quite handy, though the muzzle blast can tend to be excessive. The carbine is fitted with a pistol grip stock without grasping grooves, and the upper hand guard extends from the front of the receiver ring to just beyond the lower barrel band. The upper band is almost immediately in front of the lower barrel band, and the nose cap incorporates a German-style "H" bayonet lug. There is a swivel on the bottom of the lower band and another about four inches from the toe of the stock.

Length: 37.13"; **Weight:** 7.5 lbs.; **Barrel:** 17.32"; **Caliber:** 7.92 x 57mm; **Rifling:** 4-groove, r/hand; **Operation:** Turnbolt action; **Feed:** 5-round, staggered column, flush, box magazine; **Sights:** Tangent leaf rear sight graduated to 1400 meters. **Remarks:** Crown over initial "W" or "J", manufacturer's markings on the side rail.

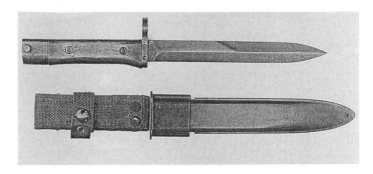

An example of the specially manufactured bayonet and scabbard that was only used with this carbine; these are quite rare and seldom seen.

Same bayonet shown attached to the carbine

The receiver ring of the Dutch FN Model 1948 Carbine, showing the crest "J" for "Juliana" (Cliff Baumann collection)

The receiver ring of the Dutch FN Model 1948 Carbine, showing the crest "W" for "Wilhelmina"

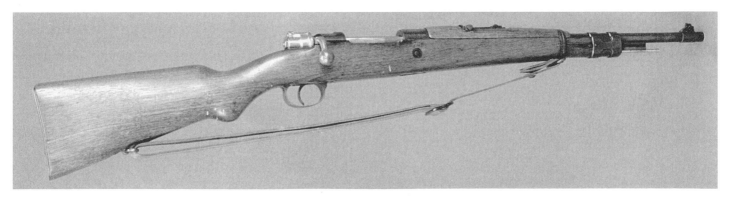

Full-length view of the Dutch FN Model 1948 Carbine (Cliff Baumann collection)

Dutch policeman, circa. 1948 with the Model 1948 Dutch carbine at left should arms; note the uniform, highly reminiscent of the German SS, which was cordially despised by the Dutch citizenry and replaced shortly thereafter.

Manufacturer's markings on the side rail of the Dutch FN Model 1948 Carbine (Cliff Baumann collection)

NICARAGUA

The early history of Nicaragua is similar to that of the rest of Central America until 1838, when the United Provinces of Central America disintegrated. The rest of the nineteenth century is a history of the incessant fighting between liberals and conservatives, with the exception of a period between 1855 and 1857 when the country was under the control of William Walker, a North American filibuster, or soldier of fortune, who succeeded in having himself made president. Infuriated, American business interests were successful in having a joint U.S.-British naval force intervene, forcing his expulsion. Walker tried once more to regain the presidency of Nicaragua, but was captured by the British, turned over to the Hondurans, and shot at dawn.

The United States continued to intervene in Nicaraguan politics, helping to remove President Zelaya in 1909 and establishing the conservatives to power. Internal strife caused the U.S. to land marines in 1912, where a legation guard remained until 1925. With the removal of the marine guard, the country lapsed into anarchy, and a recall of the marines was considered necessary, remaining in effect until 1933. Augusto Sandino led the resistance to the U.S. Marines during this intervention, and with the withdrawal of U.S. forces, Anastasio Somoza, Commander of the U.S.-trained National Guard, seized power. Sandino was assassinated in 1934, and Somoza remained in power until he was killed in 1956. The presidency of Nicaragua was passed down through the Somoza family as though by right until the regime collapsed in 1979, after a year of brutal civil war.

Nicaraguan cartouche on the left side of the buttstock of the Nicaraguan VZ 24 Short Rifle

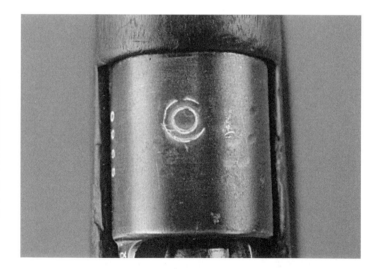

Circle within a circle receiver marking on the Nicaraguan VZ 24 Short Rifle

Side rail markings on the Nicaraguan VZ 24 Short Rifle

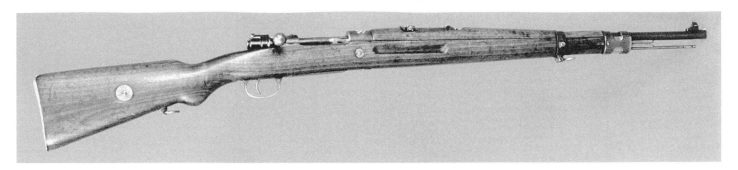

Full-length view of the Czech VZ 23 Short Rifle as used by the armed forces of Nicaragua (Bob Bennett collection)

Full-length view of the Czech VZ 12/33 Carbine as used by Nicaragua

The Sandinista clique succeeded to power after the revolution, backed by Soviet weapons and advisors. Struggles with the "Contras," supported by the United States, continued until elections, long postponed, were held in 1990. The elections were a stunning

Czech manufacturer's markings in Spanish on the side rail of the Czech Model VZ 12/33 Carbine as used by Nicaragua

defeat for the Sandinistas. The transition of power has been peaceful, but the social and economic recovery of this impoverished country will be slow in coming.

NICARAGUAN CZECH VZ 23 SHORT RIFLE: Nicaragua ordered a small number of VZ 23 Short Rifles from Czechoslovakia during the early 1930s. This rifle proved to be long-lived, serving well into the Sandinista rebellion against the Somoza regime. All pertinent information relative to this short rifle will be found under the section on Czechoslovakia.

Sandinista rebel armed with an FN Model 24 Short Rifle relaxing for a moment in Esteli (Susan Meiselas)

Sandinista rebels in the streets of Esteli, carrying FN Model 24 Short Rifles (Susan Meiselas)

NICARAGUAN CZECH VZ 12/33 CARBINE: In conjunction with the order of Czech Model VZ 23 Short Rifles, the Czech Model VZ 12/33 Carbine was also ordered at the same time. It is said that some of these carbines bear Czech markings on the receiver ring and side rail, while others were apparently delivered with the manufacturer's markings stamped in Spanish on the side rail, with the coat of arms of Nicaragua on the receiver ring. This crest consists of a background of five volcanoes, with a liberty cap on a staff arising from a seascape beneath a sunrise and a rainbow. All pertinent data on the Czech Model VZ 12/33 Carbine will be found under the section on Czechoslovakia.

NORWAY

At the end of hostilities in World War II, Norway found it necessary to equip its army with the vast stocks of German weapons surrendered by the German occupation army. Previously armed with the Krag-Jorgensen system of rifles, the German weapons were a stopgap until such time as the Norwegian army was able to reequip with the semiautomatic weapons available in the postwar years.

NORWEGIAN REISSUED GERMAN MODEL K98k CARBINE: As the only difference between this and standard German-issue weapons is the markings, pertinent data relative to the weapon will be

Stampings on the side of the barrel, receiver ring, and side rail of the Norwegian Reissue Model K98k Carbine. (Bob Bennett collection)

The receiver ring stampings on the Norwegian army target rifle as modified from the Mauser K98k action

Receiver markings on the Norwegian Reissue Model K98k Carbine. Note how the face of the receiver has been milled to accept a different size cartridge. (Bob Bennett collection)

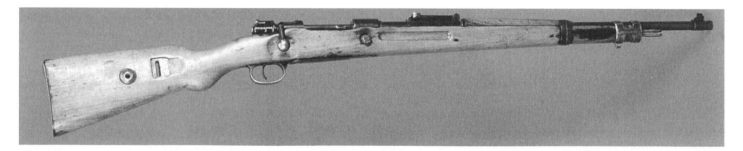

Full-length view of the Norwegian Reissue German Model K98k Carbine (Bob Bennett collection)

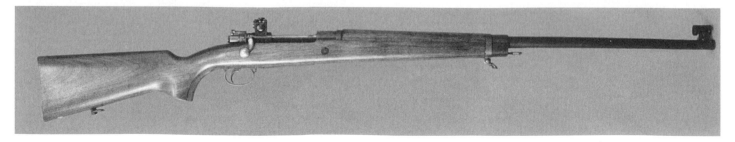

Full-length view of the Norwegian army target rifle, built around the Mauser K98k action

found under the section on Germany. These rifles were later modified to accept caliber 7.62mm NATO ammunition.

NORWEGIAN ARMY MAUSER TARGET RIFLE: For marksmanship purposes, specially selected Mauser actions were used to build target rifles for the Norwegian Army. These special rifles are not commonly encountered.

ORANGE FREE STATE - ORANJE VRIJ STAAT (OVS)

A short-lived republic in South Africa, the Orange Free State (Oranje Vrij Staat) began to arm itself in earnest after the abortive Jameson raid into the neighboring Transvaal in 1896. Contacts were made and contracts drawn with DWM (Deutsche Waffen und Muntionfabrik) in 1897 for the purchase of Model 1893 Spanish-pattern Mauser rifles, short rifles, and carbines, made with the cylindrical bolt head as opposed to the Spanish flat-bottom bolt. Records indicate that approximately eighteen thousand weapons were delivered before shipments were abruptly terminated by the advent of war.

Of particular interest is that there were several variations in the weapons delivered, with the majority of the rifles made by DWM, showing the DWM markings and "MOD. MAUSER" on the receiver ring, as well as "OVS" on the side of the receiver and stock. A small number of rifles were manufactured by Ludwig Loewe and Co. of Berlin, and were marked "MOD. MAUSER 1896" on the side rail and incorporated the Loewe crest on the receiver ring. The left side of the receiver ring is marked "OVS," as is the stock immediately below. Several thousands of rifles were in the process of completion when delivery was halted by the onset of the Boer War; these rifles were then overstamped with the crest of Chile and used to complete a contract with that country. Of those "OVS" Mauser rifles to be found, some will have bent bolt handles, while others will have a straight bolt handle. It is of interest to note that a number of the Model G 71 Mauser Rifles purchased by the Transvaal were also used during the Boer War.

The Boers acquitted themselves admirably with their Mauser rifles during the course of the ill-fated Boer War, treating the British to an astonishing show of marksmanship, coupled with introducing the British to flat-trajectory, clip loading rifles. Losses of equipment and weapons during the course of the war forced the Boers to rely upon the capture of British weapons for resupply, resulting in very few "OVS" Mauser rifles being found at the end of the war.

MODEL 1895 MAUSER RIFLE: Model 1895, 1896, and 1897 rifles and carbines used by the Boers are different from the Spanish Modelo 1893 in that minor modifications were made to the weapon, mainly a cylindrical-head bolt and a thumb recess in the left receiver wall to aid in stripping the cartridges from the clip. This rifle was equipped with a tangent leaf sight, and the upper hand guard extends from the front of the receiver ring to just beyond the lower barrel band. The upper barrel band incorporates a bayonet lug for

A posed group of Boers with both Model 1895 Rifles and Short Rifles, early in the Boer War. Note the interesting variations in how they carried their ammunition, especially the seated figure in the center.

Boer town-dwelling burghers with their newly issued Model 1895 Short Rifles and ammunition belts. In their town clothing, they hardly look ready for the veldt; clothing, however, did not make a soldier!

Posed picture of Boer burghers in the act of loading their rifles for the camera

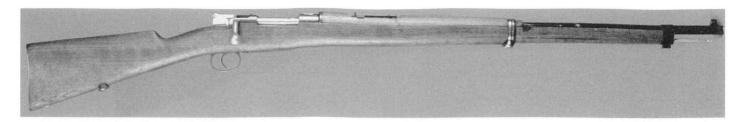

Full-length view of the "OVS" Model 1895 Mauser Rifle as overstamped for the Republic of Chile. Note that the bolt handle is bent down. These rifles will be found with both a straight and bent bolt handle.

the Model 1895 bayonet. Interestingly, while rarely seen on the battlefield, the Boers had purchased a number of Model 1871-style bayonets with a reversed "S" guard for use with some of these weapons. These are to be found in collections, and advertisements for the complete belt, buckle, frog, and bayonet plus scabbard can be seen in old Francis Bannerman catalogs as relics of the Boer War. Often, the stocks of the rifles were quite artistically carved with the owner's initials, the seal of the Orange Free State, or something equally of interest to the individual. The following data will apply to the rifles that are shown.

Length: 48.5"; **Weight:** 8.75 lbs.; **Barrel:** 29.0"; **Caliber:** 7 x 57mm; **Rifling:** 4-groove, r/hand; **Operation:** Turnbolt action; **Feed:** 5-round, staggered column, flush, box magazine; **Sights:** Tangent leaf rear sight graduated to 2000 meters. **Remarks:** Manufacturer's markings on the receiver ring and side rail, "OVS" marked on the left of the receiver ring and immediately below in the stock. Other German markings will be found on these weapons, as well as the Chilean crest.

"OVS" CHILEAN-MARKED MODEL 1895 MAUSER RIFLE:

The side rail of the "OVS" Model 1895 Mauser Rifle as sold to Chile. This picture clearly shows the location of the "OVS" markings over the serial number of the individual weapon, both on the receiver ring and the stock immediately below.

The receiver ring of the "OVS" Model 1895 Mauser Rifle showing the Chilean crest. Note the "OVS" stamping to the left.

"OVS" MARKED MODEL 1896 MAUSER RIFLE BY LOEWE:

"Along with the large number of 1895 and 1896 rifles which were purchased by the Boers (the OVS and the ZAR), there were small numbers of the Model 1895 Carbines, and fewer yet of the model 1896 Carbine. This particular Carbine has no official or distinguishing markings on it, however, it does have the original owner's name, along with "OVS" carved into the right side of the buttstock; a common practice of the Boers.

Length: 37.50"; **Weight:** 7.0 lbs.; **Barrel:** 18.0'; **Caliber:** 7x57mm; **Rifling:** 4-groove, r/hand; **Operation:** Turnbolt; **Feed:** 5-round, staggered column, flush, box magazine; **Sights:** Tangent leaf rear sight graduated to 2000 meters.; **Remarks:** Sling configuration consists of a left-side mounted swivel on the bottom band, with a left-side mounted swivel on the left buttstock with a saddle ring. "Model 1896/Ludw. Loewe & Co. Berlin" on the left side rail. No markings present on the receiver ring.

Side rail and receiver markings of the Ludwig Loewe & Co. Model 1896 Mauser Rifle

The Ludwig Loewe & Co. crest on the receiver ring of the Model 1896 "OVS" marked Mauser Rifle. The finish on this weapon is peppery due to exposure to the elements.

"OVS" MARKED MODEL 1897 MAUSER RIFLE BY DWM:

Receiver and side rail markings on the "OVS" marked Model 1897 Mauser Rifle

"DWM" script crest on the "OVS" marked Model 1897 Mauser Rifle

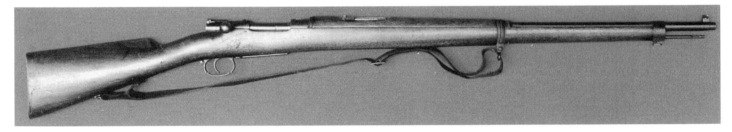

Full-length view of the Ludwig Loewe and Co. Model 1896 "OVS" marked Mauser Rifle

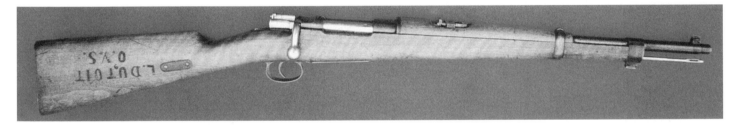

Right side view of the Model 1896 OVS Mauser Carbine; notice the carvings in the stock are not as one would expect! (John Wall collection)

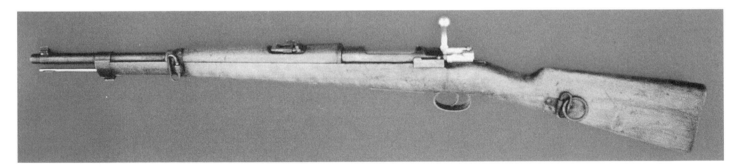

Left side view of the Model 1896 OVS Mauser Carbine, with the bolt handle in the upward position; note the saddle ring on the left side of the small of the stick. (John Wall collection)

Full-length view of the "OVS" marked Model 1897 Mauser Rifle manufactured by DWM

PARAGUAY

Colonized by the Spaniards in the sixteenth century and largely influenced by the Jesuits, both politically and economically, Paraguay was an isolated outpost of the Spanish Empire. The political elite of Asunción, the capitol city, overthrew Spanish authority in 1811 and declared the independence of Paraguay. From the time of independence until 1862, there was relatively stable rule, but with the assumption of the presidency in 1862 by Francisco Solano López, stability was a thing of the past.

From 1865 to 1870, Paraguay was the central figure in the War of the Triple Alliance, fighting against Brazil, Argentina, and Uruguay. Paraguay had attempted to intervene between Brazil and its attempt to control Uruguay, fomenting the war. This was one of the most disastrous wars recorded in the history of South America, with Paraguay losing three-quarters of its population and ninety-five percent of its males, as well as sixty thousand square miles of Paraguayan territory. Brazil also levied a war debt of two hundred million dollars, which was later excused.

Slowly struggling back to normalcy over the next four decades, Paraguayan politics developed into struggles between the Colorados and the Liberals, with power passing back and forth over the years. Problems with Bolivia began to heat up in the 1920s over the ownership of the Chaco Boreal, a one hundred thousand square mile area to the west of the Paraguay River and north of the Rio Pilcomayo. Clashes occurred between troops of both nations, with the Paraguayans launching an assault on Bolivian outpost incursions of Paraguayan territory in 1932. This precipitated the Gran Chaco War, the largest war of modern forces in South American history, with the Paraguayans, under the brilliant command of Marshal José Félix Estigarribia, victorious in 1935.

Paraguay has a long and proud history of military accomplishment, and is one of the few Latin American armies with a fighting tradition.

During the late 1890s, Paraguay purchased small quantities of Chilean-style Model 1895 Rifles from DWM (Deutsche Waffen-und Munitionfabriken). From 1907 to 1912, the Paraguayan Model 1907 Rifle (Fusil Modelo 1907 Paraguayo) was produced in caliber 7.65 x 53mm for Paraguay by DWM. These rifles are quite similar to the Gew. 98, with the exception of the heavy 1904-style cocking piece and the nose cap that accepts an export style Model 1907 bayonet with muzzle ring. Sling swivels are suspended from the un-

Youthful Boers with their new Model 1896 Mauser Rifles and ammunition. Many of the Boers went to war in their Sunday best clothes, even wearing top hats!

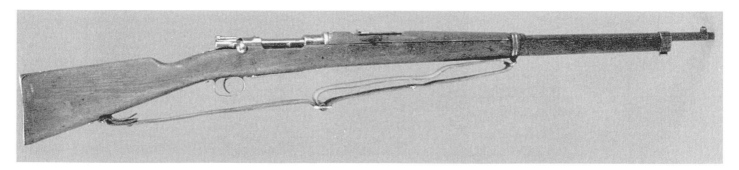

Full-length view of the Paraguayan Chilean-style Model 1895 Rifle

Full-length view of the Paraguayan Model 1907 Rifle

Paraguayan sentry post on the Pilcomayo River during the Chaco War. The sentry is armed with a Model 1895 Rifle. (Benjamin Banks collection)

derside of the lower barrel band and the bottom of the stock. The Paraguayan Model 1907 Carbine (Carabina Mauser Paraguayan Model 1907) is similar to the rifle, but is shorter, has a turned down bolt handle and a tangent leaf rear sight, and is fully stocked to the muzzle. The nose cap provides front sight protectors, and the sling is side mounted.

Ordered from the Fabrica Nacional de Armas, Oviedo, Spain, the Model 1927 Rifle (Fusil Modelo 1927), made from 1927 to 1932, was manufactured in long rifle, short rifle, and carbine configurations, all chambered for the 7.65 x 53mm round. The long rifle differs from the Model 1907 in having a bolt stop/charger guide, and requiring a bayonet with the muzzle ring set flush with the handle. In order to make use of existing stocks of Model 1895 bayonets, an auxiliary lug attachment is used. The rifle is fitted with a pistol grip stock, while the Model 1927 Short Rifle (Mosqueton Modelo 1927) has a straight-wristed stock, with the bolt handle either bent down or straight. The Model 1927 Carbine (Carabina Modelo 1927) is full stocked to the muzzle, with a turned down bolt handle and side-mounted sling. Records show that approximately 10,363 rifles were purchased at this time. Further purchases in 1930 include 7,000 Belgian Mauser Model 1889 Rifles in caliber 7.65 x 53mm.

The foregoing weapons served the Paraguayan forces for many years, being converted to caliber 7.62mm during the 1950s. According to reports from the Chaco War, Paraguayan soldiers ("pilas") cordially loathed the Spanish-made weapons, labeled "Mata Paraguayo" or "Paraguayan Killer." As soon as possible, these rifles were replaced on the field of battle with captured Czech-made 7.65 mm VZ 24 Short Rifles, and/or VZ 08/33 Short Rifles.

Standard Modell MauserRrifles and FN-made Mle. 24 "Mod. 1935" Short Rifles were acquired in the late 1930s. During the war with Bolivia, Paraguay captured enormous quantities of equipment from the enemy, including 39,000 usable rifles, 900 submachine guns, 700 heavy and 2,100 light machine guns, about 100 mortars, 50 pieces of artillery, and 3 tanks.

CHILEAN-STYLE MODEL 1895 RIFLE: DWM supplied the Paraguayan army with Chilean-style Model 1895 Rifles during the late 1890s. These rifles were kept in use and reserve from the time of acquisition through the period of the Chaco War. All specific data regarding this rifle will be found under the section on Chile.

PARAGUAYAN MODEL 1907 RIFLE: The Paraguayan Model 1907 Rifle is quite similar to the Gew. 98, with a straight bolt handle, a pistol grip stock, and the upper hand guard running from in front of the "Lange Vizier" rear sight to just beyond the lower barrel band. The action includes safety lugs and nonrotating extractor, with the heavy 1904-style cocking piece. Swivels are found on the bottom of the lower barrel band and the bottom of the buttstock. The German "H"-style bayonet lug is used, and this rifle also will be found fitted with an auxiliary bayonet lug in order that the Model 1895 bayonet can be utilized.

Length: 49.09"; **Weight:** 9.06 lbs.; **Barrel:** 28.13"; **Caliber:** 7.65 x 53mm, later converted to 7.62mm; **Rifling:** 4-groove, r/hand; **Operation:** Turnbolt action; **Feed:** 5-round, staggered column, flush, box magazine; **Sights:** "Lange Vizier" rear sight graduated to 2000 meters. **Remarks:** Paraguayan crest on the top of the receiver ring, with manufacturer's markings stamped on the left side rail.

PARAGUAYAN MODEL 1907 CARBINE: The Paraguayan Model 1907 Carbine (Carabina Mauser Paraguayana Mo. 1907) has an action identical to the Model 1907 Rifle, but with a turned down bolt handle. The carbine is fitted with a pistol grip style stock that extends to the muzzle. The simple nose cap has protecting ears for the front sight, and there is no provision for a bayonet. The buttstock is cut with a sling slot, and the lower barrel band has a side-mounted sling slot. A tangent leaf rear sight replaced the Lange Vizier rear sight of the Model 1907 Rifle.

Length: 41.25"; **Weight:** 8.1 lbs.; **Barrel:** 21.75"; **Caliber:** 7.65 x 53mm; **Rifling:** 4-groove, r/hand; **Operation:** Turnbolt action; **Feed:** 5-round, staggered column, flush, box magazine; **Sights:** Tangent leaf rear sight graduated to 1400 meters. **Remarks:** Crest of Paraguay on top of the receiver ring, with proofs and

Crest of the Republic of Paraguay on the receiver ring of the Paraguayan Model 1907 Carbine (Noel P. Schott collection)

Full-length view of the Paraguayan Model 1907 Carbine (Noel P. Schott collection)

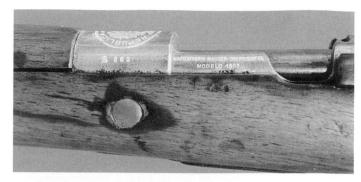

The left side rail with manufacturer's markings on the Paraguayan Model 1907 Carbine (Noel P. Schott collection)

Right side of the receiver ring of the Paraguayan Model 1907 Carbine, showing proof marks (Noel P. Schott collection)

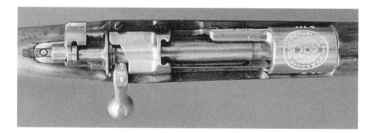

Overview of the complete action of the Paraguayan Model 1907 Carbine (Noel P. Schott collection)

Markings on the receiver ring of the Paraguayan Model 1909 Haenel Export Model Rifle

Model designation and caliber stamped on the left side rail of the Paraguayan Model 1909 Haenel Export Model Rifle

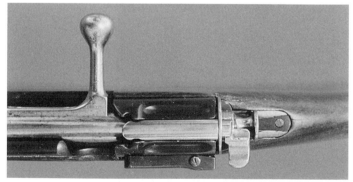

Top view of the Mauser and Commission-style action of the Paraguayan Model 1909 Haenel Export Model Rifle. Note the large gas flange on the bolt sleeve.

serial number on the left side of the receiver ring, and further proofing on the right side of the receiver ring. Manufacturer's markings on the left side rail.

PARAGUAYAN MODEL 1909 C. G. HAENEL EXPORT MODEL RIFLE: This rifle is rather obscure, and little is known other than the obvious. C. G. Haenel of Suhl made a number of rifles for export built around a modified Mauser and Commission 88 action. According to information received, some of these were purchased by Paraguay for use at the army military academy. Lightweight and quite easy to handle, these rifles are in caliber 7 x 57mm. The rifle is fitted with a pistol grip style stock, with the upper hand guard extending from the front of the receiver ring to just beyond the lower barrel

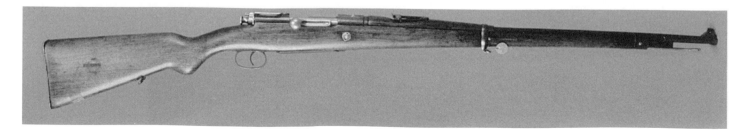

Full-length view of the Paraguayan Model 1907 Carbine (Noel P. Schott collection)

band. The forestock is unusually narrow, and is fitted with a nose-cap incorporating a simple German-style "H" bayonet lug. The lower barrel band has a swivel on the bottom, with another attached to the bottom of the stock behind the pistol grip.

Length: 44.0"; **Weight:** 6.8 lbs.; **Barrel:** 23.50"; **Caliber:** 7 x 57mm; **Rifling:** 4-groove, r/hand; **Operation:** Turnbolt action; **Feed:** 5-round, staggered column, flush, box magazine; **Sights:** Tangent leaf rear sight graduated to 2000 meters. **Remarks:** Marked "C.G. HAENEL/SUHL/1914" on the receiver ring, and "MOD. 09, 7MM" on the left side rail.

PARAGUAYAN MODEL 1927 RIFLE: Made in Oviedo, Spain at the Fabrica Nacional de Armas, the Model 1927 Rifle (Fusil Modelo 1927) is very similar to the Gew. 98, with the exception of the tangent rear sight and a curved extension on the bolt stop to hold the clip in position while loading the magazine (this allowed use of both old and new style clips). The rifle version of this weapon also has an auxiliary bayonet lug attached over the original flush lug, allowing the use of the Model 1895 bayonet. The rifle is fitted with a pistol grip stock without grasping grooves, and the upper hand guard extends to .75 inches beyond the lower barrel band. There is a magazine floorplate release in the front of the trigger guard on the example shown; however the author is unable to state with certainty that this is the case on all rifles produced.

Length: 49.0"; **Weight:** 9.0 lbs.; **Barrel:** 28.63"; **Caliber:** 7.65 x53mm, later converted to 7.62 mm; **Rifling:** 4-groove, r/hand; **Operation:** Turnbolt action; **Feed:** 5-round, staggered column, flush, box magazine ; **Sights:** Tangent leaf rear sight graduated to 2000 meters. **Remarks:** Paraguayan national crest on the top of the receiver ring, manufacturer's markings on the left side rail.

The Paraguayan crest on the receiver ring of the Paraguayan Model 1927 Rifle

The left side of the receiver ring with model designation, and left side rail with manufacturer's markings of the Paraguayan Model 1927 Rifle

Scene of Paraguayan soldiers ("pilas") in a shallow trench during the Chaco War. The first soldier appears to be using a long-barreled version of the Erma submachine gun, while the other troops are using Czech VZ 12/33 and Paraguayan Model 1927 Short Rifles. (Benjamin Banks collection)

Full-length view of the Paraguayan Model 1927 Rifle

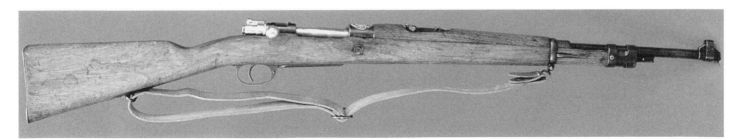

Full-length view of the Paraguayan Model 1927 Short Rifle

The left side of the action of the Paraguayan Model 1927 Short Rifle, showing the model designation and the manufacturer's markings

PARAGUAYAN MODEL 1927 SHORT RIFLE: The Paraguayan Model 1927 Short Rifle is similar to the Model 1927 Rifle with the exception of having a straight wrist stock, either a straight, or a bent bolt handle, and Spanish-style front sight protectors. The upper hand guard extends from the front of the receiver ring to approxi-mately .75 inches beyond the lower barrel band. The lower barrel band has a swivel on the bottom, and there is another on the bottom of the buttstock.

Length: 42.25"; **Weight:** 8.50 lbs.; **Barrel:** 22.50"; **Caliber:** 7.65 x 53mm, later converted to 7.62mm; **Rifling:** 4-groove, r/hand; **Operation:** Turnbolt action; **Feed:** 5-round, staggered column, flush, box magazine; **Sights:** Tangent leaf rear sight graduated to 2000 meters. **Remarks:** Paraguayan national crest on the top of the receiver ring, with model designation on the left side of the receiver ring; manufacturer's markings stamped on the left side rail.

PARAGUAYAN FN MODEL 24/30 SHORT RIFLE: This the standard export Model 24/30 Short Rifle produced by FN. The short rifle is fitted with a pistol grip stock, and the upper hand guard runs from the front of the receiver ring to the upper barrel band. Note the grasping grooves. There is a swivel on the bottom of the lower barrel band and another on the bottom of the stock behind the pistol grip.

A period of rest during the Chaco War for some Paraguayan troops. Note the covered and uncovered Vickers heavy machine guns, with the Czech VZ 23 Short Rifle leaning against the tree. (Benjamin Banks collection)

The "FN" logo on the receiver ring of the Paraguayan FN Model 24/30 Short Rifle

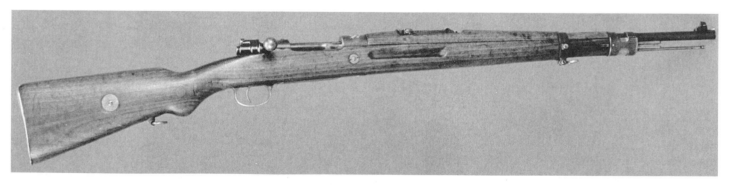

Full-length view of the Paraguayan FN Model 24/30 Short Rifle

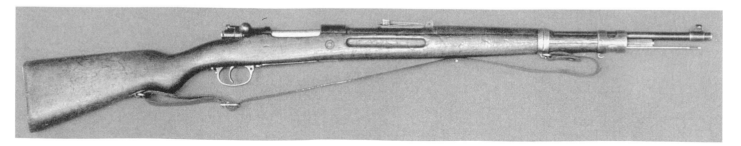

Full-length view of the Paraguayan Standard Modell Short Rifle

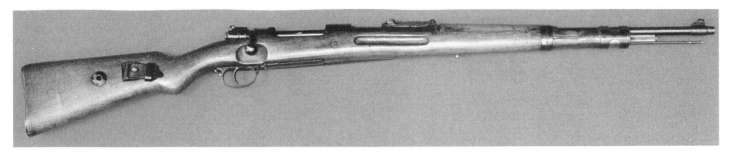

Full-length view of the Paraguayan Standard Modell Carbine

Paraguayan troops charging through arid underbrush during the Chaco War (Benjamin Banks collection)

Length: 43.25"; **Weight:** 10.0 lbs.; **Barrel:** 22.50"; **Caliber:** 7.65 x 53mm; later converted to 7.62mm; **Rifling:** 4-groove, r/hand; **Operation:** Turnbolt action; **Feed:** 5-round, staggered column, flush, box magazine; **Sights:** Tangent leaf rear sight graduated to 2000 meters. **Remarks:** "FN" logo on the receiver ring, with manufacturer's markings on the left side rail.

PARAGUAYAN STANDARD MODELL MODEL 1933 SHORT RIFLE: During the 1930s, Paraguay purchased small numbers of Standard Modell Short Rifles from Germany. All specific data on these rifles is to be found under the section on Germany.

PARAGUAYAN STANDARD MODELL MODEL 1933 CARBINE: Standard Modell Carbines were among the purchases made from Germany during the 1930s. The data for this carbine will be found in the section on Germany.

PERSIA / IRAN

Established by Cyrus the Great in 549 B.C., this troubled country has been rent by internal and external forces for centuries. Brought kicking and screaming into the twentieth century by the Shah, this nation has since attempted to turn back the clock under the Ayatollahs, while attempting to maintain military superiority in the region.

During the late nineteenth century, internal affairs in Persia became increasingly controlled by the British and the Russians, with the country divided into spheres of influence. Following World War I, Persia was recognized as an independent nation, but was virtually under a British protectorate. Reza Khan established a military dictatorship in 1921 and declared himself an hereditary monarch, Reza Shah Pahlavi, in 1925. Persia officially became Iran in 1935.

During World War II, Britain became alarmed over pro-Axis activity in Iran and occupied the country, forcing Reza Shah to abdicate in favor of his son, Mohamed Reza Shah Pahlavi. The Shah pursued a pro-Western policy of anticommunism and social and economic modernization. While popular with the business sector, the efforts of the Shah were deeply resented by the poor, as well as the rural population. The Shah was forced into exile on 16 January 1979, and after some internal struggles, the country came under the control of the Ayatollah Khomeini. The Ayatollahs and religious extremists continue to have the final say in the affairs of this unsettled country.

Persian military leaders actively and aggressively rearmed the nation during the reigns of the Reza Shah and his son. Contracts were signed with Brno for the production of the Persian Model 98/29 Rifle in caliber 8mm Mauser, which became the standard infantry weapon of the Persian army. Later, purchases were made of the VZ 24 Short Rifle and the Model 30 Carbine. The Iranians were so impressed with the Model 30 Carbine that a Czech-supervised factory was established to produce an Iranian-made version called the Model 49 Carbine. These weapons were used at various times in action against the Kurds in the northwestern regions of the country, as well as in the internal struggles that resulted In the overthrow of the Shah. Before the exit of the Shah, the army was reequipped with semiautomatic weapons.

Kurdish rebels are seen here in northwestern Iran, using Iranian Model 98/29 Rifles, and, in at least one case, a Soviet-made SKS semiautomatic carbine. (David Adamson)

Kurdish rebels, armed with Czech Model 98/29 Iranian Rifles, crossing a river in northwestern Iran, C.1960s (David Adamson)

PERSIAN MODEL 1895 RIFLE: At the beginning of the twentieth century, Persia equipped the rather meager, poorly trained Persian army with the Model 1895 Chilean-style Mauser Rifle. This rifle was the standard issue for the infantry until purchases were made of the Czech Model 98/29 Rifle in the mid-1920s. Specific data on this rifle can be found in the section on Chile.

PERSIAN FN MODEL 24/30 SHORT RIFLE: During the late 1920s, the Persian armed forces supplemented their equipment with minor purchases of the FN Export Model 24/30 Short Rifle. Full data regarding this short rifle will be found in the section on Paraguay.

PERSIAN MODEL 98/29 LONG RIFLE: Persia ordered approximately 180,000 Model 98/29 (Persian Model 1310) Long Rifles from Czechoslovakia; however, this order, which was filled from 1931 through 1938, was not completed before the takeover of Czechoslovakia by Germany. The order also included some VZ 24 Model Short Rifles, but the quantity is indeterminate.

This rifle is fitted with a pistol grip stock with grasping grooves, and the upper hand guard extends from in front of the receiver ring to just beyond the lower barrel band. There is a sling swivel on the lower barrel band and another on the buttstock, while the upper barrel band has a split type stacking swivel pivoted on the bottom. The nose cap incorporates a German-style "H" bayonet lug. The front sight has fixed sight protectors.

Length: 49.20"; **Weight:** 9.10 lbs.; **Barrel:** 29.13"; **Caliber:** 7.92 x 57mm; **Rifling:** 4-groove, r/hand; **Operation:** Turnbolt action; **Feed:** 5-round, staggered column, flush, box magazine;

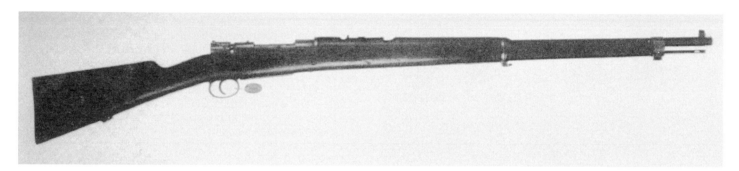

Full-length view of the Persian Model 1895 Rifle (Springfield Armory Museum)

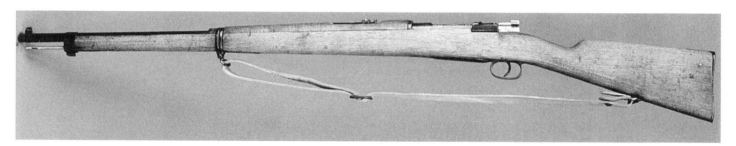

Left full-length view of the Model 1895 Rifle as used by Persia

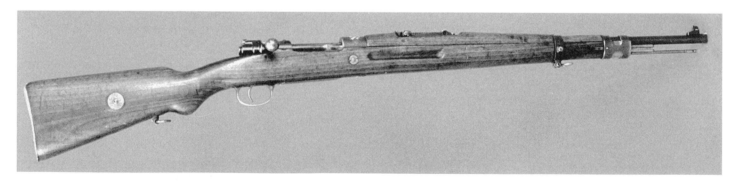

Full-length view of the FN Model 24/30 as used by Persia (Cliff Baumann collection)

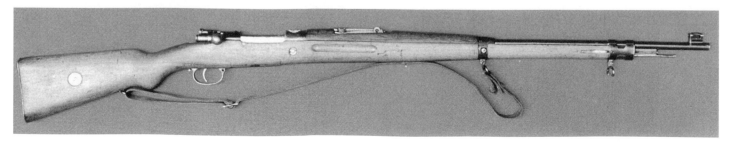

Full-length view of the Persian Model 98/29 Long Rifle (Persian Model 1310)

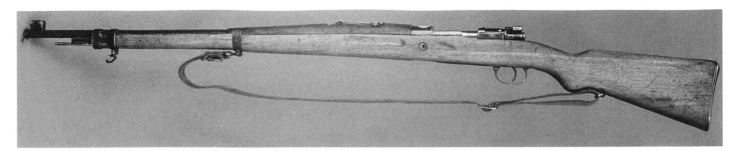

Left full-length view of the Persian Model 98/29 Long Rifle

Serial number stamped into the right side of the buttstock of the Persian Model 98/29 Long Rifle

Sights: Tangent leaf rear sight graduated to 2000 meters.
Remarks: Persian national crest on the receiver ring, with manufacturer's markings in Farsi on the left side rail.

PERSIAN CZECH MODEL VZ 24 SHORT RIFLE: Czech Model VZ 24 Short Rifles were part of the last order placed with Brno before the fall of Czechoslovakia. While some of these short rifles were re-

ceived, the total number is not known. Specific data relative to this short rifle will be found under the section on Czechoslovakia.

PERSIAN CZECH MODEL 30 CARBINE: The Persian Czech Model 30 (Persian Model 1317) Carbine is a handy, chunky weapon, fit-

Receiver ring of the Persian Model 98/29 Long Rifle showing the Persian national crest

Receiver ring of the Persian Model 98/29 Long Rifle showing the Persian national crest

ted with a pistol grip stock with grasping grooves. The upper hand guard runs from the front of the receiver ring to the upper barrel band. The upper and lower barrel bands are quite close together, with the upper one retained by a spring on the right side. The nose cap features a short German-style "H" bayonet lug. There is a swivel on the bottom of the lower barrel band, and a round, cavalry-style sling ring on the left side of the lower barrel band; another swivel is at the bottom of the buttstock. The bolt handle is bent down, and the stock has been cut out in order to facilitate operation of the bolt handle. There is a marking disk inset into the right side of the buttstock.

Length: 37.99"; **Weight:** 8.33 lbs.; **Barrel:** 17.91"; **Caliber:** 7.92 x 57mm; **Rifling:** 4-groove, r/hand; **Operation:** Turnbolt action; **Feed:** 5-round, staggered column, flush, box magazine; **Sights:** Tangent leaf rear sight graduated to 2000 meters. **Remarks:** Persian national crest on the receiver ring, with manufacturer's markings in Farsi on the left side rail.

IRANIAN MODEL 49 CARBINE: Manufactured by the Iranians in the state rifle factory set up by the Czechs in Mosalsalsasi, this is a modification of the Czech-made Model 30 Carbine. The lower and upper barrel bands are stamped from sheet steel and retained by a single spring on the right hand side. The lower barrel band incorporates a fixed sling bar on the left side, while a German-style sling slot is cut through the buttstock. The stock is made from an indigenous wood, lighter and less dense than walnut.

Rear sight graduated in Farsi of the Persian Czech Model VZ 24 Short Rifle

Manufacturer's markings stamped in Farsi on the side rail of the Persian Czech Model VZ 24 Short Rifle

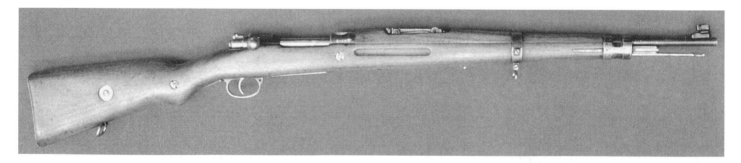

Full-length view of the Persian Czech Model VZ 24 Short Rifle

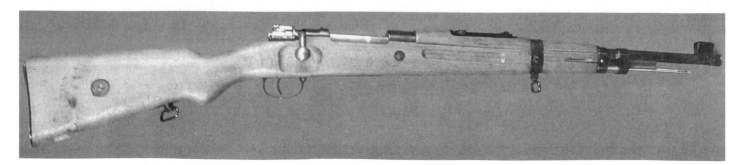

Full-length view of the Persian Czech Model 30 Carbine

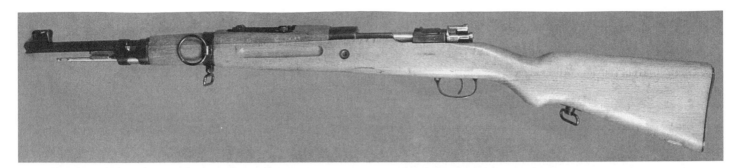

Left full-length view of the Czech Model 30 Carbine

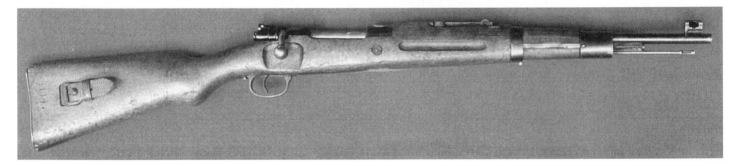

Full-length view of the Iranian Model 49 Carbine

Left side view of the receiver ring and side rail of the Iranian Model 49 Carbine, with the manufacturer's markings stamped in Farsi

Length: 38.18"; **Weight:** 8.60 lbs.; **Barrel:** 18.11"; **Caliber:** 7.92 x 57mm; **Rifling:** 4-groove, r/hand; **Operation:** Turnbolt action; **Feed:** 5-round, staggered column, flush, box magazine; **Sights:** Tangent leaf rear sight graduated to 2000 meters. **Remarks:** Iranian national crest on the receiver ring, with the manufacturer's markings stamped on the left side rail.

PERU

Peru, the site of the great Incan empire, was conquered by Francisco Pizarro of Spain in 1571. Due to its great wealth of precious metals and a compliant indigenous population, Peru quickly became a jewel in the crown of Spanish conquest. Lima, the capital city, was founded in 1535, and became the political and administrative center for the Spanish conquest of all South America. Peru achieved liberty in 1821 with the defeat of royalist forces by the armies of Bolívar and San Martín at the battles of Junin and Ayachuco.

Political growth was stormy for the new republic, and an attempt at confederation with Bolivia collapsed with the Chilean invasion of 1839. Chile defeated Peru in the War of the Pacific (1879 - 1883) and occupied Lima and Callao for two years, saddling the Peruvian nation with a crushing war debt. This debt resulted in the loss of much of the Peruvian infrastructure to foreigners.

Civilian leadership prevailed from 1895 to 1930, then there was a period of military rule until 1939, when Manuel Prado was elected president, serving until 1945. It was during Prado's presidency that Peru conducted a victorious war with Ecuador, gaining a great deal of Ecuadoran territory. This war with Ecuador was militarily outstanding due to the close cooperation between the Peruvian army, naval, and air arms. It represented the first time paratroops were actively employed in battle in South America, with close-in air support of army personnel by the Peruvian air force. The Peruvian navy, in conjunction with the drives by the army, provided close naval support.

The Peruvian military took control of the country in 1968, instituting reforms that included the nationalization of Standard Oil's International Petroleum Company holdings, as well as restructuring the economic and political power within the infrastructure. Political power was returned to civilian control in 1980. In 1985, under the leadership of president Alan García Pérez, the country started reduction of its foreign debt; however this period ushered in the brutal period of insurgency by the Shining Path ("El Sendero Luminoso"), a dedicated group of Communist-inspired rebels.

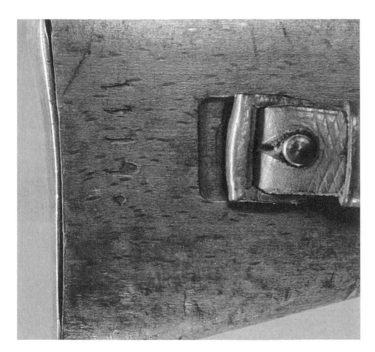

Serial number in Farsi on the butt of the Iranian Model 49 Carbine

The Peruvian national crest on the receiver ring of the Peruvian Model 1891 Rifle

Side rail of the Peruvian Model 1891 Rifle, showing the "MAUSER MODELO ARGENTINO 1891," and the "DWM" logo

With the election of president Alberto Fujimori in 1990, martial law was imposed throughout Peru, resulting in the suppression of the excesses of the Shining Path. The movement has now been reduced to ineffectualness, and the Peruvian economy is growing. Tensions have once again flared with Ecuador over the common border area, but after several skirmishes, the situation presently lies dormant.

PERUVIAN MODEL 1891 RIFLE: Between 1892 and 1895, Peru purchased a total of thirty thousand Model 1891 Rifles from Ludwig Loewe & Co. This rifle is identical to the Argentinian Model 1891 Rifle, with the exception of the markings. These rifles were originally fitted with a standard leaf rear sight, however a modernization program was instituted in 1912 to enable the weapons to handle the 7.65 x 53mm spitzer, or improved pointed-bullet ammunition. These rifles will be found with the "Lange Vizier" rear sight, similar to that of the Gew. 98.

The rifle is fitted with a straight-wristed stock, with the typical short upper hand guard extending from in front of the rear sight to the lower barrel band. The lower barrel band is fitted with a swivel on the bottom, and there is another on the bottom of the buttstock. The nose cap has a bayonet lug on the bottom for use with the Model 1895 bayonet.

Length: 48.62"; **Weight:** 9.04 lbs.; **Barrel:** 29.09"; **Caliber:** 7.65 x 53mm; **Rifling:** 4-groove, r/hand; **Operation:** Turnbolt action; **Feed:** 5-round, vertical column, box magazine; **Sights:** Lange Vizier rear sight graduated to 2000 meters. **Remarks:** Peruvian national crest on the receiver ring, with the manufacturer's markings stamped on the left side rail.

PERUVIAN MODEL 1891 CARBINE: Information obtained indicates that a number of Peruvian Model 1891 Rifles were arsenal converted to carbine configuration by the Peruvian authorities.

Aside from length and weight, these carbines are identical to the Peruvian Model 1891 Rifle, including the "Lange Vizier" rear sight.

Length: 37.25"; **Weight:** 7.0 lbs.; **Barrel:** 19.75"; **Caliber:** 7.65 x 53mm; **Rifling:** 4-groove, r/hand; **Operation:** Turnbolt action; **Feed:** 5-round, vertical column, box magazine; **Sights:** Lange Vizier rear sight graduated to 2000 meters. **Remarks:** Peruvian national crest on the receiver ring, with the model designation on the left side rail.

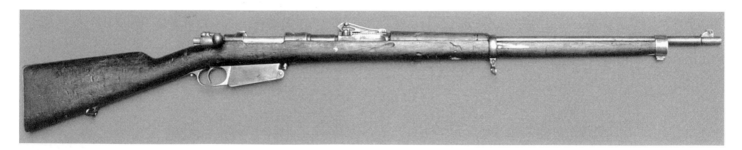

Full-length view of the Peruvian Model 1891 Rifle

Full-length view of the Model 1891 Rifle converted to Carbine configuration. This was originally an Argintinian Model 1891 Rifle converted to Carbine configuration and sold to Peru with the Peruvian crest added.

The left side rail, showing the manufacturer's markings, on the Peruvian Model 1891 Carbine

PERUVIAN MODEL 1909 RIFLE: Between 1910 and 1914, Peru purchased approximately fifty thousand Model 1909 Rifles from Waffenfabrik Mauser. The rifle is basically the export version of the Gew. 98 Rifle, including the "Lange Vizier" rear sight. The rifle is fitted with a pistol grip stock without grasping grooves, with the short style upper hand guard running from in front of the rear sight to the lower barrel band. The lower barrel band has a swivel on the bottom, and the bottom of the buttstock is fitted for a quick-release sling attachment. The upper barrel band incorporates a parade hook on the bottom for the shortening of the sling for parade use. The nose cap utilizes a German-style "H" bayonet lug that accepts the specially made Peruvian Model S 98 bayonet. The action incorporates an auxiliary locking lug, a nonrotating extractor, and the early, heavy, 1904-style cocking piece. The Peruvian Model 1909 Rifle is unusual in that the receiver ring is longer than normal, with several other dimensions deviating from that of the standard Gew. 98 Rifle.

The Peruvian national crest on the receiver ring of the Peruvian Model 1891 Carbine

Peruvian national crest on the receiver ring of the Peruvian Model 1909 Rifle (Lothar Frank collection)

PERUVIAN MODEL 1895 RIFLE: Peru acquired an unknown quantity of Chilean-style Model 1895 Rifles; these rifles are standard for this period, and all relevant data concerning the rifle may be found in the section on Chile.

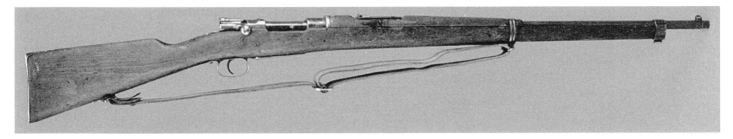

Full-length view of the Model 1895 Rifle as used by Peru

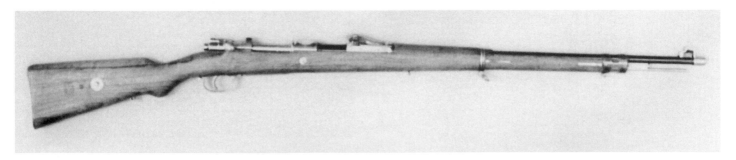

Full-length view of the Peruvian Model 1909 Rifle. Note the original Peruvian muzzle cover. (Lothar Frank collection)

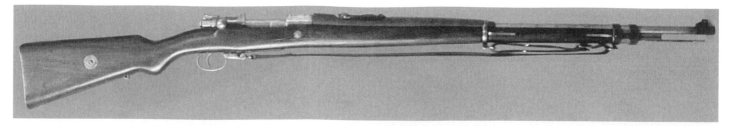

Full-length view of an unusual Peruvian Model 1909 Rifle. Note the tangent leaf rear sight rather than the usual "Lange Vizier" rear sight.

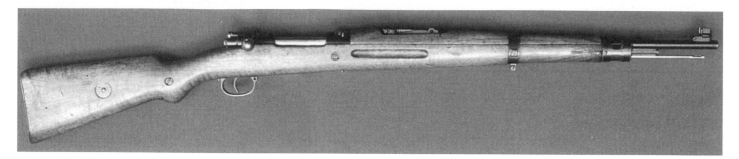

Full-length view of the Czech VZ 24 Short Rifle as used by Peru

Length: 49.2"; **Weight:** 9.0 lbs.; **Barrel:** 29.13"; **Caliber:** 7.65 x 53mm; **Rifling:** 4-groove, r/hand; **Operation:** Turnbolt action; **Feed:** 5-round, staggered column, flush, box magazine; **Sights:** "Lange Vizier" rear sight graduated to 2000 meters. **Remarks:** Peruvian national crest on the receiver ring, with manufacturer's markings stamped on the left side rail. Mauser Banner logo and proofs stamped into the right side of the stock.

PERUVIAN CZECH MODEL VZ 24 SHORT RIFLE: During 1930, Peru purchased a small number of VZ 24 Short Rifles, estimated at less than one thousand, from Czechoslovakia. These short rifles are the standard export model, and it is not known if the Peruvian crest appears on the receiver ring. All specific data relative to this short rifle can be found in the section on Czechoslovakia.

Peru placed orders with Brno for a modest number of Peruvian VZ32 Short Rifles, loosely based upon the Czech VZ 16/33, but subject to Peruvian needs and desires.

Manufacturer's markings stamped on the left side rail of the Peruvian Model 1909 Rifle (Lothar Frank collection)

Caliber markings in electric pencil on the right side of the receiver ring of the above Peruvian Model 1909 Rifle

Mauser Banner logo and proof stamped into the right side of the buttstock of the Peruvian Model 1909 Rifle (Lothar Frank collection)

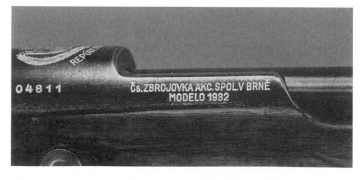

View of the side rail of the Peruvian VZ32 Short Rifle showing the markings in Czech, but plainly showing the Model 32

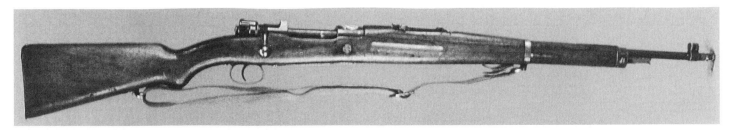

Full-length view of the right side of the Peruvian VZ32 Short Rifle; note the turned down bolt handle and the finger groove stock

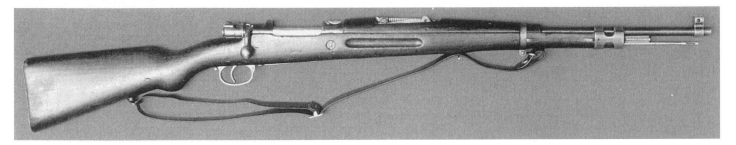

Full-length view of the Peruvian Model 1935 Short Rifle

Top view of the receiver area of the Peruvian VZ32 Short Rifle, showing the Peruvian crest

Peruvian national crest on the receiver ring of the Peruvian Model 1935 Short Rifle

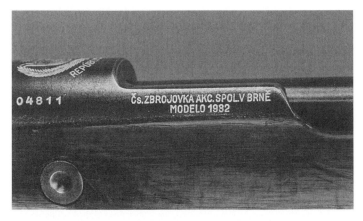

View of the side rail of the Peruvian VZ32 Short Rifle showing the markings in Czech, but plainly showing the Model 32

The side rail with manufacturer's markings on the Peruvian Model 1935 Short Rifle

PERUVIAN MODEL 1935 SHORT RIFLE: During the late 1930s, Peru purchased an indeterminate number of short rifles from FN that were designated the Peruvian Model 1935. This is a standard export model short rifle as produced for a number of countries, with one exception—the Peruvian Model 1935 has a reversed safety, with the safety being on when turned to the left.

The short rifle is fitted with a pistol grip stock with grasping grooves, and the upper hand guard extends from the front of the receiver ring to just beyond the lower barrel band. The lower barrel band has a swivel on the bottom, and there is another on the bottom of the buttstock. The nose cap incorporates a German-style "H" bayonet lug.

Length: 43.10"; **Weight:** 8.9 lbs.; **Barrel:** 23.19"; **Caliber:** 7.65 x53mm (Many later converted to .30-06 and so marked); **Rifling:** 4-groove, r/hand; **Operation:** Turnbolt action; **Feed:** 5-round, staggered column, flush, box magazine; **Sights:** Tangent leaf rear sight graduated to 2000 meters. **Remarks:** Peruvian national crest on the receiver ring, with manufacturer's markings stamped on the left side rail.

POLAND

Poland, a once strong and united kingdom, was partitioned and dismembered as a nation by Sweden, Prussia, Russia, and Austria in 1795. Long used as a pawn in territorial chess by stronger nations, Poland did not rise as a country once again until after the fall of Russia in 1917. Reconstituted by the efforts of Joséf Pilsudski, Poland wrested victory and a new nation from the Bolshevik regime of Russia.

As part of war booty from Germany and Austria following the end of the first World War, Poland received large numbers of German weapons, both Gew. 98 Rifles and Model 98AZ Carbines, in reality short rifles. Production facilities from the Danzig arsenal were established in Warsaw shortly after the end of the war, with a move made to Radom in the 1920s. The Gew. 98-style rifle produced for Poland, of which few were made, is almost indistinguishable from the German model. The Model 98AZ-style short rifle, however, differs in having a sling bar on the left side of the stock, in addition to swivels suspended under the lower barrel band and the bottom of the stock. The familiar stacking rod has a squared elbow extending from the nose cap, which also helps identify the Polish version of this weapon. These rifles were all used in the Russo-Polish War that ended in 1921.

In 1929, Poland decided that the Czech VZ 24 and the FN Mle 24 Short Rifle designs had much to recommend them, and a new

Polish cavalry troops on maneuvers prior to the outbreak of World War II. Note the cavalry-style Model 98A Short Rifles, and the use of the French "Adrian" steel helmet.

Polish short rifle, the Wz 29, was patterned on the basic design of these two weapons. This was the standard service weapon at the start of World War II, when Poland was invaded on 1 September 1939. All Wz 29 Short Rifle stocks are cut for a bent bolt handle; however, the short rifle was produced with a straight bolt handle for infantry use, while the weapon issued to the cavalry has a bent bolt handle.

When Germany overran Poland, many of the short rifles were converted to G29/40 specifications by Austrian arms plants. The use of Polish bayonets was quite widespread, helping to alleviate the chronic shortages felt by the Wehrmacht.

POLISH MODEL 98 RIFLE: Produced on machinery from the Danzig arsenal, the Polish 98 differs from the Gewehr 98 in having a tangent rear sight instead of the "Lange Vizier" rear sight of the Germans, although the first pieces off the production line were equipped with the original "Lange" rear sight. The pistol grip stock has grasping grooves, and the typical German short upper hand guard extends from the front of the rear sight to just beyond the lower barrel band. In all other respects, the rifle is identical to the Gew. 98, and specific data on the rifle can be found under the section on Germany.

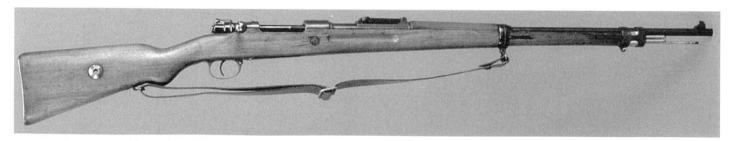

Full-length view of the Polish version of the Model 98 Rifle

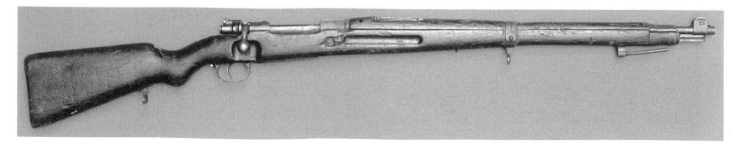

Full-length view of the Polish version of the Model 98AZ Carbine (Century International Arms, Inc.)

Polish markings on the receiver ring of the Polish version of the Model 98AZ Carbine. Note the lack of a date on this specimen. (Century International Arms, Inc.)

Close-up view of the markings "PFK WARSZAWA/1929" on the receiver ring of the Model Wz 29 Short Rifle. (Robert Jensen collection)

POLISH MODEL 98AZ CARBINE: With some minor changes, this Polish version of the German Model 98AZ Carbine is identical to that produced by the Germans in World War I. The major difference is a change in design of the stacking rod found under the nose cap; the elbow of the stacking rod is square, rather than rounded as in the German version. The other difference is the attachment of a sling bar on the left side of the stock, while still providing a swivel on the bottom of the lower barrel band and the bottom of the stock. The wood used for the stock is not usually walnut but a less dense native wood. All specific data relative to this weapon will be found in the section on Germany.

POLISH Wz 29 SHORT RIFLE: Manufactured in the Radom plant, and based upon the best of the designs of the Czech VZ 24 Short Rifle and the FN Model 24 Short Rifle, the Polish Wz 29 Short Rifle is reminiscent of both weapons. The pistol grip stock is fitted with grasping grooves and an upper hand guard that normally runs from the front of the receiver ring to the upper barrel band. In the Czech-oslovakian manner, the lower barrel band is held in place by means of a transverse screw, with a swivel suspended from the bottom; another swivel was attached to the bottom of the buttstock. Additionally, a sling bar is attached to the left side of the buttstock. The front sight is protected by sight ears. A hollow washer is set into the stock to facilitate disassembly of the firing mechanism.

A posed group of Polish soldiers, circa 1919-1925; note the stacked Polish 98 rifles with the "Lange Vizier" rear sight, indicating that not all had the tangent rear sight.

Side rail markings on the Polish-produced Model 98 AZ Carbine. The only designation is "K 98." (Century International Arms, Inc.)

Receiver markings on the Polish Model Wz 29 Short Rifle (Springfield Armory Museum)

Markings on the receiver of the Wz 29 Short Rifle made from World War I reparation parts. Note the diamond-shape Radom symbol above the C.G. Haenel markings. (Century International Arms, Inc.)

Side rail markings on the Wz 29 Short Rifle made from World War I reparation parts (Century International Arms, Inc.)

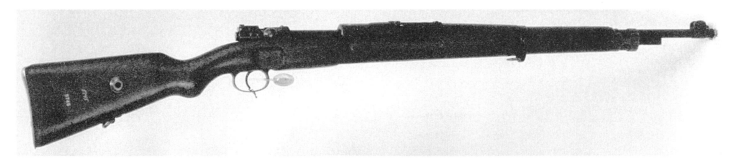

Full-length view of the Polish Model Wz 29 Short Rifle (Springfield Armory Museum)

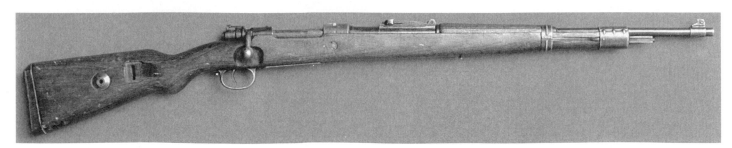

Full-length view of a Radom-marked Wz 29 Short Rifle made from World War I reparation parts (Century International Arms, Inc.)

Length: 43.40"; **Weight:** 9.0 lbs.; **Barrel:** 23.62"; **Caliber:** 7.92 x 57mm; **Rifling:** 4-groove, r/hand; **Operation:** Turnbolt action; **Feed:** 5-round, staggered column, flush, box magazine; **Sights:** Tangent leaf rear sight graduated to 2000 meters. **Remarks:** Polish crest/maker's name/date on the receiver ring, with the model designation on the side rail.

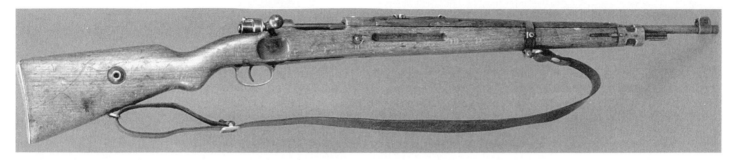

Full-length view of the Polish Wz 29 Short Rifle as issued for infantry. Note the straight bolt handle.

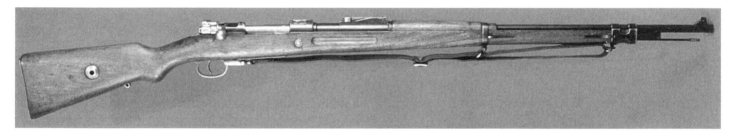

Full-length view of the Polish Wz 29 Short Rifle as issued for cavalry. Note the bent bolt handle.

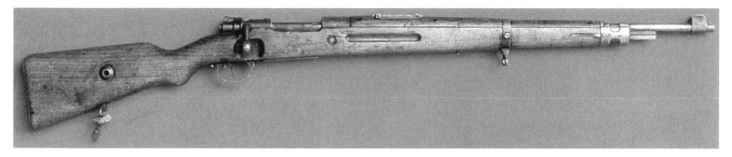

Seldom found is this Polish Model Wz 98a Rifle, which was produced in the middle to late 1930s

Full-length view of the Polish Model Wz 29 Training Short Rifle in .22 caliber. In all other respects, this is identical to the standard short rifle.

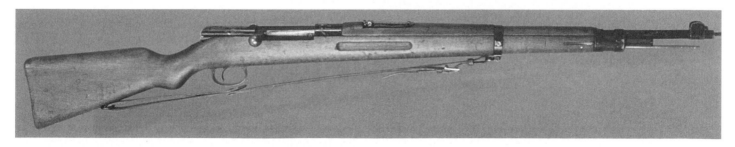

Full-length view of a purpose-built, Radom-made .22 caliber training rifle, built on the configuration of the Polish Wz 29 Short Rifle. This the Model Kbk. 8 wz31.

Receiver markings on the Polish Model Wz 98a Rifle, indicating production in 1937

Side rail markings on the Polish Model Wz 98a Rifle

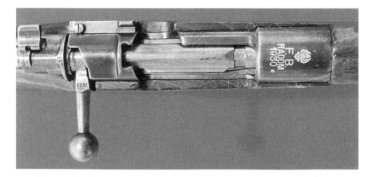

Markings on top of the receiver ring of the Polish Model Wz 29 Training Short Rifle

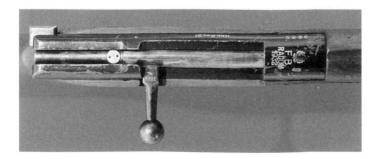

The action and the receiver markings on the .22 caliber Radom Training Rifle

Twenty-two caliber designation burned into the upper hand guard of the Polish Model Wz 29 Training Short Rifle

Side rail markings on the Polish Model Wz 98a Rifle

PORTUGAL

A fundamentally poor nation, Portugal has been independent since it won recognition as a kingdom in 1143. A seafaring nation since before Columbus, it was this expertise that gave them the status of a world empire in the fifteenth and sixteenth centuries. Portugal controlled the coast of West Africa, the countries bordering the Indian Ocean, many lands in southern Asia, as well as Brazil. However, with the rise of Spain and the Netherlands as empire builders, Portugal quickly sank to second or third rate status.

During the nineteenth century, civil wars weakened the nation, resulting in British control of their foreign policy. In 1910, Portugal became the first kingdom in the twentieth century to become a republic; however, chaos reigned, forcing the military to intervene and create a military dictatorship. In 1928, the military installed a civilian dictator, Antonio Salazar. With the backing of the military, he ruled through civilian governments, controlling the economy and the political scene for generations. In spite of the stability provided by the Salazar regime, the country was the most impoverished in Europe.

After World War II, Portugal was caught up in the storm of decolonialization. Nevertheless, it refused to consider its overseas possessions as colonies, but rather "overseas provinces." This led to tragic colonial wars, with terrible strains on the Portuguese economy and devastating military losses. The colonies won independence in spite of every means used to retain them. Following this, Portugal went through many political upheavals, until 1987 when the Social Democrats won an absolute majority. Under the principle of free enterprise, this turned the country around and it is no longer the poorest in the European Community.

In 1904, the Mauser-Vergueiro Rifle in 6.5 x 58Pmm was adopted by the Portuguese military; these weapons were all produced by DWM, and are of very high quality. Prior to this, the military had been equipped with the Kropatschek tubular magazine rifle, and before that by the Portuguese Guedes lever action rifle. The Portuguese army was well served by the Mauser-Vergueiro Rifle, but in 1937 contracted with Germany for deliveries of the Model 937-A, a short rifle in caliber 7.92 x 57mm, quite similar to the Model K98k Carbine. With the adoption of the Model 937-A, it was found desirable to convert the stocks of the 1904 Mauser-Vergueiro Rifles to more closely conform to the Model 937-A configuration. These converted weapons were designated Model 904/M39. During the Second World War, arrangements were made for the purchase of Model 1941 Carbines, which are identical to the German Model K98k Carbine, except for the markings. These shipments continued until 1943.

All of these weapons were used at one time or another in the Portuguese overseas possessions, as well as in Portugal itself. They were carried by the Portuguese "volunteers" who fought on the Nationalist side during the Spanish Civil War; others were captured by Colonel von Lettow-Vorbeck from Portuguese forces in East Africa during the First World War, and then turned against the British. No doubt some were used or held in reserve for the colonial wars fought in the 1960s.

PORTUGUESE MODEL 1904 MAUSER-VERGUEIRO RIFLE: This rifle in 6.5 x 58Pmm was designed by Vergueiro, a Portuguese officer, in conjunction with the designers at DWM. This rifle is easily recognized by the split-bridge receiver, with the bolt handle turned down in front of the bridge so that the bridge acts as a safety lug in the event of failure of the front lugs. The rifle actually combines the best features of the Gew. 98 Rifle with a split-bridge receiver and a modified Mannlicher-Schoenauer bolt.

The rifle is fitted with a shallow pistol grip stock, and the upper hand guard runs from the front of the receiver ring to the lower barrel band. The upper band is quite simple, and the nose cap incorporates a short, German-style "H" bayonet lug. There is a swivel on the bottom of the lower barrel band and another on the bottom of the stock. The rifle cocks partially on the opening and partially on the closing of the bolt. There is a magazine floor plate release in the front of the trigger guard similar to that in the Argentine Model 1909 Rifle.

Length: 48.20"; **Weight:** 8.4 lbs.; **Barrel:** 29.13"; **Caliber:** 6.5 x 58Pmm; **Rifling:** 4-groove, r/hand; **Operation:** Turnbolt action; **Feed:** 5-round, staggered column, flush, box magazine; **Sights:** Tangent leaf rear sight graduated to 2000 meters. **Remarks:** The

The crown and initial of King Carlos I on the receiver ring of the Portuguese Model 1904 Mauser-Vergueiro Rifle

The left side rail of the Portuguese Model 1904 Mauser-Vergueiro Rifle, showing the model designation and caliber in Portuguese and the manufacturer in German

crest of King Carlos I on the receiver ring, with the model designation in Portuguese on the side rail, and the manufacturer's markings also on the side rail.

PORTUGUESE MODEL 904/M39 RIFLE: In order to conform with the .792 x 57mm Portuguese Model 937-A Short Rifle purchased in the 1930s, the Portuguese Model 1904 Mauser-Vergueiro Rifle was converted to more closely conform with the configuration of the

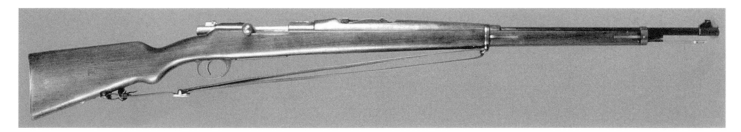

Full-length view of the Portuguese Model 1904 Mauser-Vergueiro Rifle

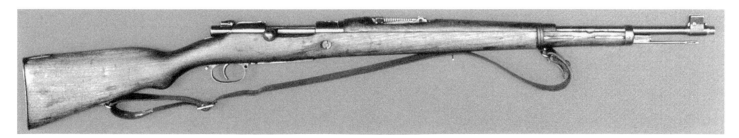

Full-length view of the Portuguese Model 937/M39 Rifle

Note that the markings on the receiver ring of the Portuguese Model 937/M39 are the same as on the Model 1904 Mauser-Vergueiro Rifle

Model 937-A Short Rifle. This consisted of reboring and rechambering the rifle to 7.92 x 57mm, shortening the barrel and the forend, and modifying the front sight by the addition of sight protectors. Markings were not changed.

Length: 42.80"; **Weight:** 8.1 lbs.; **Barrel:** 23.62"; **Caliber:** 7.92 x 57mm; **Rifling:** 4-groove, r/hand; **Operation:** Turnbolt action; **Feed:** 5-round, staggered column, flush, box magazine; **Sights:** Tangent leaf rear sight graduated to 2000 meters. **Remarks:** All markings are the same as on the Model 1904 Mauser-Vergueiro Rifle.

PORTUGUESE STANDARD MODELL MODEL 1933 MAUSER SHORT RIFLE: In order to alleviate the pressing need for more modern weapons, the Portuguese purchased an undetermined number of Standard Modell Short Rifles from Germany, especially at the time of the Spanish Civil War. These weapons are the standard export models, and do not differ in any way from other Standard Modell Short Rifles. All specific data on this rifle will be found in the section on Germany.

PORTUGUESE STANDARD MODELL MODEL 1933 MAUSER CARBINE: Portugal also ordered a number of the 1933 Standard Modell Carbines at the same time as the Standard Modell Short Rifles, but the quantity is unknown. This is the standard export model and does not differ in any manner from other Standard Modell Carbines. All information relative to this carbine will be found in the section on Germany.

PORTUGUESE MODEL 937-A SHORT RIFLE: In 1937, Portugal adopted the Model 937-A Short Rifle as the replacement for the Model 1904 Mauser-Vergueiro Rifle. This rifle is very similar to the German K98k Carbine, with only minor differences. Chief among these is a swivel on the bottom of the lower barrel band, with a sling attachment both on the bottom of the stock and on the left side of the buttstock. The front sight is also protected by sight ears.

Length: 41.43"; **Weight:** 8.73 lbs.; **Barrel:** 23.62"; **Caliber:** 7.92 x 57mm; **Rifling:** 4-groove, r/hand; **Operation:** Turnbolt action; **Feed:** 5-round, staggered column, flush, box magazine; **Sights:** Tangent leaf rear sight graduated to 2000 meters. **Remarks:** Portuguese national crest on the receiver ring, manufacturer's markings on the left side rail.

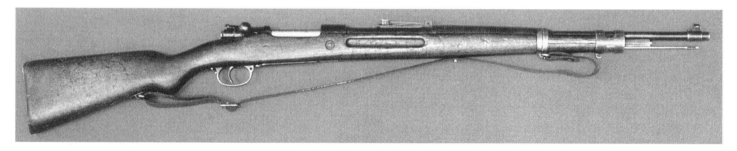

Full-length view of the Standard Modell Short Rifle as used by Portugal

Full-length view of the Standard Modell Carbine as used by Portugal

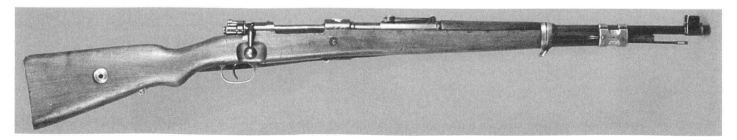

Full-length view of the Portuguese Model 937-A Short Rifle

The receiver ring of the Portuguese Model 937-A Short Rifle, showing the Portuguese national crest over the date of manufacture

Receiver ring with Portuguese crest over the date on the Portuguese Model 41 Short Rifle

Manufacturer's markings stamped on the side rail of the Portuguese Model 41 Short Rifle

The left side of the buttstock of the Portuguese Model 937-A Short Rifle, showing the quick-release sling attachment and deeply cut out section of stock

PORTUGUESE MODEL 1941 SHORT RIFLE: As production continued on the Portuguese Model 937-A, the weapon was subjected to minor changes that brought it more into conformity with the standard K98k Carbine. While referred to as the Model 41 Short Rifle, it is not clear whether this is official nomenclature. Changes in design consist of a cupped butt plate, a side bar on the lower barrel band, and a slotted stock for the typical German-style sling. The front sight retains the sight protectors that help identify this model. Stocks held in Germany in 1944 were released to the Wehrmacht.

Manufacturer's markings stamped on the side rail of the Portuguese Model 41 Short Rifle

German Waffenamt stamp on the right side of the buttstock of the Portuguese Model 41 Short Rifle

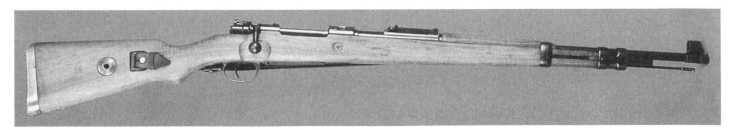

Full-length view of the Portuguese Model 41 Short Rifle

ROMANIA

Romania, for centuries one of the poorest countries in Europe, has had a turbulent and chaotic political and social history. Switching sides three times in World War I, Romania ended the war on the side of the Allies and, by the terms of the peace treaty, doubled the size of the country at the expense of its neighbors. The years between the wars were a turbulent period for Romania; in 1940, Russia took back Bessarabia and Northern Bukovina under the terms of the Hitler-Stalin pact, while Hitler forced Romania to return half of Transylvania to Hungary, her ancient enemy.

During this time, Romania was ruled by King Carol, who twice entered exile, leaving his son, Prince Michael, on the throne. At the start of the Second World War, the pro-Hitler dictator Marshal Ion Antonescu assumed power with the backing of the Romanian "Iron Guard." When the Guard attempted a coup, it was crushed by the military. Romania, though pro-Allied, was forced into the position of helping Germany invade Russia, mainly in an attempt to regain their lost provinces. Romania, under then King Michael, had the third largest Axis army, and when the country switched sides in 1944, they formed the fourth largest Allied army.

Romanian sentries armed with Romanian VZ 24 Short Rifles standing guard near the Russian border, C. 1940 (Photoworld)

During the First World War, and into the postwar years, the arms situation of the Romanian army was a supply officer's nightmare. Originally equipped with 6.5mm Model 1892 and 1893 Romanian Mannlicher Rifles and Carbines, by the end of World War I, various

The receiver ring of the Romanian Model VZ 24 Short Rifle, showing the crest of King Carol

The receiver ring of the Romanian Model VZ 24 Short Rifle, showing the crest of King Michael

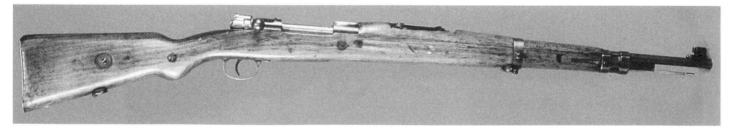

Full-length view of the Czech VZ 24 Short Rifle as used by Romania

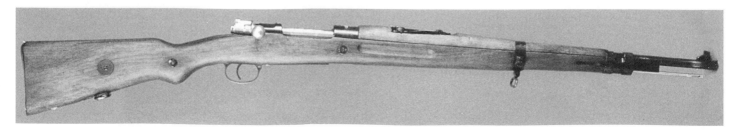

Full-length view of a later Romanian Model VZ 24 Short Rifle, as used during the reign of King Michael

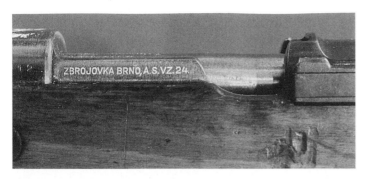

Manufacturer's markings stamped on the left side rail of the Romanian Model VZ 24 Short Rifle

military formations were armed with a huge variety of weapons, including Steyr 8mm Model 1895 Rifles and Carbines, French 8mm Model 1907 Mannlicher Berthier Rifles and Carbines, Russian Model 1891 Rifles, and at a later date, FN Model 1924 Short Rifles.

In the late 1920s and the early 1930s, Romania decided in favor of standardizing on the Czech Model VZ 24 Short Rifle in caliber 7.92 x 57mm; unfortunately, the services were not fully equipped with the new weapons at the start of the Second World War, necessitating the continued use of the other weapons held in reserve, mainly the Romanian Model 1892 and 1893 Rifles.

ROMANIAN CZECH MODEL VZ 24 SHORT RIFLE: This short rifle as used by Romania is the standard Czech VZ 24 Short Rifle of Czechoslovakia, differing only in the crests of King Carol and King Michael on the receiver ring. All relative information on this weapon can be found in the section on Czechoslovakia.

SAUDI ARABIA

In ancient times, various cultures flourished independently in certain areas of the Arabian Peninsula, especially along the coastal sections of the western rim. There was little or no cohesion amongst the peoples until the rise of Mohammed, the holy prophet of Islam. Mohammed fled from Mecca to Medina, a nearby city, in 622 A.D., which dates the start of the Islamic era. In 1517, Mecca came under the power of the Ottoman Empire, but the Turks never fully controlled Arabia.

In 1902, Ibn Saud and his family controlled Riyadh, and led a Wahabi revolt against Turkish rule in 1912 and 1913; unsuccessful at the time, the Saudis were aided by the British during the First World War. In 1915, Britain established a protectorate over the region, and consolidated her position after the war ended. Ibn Saud extended his control over the country, with his kingdom officially recognized by Great Britain in 1927. In 1932, the country was renamed Saudi Arabia.

The discovery of oil in the peninsula transformed the country from an impoverished nation to one of great mineral wealth. While paying huge subsidies to other Arab nations, the Saudis have not contributed greatly to the past anti-Israel campaigns, other than token forces to show solidarity with their Arab brothers.

In the 1930s, following the renaming of the country, an effort was made to provide a paramilitary force capable of acting in a qua-

si-police manner to control the population. It was at this time that purchases of FN Model 30 Short Rifles were made by the Saudi authorities. How many were received, or how they were marked, if at all, can only be assumed.

SAUDI ARABIAN FN MODEL 30 SHORT RIFLE: This is the standard FN Model 30 export short rifle as used by many other nations. The rifle is fitted with a pistol grip stock with grasping grooves, with the upper hand guard extending from the front of the receiver ring to just beyond the lower barrel band. The lower barrel band has a swivel at the bottom, with another at the bottom of the buttstock. The nose cap incorporates a German-style "H" bayonet lug, though whether or not a bayonet was used by the Saudi forces is open to question. The bolt handle is straight.

Length: 43.10"; **Weight:** 8.9 lbs.; **Barrel:** 23.19"; **Caliber:** 7.92 x 57mm; **Rifling:** 4-groove, r/hand; **Operation:** Turnbolt action; **Feed:** 5-round, staggered column, flush, box magazine; **Sights:** Tangent leaf rear sight graduated to 2000 meters. **Remarks:** Believed to have the FN logo on the receiver ring, with the manufacturer's markings on the side rail.

SERBIA / YUGOSLAVIA

The nucleus of the lands that composed the Roman Empire province of Illyricum in the first century A.D. was Serbia. Basically settled by South Slav migrants, the Serbian empire hit its zenith during the reign of Stephen Dushan (1331-1335) when Albania, Macedonia, Thessaly, Epirus, and Bulgaria came under Serbian control. Within thirty years of the death of Dushan, the Ottoman Empire had absorbed the territory of Serbia into its vast holdings, and Serbia was not to be independent again until 1878.

Serbia was involved in the Balkan Wars of 1912 and 1913, which led directly to the First World War. Serbia fought a brilliant campaign against the Austrians and the Germans, as well as repulsing the Bulgarians in the southeast. Eventually overwhelmed by su-

Serbia's most youthful soldier! Only 12 years old, armed with a Model 1908 Carbine, and serving in the fighting around Belgrad in the first months of World War I. (Underwood and Underwood)

Full-length view of the FN Model 30 Short Rifle as used by Saudi Arabia (Cliff Baumann collection)

Serbian troops are seen firing from a temporary trench, C. 1914. (Underwood and Underwood)

Serbian troops advancing during the First Balkan War (Foto-Tanjug)

The coming together of the Serbian and the Montenegrin armies in southern Serbia during the First Balkan War, 1912 (Foto-Tanjug)

perior forces, and unable to be supported by the Allies due to distance and logistics, the Serbian forces undertook a valiant fighting retreat through the mountains of Albania, from where they were transported by Allied naval vessels to the Greek Dodecanese islands. Here, the Serbs were eventually reequipped by the Allies and continued to fight in the Salonika campaign. Serbs were even to be found in the Allied Expedition in North Russia after the armistice was signed.

During 1918 and 1919, the Kingdom of Yugoslavia was cobbled together from the former Austrian lands of Croatia and Slovenia, Bosnia and Herzegovina, Macedonia, Montenegro, and Kossovo; together they formed the multicultural and multiethnic nation known as the Kingdom of the Serbs, Croats and Slovenes. Coexisting in a state of mutual hostility, a dictatorship was proclaimed by King Alexander in 1929, which continued after his assassination in France in 1934. With the German invasion of Yugoslavia in 1941, the Croats welcomed the German troops with open arms as their liberators from the hated Serbs. During the war, the Croats and Slovenes formed their own military forces in divisional strength that fought in conjunction with the Germans, mainly in Yugoslavia. Unfortunately, this bloody legacy has carried over to the present day, thanks in large part to long memories.

When the Serbs gained their independence from the Turks they immediately made plans to equip their fledgling army with the Model G 71 Rifle, modified to their own specifications. Approximately 120,000 were purchased. This was the Serbian Model 78/80 Rifle, also known as the Mauser-Koka or Mauser Milanovic, the name of the Serbian officer who was responsible for the modifications. This rifle, converted to handle the 7 x 57mm round, was even utilized in the First World War, and it is conceivable that it was also used by guerrillas during World War II. Four thousand weapons were produced in carbine configuration as the Model 1880. The carbine was equipped with a tubular magazine and was full stocked to the muzzle.

In 1899, Serbia contracted with DWM and Steyr for the delivery of Chilean-style Model 1895 Rifles; these rifles were delivered between 1899 and 1906, with modifications made during this time. The model designations were the M1899, M1899/07, and the Model 1899/08. Differences between the models were minor—possibly improved actions or simply designation numbers. The M1899/08 was also made in small numbers as a carbine, really a shortened version of the Steyr made rifle, for cavalry and artillery use.

A further updated rifle, the Model 1910, a typical German export-style rifle patterned after the Costa Rican Model 1910, was ordered in time for the first Balkan War. Every weapon in the Serbian arsenal was in use during the Balkan Wars and the First World War, with many serving well into World War II.

In the 1920s, the Yugoslavs acquired a number of M24B Rifles (ex-Mexican rifles) from Steyr, and the arsenal at Kragujevac converted a large number of captured Turkish Model 1890 Rifles into a short rifle configuration in caliber 7.92 x 57mm. The Serbs also purchased approximately fifty thousand FN Model 22 Short Rifles, forty thousand FN Model 24 Short Rifles, as well as FN Model 30 Short Rifles and Carbines, and approximately forty thousand Czech VZ 24 Short Rifles. The FN Model VZ 24 Short Rifle and Carbine were also produced at the arsenal of Kragujevac on machinery purchased from FN.

In 1948, Yugoslavian arsenals produced a variation of the German K98k and also converted many of the FN Model 24 Short Ri-

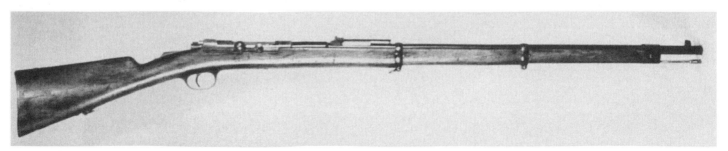

Full-length view of the Serbian Model 78/80 Rifle

fles to M24/47 configuration. The many Czech VZ 24 Short Rifles on hand were converted to VZ 24/52 configuration.

SERBIAN MODEL 78/80 RIFLE: The Serbian Model 78/80 Rifle is a modified German G 71 Rifle. Typical of the era, the rifle is long and clumsy. The rifle is fitted with a straight-wristed stock, with two screw-clamped barrel bands and a nose cap incorporating a bayonet lug on the right side. There is a swivel on the lower barrel band and another on the bottom of the buttstock. The easiest means of identification of the Serbian Model 78/80 Rifle is the long receiver tang that projects above the stock, providing support to the bolt when it is pulled to the rear. There is a groove in the tang that guides the cocking piece, preventing it from rotating. The extractor also serves as an ejector in this model, while there is also a spring surrounding the safety lock spindle. Another interesting feature of this rifle is the rifling, which is wider at the breech than at the muzzle.

Length: 50.80"; **Weight:** 9.90 lbs.; **Barrel:** 30.70"; **Caliber:** 10.15 x 62.8mm; **Rifling:** 4-groove, r/hand; **Operation:** Turnbolt action; **Feed:** Single-shot; **Sights:** V-notch rear sight adjustable to 2025 meters. **Remarks:** Manufacturer's markings either in Cyrillic or German on the left side rail.

SERBIAN MODEL 1884 MAUSER "KOKA" CARBINE: This 10.15mm black powder carbine is one of only 4,000 produced in 1884 for the Serbian cavalry by Mauser at the Oberndorf plant. It was based on the 71/84 action and has a five-round tubular magazine under the forestock, and is fitted with the typical 71/84 cartridge lifting mechanism.

It could be used with a standard carbine sling, or use a cavalry saddle ring clip attachment. For use with the standard sling, the top swivel is mounted to the left side of the bottom barrel band. Underneath and behind the wrist of the stock is a rectangular fitting which functions as an attachment point for a side-mounted standard sling, or as a sling hook attachment for an old-style cavalry saddle ring crossbelt. The carbine has front sight protective wings, and there is no provision for a bayonet.

Four thousand Short Rifles were also produced for the Serbian artillery forces; slightly longer, it has a six-round tubular magazine, and accepts the same bayonet as the Model 1878/80 Mauser-Milanovich Rifle. Due to the constant attrition to weapons used by the Serbian military, these carbines and Short Rifles were used extensively in the First and Second Balkan Wars, as well as throughout World War One.

Length: 37.75"; **Weight:** 8.00 lbs.; **Barrel:** 18.375"; **Caliber:** 10/15x63mmR; **Rifling:** 4-groove, r/hand; **Operation:** Turnbolt action; **Magazine:** Five round tubular feed, with each cartridge loaded individually; **Sling configuration:** Left side swivel and rectangular bottom sling bar at small of stock; **Remarks:** Original finish was in the white, with the left side rail marked in Cyrillic "MauserOberndorf" and "Model 1884." "Crown H" cartouche on right side of the butt, while all parts are numbered as per the practice of the period.

SERBIAN MODEL 1899 RIFLE: The Serbian Model 1899 Rifle made by DWM is very similar to the Chilean Model 1895 Rifle; however the entire Serbian M1899 series have the thumb cut in the left side rail to facilitate loading. All of the Model 1899 series, as well as the Model 1908 Carbine, have the enclosed bolt head feature of the Costa Rican Model 1910 Rifle, with the exception of the Model 1899 Rifle. The rifle is fitted with a straight-wristed stock, with the upper hand guard running from in front of the receiver ring to just beyond the lower barrel band. The nose cap is simple, with a bayonet lug on the bottom to accommodate the Model 1899 bayonet. There is a swivel on the bottom of the lower barrel band, and another on the bottom of the stock.

Manufacturer's markings in German on the left side rail of the Serbian Model 78/80 Rifle

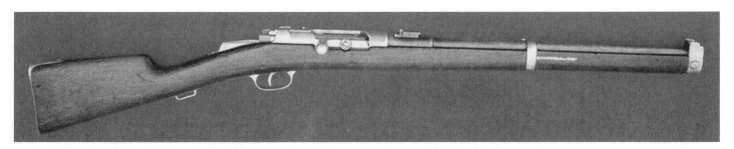

Right side view of the Model 1884 Serbian Mauser "Koka" Carbine. (John Sheehan collection)

Left side view of the Serbian Mauser "Koka" Carbine wtih the bolt withdrawn; this shows the support to the bolt of the receiver extension. (John Sheehan collection)

Serbian crest on the receiver ring of the Serbian Model 1899 Rifle (Springfield Armory Museum)

Side rail with manufacturer's markings in Cyrillic of the Serbian Model 99/07 Rifle (Noel P. Schott collection)

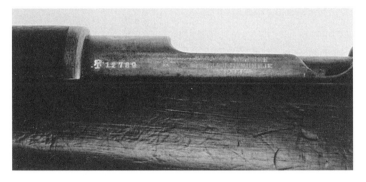

Manufacturer's markings in Cyrillic on the left side rail of the Serbian Model 1899 Rifle (Springfield Armory Museum)

Crest, showing model designation, on the receiver ring of the Serbian Model 99/07 Rifle (Noel P. Schott collection)

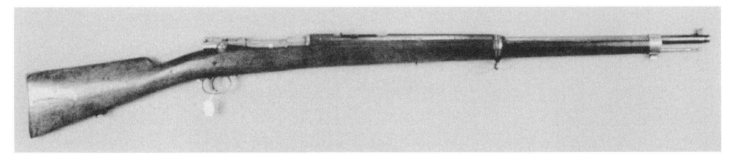

Full-length view of the Serbian Model 1899 Rifle (Springfield Armory Museum)

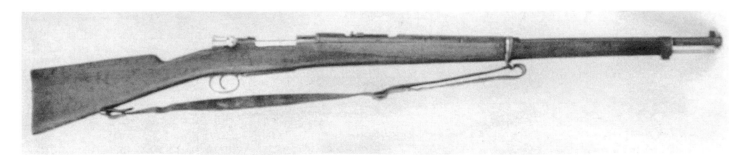

Full-length view of the Serbian Model 99/07 Rifle (Noel P. Schott collection)

The receiver ring of the Serbian Model 1899C Short Rifle, showing the Serbian crest over the model designation

Exhausted Serbian soldiers asleep where they fell during the retreat through Albania, 1915

Length: 48.50"; **Weight:** 8.9 lbs.; **Barrel:** 29.13"; **Caliber:** 7 x 57mm; **Rifling:** 4-groove, r/hand; **Operation:** Turnbolt action; **Feed:** 5-round, staggered column, flush, box magazine; **Sights:** V-notch rear sight adjustable to 2000 meters. **Remarks:** Serbian crest on the receiver ring, with the manufacturer's markings stamped in Cyrillic on the left side rail.

SERBIAN MODEL 1899C SHORT RIFLE: The Serbian Model 1899C has been configured at some time by the Yugoslavians to more closely conform to the Model 24 Short Rifle pattern as produced at the arsenal of Kragujevac. The resultant short rifle was rechambered and rebored for the 7.92 x 57mm cartridge. The rifle is fitted with a pistol grip stock without grasping grooves, and the upper hand guard runs from in front of the receiver ring to the upper band. The lower barrel band has a swivel on the side as well as the bottom. There is another swivel at the bottom of the buttstock and a pivoted swivel at the swell of the wrist. The bolt handle is straight and the action is similar to the Spanish Model 1893.

Length: 42.63"; **Weight:** 8.4 lbs.; **Barrel:** 23.25"; **Caliber:** 7.92 x 57mm, originally 7 x 57mm; **Rifling:** 4-groove, r/hand; **Operation:** Turnbolt action; **Feed:** 5-round, staggered column,

flush, box magazine; **Sights:** Tangent leaf rear sight graduated to 2000 meters. **Remarks:** Serbian crest over the model designation on the receiver ring.

SERBIAN MODEL 1908 CARBINE: While purchased in small quantities, the Serbian Model 1908 Carbine is really a shortened version of the Steyr-made rifle. The carbine is fitted with a full, muzzle-length, pistol grip stock with grasping grooves, with the simplified nose cap secured with a side screw, providing front sight protectors. The upper hand guard extends from the front of the receiver ring to just beyond the lower barrel band, which is secured with a lateral screw. The action is similar to the Chilean Model 1895 action, with the bolt handle bent down. The carbine will not accept a bayonet. There is a sling bar on the left side of the lower barrel band, with a pivoted swivel mounted on the left side of the buttstock.

Length: 37.50"; **Weight:** 6.80 lbs.; **Barrel:** 17.0"; **Caliber:** 7 x 57mm; **Rifling:** 4-groove, r/hand; **Operation:** Turnbolt action; **Feed:** 5-round, staggered column, flush, box magazine; **Sights:** Adjustable leaf rear sight graduated to 1500 meters. **Remarks:** Serbian crest over the model designation on the receiver ring, with the manufacturer's markings stamped in Cyrillic on the left side rail.

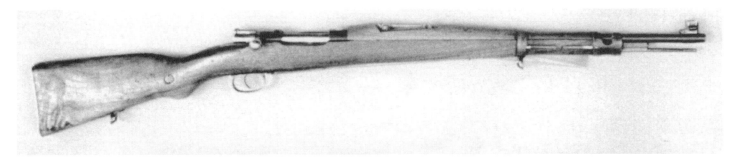

Full-length view of the Serbian Model 1899C Short Rifle

Full-length view of the Serbian Model 1908 Carbine (Noel P. Schott collection)

Receiver ring of the Serbian Model 1908 Carbine, showing the Serbian crest over the model designation. (Noel P. Schott collection)

Left side rail of the Serbian Model 1908 Carbine, showing the stamped manufacturer's markings in Cyrillic, proof marks, and rifle serial number (Noel P. Schott collection)

SERBIAN MODEL 1910 RIFLE: The Serbian Model 1910 Rifle is the standard export German Model 1910. The action is the same as the G 98 action but has the enclosed cartridge head feature of the Costa Rican Model 1910 Rifle. The rifle is fitted with a pistol grip stock without grasping grooves, a narrow lower band with swivel attached on the bottom, and another swivel on the bottom of the buttstock. The upper hand guard extends from the front of the receiver ring to just beyond the lower barrel band. The nose cap incorporates a simple bayonet lug on the bottom.

Serbian soldiers in retreat to the Adriatic coast, C. 1915

Length: 48.80"; **Weight:** 8.8 lbs.; **Barrel:** 29.13"; **Caliber:** 7 x 57mm; **Rifling:** 4-groove, r/hand; **Operation:** Turnbolt action; **Feed:** 5-round, staggered column, flush, box magazine; **Sights:** Tangent leaf rear sight graduated to 2000 meters. **Remarks:** The rifle may be marked in one of two ways—on the receiver ring with the Serbian crest over the model designation, with the manufacturer's markings on the side rail in Cyrillic; or export marked in German with "WAFFENFABRIK/MAUSER A-G/OBERNDORF a/n" on the receiver ring, with the model designation, "MAUSER MODEL 1910" on the left side rail.

Manufacturer's markings stamped in Cyrillic on the left side rail of the Serbian Model 1910 Rifle (Springfield Armory collection)

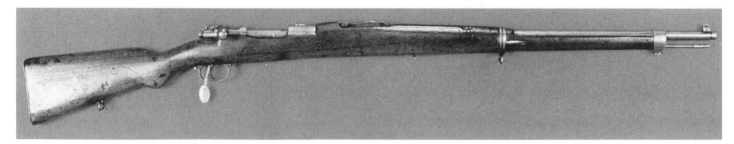

Full-length view of the Serbian Model 1910 (Marked in Cyrillic) (Springfield Armory collection)

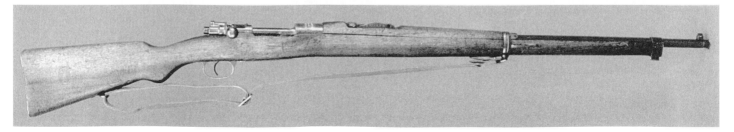

Full-length view of the German export Model 1910 Rifle

Receiver ring of the Serbian Model 1910, showing the Serbian crest over the model designation (Springfield Armory collection)

Left side rail of the German export version of the Serbian Model 1910 Rifle, showing the model designation

YUGOSLAVIAN MODEL 90(T) AND MODEL 03(T) SHORT RIFLES: Following the end of World War I, the Yugoslavs received many Turkish weapons as war reparations; these weapons were re-barreled and cut down to short rifle configuration, while all other earlier characteristics remained. The Model 90 (T) is as follows:

Receiver ring of the German export version of the Serbian Model 1910 Rifle, with manufacturer's markings stamped in German

Length: 43.13"; **Weight:** 8.6 lbs.; **Barrel:** 23.25"; **Caliber:** 7.92 x 57mm; **Rifling:** 4-groove, r/hand; **Operation:** Turnbolt action; **Feed:** 5-round, vertical column, box magazine; **Sights:** Tangent leaf rear sight graduated to 2000 meters. **Remarks:** All original markings are untouched.

The Yugoslavian Model 03(T) Short Rifle specifications are as follows:

Length: 42.75"; **Weight:** 9.0 lbs.; **Barrel:** 23.0"; **Caliber:** 7.92 x 57mm; **Rifling:** 4-groove, r/hand; **Operation:** Turnbolt action; **Feed:** 5-round, vertical column, box magazine; **Sights:** Tangent leaf rear sight graduated to 2000 meters. **Remarks:** All original markings are untouched.

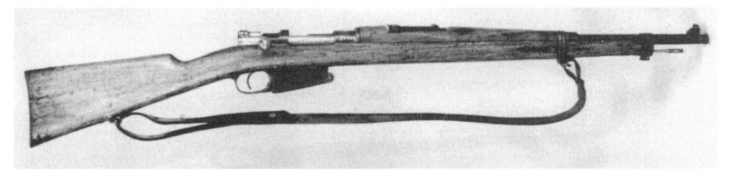

Full-length view of the Yugoslavian Model 90(T) Short Rifle (Noel P. Schott collection)

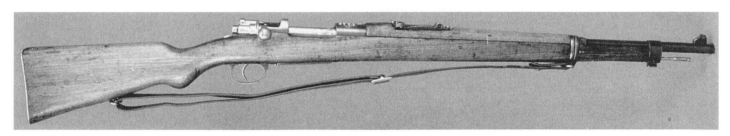

Full-length view of the Yugoslavian Model 03(T) Short Rifle (Noel P. Schott collection)

Receiver ring of the Yugoslavian Model 90(T) Short Rifle, showing the original Turkish Toghra marking. (Noel P. Schott collection)

Left side rail of the Yugoslavian Model 90(T) Short Rifle, showing the original manufacturer's markings in Turkish. (Noel P. Schott collection)

Right side of the receiver ring of the Yugoslavian Model 90(T) Short Rifle, showing the original serial number. (Noel P. Schott collection)

Receiver ring of the Yugoslavian Model 03(T) Short Rifle, showing the original markings in Turkish. (Noel P. Schott collection)

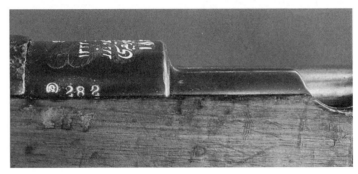

Left side view of the Yugoslavian Model 03(T) Short Rifle, showing the new serial number on the side of the receiver ring. (Noel P. Schott collection)

YUGOSLAVIAN MODEL 24 SHORT RIFLE: The Yugoslavs adopted both the FN Model 24 Short Rifle and Carbine, purchasing many from FN and producing many more at the arms factory of Kraguje-vac. The Yugoslav Model 24 features the enclosed cartridge head of the Costa Rican Model 1910 Rifle. The short rifle is fitted with a pistol grip stock, with the upper hand guard running from the front of the receiver ring to the upper barrel band. The upper and lower barrel bands are situated in close proximity to one another, with each secured by a separate spring. The nose cap incorporates the German-style "H" bayonet lug; the lower barrel band is fitted with a swivel at the bottom and a sling bar on the left side, while another pivoted swivel is found on the left side of the buttstock. The bolt handle is straight.

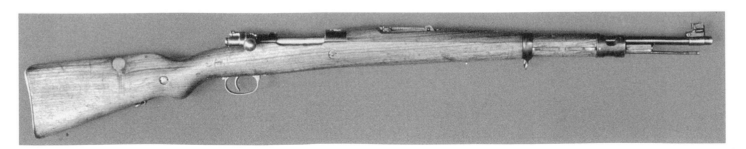

Full-length view of the Yugoslavian Model 24 Short Rifle

Yugoslavian partisans serving a captured anti-tank gun during action in Yugoslavia, C. 1944. Note the Yugoslav Model 24 Short Rifles carried by the men.

Yugoslavian crest over the model designation on the receiver ring of the Yugoslavian Model 24 Short Rifle

Manufacturer's markings stamped into the left side of the receiver and the left side rail of the Yugoslavian Model 24 Short Rifle

Dual monarchy buttstock markings on the Yugoslavian Model 24 Short Rifle

Length: 42.90"; **Weight:** 8.4 lbs.; **Barrel:** 23.25"; **Caliber:** 7.92 x 57mm; **Rifling:** 4-groove, r/hand; **Operation:** Turnbolt action; **Feed:** 5-round, staggered column, flush, box magazine; **Sights:** Tangent leaf rear sight graduated to 2000 meters. **Remarks:** Yugoslav crest over the model designation, with manufacturer's markings on the left receiver and side wall.

YUGOSLAVIAN MODEL 24 CARBINE: The Yugoslavian Model 24 Carbine is rather unusual, rarely encountered, and quite collectible. The carbine is fitted with a pistol grip stock without grasping grooves, and the upper hand guard extends from the front of the receiver ring to the combination lower/upper band; the lower band is seated partially on top of the upper band. There is a swivel at the bottom of the lower band, and another on the bottom of the buttstock. The nose cap incorporates a most unusual, dual position, German-style bayonet lug, enabling bayonets with different length handle slots to be used with the carbine. The stock is not cut out to facilitate operation of the bent bolt handle, but there is a slight recurve to the handle itself to assist in ease of operation.

Close-up view of the variant butt stock cartouche on the Yugoslavian Model 24 Short Rifle. (Robert Jensen collection)

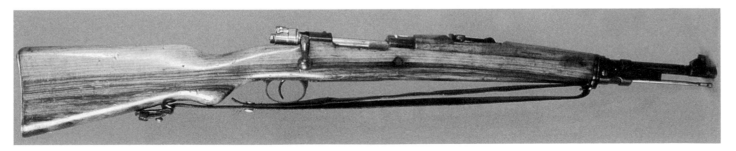

Full-length view of the Yugoslavian Model 24 Carbine

Manufacturer's markings stamped into the side of the receiver ring and the left side rail of the Yugoslavian Model 24 Carbine

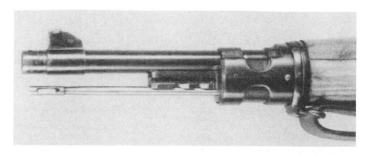

The dual position bayonet lug and the overlapping lower barrel band are seen to good effect in this view of the Yugoslavian Model 24 Carbine.

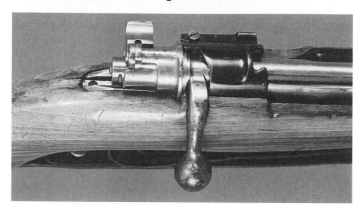

The action and the slightly recurved bolt handle on the Yugoslavian Model 24 Carbine

Length: 37.0"; **Weight:** 7.25 lbs.; **Barrel:** 16.75"; **Caliber:** 7.92 x 57mm; **Rifling:** 4-groove, r/hand; **Operation:** Turnbolt action; **Feed:** 5-round, staggered column, flush, box magazine; **Sights:** Tangent leaf rear sight graduated to 1500 meters. **Remarks:** Yugoslavian crest and model designation on the receiver ring, with the manufacturer's markings in Cyrillic on the left side of the receiver ring and the left side rail.

YUGOSLAVIAN FN MODEL 30 SHORT RIFLE: In 1935, Yugoslavia purchased an unknown quantity of FN Model 30 Short Rifles and Carbines; these are the typical export models as produced by FN for many other countries. The Model 30 Short Rifle is fitted with a pistol grip stock, with the upper hand guard running from in front of the receiver ring to just beyond the lower barrel band. The lower barrel band is fitted with a swivel on the bottom, and there is another on the bottom of the buttstock. The bolt handle is straight. No information has been forthcoming on exactly how, or even if, these short rifles were marked. Additional details on the FN export Model 24 and Model 30 can be found in the section on China.

YUGOSLAVIAN FN MODEL 24 CARBINE: The FN Model 24 Carbine was not purchased in large quantities, and the one pictured in this section is somewhat different than the standard export model.

Yugoslavian crest and model designation in Cyrillic on the receiver ring of the Yugoslavian Model 24 Carbine

This particular carbine was produced specifically for the gendarmerie of the city of Nish, a town of approximately twenty thousand inhabitants at the time.

The carbine is fitted with a pistol grip stock and an upper hand guard that runs from the front of the receiver ring to just beyond the lower barrel band, which is placed quite close to the upper band. There is a swivel on the bottom of the lower barrel band, and another on the bottom of the buttstock. There is no provision for a bayonet. On the right side of the buttstock is a carbine clip, attached by screws.

Length: 37.0"; **Weight:** 7.8 lbs.; **Barrel:** 17.50"; **Caliber:** 7 x 57mm; **Rifling:** 4-groove, r/hand; **Operation:** Turnbolt action; **Feed:** 5-round, staggered column, flush, box magazine; **Sights:** Tangent leaf rear sight graduated to 1400 meters. **Remarks:** Yugoslavian crest over model designation over the Cyrillic wording for "Nish Gendarmerie" on the top of the receiver ring. Belgian proof marks on the left upper side of the receiver ring, with manufacturer's markings on the left side rail. The serial number, # 16, is on the lower right side of the receiver ring.

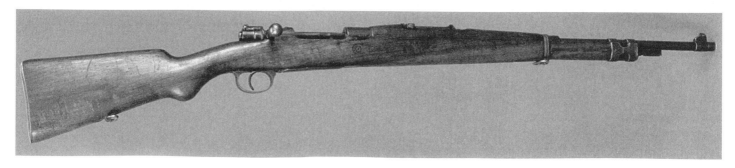

Full-length view of the FN Model 30 Short Rifle as used by Yugoslavia (Cliff Baumann collection)

Full-length view of the Yugoslavian FN Model 24 Carbine, marked for the city of Nish gendarmerie (Noel P. Schott collection)

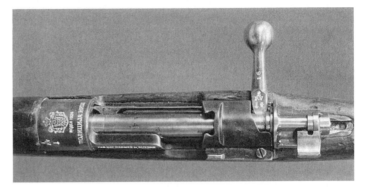

Overview of the complete action of the Yugoslavian FN Model 24 Carbine (Noel P. Schott collection)

Chetnik guards relaxing; the man to the right holds a Yugoslav Mauser M24B carbine, while the other two men have M95 Mannlicher straight-pull carbines.

The receiver ring of the Yugoslavian FN Model 24 Carbine, showing the Yugoslavian crest, the model designation, and the Cyrillic wording for the Nish gendarmerie. (Noel P. Schott collection)

Carbine serial number on the right side of the receiver ring of the Yugoslavian FN Model 24 Carbine (Noel P. Schott collection)

The Belgian proofs on the receiver ring and the manufacturer's markings on the left side rail of the Yugoslavian FN Model 24 Carbine (Noel P. Schott collection)

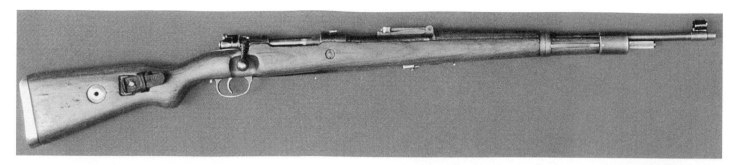

Full-length view of the Yugoslavian Model 48 Short Rifle

YUGOSLAVIAN MODEL 1948 98k SHORT RIFLE: The last Mauser rifle produced by Yugoslavia at the Kragujevac arsenal is the Model 48 Short Rifle, quite similar to the German 98k Carbine. The short rifle is fitted with a pistol grip stock, with a typical German-style short upper hand guard extending from the front of the rear sight to the lower barrel band. The lower barrel band has a side bar sling slot, with a slot through the buttstock for attachment of the sling. The front sight has a German-style front sight cover, while the nose cap has an "H" style bayonet lug. The bolt handle is bent, with the stock cut for easier operation of the bolt.

Markings on the side of the receiver and the left side rail of the Yugoslavian Model 48 Short Rifle

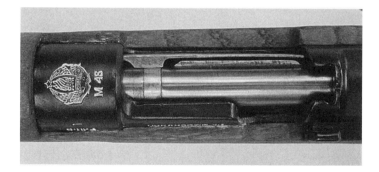

Close-up view of the variant Communist markings on the receiver ring of the Yugoslavian Post-WWII Model 48 Short Rifle

Variant side rail markings on the Yugoslavian Model 48 Short Rifle

The Communist Yugoslavian crest on the receiver ring of the Yugoslavian Model 48 Short Rifle

Length: 43.50"; **Weight:** 10.0 lbs.; **Barrel:** 23.25"; **Caliber:** 7.92 x 57mm; **Rifling:** 4-groove, r/hand; **Operation:** Turnbolt action; **Feed:** 5-round, staggered column, flush, box magazine; **Sights:** Tangent leaf rear sight graduated to 2000 meters. **Remarks:** Communist Yugoslavian crest on the receiver ring, with "PREDUZECE 44" on the left side of the receiver and the model designation on the left side rail.

YUGOSLAVIAN MODEL 24/52C SHORT RIFLE: Yugoslavian authorities reconditioned many of their prewar rifles during the late 1940s and 1950s. These weapons had minor changes made to their prior configuration, and were remarked with the Yugoslavian Communist crest. In all other respects, the short rifles are the same as the Model 24 Short Rifle, and the same data will apply.

The Yugoslavian Communist crest over the model designation on the receiver ring of the Model 24/52C Short Rifle (Century International Arms, Inc.)

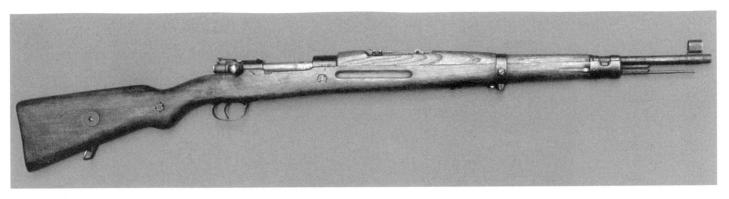

Full-length view of the Yugoslavian Model 24/52C Short Rifle (Century International Arms, Inc.)

The Slovak Republic crest on the right side of the receiver ring of the Slovak Republic Short Rifle

Side rail arsenal markings on the Yugoslavian Model 24/52C Short Rifle (Century International Arms, Inc.)

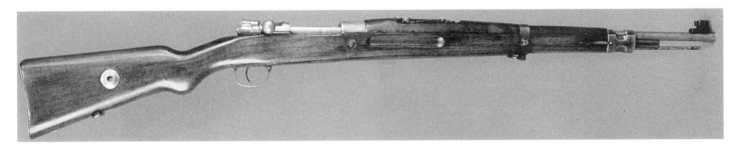

Full-length view of the Slovak Republic VZ 24 Short Rifle

Chetnik officers and men in a posed picture. The soldiers appear to be armed with Yugoslav Model 24 Short Rifles.

SLOVAK REPUBLIC

In order to destroy Czechoslovakia after its annexation by Germany, the Slovak Republic was forced into being by Hitler during World War II. If the Slovaks had not acceded to Hitler's demands, much of their territory would have been given to Hungary. Left with no other options, a one-party state was established by Monsignor Jozef Tiso, a staunch fascist, whose Hlinka Guards were modeled on the storm troopers of Hitler's Germany. Allowed their own national army, the Slovaks inherited all of the former Czechoslovakian material within their borders and were able to field three divisions at the start of the war.

Highly professional, the Slovak army fought alongside the German armies during the attack on Poland and the attack against Russia.

Some units also served in Hungary, Romania, and Italy. In 1944, a premature uprising was staged by partisans in central Slovakia, but they could only hold their ground until October of the same year. With the end of the war, the Czechoslovakian Republic was reestablished.

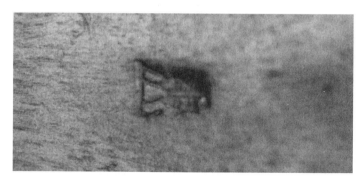

Full-length view of the right side of the Slovak Republic VZ 24 Short Rifle with variant turned-down bolt handle and inletted stock. (Robert Jensen collection)

Close-up view of the right side of the receiver ring on the Slovak Republic variant Model VZ 24 Short Rifle, shwoing a different version of the Slovak Republic Tatra Mountain crest. (Robert Jensen collection)

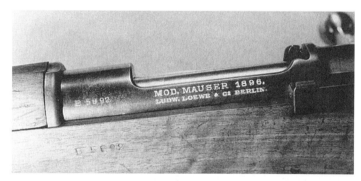

Stock cartouche impressed in the Slovak Republic VZ 24 Short Rifle. (Robert Jensen collection)

Among the equipment that was available to the new Slovak army were the large quantities of Czech VZ 24 Short Rifles. Many of the rifles used by troops of the Slovak Republic were inconspicuously marked with a very small Slovak crest on the right or left side of the receiver.

SLOVAK REPUBLIC VZ 24 SHORT RIFLE: In all respects, this short rifle is identical to the Czech VZ 24 Short Rifle. Specifications on this weapon will be found in the section on Czechoslovakia.

SOUTH AFRICAN REPUBLIC-Z.A.R.
(ZUID-AFRICAANSCHE REPUBLICK)

Before the Boer War of 1899-1901, the South African Republic purchased a total of 47,000 Mauser Model 1895 7mm rifles and carbines from DWM and Ludwig Loewe. 10,000 rifles, serial number A1-10,000 marked on the side rail "Mod. Mauser 1896" over "Ludw. Loewe & Ce Berlin" with no marking on the receiver ring were shipped to the ZAR during July, August and September of

1896. These rifles had the 29-inch barrel, and were reported by Bester (page 144) to have German military-style quality inspection marks (a crown over a faktur letter) on the left of the buttstock, on the left side of the receiver near the serial number, the top of the bolt handle, and on top of the barrel under the handguard. There was no circular cartouche stamp.

Ten thousand rifles, serial numbers B1-10,000, and 5,000 18-inch barreled carbines, serial numbers 1-5,000 without a prefix letter, were shipped from Germany in September of 1896. The carbines were marked "Mod. Mauser 1896" over "Ludwig Loewe & Ce Berlin" on the left side rail, and were unmarked on the receiver ring. Inspection marks were as noted for the rifles, the bolt handle was bent and the carbines were fitted with the short carbine sight, graduated from 400 to 1,400 meters. Also shipped during this period was a shipment of 10,000 rifles with the 29-inch barrel, serial number 1-10,000 without a letter prefix; these rifles were marked

Left side view of the ZAE M1896 "B" series Mauser Rifle manufactured by Ludwig Loewe, showing the receiver without crest and the serial number on the receiver and stock. (John Wall collection, photo by John M. Leone)

View of the German military quality inspection mark on the root of the bolt handle, with the serial number on the bolt handle of the M1896 ZAR Mauser rifle. (John Wall collection, photo by John M. Leone)

The German military inspection mark of a crown over a fraktur letter on the barrel (under the handguard) of the M1896 ZAR Loewe manufactured long rifle. (John Wall collection, photo by John M. Leone)

Left side view of the receiver of a "C" series M1895/1896 illustrating the unusual circle mark found on many ZAR and OVS Mauser rifles. Its meaning is not known at this time. (John Wall collection, photo by John M. Leone)

View of the wrist of a "C" series Mauser rifle, showing the unusual circle marking as found on the receivers of many ZAR and OVS Mauser rifles. (John Wall collection, photo by John M. Leone)

"Deutsche Waffe-und-Munitionsfabriken" over "Berlin" on the left side rail. Inspection marks are found as for the first shipment of rifles. In March, 1897, 2,000 rifles , serial number 5,001-7,000 were shipped to the ZAR, while in May and June, 1897, 8,000 more rifles and 2,000 more carbines marked from DWM were received by the ZAR. No German military inspection marks are to be found on the carbines, while the circular cartouche is present stamped on the left buttstock, stock wrist, next to the serial number, on the bolt knob and on the barrel under the handguard.

Further weapons were shipped from Germany, but were turned back by the British blockade and later sold to Chile, having had the Chilean crest applied.

SPAIN

Despite the loss of the Spanish Armada in the war with England, Spain reached the height of its prestige and power around the year 1600. At that time, the empire of Spain covered all of South America (with the exception of Brazil), along with Central America, Mexico, western North America, the Philippines, and smaller territories in Asia and Africa.

With installation of Napoleon's brother as king in 1808, the power of Spain went into a downward spiral. After the defeat of Napoleon at Waterloo, the nineteenth century witnessed the loss of the South American, Central American, and Mexican colonies, as well as the holdings in western North America. The crowning blow to Spanish colonialism was the defeat of Spain in the Spanish-American War, with the resultant loss of Cuba, Puerto Rico, and the Philippines.

During the first half of the twentieth century, Spain seesawed back and forth between right and left wing governments, and found itself deeply involved in a continuous brush war with the Rifs of Morocco, where Spain had territorial holdings. Political events of the early 1930s rapidly led to a situation where there was almost no alternative to the terrible, deadly, nation-crushing civil war that was fought from July of 1936 to the spring of 1939. This war was used by the Germans, Italians, and Russians as a wonderful testing ground for their military theories and their latest equipment. To many, this was the last pure test of good against evil, with thousands of men flocking to fight on the side of the Spanish Republic against the Fascist dictatorship of Francisco Franco. Unfortunately, in this war, Fascism triumphed, and the Republic was crushed.

Neutral during World War II, Franco allowed a volunteer Spanish "Blue Division" to fight in Russia alongside the Germans; Spanish air force units also fought on this grueling battlefront. Following the end of the war, Spain was slowly welcomed back into the European community, and with the death of Franco in 1975, Prince Juan Carlos ascended the Bourbon throne as King Carlos. Since then, Spain has been a full participant in European affairs, with all pluses and minuses that membership involves.

Spain has always been an arms producing nation, with a large national arsenal at Oviedo in northwestern Spain. The Spanish army has followed small arms development quite closely over the years, Mauser rifles having been submitted for trial almost continuously. Apparently, some Turkish Model 1887 models were submitted for troop trials; however they proved unsatisfactory. The Model 1891 Rifle in caliber 7.65 x 53mm was adopted for trial, as was the Model 1891 Carbine; these were almost identical to the Turkish models. In 1892, improvements and a change in caliber to 7 x 57mm

A group picture of Spanish soldiers in Manila, P. I. prior to the Spanish-American War. They are equipped with Model 1893 Rifles.

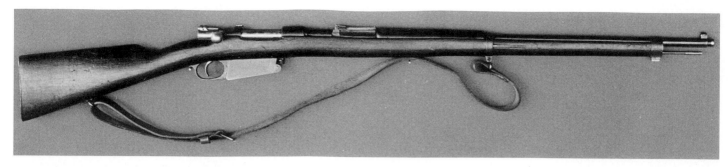

Full-length view of the Spanish Model 1891 Rifle

brought a recommendation for adoption by the Spanish authorities. Few were made, however, due to the introduction of the world famous Model 1893 Rifle and Carbine.

The Model 1893 Rifle introduced a major improvement with the 5-round, staggered column, flush box magazine, which gives the rifle a much neater and more compact appearance, as well as protecting the magazine box. The Spaniards were so pleased with the Model 1893 Rifle that Paul Mauser was awarded the Grand Cross of the Order of Military Merit. The initial order from the Spanish Army was for approximately 252,000 rifles and 25,000 carbines. These weapons saw service in all of the major campaigns fought by the Spanish Army, including the Spanish-American War, the Riffian Wars, the Spanish Civil War, and some were still employed into the 1950s. 1895 saw the advent of the Model 1895 Carbine, while the Model 1916 Short Rifle was in production from 1916 to 1951. In 1943, Spain adopted the Model 43, a modified German-style K98k Short Rifle. In the 1950s, Model 1916 Short Rifles and Model 43 Short Rifles were modified by Spanish arsenals into lightweight, compact weapons designated the FR-7 and FR-8.

With the advent and easy availability of semiautomatic weapons after World War II, Spain gradually found no further use for the Mauser rifle as a standard weapon.

SPANISH MODEL 1891 RIFLE: The Spanish Model 1891 Rifle is almost identical with the Turkish Model 1890 Rifle, and is also in caliber 7.65 x 53mm. The rifle is fitted with a straight wrist stock, with a short upper hand guard running from in front of the rear sight base to the lower barrel band. The lower barrel band has a swivel on the bottom, and there is another on the bottom of the buttstock. The simple nose cap incorporates a bayonet lug on the bottom. The

Model 1891 Rifle introduced an action improvement that prevented double loading by undercutting on the bolt face and placing a spring-loaded plunger in the right locking lug. Approximately twelve hundred Model 1891 Rifles were made for Spain by Waffenfabrik Mauser A-G. The carbine was produced in much larger numbers, is marked with the Spanish crest on the receiver ring, and is identical to the Argentine Model 1891 Carbine.

Length: 48.60"; **Weight:** 8.8 lbs.; **Barrel:** 29.13"; **Caliber:** 7.65 x 53mm; **Rifling:** 4-groove, r/hand; **Operation:** Turnbolt action; **Feed:** 5-round, vertical box magazine; **Sights:** V-notch adjustable rear sight graduated to 2000 meters. **Remarks:** It is believed that the Model 1891 Rifle was not marked on the receiver, and that the manufacturer's markings are stamped on the left side rail.

SPANISH MODEL 1892 RIFLE: The Spanish Model 1892 Rifle incorporates improvements made during the troop trials of the Model 1891 Rifle. These improvements were a non-rotating 1892-patent extractor, a trigger system that was altered so that the striker would not be released unless the bolt was fully locked, a detachable floor plate and follower, a guide rib in the left side of the receiver, a cocking piece that was attached to the firing pin with interrupted lugs, and a safety catch that was fitted with a third position to assist in dismantling. The basic description of the rifle is the same as for the Model 1891.

SPANISH MODEL 1892 CARBINE: Approximately ten thousand Spanish Model 1892 Carbines were purchased from Ludwig Loewe & Co. between 1893 and 1895. The carbine is fitted with a straight wrist stock to the muzzle, with an upper hand guard running from the front of the receiver ring to the lower barrel band. There is a sim-

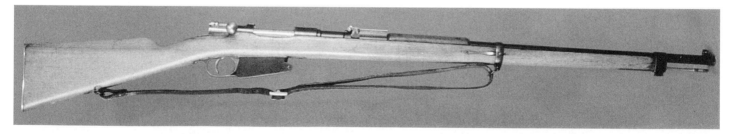

Full-length view of the Spanish Model 1892 Rifle

Full-length view of the Spanish Model 1892 Carbine (Cliff Baumann collection)

ple nose cap with no provision for a bayonet. The bolt handle is turned down for compactness, and there is a sling bar and ring under the wrist of the stock.

Length: 37.0"; **Weight:** 7.2 lbs.; **Barrel:** 17.63"; **Caliber:** 7 x 57mm; **Rifling:** 4-groove, r/hand; **Operation:** Turnbolt action; **Feed:** 5-round vertical box magazine; **Sights:** Leaf rear sight graduated to 1200 meters. **Remarks:** Spanish crest on the receiver ring, with the manufacturer's markings stamped in the left side rail.

German manufacturer's markings on the left side rail of the Spanish Model 1892 Rifle

Manufacturer's markings on the left side rail of the Spanish Model 1892 Carbine (Cliff Baumann collection)

Spanish crest on the receiver ring of the Spanish Model 1892 Carbine (Cliff Baumann collection)

SPANISH MODEL 1893 RIFLE: Probably one of the best known Mauser rifles of all time, this veteran has seen service in the jungles of Mindanao and Cuba, the mountains of Morocco, and the length and breadth of Spain. Adopted on 7 December 1893, it was the first Mauser rifle to have a clip-loaded magazine entirely within the

Battle scene from Spanish Morocco, C. 1920. While armed with the Model 1893 Rifle, the troops use British web equipment bought as war surplus. (Agencia Efe)

Typical Spanish outpost in Spanish Morocco during the Rif War of the 1920s. Troops are armed with Model 1893 Rifles. Note the Spanish Hotchkiss machine gun being served in the right side of the picture. (Agencia Efe)

Spanish crest over "BERLIN 1896" on the receiver ring of the Spanish Model 1893 Rifle

Manufacturer's markings stamped in Spanish on the left side rail of the Spanish Model 1893 Rifle

stock. The lower portion of the bolt face was squared in order to insure improvement in feeding of cartridges (this feature was discarded in later Mauser rifles), clip guides were milled into the front of the receiver bridge, and the safety could be applied only when the action was cocked. The rifle is fitted with a straight wrist stock, and the upper hand guard extends from the front of the receiver to the lower barrel band. The upper band is simple, with a bayonet lug on the bottom for use with the Model 1893 sword bayonet. There is a swivel on the bottom of the lower barrel band, and another on the bottom of the buttstock. The bolt handle is straight.

Length: 48.60"; **Weight:** 8.80 lbs.; **Barrel:** 29.06"; **Caliber:** 7 x 57mm; **Rifling:** 4-groove, r/hand; **Operation:** Turnbolt action; **Feed:** 5-round, staggered column, flush, box magazine; **Sights:** V-notch leaf rear sight graduated to 2000 meters. **Remarks:** Spanish crest on top of the receiver ring, with the manufacturer's markings stamped on the left side rail.

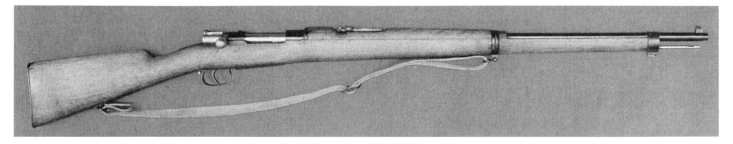

Full-length view of the standard issue Spanish Model 1893 Rifle

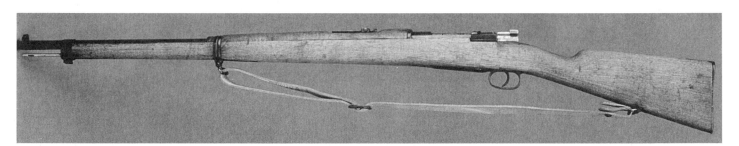

Left full-length view of the Spanish Model 1893 Rifle

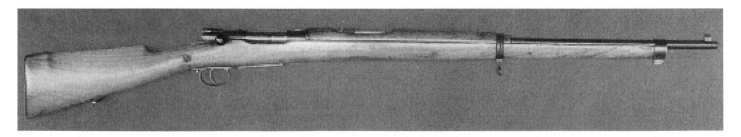

Full-length view of another, slightly different issue Spanish Model 1893 Rifle. Note the reinforcing lug at the small of the wrist.

Full-length view of the Spanish Model 1893 Carbine. Note the manner in which the forend is formed. (Cliff Baumann collection)

SPANISH MODEL 1893 "TRUE" CARBINE: According to information received, this is the original configuration of a "true" Model 1893 Carbine that is not arsenal or gunsmith converted. The carbine is fitted with a straight wrist stock, with an upper hand guard extending to slightly beyond the barrel band. There is no upper barrel band, nose cap, or provision for bayonet attachment. There is a sling bar and ring on the bottom of the stock at the wrist, and the bolt handle is bent.

Length: 37.0"; **Weight:** 6.50 lbs.; **Barrel:** 17.0"; **Caliber:** 7 x 57mm; **Rifling:** 4-groove, r/hand; **Operation:** Turnbolt action; **Feed:** 5-round, staggered column, flush, box magazine; **Sights:** V-notch leaf rear sight graduated to 1400 meters. **Remarks:** Spanish crest on top of the receiver ring, with the manufacturer's markings stamped into the left side rail.

SPANISH MODEL 1895 CARBINE: Despite that many specimens bear earlier dates, the carbine model of the Model 1893 Rifle was not approved until 1895, thus the Model 1895 designation. The

The left side rail of the Spanish Model 1893 Carbine, showing the manufacturer's markings stamped in Spanish. (Cliff Baumann collection)

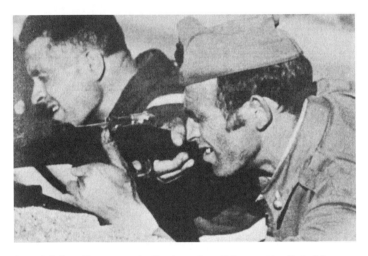

Spanish Loyalist troops in the trenches firing on the Rebel forces

The Spanish crest on top of the receiver of the Spanish Model 1893 Carbine (Cliff Baumann collection)

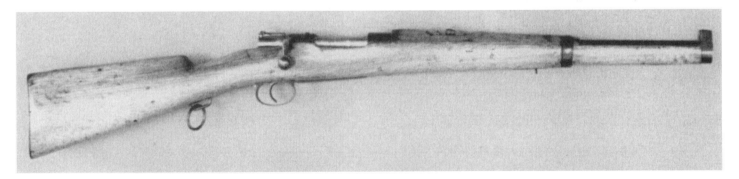

Full-length view of the Spanish Model 1895 Carbine

Full-length view of a presentation Spanish Model 1895 Carbine from the Spanish government to the government of the United States, 1906 (Springfield Armory Museum)

Presentation medallion on the right side of the buttstock on the presentation Spanish Model 1895 Carbine. (Springfield Armory Museum)

Manufacturer's markings, arsenal, and date on the receiver ring of the presentation Spanish Model 1895 Carbine. (Springfield Armory Museum)

SPANISH MODIFIED GEW. 98 RIFLE: After the First World War, a number of ex-German G 98 Rifles were modified at Oviedo, Spain for use by the Spanish army. In all respects except for the tangent rear sight that replaced the "Lange Vizier" rear sight, the rechambering and reboring of the rifle to 7 x 57mm, and Spanish markings, the modified rifle was identical to the G 98 Rifle. Specific data on this rifle may be found in the section on Germany.

Spanish Militia troops preparing to depart from Aragon. Among them are some "regulares," or regular army troops. Note the Spanish Model 1926 helmets being worn and carried. (Cushing collection)

carbine is full stocked to the muzzle, has a turned down bolt handle, and has a sling bar and ring on the bottom of the stock at the wrist. The simple nose cap has sight protectors for the front sight, and there is no provision for a bayonet. Weapons made after 1896 have a sling ring on the left side of the barrel band, and a sling bar attached to the left side of the buttstock, in addition to the sling bar and ring at the wrist.

Length: 37.0"; **Weight:** 7.50 lbs.; **Barrel:** 17.56"; **Caliber:** 7 x 57mm; **Rifling:** 4-groove, r/hand; **Operation:** Turnbolt action; **Feed:** 5-round, staggered column, flush, box magazine; **Sights:** V-notch adjustable leaf rear sight graduated to 1400 meters. **Remarks:** Spanish crest on the receiver ring, with manufacturer's markings stamped on the left side rail.

Spanish markings that have replaced the original German markings on the Spanish modified G 98 Rifle. (Springfield Armory Museum)

Full-length view of the Spanish modified G 98 Rifle (Springfield Armory Museum)

SPANISH MODEL 1916 SHORT RIFLE: Adopted to replace the Model 1895 Carbine, which was not suited to the ballistics of the improved Model 1913 ammunition, the Spanish Model 1916 Short Rifle was produced by Fabrica de Armas of Oviedo from 1916 to 1951, and by the Industrias de Guerra de Cataluna from 1936 to 1939.

The Spanish Model 1916 is basically a shortened version of the Model 1893 Rifle, fitted with a straight wrist stock and an upper hand guard that extends from the front of the receiver ring to approximately one inch beyond the lower barrel band. There is a pivoting swivel on the left side of the lower band and a sling bar on the left side of the buttstock. A full-depth cutout on the left side rail was employed to improve stripping cartridges from the clip, while additional gas escape holes have been incorporated in the bolt body and the chamber. On the first pattern Model 1916 Short Rifle, the "Lange Vizier" rear sight was employed; this was replaced during the Spanish Civil War by a more conventional tangent leaf rear sight. The nose cap, which incorporates a bayonet lug on the bottom, is retained by a flat spring on the bottom of the forend. The bolt handle is bent, without the stock being recessed to facilitate operation.

In 1918, front sight protectors were adopted. During 1943, some surviving specimens were converted to caliber 7.92 x 57mm in order to conform more closely to the Model 1943 Rifle introduced at that time.

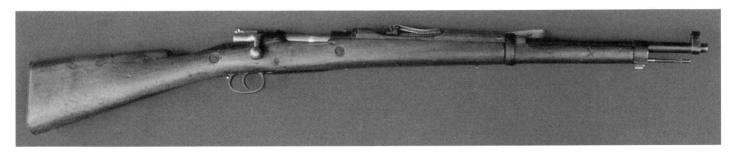

Full-length view of the Spanish Model 1916 Short Rifle, first pattern

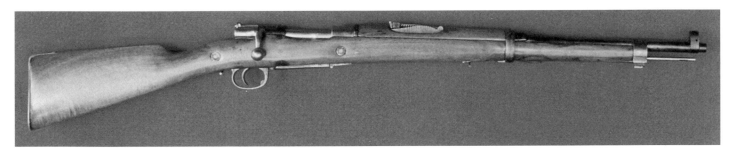

Full-length view of the Spanish Model 1916 Short Rifle, second pattern

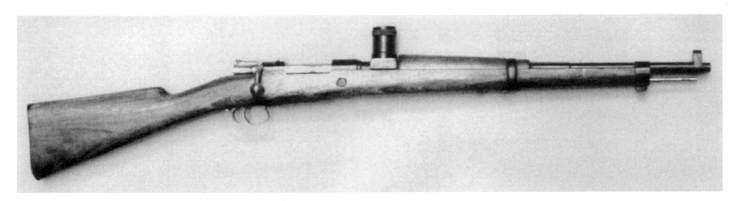

Full-length view of a Spanish Model 1916 Short Rifle converted for use as a pressure test rifle (Century International Arms, Inc.)

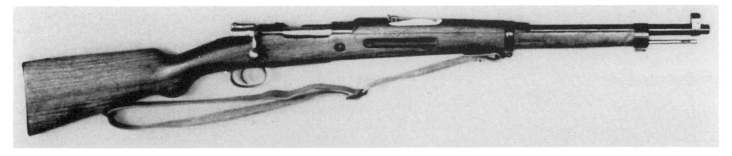

Full-length view of a Model 1916 Short Rifle modified during 1943 to more closely conform to the new Model 1943 Rifle. Note the pistol grip stock and grasping grooves, as well as the swivels on the bottom of the lower barrel band and the bottom of the stock. This short rifle has been rebored and rechambered for the 7.92 x 57mm cartridge.

Spanish Foreign Legion troops attacking on the outskirts of Madrid during the Spanish Civil War. They are armed with Model 1893 Rifles and Model 1916 Short Rifles. (Keystone)

Length: 41.30"; **Weight:** 8.3 lbs.; **Barrel:** 21.75"; **Caliber:** 7 x 57mm; **Rifling:** 4-groove, r/hand; **Operation:** Turnbolt 1893-style action; **Feed:** 5-round, staggered column, flush, box magazine; **Sights:** First pattern, "Lange Vizier" rear sight graduated to 2000 meters; second pattern, tangent leaf rear sight graduated to 2000 meters.

Spanish crest over "LA CORUÑA" on the receiver ring of the modified Spanish Model 1916 Short Rifle (previous page, bottom photo)

Spanish "Falangist" crest on the receiver of a Model 1916 Short Rifle

Caliber designation and "ESPECIAL" marking on the left side rail of the modified Spanish Model 1916 Short Rifle. Note the low serial number 32.

SPANISH "TRUE" MODEL 1916 CARBINE: This carbine was produced at Oviedo arsenal, and according to the information received, the configuration is original and not arsenal refinished in any manner. The carbine is fitted with a straight wrist stock, which is standard, with an upper hand guard extending from the front of the receiver ring to just beyond the lower barrel band. There is no upper

Spanish markings on the top of the receiver ring as well as those visible on the left side rail of the Spanish Model 1916 "True" Carbine (Cliff Baumann collection)

Full-length view of the Spanish Model 1916 "True" Carbine. Note the configuration of the top of the upper hand guard, as well as the forend. (Cliff Baumann collection)

band or nose cap, and the carbine is not made to accept a bayonet. There is a pivoted swivel on the left side of the lower barrel band, with a sling bar on the left side of the stock. The bolt handle is bent.

Length: 37.0"; **Weight:** 6.75 lbs.; **Barrel:** 17.0"; **Caliber:** 7 x 57mm; **Rifling:** 4-groove, r/hand; **Operation:** Turnbolt 1893 style action; **Feed:** 5-round, staggered column, flush, box magazine; **Sights:** Tangent leaf rear sight graduated to 2000 meters. **Remarks:** Spanish crest/OVIEDO/1923 on the receiver ring, "P.A.C." and the serial number on the left side rail.

STANDARD MODELL MODEL 1933 SHORT RIFLE USED BY SPAIN: Small numbers of the German Standard Modell Short Rifle were purchased by Spain, both prior to, and during the Spanish Civil War. This Short Rifle has been fitted with a straight wrist stock, with an upper hand guard that extends from the front of the receiver ring

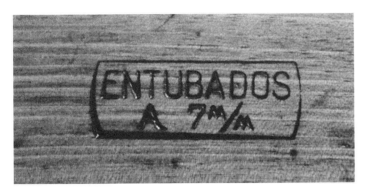

Marking on both sides of the buttstock of the Standard Modell Short Rifle used by Spain. This warns users that the rifle has been rebarreled for the 7 x 57mm cartridge.

Spanish Nationalist (Rebel) troops during a firefight on the outskirts of Madrid (Cushing collection)

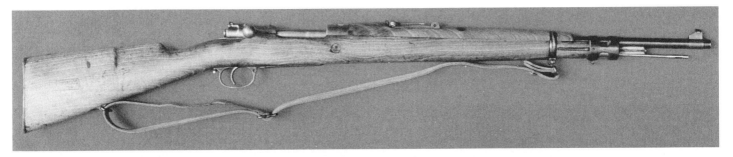

Full-length view of the Standard Modell Short Rifle as used by Spain. Note the very short distance between the lower and upper barrel bands.

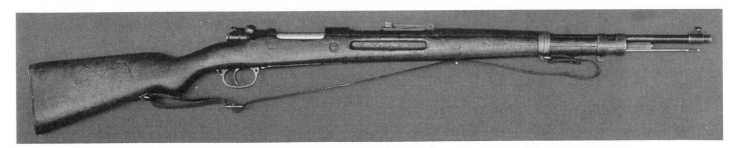

M1933 Standard Modell Short Rifle as used in Spain by the Condor Legion. This short rifle is in caliber 7.92 x 57mm.

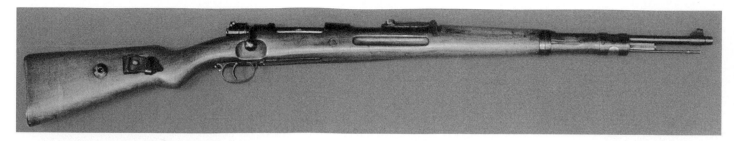

M1933 Standard Modell Carbine, used in Spain by the Condor Legion and other military formations. The caliber is 7.92 x 57mm.

Markings on the receiver ring of the Standard Modell Short Rifle as used by Spain

to just beyond the lower barrel band, which is extremely close to the upper barrel band. The upper band is fitted with a parade hook, and the nose cap incorporates a typical "H"-style bayonet lug. There is a swivel on the bottom of the lower barrel band, and another on the bottom of the stock. The bolt handle is straight.

Length: 42.0"; **Weight:** 8.20 lbs.; **Barrel:** 22.0"; **Caliber:** 7 x 57mm; **Rifling:** 4-groove, r/hand; **Operation:** Turnbolt action; **Feed:** 5-round, staggered column, flush, box magazine; **Sights:** Tangent leaf rear sight graduated to 2000 meters. **Remarks:** Mauser banner logo over the date of manufacture on the receiver ring, "ENTUBADOS A 7m/m" in a rectangle on each side of the buttstock.

SPANISH MODEL 1943 SHORT RIFLE: As a result of the infusion of German weapons, as well as other weapons chambering the 7.92 x 57mm cartridge, the Model 1943 Short Rifle was adopted to replace the Model 1916 Short Rifle, as well as those Model 1893 Rifles still in use. This is a conventional 98 style weapon, with dimensions and specifications quite close to the German K98k, other than the straight bolt handle and the grasping grooves in the forestock. Fitted with a pistol grip stock, the upper hand guard extends from the front of the receiver ring to approximately one inch beyond the lower barrel band. The lower barrel band has a swivel on the bottom and on the left side, while there is another swivel on the bottom of the stock, as well as a sling attachment bar on the left side of the buttstock. The nose cap is fitted with an "H" style bayonet lug; however this short rifle will be most often found with an auxiliary bayonet lug, similar to that on the Argentine Model 1909, for use with older bayonets.

Length: 43.50"; **Weight:** 8.6 lbs.; **Barrel:** 23.62"; **Caliber:** 7.92 x 57mm; **Rifling:** 4-groove, r/hand; **Operation:** Turnbolt action; **Feed:** 5-round, staggered column, flush, box magazine; **Sights:** Tangent leaf rear sight graduated to 2000 meters. **Remarks:** Spanish crest within "FABRICA DE ARMAS" curved around the top/the arsenal/year of manufacture.

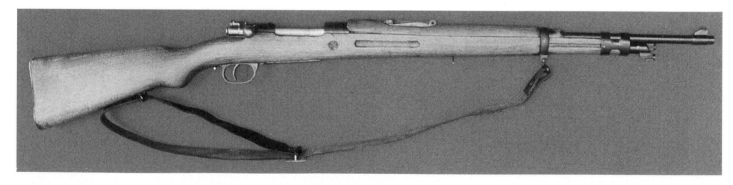

Full-length view of the Spanish Model 43 Short Rifle as made for the Spanish army

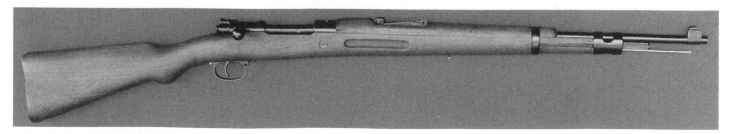

Full-length view of the Spanish Model 1944 Short Rifle as made for the Spanish Air Force. Note that the air force model does not have the auxiliary bayonet lug.

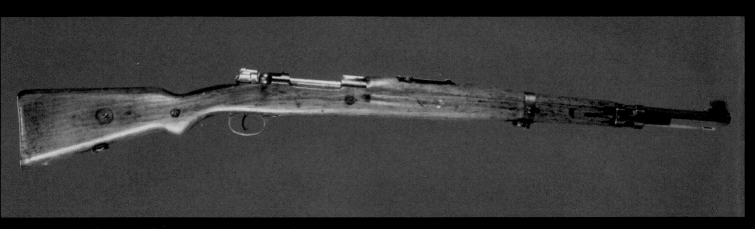

Czech VZ 24 Short Rifle as used by Romania

The receiver ring of the Romanian Model VZ 24 Short Rifle, showing the crest of King Carol

The receiver ring of the Romanian Model VZ 24 Short Rifle, showing the crest of King Michael

Serbian Model 78/80 Rifle

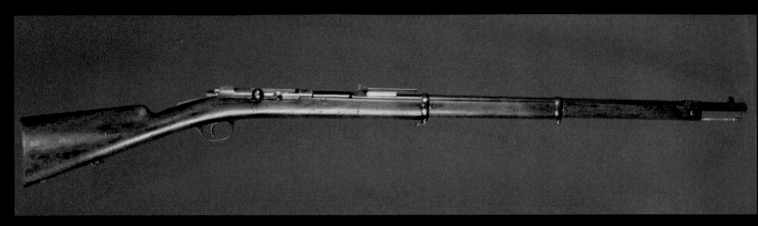

Manufacturer's markings in German on the left side rail of the Serbian Model 78/80 Rifle

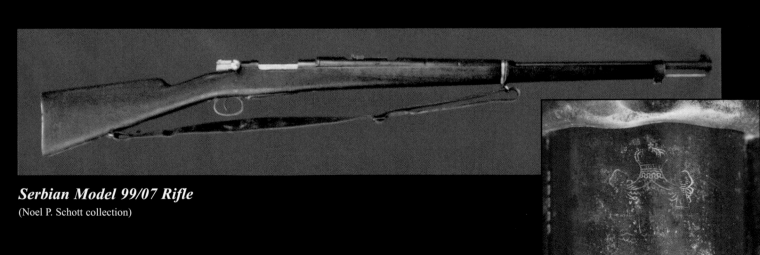

Serbian Model 99/07 Rifle

(Noel P. Schott collection)

Crest, showing model designation, on the receiver ring of the Serbian Model 99/07 Rifle

(Noel P. Schott collection)

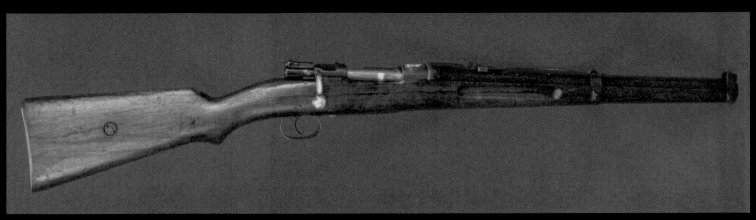

Serbian Model 1908 Carbine

(Noel P. Schott collection)

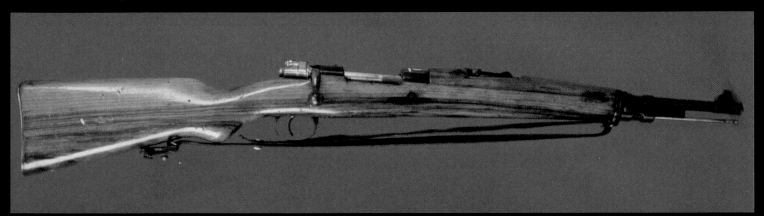

Yugoslavian Model 24 Carbine

Yugoslavian crest and model designation in Cyrillic on the receiver ring of the Yugoslavian Model 24 Carbine

Yugoslavian FN Model 24 Carbine, marked for the City of Nish Gendarmerie
(Noel P. Schott collection)

The receiver ring of the Yugoslavian FN Model 24 Carbine, showing the Yugoslavian crest, the model destination, and the Cyrillic wording for the Nish Gendarmerie
(Noel P. Schott collection)

Close-up view of the variant Communist markings on the receiver ring of the Yugoslavian Post-World War Two Model 48 Short Rifle.

Variant side rail markings on the Yugoslavian Model 48 Short Rifle.

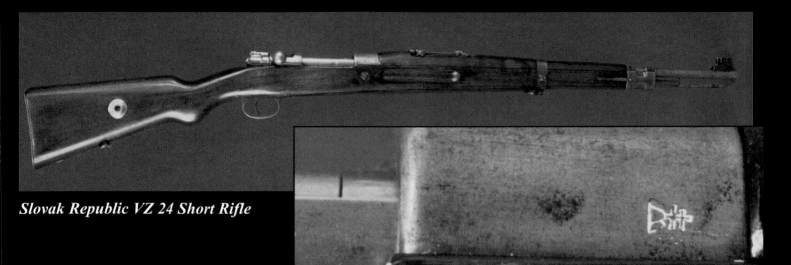

Slovak Republic VZ 24 Short Rifle

The Slovak Republic crest on the right side of the receiver ring of the Slovak Republic Short Rifle

Spain

Spanish Model 1893 Carbine. Note the manner in which the forend is formed.
(Cliff Baumann collection)

The Spanish crest on top of the receiver of the Spanish Model 1893 Carbine
(Cliff Baumann collection)

Spain

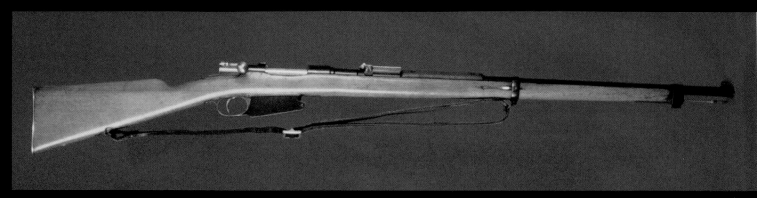

Spanish Model 1892 Rifle

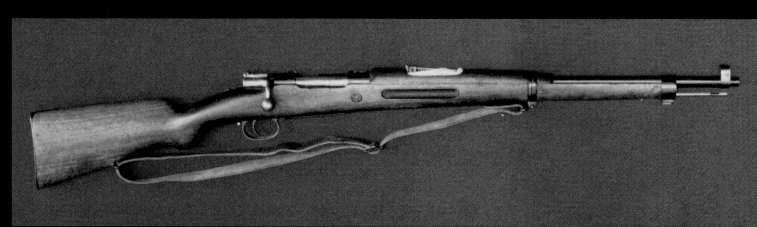

Model 1916 Short Rifle modified during 1943 to more closely conform to the new Model 1943 Rifle. Note the pistol grip stock and grasping grooves, as well as the swivels on the bottom of the lower barrel and band and the bottom of the stock. This short rifle has been rebored and rechambered for the 7.92 x 57mm cartridge.

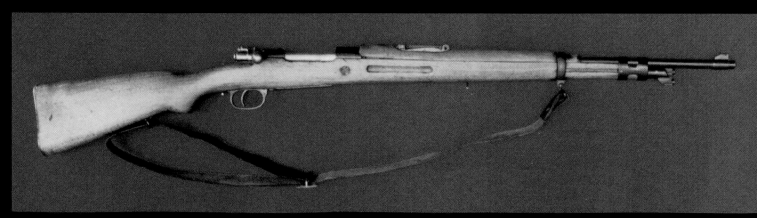

Spanish Model 43 Short Rifle as made for the Spanish army

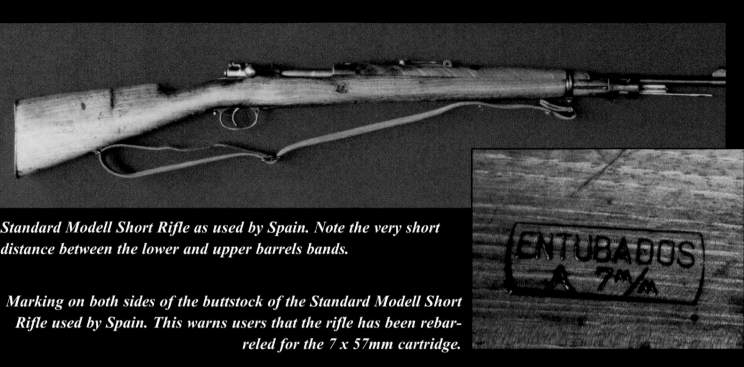

Standard Modell Short Rifle as used by Spain. Note the very short distance between the lower and upper barrels bands.

Marking on both sides of the buttstock of the Standard Modell Short Rifle used by Spain. This warns users that the rifle has been rebarreled for the 7 x 57mm cartridge.

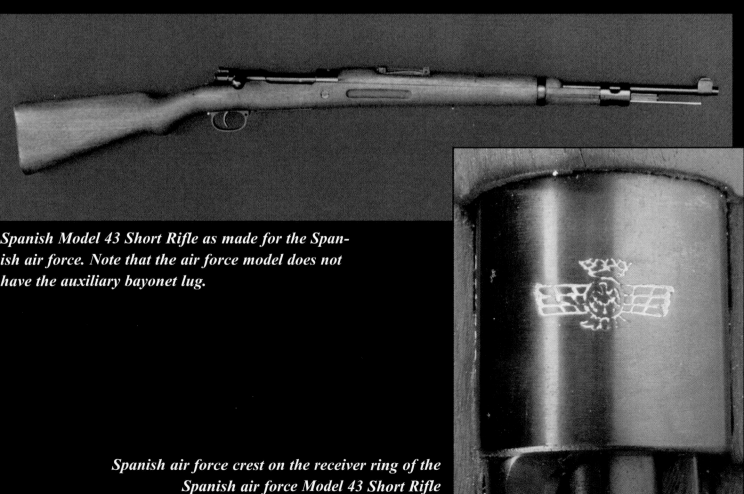

Spanish Model 43 Short Rifle as made for the Spanish air force. Note that the air force model does not have the auxiliary bayonet lug.

Spanish air force crest on the receiver ring of the Spanish air force Model 43 Short Rifle

Swedish Model 1894 Carbine as modified in 1917 by the addition of a bayonet lug
(Lothar Frank collection)

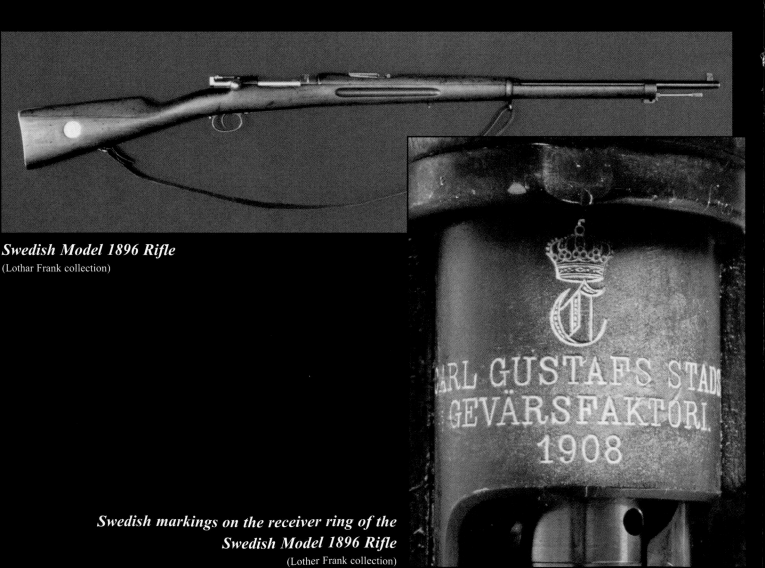

Swedish Model 1896 Rifle
(Lothar Frank collection)

Swedish markings on the receiver ring of the
Swedish Model 1896 Rifle
(Lother Frank collection)

ARL GUSTAFS STADS
GEVÄRSFAKTORI.
1908

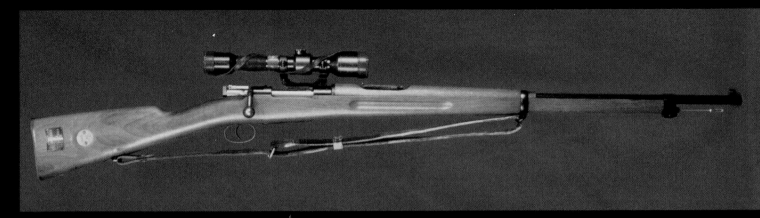

Swedish Model 1896 Sniper Rifle fitted with the Model 41 AGA scope. Note the bent bolt for clearance.

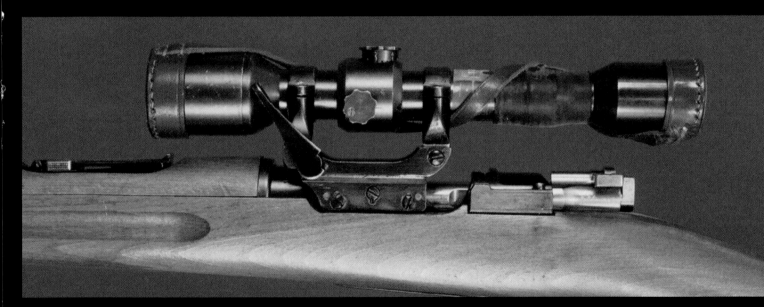

View of the left side of the Swedish Model 1896 Sniper Rifle fitted with the Model 41 AGA scope

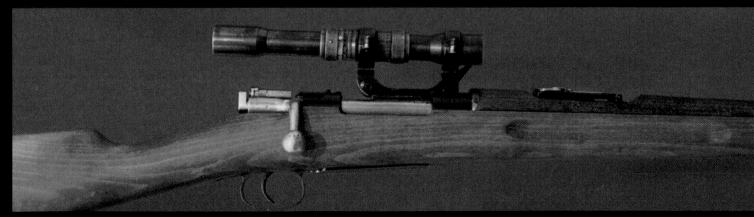

View of the right side of the Swedish Model 1896 Sniper Rifle fitted with the Model 42 AGA scope,

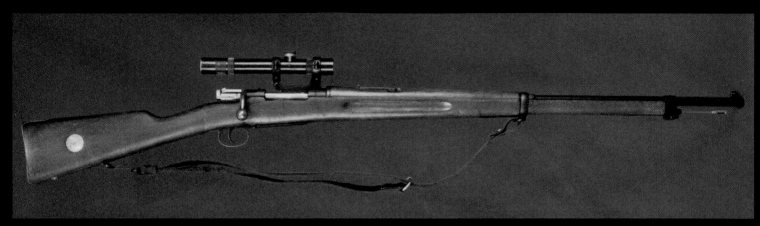

Swedish Model 1896 Sniper Rifle fitted with the Model 44 AGA scope, which is also 3 x 65mm

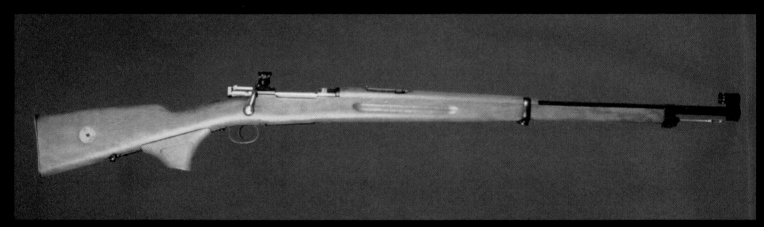

Swedish Model 1896 Military Target Rifle fitted with special target front and rear sights

Swedish Model 1938 Short Rifle
(Lothar Frank collection)

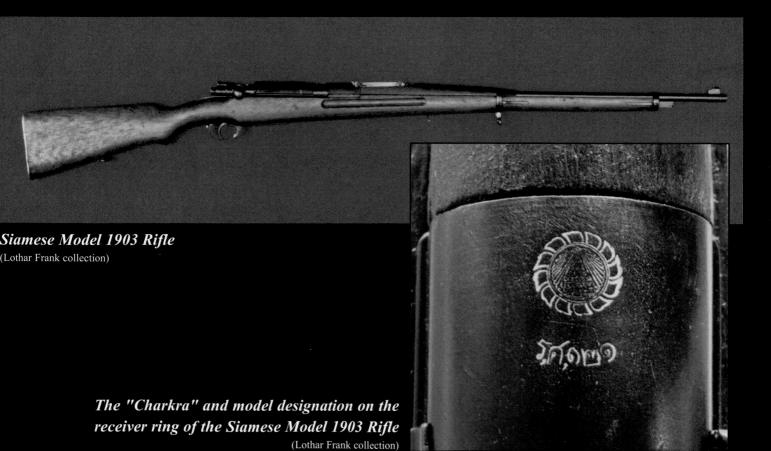

Close-up view of the Syrian Model 1948 bolt handle, showing the angle of the handle, as well as the flattened bottom of the bolt knob; note also the laminations of the stock.

 # Thailand/Siam

Siamese Model 1903 Rifle
(Lothar Frank collection)

The "Charkra" and model designation on the receiver ring of the Siamese Model 1903 Rifle
(Lothar Frank collection)

Thailand/Siam

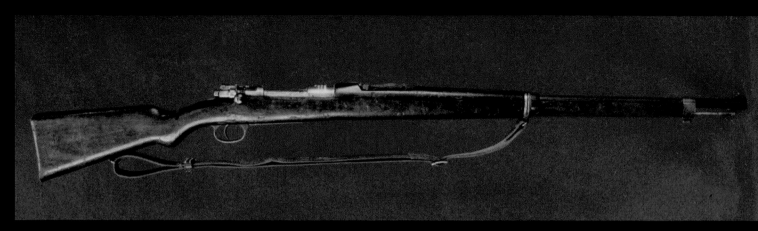

Siamese Model 1904 Rifle

(Noel P. Schott collection)

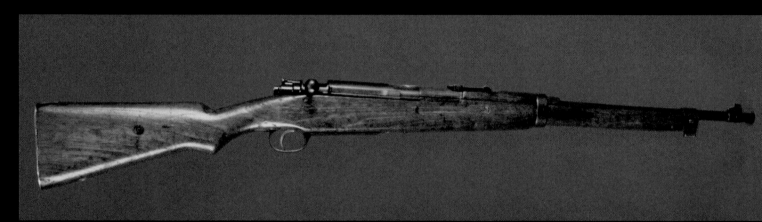

Siamese Model 1923 (Type 66) Short Rifle, with the bolt cover closed

"Charkra" and model year in Siamese numerals on the receiver ring of the Siamese Model 1923 (Type 66) Short Rifle

Turkish-marked Turkish Model 1887 Rifle
(Cliff Baumann collection)

Barrel flat markings in Turkish on the Turkish Model 1887 Rifle
(Cliff Baumann collection)

Left side rail of the Turkish Model 1887 Rifle, showing the manufacturers markings in German

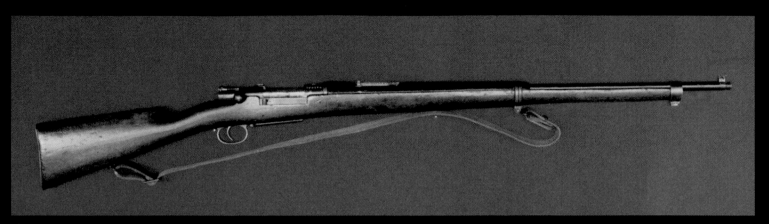

Turkish Model 1893 Rifle

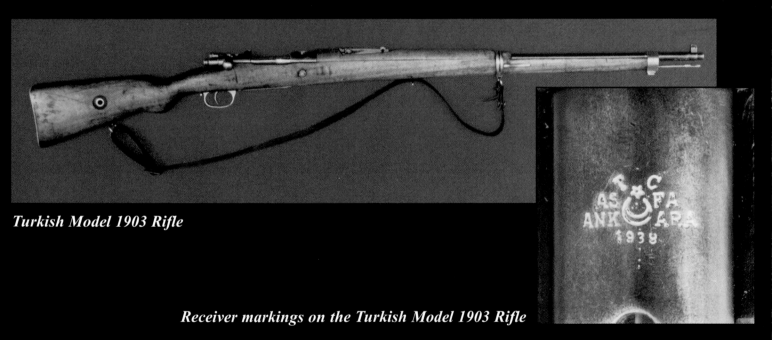

Turkish Model 1903 Rifle

Receiver markings on the Turkish Model 1903 Rifle

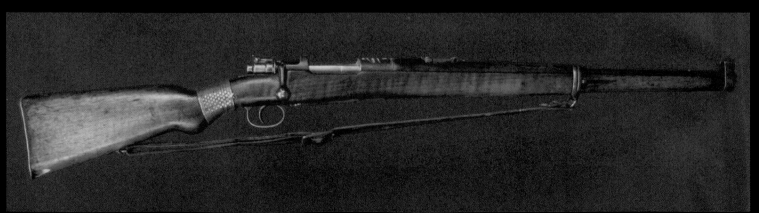

Turkish Model 1905 Carbine. Note how the wrist of the stock has been very artfully wrapped with wire to reinforce a presumed crack or break.

(Noel P. Schott collection)

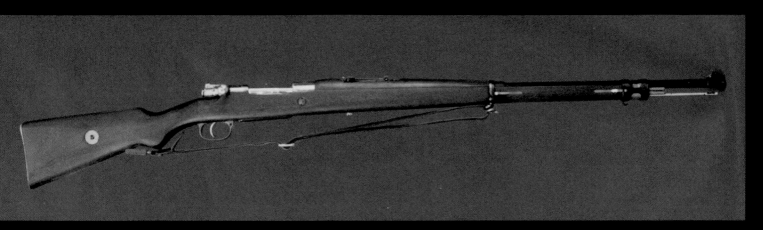

Uruguayan Model 1908 Rifle
(Noel P. Schott collection)

Uruguayan Model VZ 37 ("937") Short Rifle
(Noel P. Schott collection)

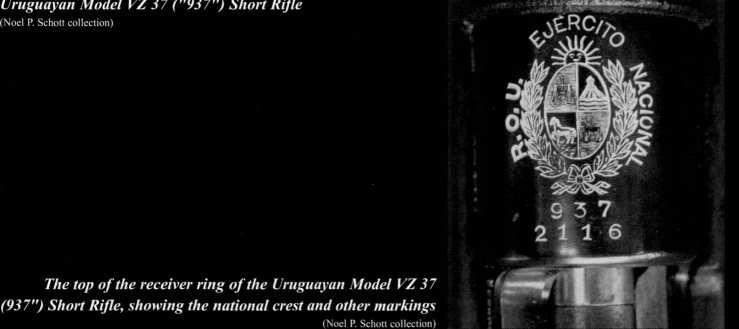

***The top of the receiver ring of the Uruguayan Model VZ 37
("937") Short Rifle, showing the national crest and other markings***
(Noel P. Schott collection)

Venezuela

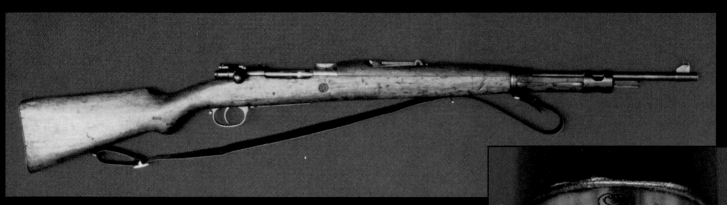

Venezuelan FN Model 24/30 Short Rifle

**Venezuelan crest on the receiver ring of the Venezuelan
FN Model 24/30 Short Rifle**

Z.A.R./South Africa

*View of the German military
quality inspection mark on the
root of the bolt handle, with the
serial number on the bolt handle
of the M1896 ZAR Mauser rifle.*
(John Wall Collection, photo by John M. Leone.)

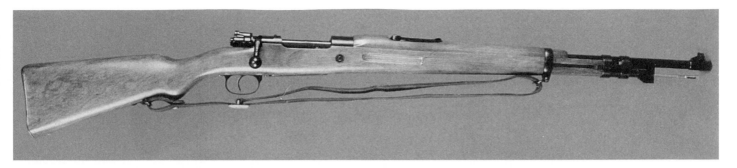

Full-length view of a variant of the Spanish Model 43 Short Rifle. In this case, the rifle was produced with a turned down bolt handle.

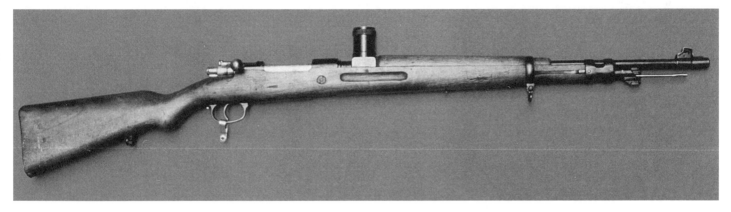

Full-length view of a pressure test Spanish Model 43 Short Rifle (Century International Arms, Inc.)

Spanish air force crest on the receiver ring of the Spanish air force Model 43 Short Rifle

Markings stamped on the side of the receiver and left side rail of the Spanish air force Model 43 Short Rifle

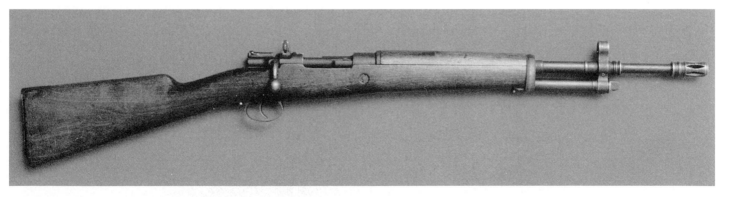

Full-length view of the FR7 Spanish Special Purpose Rifle. Note the straight wrist stock and the bent bolt handle of the Model 1916 Short Rifle. (Century International Arms, Inc.)

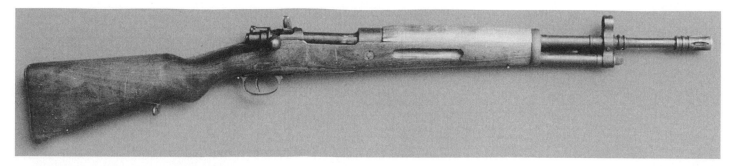

Full-length view of the FR8 Spanish Special Purpose Rifle. Please note the grasping grooves, straight bolt handle, and the pistol grip stock of the Spanish Model 43 Short Rifle. (Century International Arms, Inc.)

A Republican force on the skirmish line, armed with Model 1893 Rifles (Cushing collection)

SPANISH SPECIAL PURPOSE RIFLES, FR7 AND FR8: During the 1950s, a limited number of Spanish Model 1916 and Model 43 Short Rifles were arsenal converted to transition training rifles for the CETME rifle. These SP rifles are handy, lightweight, and reliable, and apparently saw considerable troop use with Spanish Special Forces. Both rifles retained their stock configuration, but were shortened to 38.8 inches overall, with an 18.5-inch barrel; the weight was reduced to 7.5 lbs, and the barrel is fitted with a flash suppresser. The tube under the barrel holds the bayonet adapter and is also used to store cleaning equipment. The rifles have been converted to fire the .308 Winchester round.

SWEDEN

Sweden, slightly larger than the state of California, has a long history of military involvement in northwestern Europe. In the seventeenth century, Sweden became the champion of Protestantism in Europe. The Swedes waged war against the Hapsburgs in the Thirty Years War, emerging as victors. Sweden also fought successful wars against Denmark and Poland, creating a great northern empire and virtually turning the Baltic into a Swedish lake.

During the eighteenth century, Sweden's kings became despotic and completely weakened the country, both economically and polit-

ically. During the Napoleonic Wars, Sweden joined with the other European powers against Napoleon, and, upon the victorious conclusion of the war, Sweden was awarded Norway. Norway finally regained its independence in 1906.

Sweden remained neutral during both the First and Second World Wars, and after the conclusion of World War II, became a charter member of the U.N., joining the European Union in 1944.

The Swedish Army has also had a keen interest in maintaining parity with other nations in regard to armaments, based upon the theory that the best way to keep peace is to be prepared for war. The Swedes adopted the Mauser system after strenuous testing of Mauser, Mannlicher, Krag-Jorgensen, Lee and many other pattern rifles. Fortunately for the Swedes, the weapons have never had to undergo trial by warfare.

SWEDISH MODEL 1894 CARBINE: From 1894 to 1896, Waffenfabrik Mauser manufactured a total 12,185 carbines for Swedish use, while the Carl Gustafs Stads Gevarsfactori and the commercial firm Husqvarna Vapenfabriks. A.B. (Husqvarna Arms Factory, Inc.) produced many more of the carbine model. This is the first of the Swedish Mauser series, and is a very attractive and handy weapon.

The markings on the receiver ring of the Swedish Model 1894 Carbine (Lothar Frank collection)

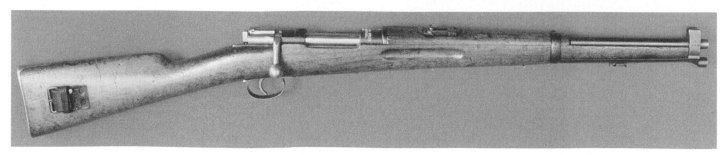

Full-length view of the Swedish Model 1894 Carbine as modified in 1917 by the addition of a bayonet lug (Lothar Frank collection)

The right side view of the bayonet lug on the variant Model 1894 Swedish Navy Carbine. (Noel Schott collection)

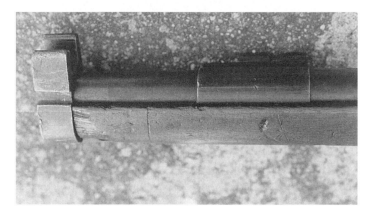

Left side view of the bayonet lug attachment on the Swedish Navy Model 1894 Carbine. (Noel Schott collection)

Property plate on the bottom of the stock of the Swedish Navy Model 1894 Carbine. (Noel Schott collection)

The action is very similar to the Spanish Model 1893 Rifle; however there is a notch on the cocking piece in order for the safety to be engaged while the firing pin is almost completely forward. There is a distinctive angular extension on the cocking piece. The carbine is fitted with a straight wrist stock to the muzzle, with an upper hand guard that extends from the front of the receiver ring to just beyond the lower barrel band. The stock has grasping grooves, and there is a sling slot cut through the stock. The lower swivel has a sling slot on the left hand side, while the nose cap forms protective ears for the front sight. After the adoption of the Model 1896 Rifle, the carbine was revised by providing a cutout in the left side rail. In 1917, the nose cap was modified by the addition of a bayonet lug on the order of the British SMLE No. III, as well as a long extension under the forend with an attachment lug.

Length: 37.40"; **Weight:** 7.3 lbs.; **Barrel:** 17.38"; **Caliber:** 6.5 x 55mm; **Rifling:** 4-groove, r/hand; **Operation:** Turnbolt 1893-style action; **Feed:** 5-round, staggered column, flush, box magazine; **Sights:** V-notch adjustable rear sight graduated to 1600 meters. **Remarks:** Swedish crest, name of manufacturer, and date of manufacture on the receiver ring, with the serial number on the left side rail.

SWEDISH MODEL 1896 RIFLE: In 1896, Sweden adopted as standard the Model 1896 Rifle. Fitted with a straight wrist stock with grasping grooves, the upper hand guard extends from the front of the receiver ring to just beyond the lower barrel band. There is a simple nose cap with a bayonet lug on the bottom. The lower barrel band has a swivel on the bottom and another on the bottom of the stock. There is a full-depth rounded cut in the left side wall of the receiver, and the bolt has the right-angled cocking piece projection.

Swedish markings on the receiver ring of the Swedish Model 1896 Rifle (Lothar Frank collection)

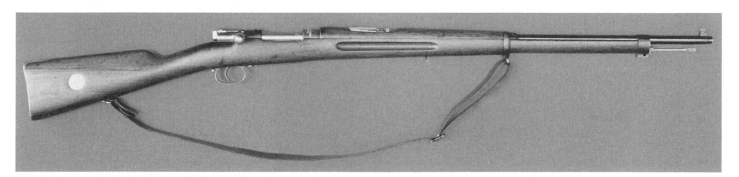

Full-length view of the Swedish Model 1896 Rifle (Lothar Frank collection)

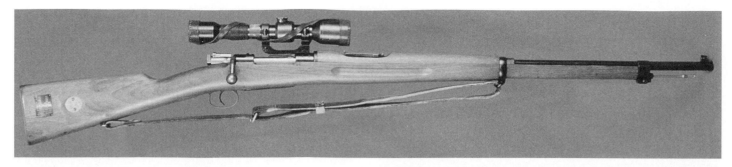

Full-length view of the Swedish Model 1896 Sniper Rifle fitted with the Model 41 AGA scope. Note the bent bolt for clearance.

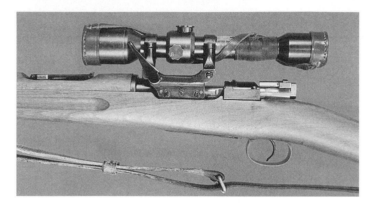

Close-up view of the left side of the Swedish Model 1896 Sniper Rifle fitted with the Model 41 AGA scope

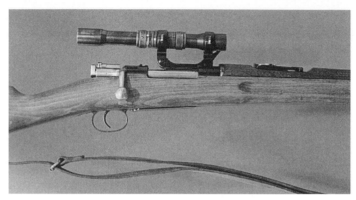

Close-up view of the right side of the Swedish Model 1896 Sniper Rifle fitted with the Model 42 AGA scope, which is 3 x 65mm

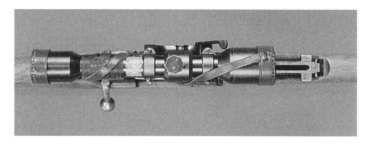

Top view of the scope and action of the Swedish Model 1896 Sniper Rifle fitted with the Model 41 AGA scope

Due to the depth of the cut in the left side wall, the guide rib is on the bolt instead of on the receiver. The rear sight differs from earlier Mauser sights in that the leaf is pivoted to the front of the sight base instead of the rear. There is a hole at the bottom of the upper barrel band for the attachment of a monopod, and the stock has a metal disc on the right side for marking purposes.

Length: 49.50"; **Weight:** 9.0 lbs.; **Barrel:** 29.10"; **Caliber:** 6.5 x 55mm; **Rifling:** 4-groove, r/hand; **Operation:** Turnbolt 1894-style action; **Feed:** 5-round, staggered column, flush, box magazine; **Sights:** V-notch or U-notch leaf rear sight graduated to 2000 meters. **Remarks:** Swedish crest over name of manufacturer over date of manufacture on the receiver ring, with the serial number on the left side rail.

SWEDISH MODEL 1938 SHORT RIFLE: In 1938, the Swedes adopted a short rifle that was identical to the Model 1896 with the exception of smaller dimensions and a bent bolt handle. This is the Model 1938 Short Rifle.

Length: 44.10"; **Weight:** 9.1 lbs.; **Caliber:** 6.5 x 55mm; **Rifling:** 4-groove, r/hand; **Operation:** Turnbolt action; **Feed:** 5-round, staggered column, flush, box magazine; **Sights:** U-notch adjustable rear sight graduated to 1600 meters. **Remarks:** Name of the manufacturer over the date of manufacture on the receiver ring.

Close-up view of the left side of the Swedish Model 1896 Sniper Rifle fitted with the Model 42 AGA scope

Top view of the Model 42 AGA scope, action, and rear sight of the Swedish Model 1896 Sniper Rifle

The Swedes held the distinction of having the world's most powerful bolt action infantry rifle when they adopted the Swedish Model 40, a standard Model K98k carbine re-chambered for the Swedish Model 32 8mm machinegun cartridge. This carbine was intended for use by the troops manning the machine guns, based on the theory that they would be utilizing the same cartridge as the machine guns. Due to the size of the cartridge, the magazine capacity was reduced to four rounds, and, due to the excessive recoil from the powerful Model 32 cartridge, it was necessary to equip the carbines with a muzzle brake...all in all, a handful for any soldier to fire!

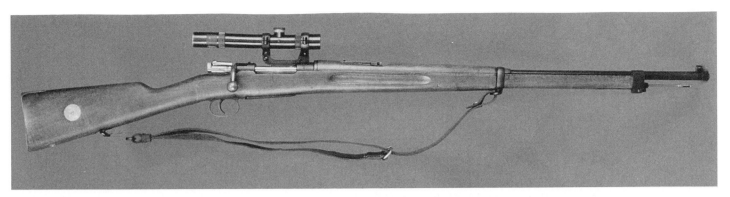

Full-length view of the Swedish Model 1896 Sniper Rifle fitted with the Model 44 AGA scope, which is also 3 x 65mm

Full-length view of the Swedish Model 1896 Sniper Rifle fitted with the Model 44 AGA scope, which is also 3 x 65mm

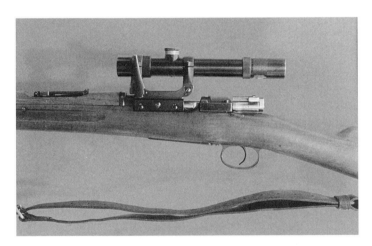

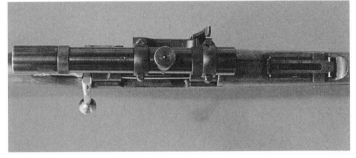

Top view of the Model 44 AGA scope, action, and rear sight of the Swedish Model 1896 Sniper Rifle

Close-up view of the left side of the Swedish Model 1896 Sniper Rifle fitted with the Model 44 AGA scope

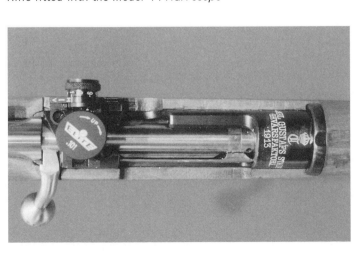

Top view of the action and special target rear sight of the Swedish Model 1896 Military Target Rifle

Markings on the receiver ring of the Swedish Model 1896 Military Target Rifle

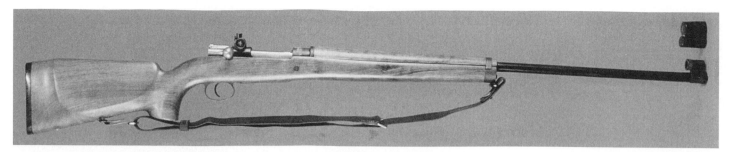

Full-length view the Swedish heavy-barreled Model 1896 Target Rifle. Note the muzzle cover, which also covers the front sight.

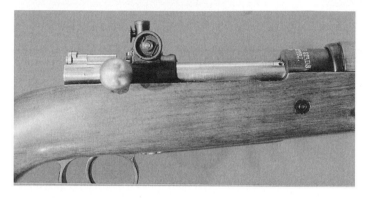

Close-up view of the action and receiver bridge sight on the heavy-barreled version of the Swedish Model 1896 Target Rifle

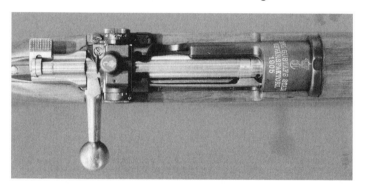

Top view of the action and rear sight of the heavy-barreled version of the Swedish Model 1896 Target Rifle

Manufacturer's name and date of manufacture on the receiver ring of the Swedish Model 1938 Short Rifle. (Lothar Frank collection)

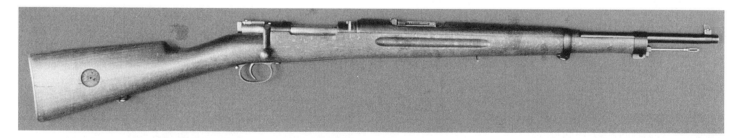

Full-length view of the Swedish Model 1938 Short Rifle (Lothar Frank collection)

Full-length view of the Swedish Model 40 98k Carbine as used by Swedish machine gun troops; note the muzzle brake used to help control the heavy recoil. (Robert Jensen collection)

Full-length view of the Syrian Model 1948 Short Rifle (Century International Arms, Inc.)

SYRIA

As the Ottoman Empire crumbled during the First World War, Syrian national ambitions began to be realized. Backed by the British, the Syrians were encouraged to rebel against the Turks. Unfortunately for the Syrians, France governed Syria after the war under a mandate from the League of Nations, splitting off Lebanon, which became independent in 1926. The Syrians rebelled against the French, but were completely unsuccessful in overthrowing them. In 1940, the French authorities in Syria declared for Vichy, prompting an invasion by British and Free French troops in 1941. As a result of this invasion, an independent Syrian Republic was declared in September, 1941.

Syria was a founding member of the Arab League, and was deeply involved in the Arab-Israeli War of 1948; an armistice was signed with Israel in 1949. There was a brief, abortive attempt at a union between Syria and Egypt, from which Syria seceded in 1961. In all of the succeeding wars with Israel, Syria has been an active leader. From the time of the Yom Kippur War (1973), Syria has defiantly rejected any attempts at reconciliation or peace in the region. In 1994, however, Syria did make serious efforts at normalizing relations in exchange for the return of the Golan Heights.

Syria's army, until the influx of Russian equipment and advisors after the first Arab-Israeli conflict, could best be described as woefully lacking in any homogeneous effort to field an effective force. Armaments were mainly French World War I and II leftovers, with supplies of war surplus German K98k Carbines coming off the deserts of North Africa. In order to flesh out its fledgling forces, Syria turned to the Yugoslavs for equipment, purchasing the Model 1948 copy of the German K98k Carbine. These weapons became redundant with the commencement of the Russian arms deals.

SYRIAN MODEL 1948 SHORT RIFLE: The Model 48 is very similar to the German K98k, the rifle being fitted with a pistol grip stock without grasping grooves, and the upper hand guard extending from the front of the receiver ring to the upper barrel band (as in the Yugoslav Model 24). The lower barrel band has a sling bar on the left, with a sling slot cut through the buttstock.

Length: 42.90"; **Weight:** 8.62 lbs.; **Barrel:** 23.30"; **Caliber:** 7.92 x 57mm; **Rifling:** 4-groove, r/hand; **Operation:** Turnbolt action; **Feed:** 5-round, staggered column, flush, box magazine; **Sights:** Tangent leaf rear sight graduated to 2000 meters. **Remarks:** Syrian national crest on top of the receiver ring.

THAILAND (SIAM)

The kingdom of Siam came into existence around 1000 A.D., with the unification of the petty states of the region in Southeast Asia. From 1511, European traders and missionaries were active in the kingdom. By skillful political manipulation, the Thai monarchy enabled the country to be the only country in Southeast Asia that did not come under the political domination of, or be colonized by, a European power.

The absolute monarchy ended by military coup in 1932, and in December 1941, Siam was occupied by the Japanese forces. Under pressure, Siam concluded an alliance with Japan and declared war on Great Britain and the United States. At the same time, the mon-

The receiver ring showing the Syrian national crest on the Syrian Model 1948 Short Rifle (Century International Arms, Inc.)

Close-up view of the Syrian Model 1948 bolt handle, showing the angle of the handle, aw well as the flattened bottom of the bolt knob; note also the laminations of the stock.

archy supported a secret war of resistance against the Japanese. Since the end of World War II, Thai politics have been largely democratic, but closely tied to a military-civilian oligarchy.

The Thai army has always had a close interest in maintaining military equality with its neighbors, and the influence of the Mauser rifle has been felt since the 1870s. At the turn of the century, some specimen rifles of a variation on the G 98 design were produced by Waffenfabrik Mauser for troop trials. With the successful completion of field trials, production of the new rifle, specified as the Model 1903 (Type 45) Siamese Mauser Rifle, was undertaken at the Tokyo arsenal, Japan. In 1923, an artillery and cavalry model, the Model 1923 (type 66) Short Rifle, based upon the 1903 Rifle, was

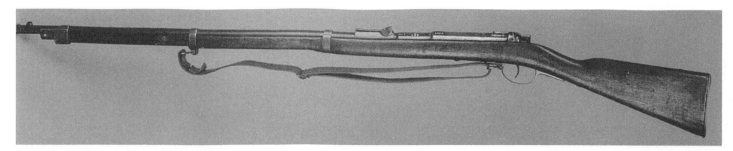

Left full-length view of the German Model G 71 Rifle as used by Siam

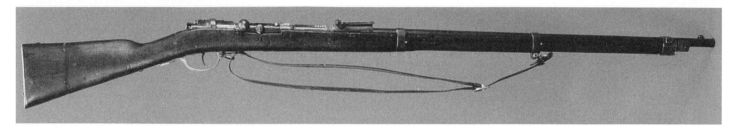

Full-length view of the Siamese Model G 71 Rifle

also produced in Japan. These weapons were used by the Thai resistance during World War II; however, most will be found in very good condition.

GERMAN MODEL G 71 RIFLE: This rifle represents the first efforts of the Siamese to arm themselves with modern weapons. These rifles were purchased from Germany shortly after they were accepted by the German armed forces and were considered standard for many years. Other than being marked on top of the receiver with the Siamese "Charkra," or symbolic throwing weapon, all of the other

Model designation on the left side rail of the Siamese Model G 71 Rifle

Siamese "Charkra" and manufacturer's markings and proofs on the receiver ring and barrel of the Siamese Model G 71 Rifle

markings are strictly according to German practice. Specific data on this rifle will be found in the section on Germany.

SIAMESE MODEL 1903 (TYPE 45) RIFLE: This rifle is most unusual; it is chambered for a rare size 8mm Siamese rimmed cartridge, and is equipped with a sliding bolt cover designed to keep dirt from the action. By lifting the cover latch, the cover can be slid forward to expose the action. The top and bottom tangs lend reinforcement to the stock, and the magazine is slanted in order that the rimmed cartridges can feed properly.

The rifle is fitted with a pistol grip stock with grasping grooves and an upper hand guard extending from the front of the receiver ring to just beyond the lower barrel band. The simple nose cap/upper barrel band is fitted with a short "H"-style bayonet lug. The lower barrel band has a swivel on the bottom and another at the bottom of the buttstock. All of the markings are in Siamese. Ammunition for these rifles is virtually unobtainable, and many in the U.S. have been professionally rechambered for the .45-70 cartridge.

The "Charkra" and model designation on the receiver ring of the Siamese Model 1903 Rifle (Lothar Frank collection)

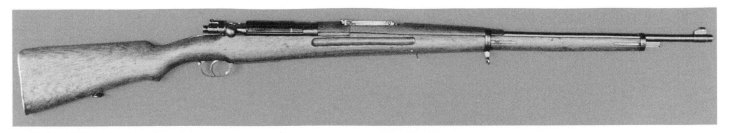

Full-length view of the Siamese Model 1903 Rifle (Lothar Frank collection)

The receiver bridge and the sliding bolt cover latch (on the right) of the Siamese Model 1903 Rifle (Lothar Frank collection)

The action, with sliding bolt cover open, of the Siamese Model 1903 Rifle (Lothar Frank collection)

Length: 49.10"; **Weight:** 8.50 lbs.; **Barrel:** 29.13"; **Caliber:** 8 x 50mm Siamese rimmed; **Rifling:** 4-groove, r/hand; **Operation:** Turnbolt 98-style action; **Feed:** 5-round, staggered column, flush, box magazine; **Sights:** Tangent leaf rear sight graduated to 2000 meters. **Remarks:** The receiver ring is marked with the Siamese "Charkra" over the Siamese markings for the model year, which translates into "R.S. 121," (Ratanakos 121), the year of adoption of the dynasty, or the Christian year 1903. All markings are in Siamese.

SIAMESE MODEL 1904 RIFLE: Prior to 1914, Siamese authorities purchased an undetermined number of export Model 1904 Rifles produced by Waffenfabrik Mauser. The rifles made for Siam appear to differ slightly in several areas, mainly in weighing almost a full pound more than the standard export model, and in having a slightly longer barrel.

The Siamese Model 1904 Rifle is fitted with a pistol grip stock, with the upper hand guard extending from the front of the receiver ring to just beyond the lower barrel band. The lower barrel band is fitted with a swivel on the bottom, with another at the bottom of the buttstock. There is a simple nose cap with a bayonet lug on the bottom.

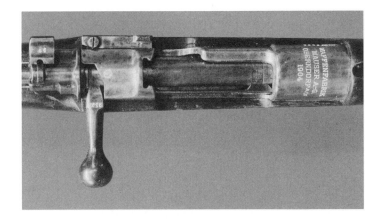

Overall view of the action of the Siamese Model 1904 Rifle, showing manufacturer's markings and the Siamese "Charkra" marking on the receiver bridge (Noel P. Schott collection)

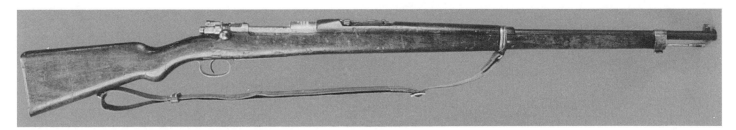

Full-length view of the Siamese Model 1904 Rifle (Noel P. Schott collection)

Left side of the receiver of the Siamese Model 1904 Rifle, showing the weapon serial number and the proof marks. (Noel P. Schott collection)

Close-up view of the Siamese "Charkra" marking on the receiver bridge of the Siamese Model 1904 Rifle. (Noel P. Schott collection)

Length: 48.78"; **Weight:** 9.8 lbs.; **Barrel:** 29.25"; **Caliber:** 7 x 57mm; **Rifling:** 4-groove, r/hand; **Operation:** Turnbolt action; **Feed:** 5-round, staggered column, flush, box magazine; **Sights:** Tangent leaf rear sight graduated to 2000 meters. **Remarks:** Manufacturer's markings appear in German on top of the receiver ring over the model designation, with the serial number and proofs on the left side of the receiver ring. The Siamese "Charkra" marking is on the receiver bridge.

SIAMESE MODEL 1923 (TYPE 66) SHORT RIFLE: These short rifles were produced in Japan, and there is some conjecture that many of them were cut down from the Model 1903 Rifle. This short rifle is fitted with a pistol grip stock, with an upper hand guard extending from the front of the receiver ring to just beyond the lower barrel band. There is a sling slot on the left side of the lower barrel band, and a swivel on the left side of the buttstock. The simple nose cap incorporates a bayonet stud on the bottom. The action is identical to the Model 1903 Rifle.

Length: 41.92"; **Weight:** 8.05 lbs.; **Barrel:** 22.05"; **Caliber:** 8 x 52mm rimmed; **Rifling:** 4-groove, r/hand; **Operation:** Turnbolt action; **Feed:** 5-round, staggered column, flush, box magazine; **Sights:** Tangent leaf rear sight believed to graduated to 1200 meters. **Remarks:** All model designations and manufacturer's markings are in Siamese.

NOTE: When the Model 1903 (Type 45) Rifle was adopted, the cartridge for which the rifle was chambered was an 8 x 50mm bottleneck rimmed case, with a round-nose, metal-jacketed bullet.

"Charkra" and model year in Siamese numerals on the receiver ring of the Siamese Model 1923 (Type 66) Short Rifle

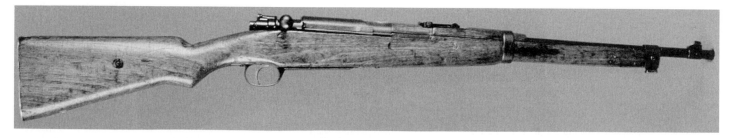

Full-length view of the Siamese Model 1923 (Type 66) Short Rifle, with the bolt cover closed

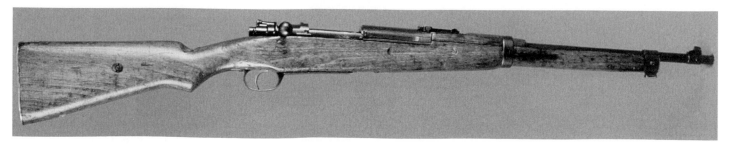

Full-length view of the Siamese Model 1923 (Type 66) Short Rifle, with the bolt cover open

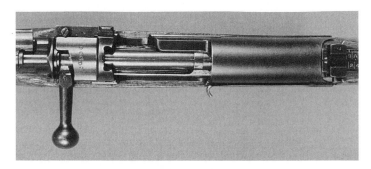

Full view of the action with open bolt cover of the Siamese Model 1923 (Type 66) Short Rifle

With the advent of the Model 1923 Short Rifle (Type 66), the short rifles were chambered for the 8 x 52mm cartridge with a pointed bullet. These cartridges are not interchangeable.

THE TRANSVAAL

The Cape of Good Hope was discovered by the Portuguese explorer Bartholomew Dias in 1488. The Dutch East India Company, always taking advantage of a good thing, established a large, permanent settlement for the furthering of trade with the East Indies in 1652. This settlement attracted Protestant settlers from around Europe, who found it necessary to do battle with the various tribal nations who were in possession of the lands prior to the white influx.

Control of the Cape of Good Hope became a matter of dissension between Great Britain and the Dutch settlers during the eighteenth century; to escape the intrusive British lion, the settlers embarked upon what became known as the Great Trek, moving the predominantly Dutch settlers to the north, away from the British encroachments. These pioneers later became known as the Boers (farmers), who had to do battle with the mighty Zulu tribes to establish themselves in the region. Two provinces were formed, the Orange Free State and the Transvaal.

When diamonds were discovered in the Orange Free State and gold in the Transvaal, the area was inundated by British interests and workers, provoking Boer rebellions. Seeking to arm themselves, the Boers secretly ordered quantities of the German G 71 Rifle, which were used in the first Anglo-Boer War of 1881-1882. During the later, better known Boer War of 1899-1902, these same weapons were to be found in the hands of some of the Boer commandos.

GERMAN MODEL G 71 RIFLE: This was the standard issue German infantry rifle, with typical German manufacturer's markings and proofs. As far as can be determined, there were no special markings of any kind, other than perhaps informal carvings in the stocks to indicate usage in the Transvaal. All specific data on this rifle will be found in the section under Germany.

TURKEY

Located partly in southeastern Europe and partly in western Asia, the nation of Turkey was a Hittite empire for thousands of years before the birth of Christ, controlling most of present-day Turkey. All of the provinces that comprised Turkey, including Galatia, Cappadocia, Cilicia and smaller provinces, were incorporated into the Roman Empire by the end of the first century A.D. Following the decline of the Roman Empire, the Eastern Roman (Byzantine) Empire controlled the entire area.

After the Mongol invasions of the thirteenth century, the Ottomans, a small tribe in central Anatolia, expanded from their base, and within the space of a century, had captured most of Turkey, Serbia, and Bulgaria. By the middle of the sixteenth century, the Ottoman Empire included most of Arabia, Egypt, the Middle East, Iran, and southeastern Europe into the Crimea.

The Ottoman Empire, at one time a commanding figure in the balance of power in Europe, gradually became known as the "Sick Old Man of Europe," adopting a liberal constitution in 1876, which was largely ignored by the sultan until a revolution of "Young Turks" in 1908 forced observance of the terms of the constitution. Angered by what they perceived as mistreatment of Greek citizens during an uprising in Crete in 1896, Greece forced Turkey into a war in 1897, one that proved disastrous for the Greeks. Fighting on two fronts, in Crete and Thessaly, the Turkish forces were consistently victorious, forcing the Greeks to accept an armistice in May 1897, which resulted in Greece losing part of Thessaly and paying a large indemnity.

Turkey found itself embroiled in a two-year war (1911-1912) with Italy after the Italian invasion of Libya, ending in a defeat for Turkey. Just days after concluding peace with Italy, Turkey was attacked by the Balkan League, consisting of Serbia, Bulgaria, and Greece, later joined by Montenegro. United in a common cause, the members of the League attempted to wrest away the balance of Turkey's Balkan possessions. Greece drove the Turks out of Salonika, while the Bulgarians were successful in defeating the Turks at Kirk Killisa and Lule Burgas. The Turks managed to hold onto Adrianople and Constantinople in Europe proper, due to Bulgarian supply problems. Enraged at the terms of the armistice, the Young Turks seized control of the government and resumed fighting. The Greeks forced the surrender of the Turks at Yannina. Three weeks later, a combined Serbian-Bulgarian army defeated the Turks at Adrianople,

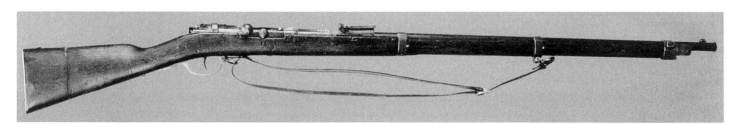

Full-length view of the German Model G 71 as used in the Transvaal

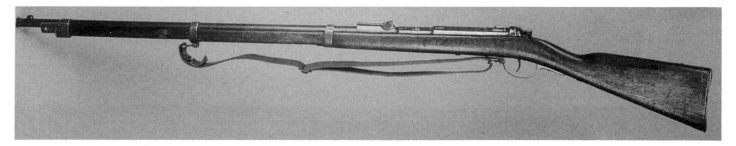

Left full-length view of the German Model G 71 Rifle as used in the Transvaal

while Scutari fell to Montenegrin troops. This forced the Turks to accept the peace terms of the London conference, with Turkey losing Crete and its European possessions, not including the Chatalja and Gallipolis peninsulas.

Entering World War I on the side of the Central Powers, the loss of the war reduced the Turkish empire to a small part of northern Anatolia. Before the treaty concerning the peace terms could be ratified, Kemal Ataturk seized power and denounced the sultan and his acquiescence to the victorious Allies. In a masterful series of diplomatic and military moves, Ataturk, known later as the "Father of Modern Turkey," restored much of the lost territories, fixing the boundaries of modern-day Turkey. Turkey became a republic in October 1923.

Greece, under the terms of the Treaty of Sevres, was granted control of Smyrna (Izmir); Greece, however, wanted to control much more, and set about annexing as much of western Anatolia as possible, precipitating the Turkish War of Independence (1920-1922). Despite inadequate preparations, the Greeks forged eastward. Twice defeated in battles at Inonu, the Greeks were severely defeated in an epic three-week battle at the Sakarya River. Then began an agonizing, year-long retreat to Smyrna, from which the Greeks were forced by the armies of Ataturk. Thousands upon thousands of Greek civilians and military were killed by the Turks, in return for similar depredations by the Greeks. The Treaty of Lausanne (24 July 1923) ended the war, requiring the return of eastern Thrace by the Greeks, return of the Turkish islands, and the exchange of the Greek inhabitants of the Turkish Republic for those Turkish inhabitants living in Greece.

Turkey remained neutral during World War II; however, as a member of the United Nations, Turkey fielded a contributory force to the United Nations troops fighting in Korea. Continuing problems with the Kurdish population of southeastern Turkey remain a problem even as this book is being written.

The Turkish army has been keenly concerned with maintaining an army with the most up-to-date weapons since the days of the first Mauser rifles. The Turks were the first to order a magazine rifle in sizable quantities; trials were held in 1886 to find a replacement for the single-shot Peabody-Martini Rifles with which the army had been armed. In 1887, the first magazine rifle was ordered from Waffenfabrik Mauser and Ludwig Loewe & Co. The Turks, not to be taken advantage of, included a clause in their contract that if a better rifle was developed, it would replace those yet to be filled under the terms of the contract. This clause was exercised in the case of the Model 1887 Rifle, which was replaced by the small-bore Model 1890 Rifle. These initial purchases were followed by the Model

1890 Rifle, the Model 1893 Rifle, the Model 1903 Rifle, the Model 1905 Carbine, the Model G 98 Rifle, as well as the Czech Model 98/22 Rifle. During the 1930s, many of these rifles were arsenal refinished to a short rifle configuration.

TURKISH MODEL 1887 RIFLE: Joined by Isidor Loewe, Paul Mauser went to Constantinople, Turkey to convince the Turkish authorities to purchase a variation of the German Model 71/84 Rifle. In February, 1887, they were successful in this venture, obtaining an initial contract for five hundred thousand Model 1887 Rifles, and fifty thousand carbines in caliber 9.5 x 60mm. Mauser and Loewe were to share the contract, but it turned out that Loewe's share of the contract eventually went to Mauser Waffenfabrik.

Barrel flat markings in Turkish on the Turkish Model 1887 Rifle (Cliff Baumann collection)

Full-length view of a Turkish-marked Turkish Model 1887 Rifle (Cliff Baumann collection)

Full-length view of the Turkish Model 1887 Rifle, marked in German

Manufacturer's markings in Turkish over the serial number on the left side rail of the Turkish Model 1887 Rifle. (Cliff Baumann collection)

Left side rail of the Turkish Model 1887 Rifle, showing the manufacturer's markings in German

The Turkish Model 1887 Rifle is basically a reworked G 71/84, in the optimum black powder caliber of 9.5 x 60mm. The trigger guard is smaller than on the G 71/84, and the double locking arrangement of the bolt handle, which locks against the receiver bridge, and also has a locking lug that engages a shoulder in the left lower side of the receiver, differs from the G 71/84. The comb of the buttstock is noticeably higher than that of the G 71/84.

Length: 49.30"; **Weight:** 9.3 lbs.; **Barrel:** 29.97"; **Caliber:** 9.5 x 60mm Turkish; **Rifling:** 4-groove, r/hand; **Operation:** Turnbolt action; **Feed:** 8-round, tubular feed magazine; **Sights:** V-notch adjustable rear sight graduated to 1600 meters. **Remarks:** On Turkish marked specimens, the Turkish "Toughra" is on the upper flat of the barrel as it enters the receiver, with Turkish proof marks on the left and right flats. The manufacturer's markings in Turkish on the left side rail. Those pieces marked in German will have the manufacturer's markings on the left side rail over the serial number.

TURKISH MODEL 1890 RIFLE: In 1890, shortly after the Belgians adopted the Model 1889 Rifle, the Turkish authorities took advantage of the escape clause in their contract for the Model 1887 Rifle (now obsolete, due to smokeless powder), and required Mauser to complete the contract with the Model 1890 Rifle in caliber 7.65 x 53mm. The contract on the Model 1887 stopped at approximately

220,000 completed rifles, with the balance of the contract (280,000 pieces) filled with the new Model 1890 Rifle.

The Turkish Model 1890 incorporates several improvements over the Belgian Model 1889 Rifle. The rifle is fitted with a straight-wristed stock without grasping grooves. The tubular metal hand guard of the Model 1889 was removed, and is replaced by a short wooden hand guard that extends forward from the front of the rear sight base approximately half way to the lower barrel band. The Model 1890 Rifle incorporates the first successful attempt at "stepping" the barrel and relieving the stock cuts to accommodate the expansion of the barrel during heavy firing.

The rear sight incorporates improvements over the Model 1889 Rifle, and the bolt includes a one-piece sear. The magazine, while meant to remain in place, is removable by depression of the spring-loaded catch located in the trigger guard.

Rear sight of the Turkish Model 1890 Rifle, illustrating the Turkish numbering (Noel P. Schott collection)

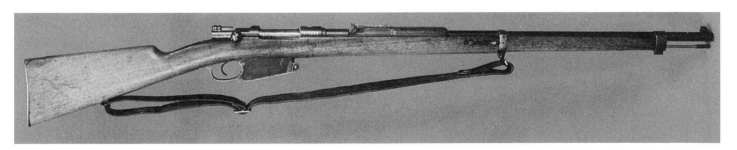

Full-length view of the Turkish Model 1890 Rifle (Noel P. Schott collection)

The left side rail of the Turkish Model 1890 Rifle, showing the manufacturer's markings in Turkish (Noel P. Schott collection)

Right side of the receiver ring showing the serial number of the rifle in Turkish (Noel P. Schott collection)

Length: 48.60"; **Weight:** 8.8 lbs.; **Barrel:** 29.13"; **Caliber:** 7.65 x 53mm; **Rifling:** 4-groove, r/hand; **Operation:** Turnbolt action; **Feed:** 5-round, staggered column, flush, box magazine; **Sights:** V-notch adjustable rear sight graduated to 2000 meters. **Remarks:** Turkish "Toughra" on the top of the receiver ring, serial number in Turkish on the right side of the receiver ring, manufacturer's markings in Turkish on the left side rail. The rear sight is marked in Turkish numerals.

TURKISH MODEL 1893 RIFLE: Ever conscious of new developments in the field of arms making, the Turks were to prove among the best of Mauser's customers. With the introduction of the Spanish Model 1893 Rifle with all of its innovations, the Turks were quick off the mark to order a total of 201,100 rifles. While very similar to the Spanish Model 1893 Rifle, this was the only rifle to be manufactured in quantity with a magazine cutoff; this allowed the contents of the magazine to be held in reserve, while the weapon

Turkish sentry armed with a Turkish Model 1890 Rifle keeping cholera victims away from an uncontaminated well and fountain during the First Balkan War

Receiver ring of the Turkish Model 1890 Rifle, showing to good effect the Turkish "Toughra" marking (Noel P. Schott collection)

The soldiers shown in this picture are typical of the hard-fighting, seasoned Turkish infantry. They were to be encountered during the First and Second Balkan Wars, World War I, and the Turkish War of Independence. This picture is C. 1912, and the men appear to be armed with the Turkish Model 1893 Rifle.

A lone Turkish infantryman in a trench before Lule Burgas during the First Balkan War

Manufacturer's markings in Turkish on the left side rail of the Turkish Model 1893 Rifle. Note the extension on the bolt stop, which acts as a charger guide.

was loaded with single rounds. This lever, located on the right side of the action, is spring loaded, and when engaged lowers the magazine follower so that the forward movement of the bolt will not pick up cartridges from the magazine well.

The rifle is fitted with a straight-wristed stock without grasping grooves, and the upper hand guard extends from the front of the receiver ring to just beyond the lower barrel band. The lower barrel band has a swivel on the bottom, and there is another at the bottom of the buttstock. Like the Spanish model, the nose cap is a simple affair with a bayonet lug on the bottom.

Length: 48.60"; **Weight:** 8.8 lbs.; **Barrel:** 29.06"; **Caliber:** 7.65 x 53mm (later converted to 7.92 x 57mm); **Rifling:** 4-groove, r/hand; **Operation:** Turnbolt 1893-style action; **Feed:** 5-round, staggered column, flush, box magazine; **Sights:** V-notch rear sight graduated to 2000 meters. **Remarks:** Turkish "Toughra" on top of the receiver ring, manufacturer's markings in Turkish on the left side rail.

Turkish markings on the sight leaf of the rear sight of the Turkish Model 1893 Rifle

The Turkish "Toughra" on the receiver ring of the Turkish Model 1893 Rifle

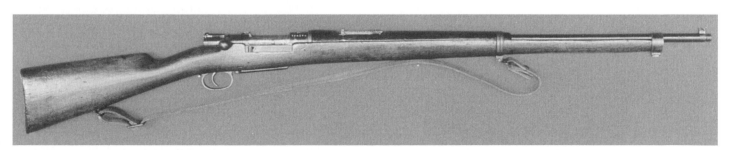

Full-length view of the Turkish Model 1893 Rifle

Turkish Model 1903 Rifle, showing the markings on the receiver ring. (Robert Jensen collection)

Turkish troops charging from trenches at Gallipolis. It appears that they are armed with Model 1903 Rifles.

TURKISH MODEL 1903 RIFLE: Turkey paid strict attention to weapons development in Germany; this policy caused the Turks to purchase large quantities of the Model 1903 Rifle—a variation of the G 98 Rifle—from Germany prior to the First World War.

Fitted with a pistol grip stock, the rifle has an upper hand guard that extends from the front of the receiver to the lower barrel band. The nose cap is simple, with a bayonet lug on the bottom for the older model bayonets in the Turkish arsenal. There is a swivel on the bottom of the lower barrel band and another on the bottom of the buttstock. The rear sight is the improved tangent leaf sight rather than the "Lange Vizier"-style German sight.

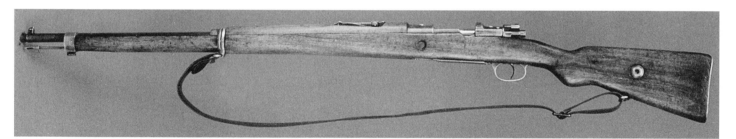

Left full-length view of the Turkish Model 1903 Rifle

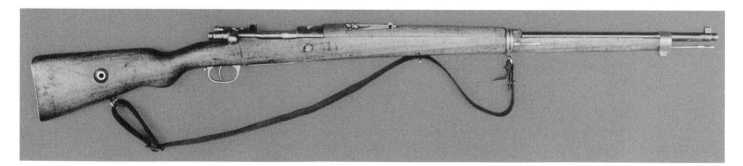

Right full-length view of the Turkish Model 1903 Rifle

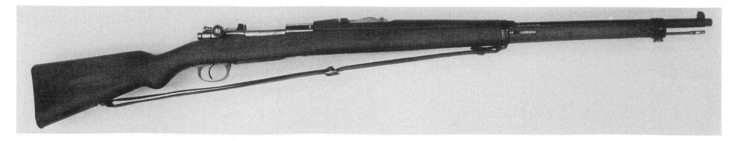

A full-length view of the right side of a Turkish Model 1903 Rifle with a variant stock; note the lack of the stock disk. (Robert Jensen collection)

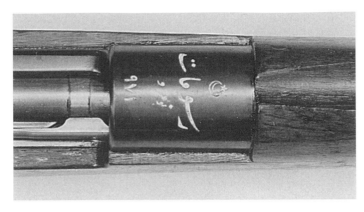

Variant markings on a Turkish Model 1903 Rifle. (Robert Jensen collection)

Poorly-clad Turkish infantrymen in a shallow trench in front of Adrianople during the First Balkan War

One of the main differences between the G 98 and the Turkish Model 1903 Rifle is the curved arm on the bolt stop that projects upward, putting pressure on the left side of the cartridge clip to keep it in position while the cartridges are stripped from the clip. The receiver is slightly larger than the G 98, and a longer cocking piece and firing pin are incorporated into the design. The Turkish Model 1903 Rifle is also without guard screws.

The Model 1903 Rifle has had a long and varied life with the Turkish army, having been used in the Italo-Turkish War of 1911-1912, the First and Second Balkan wars, the First World War on all Turkish battlefronts, the Greco-Turkish War, better known as the Turkish War of Independence (1920-1922), and finally serving out the Second World War as one of the many standard rifles in the Turkish army.

Length: 49.0"; **Weight:** 9.2 lbs.; **Barrel:** 29.13"; **Caliber:** 7.65 x 53mm, later rechambered for 7.92 x 57mm; **Rifling:** 4-groove, r/hand; **Operation:** Turnbolt action; **Feed:** 5-round, staggered column, flush, box magazine; **Sights:** Tangent leaf rear sight graduated to 2000 meters. **Remarks:** Turkish crescent and star, manufacturer's markings, arsenal, and date on the receiver ring. Turkish numbering.

TURKISH MODEL 1905 CARBINE: From 1903 to 1906, Waffenfabrik Mauser, Oberndorf, produced the Model 1905 Carbine (almost a short rifle!) for the Turkish cavalry and artillery. The total quantity manufactured is unknown, though estimates range in the area of twenty thousand. These weapons are rarely encountered today.

The carbine is fitted with a full-length pistol grip stock, with an upper hand guard extending from the front of the receiver ring to just beyond the lower barrel band. The lower barrel band has a swivel on the bottom, and there is another on the bottom of the buttstock. There is a simple nose cap with sight protectors, and no provision for the attachment of a bayonet.

Length: 41.40"; **Weight:** 8.26 lbs.; **Barrel:** 21.65"; **Caliber:** 7.65 x 53mm, later rechambered to 7.92 x 57mm; **Rifling:** 4-groove, r/hand; **Operation:** Turnbolt action; **Feed:** 5-round, staggered column, flush, box magazine; **Sights:** Tangent leaf rear sight graduated to 1600 meters. **Remarks:** Turkish "Toughra" and markings on the receiver ring.

Full-length view of the Turkish Model 1905 Carbine. Note how the wrist of the stock has been very artfully wrapped with wire to reinforce a presumed crack or break. (Noel P. Schott collection)

Full-length view of the Turkish Model 1905 Carbine, shown with a variant stock. (Robert Jensen collection)

The receiver ring with Turkish markings and "Toughra" on the Model 1905 Carbine (Noel P. Schott collection)

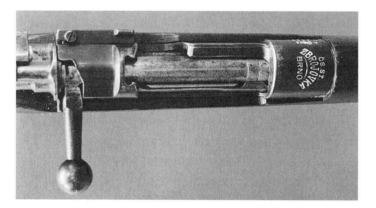

Full view of the action of the Czech Model 98/22 Rifle as used by Turkey. Note the arched Czech receiver ring marking.

TURKISH MODEL 98/22 RIFLE: Following the Turkish War of Independence (1920-1922), Turkey rearmed with Czechoslovakian Model 98/22 Rifles produced by Brno. These rifles can be found with either Turkish markings in addition to the Czech receiver markings, or with only the original Czech markings. All specific data on this rifle may be found in the section on Czechoslovakia.

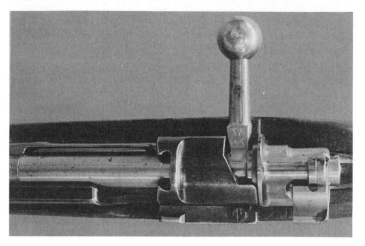

Close-up view of the action of the Czech Model 98/22 Rifle as used by Turkey. Note the Turkish markings on bolt knob, base of the bolt handle, and top of the bolt sleeve.

Close-up view of the left side of the receiver of the Czech Model 98/22 Rifle in Turkish service, showing Czech proof marks, as well as the rifle serial number

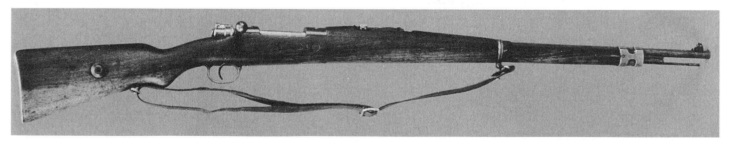

Full-length view of the Czech Model 98/22 Rifle as used by Turkey

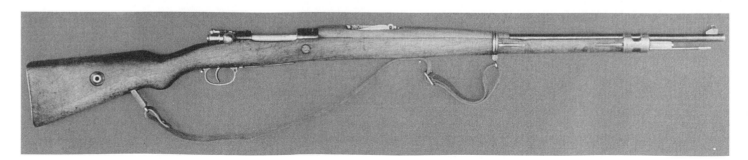

Full-length view of another Czech Model 98/22 Rifle used by Turkey, but with all markings in Czechoslovakian

Turkish numerals on the rear sight of the Czech Model 98/22 Rifle in Turkish service

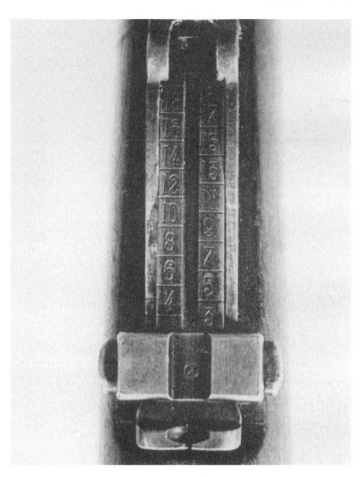

Rear sight leaf with Arabic numerals on the Czech Model 98/22 Rifle used by Turkey

Close-up view of the Turkish markings on the receiver ring of the Turkish Model 38 Short Rifle

TURKISH MODEL 38 SHORT RIFLE: In the late 1930s, in order to standardize in some fashion, the Turks took the many different varieties of weapons in their armories and had many of them arsenal reworked to a more convenient style, namely a short rifle configuration. Many different weapons, such as the G 98, Czech 98/22, Model 1903, and Model 1893, were altered in some manner or other at this time, mainly to make them appear similar to the Model 1903 Rifle.

The Gew 98AZ Carbine was the main weapon to fall under the Model 38 guidelines, with the short rifle retaining a pistol grip stock and an upper hand guard that extends from the front of the receiver ring to just beyond the lower barrel band. There is a swivel under the lower barrel band and another under the buttstock; a sling slot in the German fashion is also cut through the buttstock. The front sight protectors are retained, but the simple nose cap now incorporates a bayonet lug on the bottom to accommodate the older bayonets still available. The following specifications may vary slightly by weapon.

Length: 44.0"; **Weight:** 9.0 lbs.; **Barrel:** 24.0"; **Caliber:** 7.92 x 57mm; **Rifling:** 4-groove, r/hand; **Operation:** Turnbolt action;

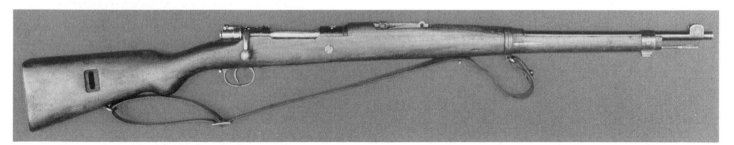

Full-length view of the Turkish Model 38 Short Rifle

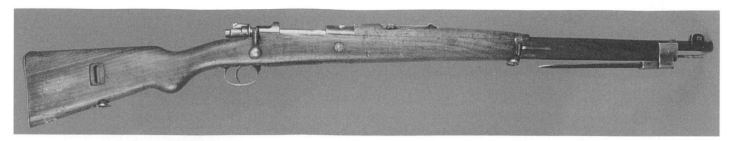

Full-length view of a Turkish Model 38 Short Rifle fitted with an unusual and rarely seen folding bayonet

Receiver markings on the Turkish Model 38 Short Rifle with folding bayonet

Feed: 5-round, staggered column, flush, box magazine; **Sights:** Tangent leaf rear sight graduated to 2000 meters. **Remarks:** All original markings have been professionally ground off, with the receiver now marked in Turkish with the Star and Crescent, arsenal markings, and the date of renovation.

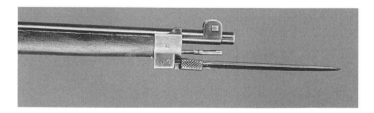

Close-up side view of the folding bayonet on the Turkish Model 38 Short Rifle

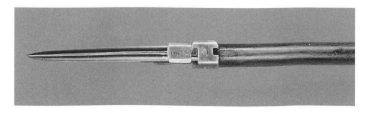

Bottom view of the folding bayonet on the Turkish Model 38 Short Rifle. Note the fluting on the bayonet blade.

URUGUAY

Uruguay, the smallest of the original independent states of South America, lies between Argentina to the west and Brazil to the north and northeast. From the late 1600s, there was continuous contention between the Spaniards moving to the east and the Brazilians pushing southward from Brazil. Eventually coming under the influence of the Argentinians, Uruguay proclaimed itself independent of Buenos Aires one year after Argentina separated itself from Spain. In 1811, Uruguay declared itself a republic; this was followed by the invasion of an army of Argentinian nationalists who were eventually driven from the country by the army of Uruguay. In 1815, the revolutionary government of Buenos Aires recognized the independence of Uruguay.

The early years of independence were filled with struggles to preserve that independence from the attempts of both the Brazilians and the Argentinians to wrest it away. Following recognition of the independence of Uruguay by both countries, internal struggles between conservatives and liberals fomented a costly civil war and political upheavals that continued for generations. In 1865, due to the aspirations of the Paraguayan dictator, Solano López, Uruguay found itself allied with Argentina and Brazil against Paraguay in the terribly costly War of the Triple Alliance. The political situation in Uruguay remained extremely unsettled until the presidency of José Battles y Ordonez in 1903. Following a civil war, the country started down the path to what is now modern Uruguay.

Uruguay, while not engaging in a military manner, supported the Allies in both the First and Second World Wars. With the advent of President Juan Peron to the presidency of Argentina, Uruguay, with the aid of the United States, successfully opposed the expansionist plans of Peron to create a "Greater Argentina" by annexing Uruguay. Due to the polarization of Uruguayan politics in the 1960s and 1970s, urban warfare broke out between the government and the leftist National Liberation Movement (MLN), or the "Tupamaros." Unable to control the violence, the government increasingly relinquished control to the army, which was effectively in control of the country by 1973, dissolving the Congress. After a brutally repressive period that tore at the very soul of the country, the violence was brought under control, but at a heavy cost. In 1980, the army held a plebiscite on a new constitution that would have amounted to full military control of the country; this was defeated, and the country continues to undergo the slow transition to civilian rule even at this date.

The Uruguayan army, which numbers approximately twenty-two thousand, was under the influence of French military missions following the First World War. With the advent of the Second World War, American military influence replaced that of the French. Uruguay experimented with the Mauser rifle by purchasing an unknown quantity of G 71 Mauser Rifles in the late 1870s and 1880s. These purchases were later followed by the introduction of the Daudetau-Mauser Rifle, a French converted 1871 pattern Mauser rifle. Remington Rolling Block Rifles were also purchased in quantity. In the late 1890s, Uruguay purchased an unknown quantity of Model 1895 Mauser Rifles patterned after the Spanish Model 1893 Rifle.

Prior to the First World War, Uruguay contracted for, and took delivery of, a sizable quantity of Model 1908 Rifles and Short Rifles. These are patterned after the G 98 Rifle, but with modifications for export.

During the 1930s, approximately five thousand FN Model 24 Short Rifles were purchased from Belgium, but it is unknown as to exactly how, or if, these weapons were marked. At about the same time, approximately six thousand VZ 12-33 Model "937" Carbines and Model VZ 37 ("937") Short Rifles were purchased from Czechoslovakia. At the end of World War II, U.S. military equipment had replaced the Mauser rifles on hand, which were put in reserve and eventually sold. U.S. weapons have since been replaced by the FN FAL in 7.62mm.

URUGUAYAN MODEL G 71 RIFLE: In the late 1870s and early 1880s, Uruguay contracted for a shipment of G 71 Rifles from Waffenfabrik Mauser. Indications are that these rifles were only marked with the standard German manufacturer's markings; however the possibility exists that the right side of the buttstock was marked with the "REPUBLICA ORIENTAL de URUGUAY" stamp sometimes used by Uruguayan authorities. All specific data relative to these rifles will be found in the section on Germany.

URUGUAYAN MODEL 1895 RIFLE: In the late 1890s, Uruguay purchased an unknown quantity of Model 1895 Rifles in caliber 7 x 57mm from FN. According to specimens observed, there are no markings on the receiver ring, and only manufacturer's markings on the side rail. The right side of the buttstock is stamped with an entwined "ROU" (Republic Oriental de Uruguay) with a property number above. All specific data relative to the Model 1895 Rifle may be found in the section on Chile.

URUGUAYAN MODEL 1908 RIFLE: Prior to 1914, Uruguay purchased Model 1908 Rifles and Short Rifles based on the design of the Brazilian Model 1908. The quantities obtained from DWM are unknown. These weapons served the Uruguayan armed forces through the 1940s and into the 1950s.

The rifle is fitted with a pistol grip stock, with the upper hand guard extending from the front of the receiver ring to about one inch beyond the lower barrel band. The lower barrel band has a swivel on the bottom, and there is another on the bottom of the buttstock.

Uruguayan stamping under the property number on the buttstock of the Uruguayan FN Model 1895 Rifle

The upper band has a parade hook on the bottom, and the nose cap incorporates a German-style "H" bayonet lug. There is a marking disk in the right side of the buttstock.

Length: 49.25"; **Weight:** 10.0 lbs.; **Barrel:** 28.75"; **Caliber:** 7 x 57mm; **Rifling:** 4-groove, r/hand; **Operation:** Turnbolt action; **Feed:** 5-round, staggered column, flush, box magazine; **Sights:** Tangent leaf rear sight graduated to 2000 meters. **Remarks:** Uruguayan crest on top of the receiver ring, over the date of manufacture; model designation on the right side of the receiver ring, with weapon serial number and proofs on the left side of the receiver ring. Manufacturer's markings on the left side rail.

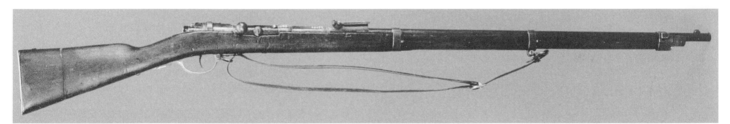

Full-length view of the Mauser G 71 Rifle as used by Uruguay

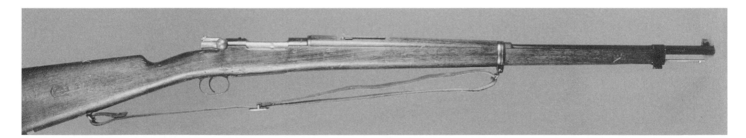

Full-length view of the Uruguayan FN Model 1895 Rifle

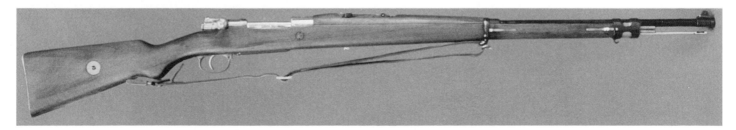

Full-length view of the Uruguayan Model 1908 Rifle (Noel P. Schott collection)

Top of the receiver ring of the Uruguayan Model 1908 Rifle, showing the Uruguayan crest over the date of manufacture (Noel P. Schott collection)

Overview of the receiver bridge and bolt handle of the Uruguayan Model 1908 Rifle, showing the serial number and proof mark (Noel P. Schott collection)

URUGUAYAN MODEL 1908 SHORT RIFLE: Purchased at the same time as the Model 1908 Rifle, the Model 1908 Short Rifle is a virtual copy of the Model 1908 Rifle except for size and a turned down bolt handle.

The Model 1908 Short Rifle is fitted with a pistol grip stock, and the upper hand guard extends from the front of the receiver ring to just beyond the lower barrel band. The lower barrel band has a swivel at the bottom, with another at the bottom of the buttstock. The upper barrel band incorporates a parade hook at the bottom

Left side of the action of the Uruguayan Model 1908 Rifle, showing the serial number and proofs on the receiver ring and the manufacturer's markings on the side rail. (Noel P. Schott collection)

Right side of the receiver ring of the Uruguayan Model 1908 Rifle, showing the model designation (Noel P. Schott collection)

rear, and the nose cap has a short, German-style "H" bayonet lug. There is a marking disk inset into the right side of the buttstock.

Length: 41.75"; **Weight:** 8.2 lbs.; **Barrel:** 23.0"; **Caliber:** 7 x 57mm; **Rifling:** 4-groove, r/hand; **Operation:** Turnbolt action; **Feed:** 5-round, staggered column, flush, box magazine; **Sights:** Tangent leaf rear sight graduated to 1400 meters. **Remarks:** Uruguayan crest on top of the receiver ring, over the date of manufacture, with the model designation on the right side of the receiver ring, the serial number and proofs on the left side. The manufacturer's markings will be found on the left side rail.

Right side of the receiver of the Uruguayan Model 1908 Short Rifle, showing the model designation (Noel P. Schott collection)

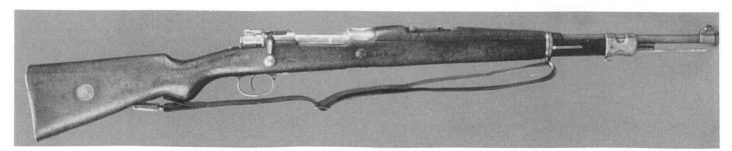

Full-length view of the Uruguayan Model 1908 Short Rifle (Noel P. Schott collection)

The left side of the action of the Uruguayan Model 1908 Short Rifle, showing the proofs and serial number on the side of the receiver and the manufacturer's markings on the left side rail (Noel P. Schott collection)

Uruguayan crest on the top of the receiver ring of the Uruguayan Model 1908 Short Rifle (Noel P. Schott collection)

URUGUAYAN FN MODEL 24 SHORT RIFLE: As many countries did after the First World War, Uruguay supplemented its weapons needs from the mail order list offered by FN. Quantities purchased have not been determined, nor has it been possible to ascertain if, and how, the weapons were marked. All specific data relative to the FN Model 24 Short Rifle can be found under the section on Mexico.

URUGUAYAN MODEL VZ 37 ("937") SHORT RIFLE: Just prior to the takeover of Czechoslovakia by Germany, the Uruguayan military establishment ordered both short rifles and carbines from the Czechs. This was in keeping with Uruguayan military planning in attempting to keep abreast of development in weaponry in spite of the small size of the military forces of the country.

The Uruguayan Model VZ 37 Short Rifle is fitted with a pistol grip stock with grasping grooves, with the upper hand guard extending from the front of the receiver ring to the upper barrel band. In the Czech fashion, the lower barrel band is held in place by a trans-

Right side of the buttstock of the Uruguayan Model 1908 Short Rifle, showing the rifle property mark next to the marking disk (Noel P. Schott collection)

verse screw and is fitted with a side swivel and a swivel located at the bottom of the band; another swivel is located on the left side of the buttstock, with yet another at the bottom. The nose cap incorporates a German-style "H" bayonet lug, while the front sight has a detachable sight protector held by a screw.

Length: 43.25"; **Weight:** 9.9 lbs.; **Barrel:** 23.25"; **Caliber:** 7 x 57mm; **Rifling:** 4-groove, r/hand; **Operation:** Turnbolt action; **Feed:** 5-round, staggered column, flush, box magazine; **Sights:**

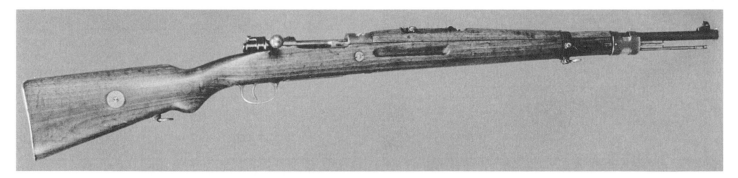

Full-length view of the FN Model 24 Short Rifle as used by Uruguay (Cliff Baumann collection)

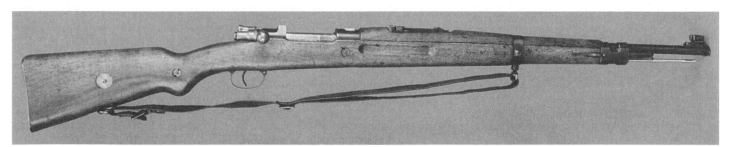

Full-length view of the Uruguayan Model VZ 37 ("937") Short Rifle (Noel P. Schott collection)

The top of the receiver ring of the Uruguayan Model VZ 37 ("937") Short Rifle, showing the national crest and other markings (Noel P. Schott collection)

Left side of the action of the Uruguayan Model 37 ("937") Short Rifle, showing the proof marks and the manufacturer's markings in Czech (Noel P. Schott collection)

Tangent leaf rear sight graduated to 2000 meters. **Remarks:** The crest of Uruguay is stamped on the top of the receiver ring, surrounded by "R.O.U. EJERCITO NACIONAL," which is over the model designation, over the serial number of the rifle. Proof marks are on the left side of the receiver ring, while the manufacturer's markings in Czech are on the left side rail.

URUGUAYAN MODEL VZ 37 ("937") CARBINE: Included with the purchase of weapons from the Czechs was an undetermined number of Model VZ 37 ("937") Carbines, very similar to the Czech VZ 12/33 Short Rifle. The carbine is fitted with a pistol grip stock with grasping grooves, and the upper hand guard extends from the front of the receiver ring to the upper barrel band. The upper band is secured by means of a transverse screw, and the nose cap incorporates a simple German-style "H" bayonet lug. The front sight is fitted

Rifle serial number of the Uruguayan Model VZ 37 ("937") Short Rifle stamped into the bottom of the buttstock behind the lower sling swivel (Noel P. Schott collection)

with sight protectors. The lower barrel band is spring retained, with a sling slot on the left side and a swivel on the bottom. There is another swivel at the bottom of the buttstock. On the left side of the buttstock is a large carbine ring.

Length: 37.875"; **Weight:** 7.8 lbs.; **Barrel:** 18.0"; **Caliber:** 7 x 57mm; **Rifling:** 4-groove, r/hand; **Operation:** Turnbolt action; **Feed:** 5-round, staggered column, flush, box magazine; **Sights:** Tangent leaf rear sight graduated to 1400 meters. **Remarks:** On the top of the receiver ring is the Uruguayan crest, surrounded by "R.O.U. EJERCITO NACIONAL" over the model designation over the serial number of the weapon. Proofs are found on the left side of the receiver ring, with manufacturer's markings in Czech on the left side rail. A property mark is stamped into the right side of the buttstock.

The left side of the action of the Uruguayan Model VZ 37 ("937") Carbine, showing the proof marks and the manufacturer's markings in Czech (Noel P. Schott collection)

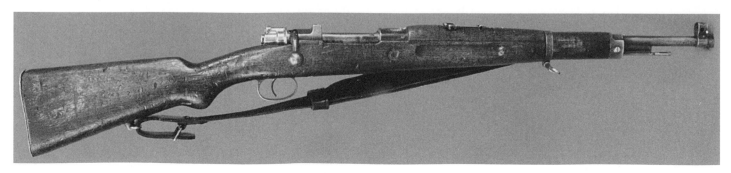

Full-length view of the Uruguayan Model VZ 37 ("937") Carbine (Noel P. Schott collection)

Property mark stamped into the right side of the buttstock of the Uruguayan Model VZ 37 ("937") Carbine. (Noel P. Schott collection)

Uruguayan crest and markings on the top of the receiver of the Uruguayan Model VZ 37 ("937") Carbine. (Noel P. Schott collection)

VENEZUELA

Permanently settled by the Spanish in 1520, Venezuela was a neglected backwater of the Spanish crown colonies for most of the colonial period. It was subject to the depredations of English pirates who roamed freely through the Caribbean, with Henry Morgan sacking the city of Maracaibo in 1669. This lack of colonial interest by the Spanish helped foster the desire for independence in Venezuelan society.

The battles for independence were particularly destructive for Venezuela; however, by 1821, the Spaniards had been defeated soundly at Carabobo, and independence was won for the region. With Simón Bolívar's liberation of Colombia from Spanish control, Colombia and Venezuela formed the Republic of Gran Colombia, later to be joined by Ecuador. In 1829, Venezuelans declared their independence from Gran Colombia, followed by Ecuador the next year.

Of a total of eight hundred thousand inhabitants, Venezuela lost over three hundred thousand lives in the Wars of Independence, leaving the country broken and prostrate. For nearly a century, periods of near anarchy alternated with periods of repressive dictator-

ship. In 1902, Venezuela was blockaded by naval units of Britain, Germany, and Italy when the then president, Cipriano Castro, defaulted on the country's foreign debt. The bloodiest tyrant in South America, Juan Vicente Gomez ruled as president of Venezuela from 1908 to 1935. Nevertheless, while one of the most brutal dictators in the history of Latin America, he managed to begin the exploitation of the country's vast oil resources. This attracted foreign investment and laid the groundwork for Venezuela to become a modern state.

Following the reign of Gomez, there have been many progressive, if not especially democratic leaders of the country, with free elections finally held in 1941. Leadership of the country has alternated between the Christian Democrats and Democratic Action, punctuated by several military coups, as well as attempted overthrows of the government. The present leader of Venezuela, Rafael Caldera, has been faced with severe economic problems, which have led to the suspension of constitutional guarantees, and the imposition of price and currency controls, thus sending Venezuela into another period of unsettled crisis.

The Venezuelan army became a more effective, efficient power base with the initial engagement of a German military mission, followed by a Chilean military mission, both of which took place during the early 1900s. When Gomez assumed the presidency, the army was a relatively proficient force of nearly six thousand men, armed with German G 71/84 Rifles. Under Gomez, training and improvement in the quality of equipment continued, with approximately six thousand Mauser Model 1910 Rifles being acquired from Germany. French military missions were active in Venezuela following World War I, remaining until 1923. In the early 1930s, indeterminate quantities of Czech VZ 24 Short Rifles were acquired from Czechoslovakia, while numbers of the FN Model 24/30 Short Rifle and Carbine were purchased from Belgium. World War II saw the start of U.S. influence with the Venezuelan army, with many American weapons acquired under lend-lease. The Mauser rifle was finally replaced by the Belgian SAFN M1949 in 7 x 57mm, which was, in turn, replaced by the Belgian FN FAL in 7.62mm. The present Venezuelan army stands at approximately twenty-five thousand plus men.

GERMAN MODEL 71/84 RIFLE: The German Mauser Model 71/84 Rifle was the standard German army issue weapon. Declared obsolete, it is virtually certain that the twenty-seven thousand piec-

Venezuelan Military Academy cadets armed with Model 1910 Rifles during a passing out parade (Venezuelan Army Review)

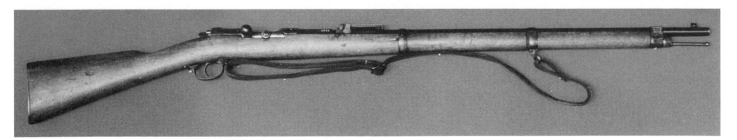

Full-length view of the G 71/84 Rifle as used by Venezuela

Model designation on the left side rail of the Model 1910 Rifle used by Venezuela

es acquired by Venezuela were from German army surplus stores, and were not marked in any manner for the Venezuelans. All specific data on this rifle can be found in the section on Germany.

VENEZUELAN MODEL 1910 RIFLE: Prior to 1914, Venezuela purchased six thousand Model 1910 Mauser Rifles from Waffenfabrik Mauser. This rifle is the typical export model similar to the rifles used by Costa Rica and Serbia. Detailed data on this rifle can be found in the section on Serbia.

CZECH VZ 24 SHORT RIFLE USED BY VENEZUELA: During the 1930s, Venezuela augmented its supply of rifles with purchases of the Model VZ 24 Short Rifle in caliber 7 x 57mm from Czechoslovakia. This is the standard model as used by the Czech armed forces, and complete data on this short rifle can be found under the section on Czechoslovakia.

VENEZUELAN FN MODEL 24/30 SHORT RIFLE: The Venezuelan authorities negotiated with FN during the mid-1930s, and eventually purchased an initial order of 16,500 Short Rifles and Carbines during 1934-1935. Smaller orders to FN continued up to the Second World War, with total quantities purchased unknown.

Chamber markings in German on the Model 1910 Rifle used by Venezuela

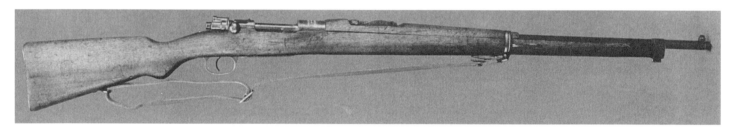

Full-length view of the Model 1910 Rifle as used by Venezuela

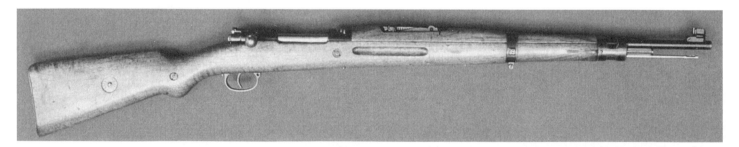

Full-length view of the Czech Model VZ 24 Short Rifle used by Venezuela

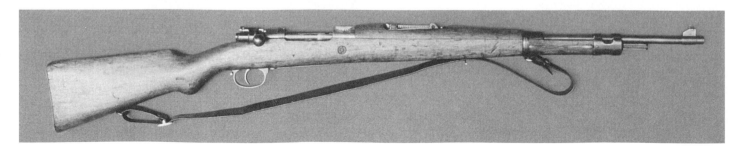

Full-length view of the Venezuelan FN Model 24/30 Short Rifle

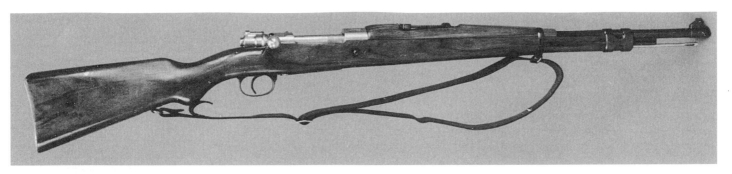

Full-length view of the Venezuelan FN Model 24/30 Short Rifle, but with slight variations. Note that the wrist of the stock is somewhat slimmer, with a less "chunky" look to it. Also note the location of the lower sling swivel in relation to the one shown previously. It is much closer to the wrist than normal. (Lothar Frank collection)

The Venezuelan national crest on the receiver ring of the Venezuelan FN Model 24/30 Short Rifle

The Venezuelan FN Model 24/30 Short Rifle is fitted with a pistol grip stock without grasping grooves, and the upper hand guard extends from the front of the receiver ring to approximately one inch beyond the lower barrel band. There is a swivel on the bottom of the spring-retained lower barrel band, with another on the bottom of the buttstock. The nose cap incorporates the typical German-style "H" bayonet lug. These are sturdy, dependable weapons, once common

Manufacturer's markings stamped into the left side rail of the Venezuelan FN Model 24/30 Short Rifle

to the U.S. surplus market, but becoming increasingly hard to find as the years go by—especially in decent condition!

Length: 43.20"; **Weight:** 9.0 lbs.; **Barrel:** 23.19"; **Caliber:** 7 x 57mm; **Rifling:** 4-groove, r/hand; **Operation:** Turnbolt action; **Feed:** 5-round, staggered column, flush, box magazine; **Sights:** Tangent leaf rear sight graduated to 2000 meters. **Remarks:** The Venezuelan national crest on top of the receiver ring, with the manufacturer's markings stamped into the left side rail.

VENEZUELAN FN MODEL 24/30 CARBINE: The Venezuelan FN Model 24/30 Carbine is a compact, handy weapon. Many of these were used by the Venezuelan rural police forces and did not receive the best of attention. The carbine is fitted with a pistol grip stock without grasping grooves and an upper hand guard that extends from the front of the receiver ring to just beyond the lower barrel band. There is a swivel on the bottom of the lower barrel band with

The Venezuelan national crest on the receiver ring of the Venezuelan FN Model 24/30 Short Rifle

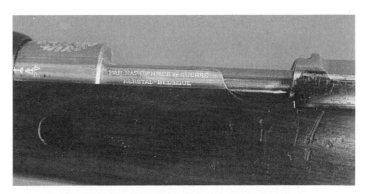

Side rail markings on the Venezuelan FN Model 24/30 Short Rifle (Lothar Frank collection)

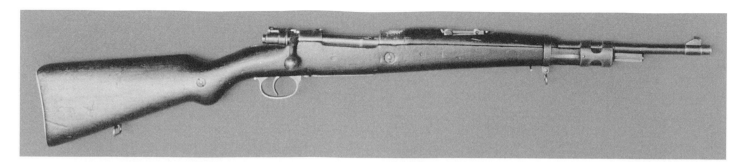

Full-length view of the Venezuelan FN Model 24/30 Carbine

The Venezuelan national crest on the receiver ring of the Venezuelan FN Model 24/30 Carbine

Left side of the action of the Venezuelan FN Model 24/30 Carbine, showing the markings of the Venezuelan army on the left side of the receiver, with the manufacturer's markings on the left side rail

National crest of Venezuela on top of the receiver ring, with "FUERZAS ARMADAS de VENEZUELA" (Armed Forces of Venezuela) on the left side of the receiver ring and the manufacturer's markings stamped into the left side rail.

VENEZUELAN FN MODEL 24/30 TARGET RIFLE: A small number of specially-chosen Venezuelan FN Model 24/30 Short Rifles were arsenal converted to target rifles for training for the Olympics. The main difference is a barrel approximately six inches longer than usual, while the balance of the configuration remains the same.

a sling slot on the left hand side, a swivel on the bottom of the buttstock, and another swivel on the left side of the stock at the pistol grip. The lower and upper barrel bands are retained by a single spring, with the nose cap incorporating a German-style "H" bayonet lug. There is a recoil lug at the chamber and another at the pistol grip.

Length: 37.50"; **Weight:** 8.50 lbs.; **Barrel:** 17.63"; **Caliber:** 7 x 57mm; **Rifling:** 4-groove, r/hand; **Operation:** Turnbolt action; **Feed:** 5-round, staggered column, flush, box magazine; **Sights:** Tangent leaf rear sight graduated to 1400 meters. **Remarks:**

Venezuelan army markings on the left side of the receiver, and the manufacturer's markings on the left side rail of the Venezuelan FN Model 24/30 Target Rifle

Venezuelan national crest on the receiver ring of the Venezuelan FN Model 24/30 Target Rifle

Full-length view of the Venezuelan FN Model 24/30 Target Rifle

YEMEN

Known as Sheba or Saba in ancient times, Yemen is strategically located on the southwestern coast of the Arabian peninsula, right by the southern end of the Red Sea. Due to its location, Yemen has for centuries dominated the trade routes between India and Africa and the Middle East. Aden has been the most important port in Yemen for countless generations, and has been the central point of dissension between the Yemenis, the Portuguese, the Ottoman Turks, and the British. Aden became a British crown colony in 1839.

Under the control of the Ottoman Empire for several hundred years from the mid-sixteenth century, Yemen became an independent kingdom in 1918. The country's independence was threatened by a short-lived invasion from Saudi Arabia in 1934, and again in the 1954 dispute with Great Britain over the status of Aden. A struggle for independence in Aden was the cause of a civil war between two opposing factions, with the British withdrawing in 1967, and the country of South Yemen coming into being the same year. The rest of the country became North Yemen. Both countries underwent political upheaval and instability, with continuous incursions against one another. In 1990, the countries merged once again into the consolidated country of Yemen; this has not brought about peace, as full scale civil war commenced once again in 1994.

The military background of Yemen is indistinct, with little in the way of a national army in the early days before the Second World War. It is known that the government purchased a substantial number of Model 30 Short Rifles from FN during the middle to late 1930s. It is not known if these purchases were marked in any manner, but they are believed to have been in caliber 7.92 x 57mm.

The Model 30 Short Rifle is the standard FN export model short rifle, and full data can be found under the section on Greece.

Full-length view of the FN Model 30 Short Rifle as used by Yemen

Mauser Curiosa

As every collector knows, there are times when we will encounter a particular weapon that cannot be assigned a comfortable niche—perhaps an experimental or a trial piece, but one that has impacted upon development, or instigated the turn to a different direction, and, thus, is still a remote relative of the Mauser family. While there are undoubtedly many other specimens out there that deserve inclusion in this section, included here are but a few of the more interesting weapons and accessories that have been uncovered while compiling this book.

A very interesting attempt to increase the cartridge capacity of single-shot rifles is shown here in this experimental magazine that was incorporated into a Dreyse-made G 71 Rifle of the period. This magazine is hinged on the left side at the top, so that when released, it swings down in a quarter circle to the left, which allows it to be filled from the right side. While never adopted, this is an interesting attempt to solve the problem of increased cartridge capacity.

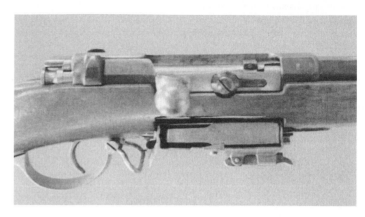

Close-up view of the right side of the Dreyse-made experimental magazine rifle, with the magazine in the open position, ready for loading. The follower appears to be in a reversed position.

Right side, close-up view of the magazine and action of the Dreyse-made experimental magazine rifle. Note the modifications made to allow for extraction and ejection of the spent cartridge. It also appears that the lower sling swivel would be useless in its present location.

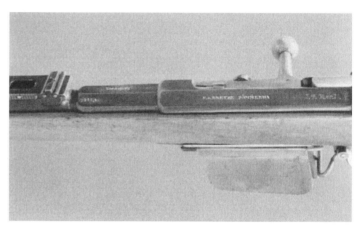

The action of the Dreyse-made experimental magazine rifle from the left side, showing the markings to good effect

Full-length view of the Dreyse-made G 71 experimental rifle with magazine

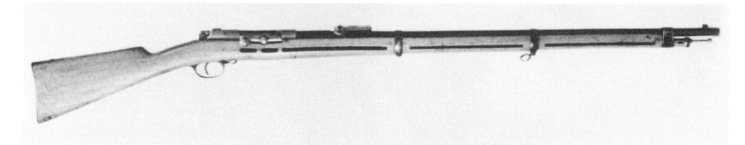

Full-length view of the G 71/84 Cutaway Rifle, showing the visual aid cuts down the length of the fore stock

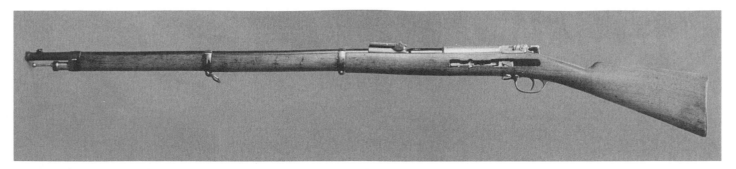

Left full-length view of the G 71/84 Cutaway Rifle, showing the cuts in the action area of the rifle

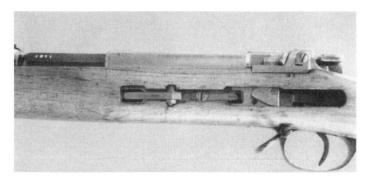

Close-up view of the left side of the action, allowing the internal working of the cutoff to be easily seen

A seldom-encountered piece of history is this G 71/84 Cutaway Rifle, which differs in a number of details from the final production models. This specimen probably dates from 1884, since the magazine cutoff and ejector match the patents of that period. The cutoff on the production G 71/84 differs from the one on this model: On the production model, the magazine holds eight cartridges, and the magazine tube is flush with the end of the stock; the cutaway model illustrated has a capacity of nine cartridges, and the magazine tube extends beyond the end of the stock by almost a full inch. Interestingly, the barrel of a G 71 Rifle was used in assembling this cutaway.

The following piece is a Steyr-made G 71/84 Short Rifle; however, the magazine lifting arm has been permanently adjusted to remain in the "up" position. The magazine cutoff has no effect upon the action whatsoever. Perhaps a training weapon?

Of compelling interest are the two special test model Mauser rifles in U.S. caliber 30-40 Krag submitted in the U.S. magazine rifle test of 1892. Model #3 had the magazine cutoff, the long non-rotary extractor, and the guide rib in the left wall of the receiver. The cutoff is a lever pivoted to the right forward portion of the trigger guard; when pivoted downward, the magazine is depressed enough that the bolt does not engage the top cartridge.

Model #5 incorporates the magazine cutoff and all of the other features; however, the cutoff on this model consists of an inner vertically moveable box magazine within a fixed outer box magazine.

Pivoting the cutoff lever downward lowers the inner box magazine, thus preventing the bolt from picking up the top cartridge.

Model #3 experienced some difficulties in the test, while Model #5 did exceptionally well, calling for further testing by the test board. In the end, the Krag-Jorgensen rifle was chosen.

The rifles are extremely close in appearance to the Belgian Model 1889 Rifle and the Spanish Model 1891 Rifle. Each rifle is fitted with a straight-wristed stock, with an extremely short upper hand guard that extends approximately six inches from the front of the base of the rear sight. There is a single lower barrel band with a swivel on the bottom, and there is another swivel on the bottom of the buttstock. A simple nose cap with bayonet lug on the bottom is fitted to the forend.

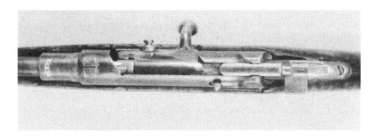

Top view of the Styer-made G71/84 Short Rifle with the action closed

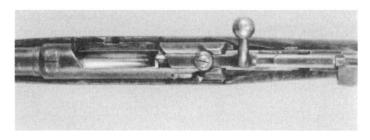

Top view of the Styer-made G71/84 Short Rifle with the action open, showing the magazine ramp in the "up" position

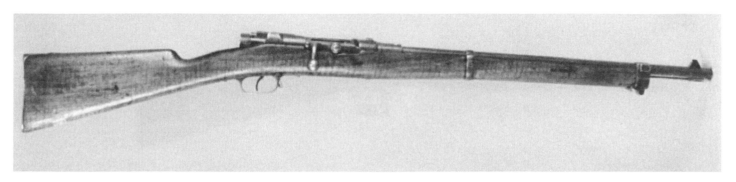

Full-length view of the Styer-made G 71/84 Short Rifle

Full-length view of special test Model #3 1892 Mauser Rifle. Note that the rear sling swivel is missing from this rifle. (Springfield Armory Museum)

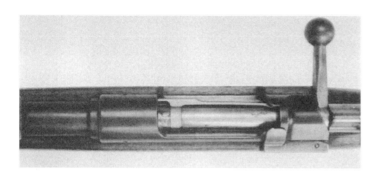

Top view of the action of the special test Model #3 1892 Mauser Rifle (Springfield Armory Museum)

Length: #3, 48.50"; #5, 48.25"; **Weight:** 8.80 lbs.; **Barrel:** 29.25"; **Caliber:** Experimental .30-40 Krag; **Rifling:** 4-groove, r/hand; **Operation:** Turnbolt action; **Feed:** 5-round, fixed vertical box magazine, with cutoff; **Sights:** V-notch adjustable rear sight graduated to 2000 meters. **Remarks:** With the exception of the serial number "641" on Model #5, neither rifle is marked in any other fashion.

A very interesting weapon is this "salesman's sample" Model 1904 Export Rifle that incorporates features presumably ordered from stock. The rifle is fitted with a pistol grip stock without grasping grooves, with the upper hand guard extending from the front of the receiver ring to the very thin lower barrel band. Note the simple, short, upper band with parade hook and the "T" shaped bayonet lug.

Length: 49.0"; **Weight:** 8.75 lbs.; **Barrel:** 28.50"; **Caliber:** 7 x 57mm; **Rifling:** 4-groove, r/hand; **Operation:** Turnbolt action; **Feed:** 5-round, staggered column, flush, box magazine; **Sights:** Tangent leaf rear sight graduated to 2000 meters. **Remarks:** This special model is marked on top of the receiver ring with the caliber, and the manufacturer's markings immediately below. There are no other markings, other than proofs and Mauser Banner on the stock.

Close-up view of the right side of the special test Model #3 1892 Mauser Rifle, showing the cutoff lever pivoted upwards (Springfield Armory Museum)

Close-up view of the right side of the special test Model #5 1892 Mauser Rifle, showing the pivoted cutoff lever in the "up" position. Note the difference in the detents of the cutoff levers between the two models. (Springfield Armory Museum)

Full-length view of the special test Model #5 1892 Mauser Rifle (Springfield Armory Museum)

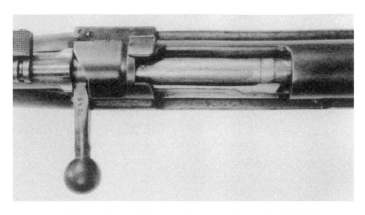

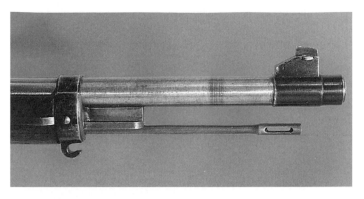

Top view of the action of the special test Model #5 1892 Mauser Rifle. Note the serial number "641" on the base of the bolt handle. (Springfield Armory Museum)

The muzzle and forend of the German Model 1904 "Salesman's Sample" Export Rifle, showing the short, simple upper band and the "T" shaped bayonet lug

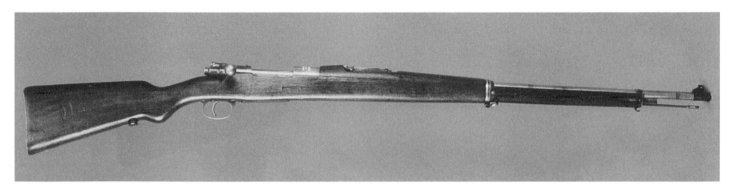

Full-length view of the German Model 1904 "Salesman's Sample" Export Rifle

Right side view of an experimental Model rifle. This Mauser Model 1892-93 Experimental Rifle was manufactured in an unknown caliber 6.5MM, and has no markings whatsoever other than the serial number. The rifle has the standard fixed magazine, without a follower stop, and the action cocks on closing. The sights are adjustable from 500 to 2000 meters. The rifle weighs 8.11 lbs., with a barrel length of 29.125" and an overall length of 49.875". (John Wall collection)

Left side view of the Model 1892-93 Experimental Rifle, with the bolt in the open position, and the rear sight extended. (John Wall collection)

Top view of the action of the German Model 1904 "Salesman's Sample" Export Rifle, showing the caliber and manufacturer's markings on top of the receiver ring

Proof and Mauser Banner logo stamped into the stock of the German Model 1904 "Salesman's Sample" Export Rifle

Developed as a means of firing a rifle from a trench without being exposed to return fire, the device below was used, to some extent, by both sides. This piece is a rare, German-developed firing device that uses a periscope as a means of aiming the rifle, while a remote firing attachment utilized a wire running from the auxiliary trigger to the trigger of the rifle. One would assume that, while not particularly accurate for generally letting off a few rounds in the direction of the enemy, zeroed in on a particular area of a trench—such as an observation slit, look-out point, or the like—it could nevertheless be deadly.

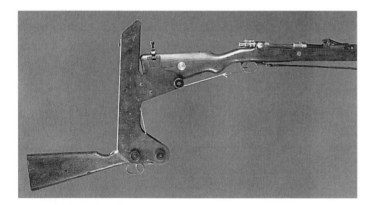

The right side of the German trench rifle-firing device as it would look when ready for use

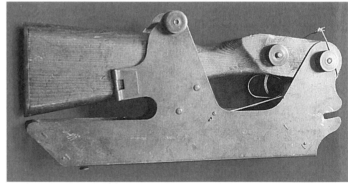

Right side view of the German trench rifle-firing device in its folded, carrying position

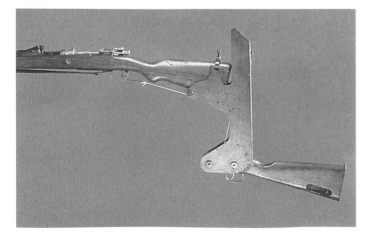

The left side of the German trench rifle-firing device

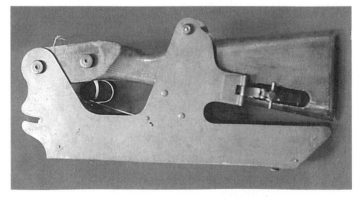

Left side view of the German trench rifle-firing device in the folded, carrying position. Note how the rifle clamping attachment is housed in the cutout on the left side of the auxiliary stock.

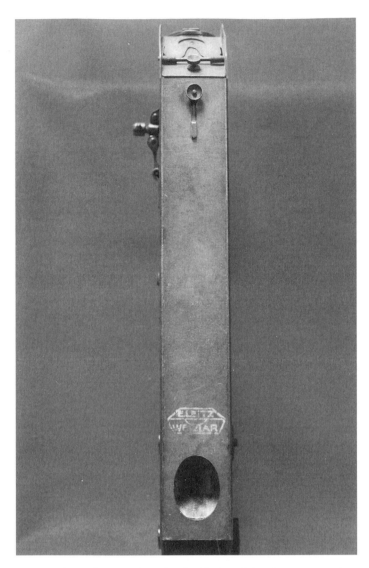

The eyepiece of the periscopic viewfinder of the German trench rifle-firing device

Undoubtedly one of the most unusual uses of a Mauser rifle is this Torpedo Boat 5cm cannon subcaliber device developed around the action of a J 71 rifle. This was used for training practice and to conserve the larger caliber ammunition. This device is fitted into the barrel of the boat's cannon by means of the ring fittings on the front and rear of the barrel, as well as by the seating of the subcaliber device into the action of the cannon.

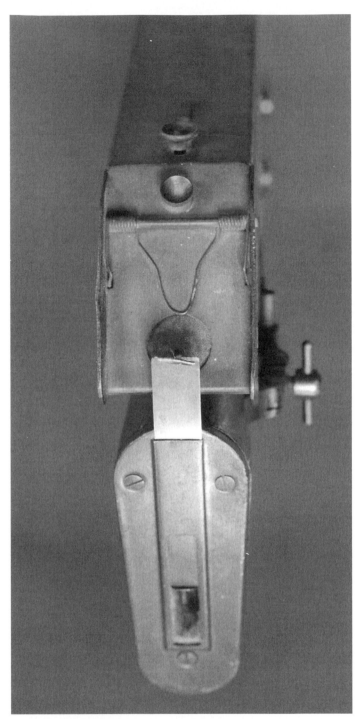

The storage trap in the butt of the auxiliary stock of the German trench rifle-firing device

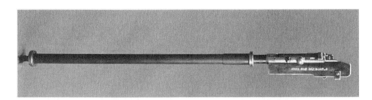

The German Torpedo Boat 5cm cannon subcaliber device

Left side view of the German Torpedo Boat 5cm subcaliber device

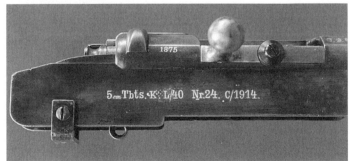

Close-up of the right side of the action and its markings on the German Torpedo Boat 5cm cannon subcaliber firing device

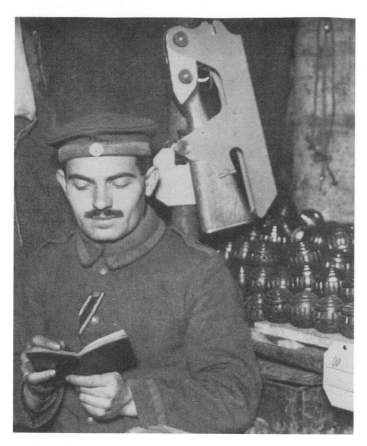

Stampings on the front fitting of the German Torpedo Boat 5cm cannon subcaliber firing device

World War I photo showing the trench device for firing the Gew 98 from within the trench using a periscope sighting device. Note the piles of grenades in the background.

The unusual piece at the top of the next page seems to have been assembled with a little bit of everything! This is basically a Model 1917 Enfield action, with a Steyr barrel, while the stock could be any one of a number of earlier-style German stocks. The weapon measures 40.75 inches overall, with a 20.0-inch long barrel, weighing in at 7.50 lbs.

A most unusual item is the below post-WW I shortened, cutaway training 98a carbine made for police use. As a training aid for new recruits, cutaway weapons that show the means of assembly and firing are invaluable.

This FN Model 30 Short Rifle is considered unusual only in respect to the markings on top of the receiver ring—crossed cannons

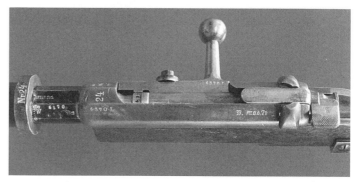

Top view of the action and markings of the German Torpedo Boat 5cm cannon subcaliber firing device

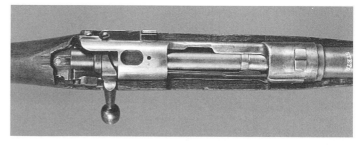

Top view of the action of the hybrid short rifle built on the action of the Model 1917 Enfield

The receiver ring of the Dutch East Indies private security force marked FN Model 1930 Carbine

on a furled anchor, which would lead one to suspect that the weapon was issued and marked to a naval artillery unit—but what unit and what country?

One of the more unusual FN Model 30 Carbines uncovered is the one which has the "IOB" markings within an almost diamond outline. The marking 'I.O.B.' stands for "Indische Ondernemers Bond," or in English, "Indies Business Union," a planter's organization. About 2,700 of these carbines were procured after World War Two, between the years 1946 to 1950, and were modified at the State Arsenal for the .308 cartridge, to be used in the then Netherlands East Indies. These carbines were fitted with a new and quite rare bayonet.

Full-length view of the hybrid short rifle built on a Model 1917 Enfield action with a Steyr barrel

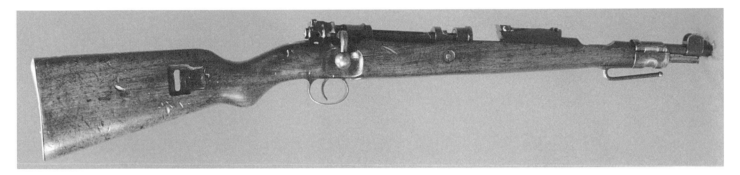

Full-length view of the German post-WW I Police 98a cutaway training carbine

Left side view of the German post-WW I Police 98a cutaway training carbine

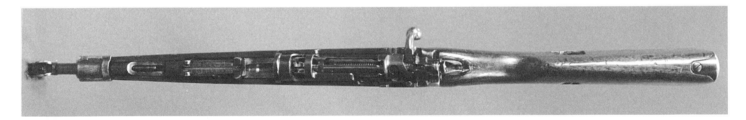

Top view of the German post-WW I Police 98a cutaway training carbine

Full-length view of the Dutch East Indies private security force marked FN Model 30 Carbine

Full-length view of the German cutaway 98k Carbine

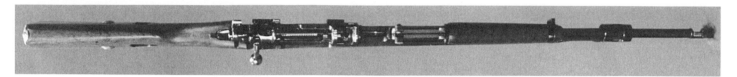

Top view of the German cutaway 98k Carbine, showing the illustrative cuts made from the muzzle to the receiver bridge

Bottom view of the German cutaway 98k Carbine, further showing the visual aid cuts to great effect

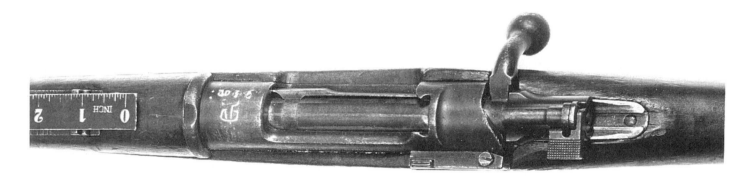

Top view of a DWM-made Model 1895 Carbine in 7.65MM as produced for some unknown Arabic nation (John Wall collection)

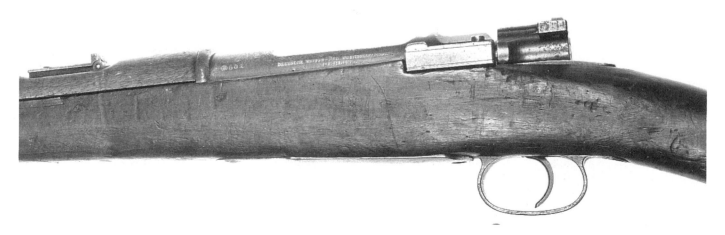

Left side view of the Model 1895 Carbine showing the DWM side rail markings as well as the serial number "601" (John Wall collection)

Full-length view of the left side of the DWM Model 1895 Carbine in caliber 7.65MM. (John Wall collection)

Full-length view of the right side of the DWM Model 1895 Carbine in caliber 7.65MM. (John Wall collection)

Developed for training recruits in the pre-WW II revived German Army, this cutaway 98k Carbine is built on a WW I double-dated action.

Not often seen is the "granddaddy" of cleaning kits, in this case, the RG-34 Lg. Anti-Tank Rifle cleaning kit. This one was originally for the Pz.B 35 (p) anti-tank rifle, but later was used for the Pz B 38 and 39, which became the Gr. B 41 (Grenade Rifle). Very few of these survived the war, so it is most unusual to find one in this condition.

The double-dated WW I G 98 receiver on the German cutaway 98k Carbine

The carrying case with all components inside (Henry Wichmann collection)

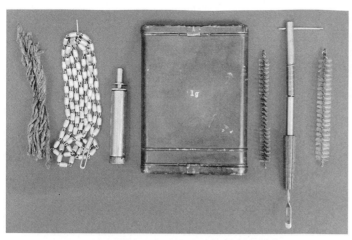

Left: The carrying case and all of its components: from left to right, a handful of "tow" that is used as a cleaning patch; the beaded chain pull-through; oiler; carrying case; barrel brush; chamber tool; and lastly, the chamber brush. (Henry Wichmann collection)

This concludes my efforts to add to and consolidate information pertinent to the world of Mauser military rifles. Undoubtedly, as this book comes off the press, there will be other collectors out there who will have unearthed yet another example of a previously undiscovered, or forgotten, foreign contract Mauser rifle, or a bit of new lore concerning a German issue weapon. One of the most fascinating aspects of collecting is trying to determine where, and in what battles, a particular weapon might have been used. You are holding a piece of history in your hands and can only plaintively wish that it could talk! That's what makes collecting in any field so enjoyable...you can never own— or even see—them all, but you continue the search and keep on hoping!

Reichswehr soldier in training with two instructors; the soldier is firing a transitional Gew 98 with the wide lower barrel band and the tangent rear sight.

WWII German soldier wearing a belt with Czech ammunition pouches and carrying a Czech VZ 24 over his right shoulder.

Reichswehr cavalry trooper (note the scalloped helmet!) on horseback, armed with a Kar 98b in a special shoe scabbard on the left rear of the horse.

Bibliography

anon. *Instruction uber das Infanterie-Gewehr M/71 und dessen Munition.* Berlin, n.p., 1878.

Atkin, Ronald. *Revolution!* New York: John Day Co., 1970.

Baer, Ludwig. *Die leichten Waffen der deutschen Armeen von 1841-1945.* Schwabisch Hall: Schwend, 1991.

Beals, Carleton. *Great Guerrilla Warriors.* Englewood, N.J.: Prentice-Hall Inc., 1970.

Blackler, Irwin R. *Irregulars, Partisans, Guerrillas.* New York: Simon and Schuster, 1954.

Boger, Jan. *Jager und Gejagte: die Geschichte der Scharfschutzen.* Stuttgart, Germany: Motorbuch, 1980.

Boudriot, Jean. *Armes a feu Francaises.* Paris: Boudriot, 1961-1971.

Bridgeman, John M. *The Revolt of the Herros.* Berkeley and Los Angeles: University of California Press, 1981.

Calvo, Juan. *Armamento Reglamentario y Auxiliar del Ejercito Espanol Libros 1-4.* Barcelona, Spain: Calvo, 1975-1981.

Chamberlin, Peter and Terry Gander. *Axis Pistols, Rifles, and Grenades.* New York: Arco Pub. Co., 1976.

Coombes, J.E. *Gew 98: German Mauser Rifle Model of 1898.* New York: Bannerman, 1921.

Datig, Fred. *D.W.M. Cartridges 1896-1956.* Beverly Hills, CA: Fadco, 1962.

English, Adrian. *Armed Forces of Latin America.* London: Jane's Pub. Co., Ltd., 1984.

Estigarribia, José Felix, Marshal of Paraguay. *The Epic of the Chaco.* New York: Greenwood Press, Pubs., 1969.

Federoff, Basil. *Dictionary of Explosives, Ammunition and Weapons (German section): Picatinny Arsenal Technical Report No. 2510.* Dover, DE: Picatinny, 1958.

Fischer, Karl. *Waffen und Schiesstechniescher Leitfaden f. d. Ordungspolizei.* Berlin: Eisenschmidt, 1944.

Gazette Des Armes (journal). *Paul Mauser et ses Armes. Numero Special no. 7.* Paris: Gazette des Armes, 1978.

Germany. Army. *Oberkommando des Herres. Heereswaffenamt Wa Z 2 Liste der Fertigungskemnzeichen fur Waffen, Munition und Gerat.* Berlin: I.K.H./Wa Z2, 1944.
Gotz, Hans Dieter. *Deutschen Militargewehr und Maschinenpistolen 1871-1945.* Stuttgart, Germany: Motorbuch, 1974.

Gotz, Hans Dieter. *German Military Rifles and Machine Pistols, 1871-1945.* Atglen, PA: Schiffer Pub. Ltd., 1990.

Great Britain. War Office. General Staff. *Textbook of Small Arms.* London: H.M.S.O., 1929.

Great Britain. War Office. General Staff. *Handbook of the German Army in War, January 1917.* London: H.M.S.O., 1917.

Great Britain. War Office. General Staff. British Intelligence Objectives Sub-Committee. *German S.A.A. Factories.* London: H.M.S.O., 1945.

Great Britain. War Office. General Staff. Combined Intelligence Objectives Sub-Committee. *German Tracer Compositions.* London: H.M.S.O., 1945.

Gumucio, Mariano Baptista. *Historia Grafica de la Guerra del Chaco*, 4th ed. La Paz, Bolivia: Ulitma Hora.

Gutierrez, Alberto Ostria. *The Tragedy of Bolivia.* New York: Devin-Adair Co., 1958.

Hahn, Fritz. *Waffen und Geheimwaffen des Deutschen Heeres 1933-45. Bde, 1-2.* Koblenz, Germany: Bernard & Graefe, 1986/1987.

Hatcher, Julian S. *Hatcher's Notebook.* Harrisburg, PA: Stackpole, 1947.

Heinrich, Dieter. *Die Ausstellungen der Wehrtechnischen Studiensammlung des Bundesamtes fur Wehrtecnik und Beschaffung, Teil 1. Die Technische Entwicklung der Handfeuerwaffen. Band 1, Die Handfeuerwaffen von ihrem ersten Aufkommen bis zu den Repetierwaffen (1985).* Herford: Mittler.

Hoffman, R.A. and Noel P. Schott. *Handbook of Military Rifle Marks, 1870-1950.*

Hoffschmidt, E.J. *Know your Anti-Tank Rifles.* Stamford, CT: Blacksmith, 1977.

Hogg, Ian, and John Weeks. *Military Small Arms of the Twentieth Century.* Chicago: Follett Pub. Co., 1973.

Hoyt, Edward P. *Guerrilla.* New York: MacMillan Pub. Co., 1981.

Huges, James B. Jr. *Mexican Military Arms, The Cartridge Period, 1866-1967*. Houston: Deep River Armory, 1968.

Johnson, George and Hans Lockhoven. *International Armament*, Vol. I, 1st Ed. Cologne, Germany: International Small Arms Pubs., 1965.

Johnson, George B. *International Armament*. Koln, Germany: International Small Arms Publishers, 1965.

Kent, Daniel W. *German 7.9mm Military Ammunition 1888-1945*. Ann Arbor, MI: Edwards, 1990.

Knotel, Knotel and Sieg. *Uniforms of the World*. New York: Chas. Scribner's Sons, 1980.

Kohn, George C. *Dictionary of Wars*. Garden City, NY: Anchor Press/Doubleday, 1987.

Korn, R.H. *Mauser-Gewehre und Mauser-Patente*. Berlin: Eckstein, 1908.

Lamb, Dean Ivan. *The Incurable Filibuster*. New York: Farrar and Rinehart, 1934.

Law, Richard D. *Backbone of the Wehrmacht: The German K98k Rifle 1934-1945*. Cobourg, Germany: Collector Grade Publications, 1996.

Lieberson, Goddard, prod. *The Irish Uprising, 1916-1922*. CBS Legacy Collection, 1966.

McFarland, Philip. *World's Guns and Other Weapons*. Pasadena, CA: Golden State Arms, Inc., 1958.

von Menges. *Bewaffnung d. Preussischen Fusstruppen mit Gewehren (Buchsen) von 1809 bis zur Gegenwart*. Oldenburg, Germany: Stalling, 1913.

Morawietz, Otto. *Handfeuerwaffen d. Brandenburgisch-Preussisch-Deutschen Heeres, 1640-1945*. Hamburg, Germany: Schultz, 1973.

Morawietz, Otto. *Beitrage zur Geschichte und Technik der handwaffen und Maschinengewehre*. Osnabruck, Germany: Biblio, 1973.

Myatt, Frederick. *Modern Small Arms*. New York: Crescent Books, 1978.

Olson, Ludwig. *Mauser Bolt Rifles*, 3rd ed. Montezuma, IA: F. Brownell & Son, Pubs., 1976.

von Pflougk-Hartung, J., ed. *Heere und Flotten der Gegenwart*. Bd. 1. Deutschland. Berlin: Schall & Grund, 1896.

Pietsch, Paul. *Formations- und Uniformierungsgeschichte des Preussischen Heeres 1808-1914*. Hamburg, Germany: Schultz, 1963.

Preussen. Kriegsministerium. *Das Konigl. Preussische Kriegministerium 1809-1909*. Berlin: Kommissions-Vlg., 1909.

Reitz, Deneys. *Commando*. New York: Praeger Publishers, 1970.

Robinson, Donald, ed. *The Dirty Wars*. New York: Delacorte Press, 1968.

Schroeder, Joseph J. *Gun Collector's Digest*, 3rd ed. Northfield, IL: DBI Books, 1981.

Schwing, Ned and Herbert Houze. *Standard Catalog of Firearms*, 3rd ed. Iola, WI: Krause Publications, 1993.

Seel, Wolfgang. *Bibliography of the Technology and History of Small Arms and Machine Guns: Part. 1: Periodical Literature in the German Language from 1755-1975*. Schwabisch Hall, Germany: Schwend, 1978.

Seel, Wolfgang. *Mauser: von der Waffenschmiede zum Weltunternehmen*. Zurich: Stocker-Schmidt, 1986.

Senich, Peter. *German Sniper*. Wickenburg, Germany: Normount, 1975.

Senich, Peter R. *The German Sniper 1914-1945*. Boulder, CO: Paladin, 1982.

Smith, W.H.B. *Book of Rifles*. Harrisburg, PA: Stackpole, 1963.

Smith, W.H.B. *Mauser Rifles and Pistols*. Harrisburg, PA: Stackpole, 1946.

Smith, W.H.B. *Small Arms of the World*. Harrisburg, PA: Stackpole, 1969.

Smith, W.H.B. *Small Arms of the World*, 9th ed. Harrisburg, PA: Stackpole Books, 1969.

Tanner, Hans, ed. *Guns of the World*. New York: Bonanza Books, 1977.

Thord-Gray, I. *Gringo Rebel*. University of Miami Press, 1961.

U.S. Army. John F. Kennedy Center for Special Warfare (Airborne). *U.S. Army Special Forces Foreign Weapons Handbook*. Fort Bragg, NC: O.A. C. of S., G2, 1967.

U.S. Army. Ordnance School, Aberdeen, Maryland. *Rifles*. Aberdeen, MD: U.S.A.O.S., 1958.
Walter, John. *German Rifle . . . 1871-1945*. London: Arms & Armour, 1979.

Walter, John. *The German Rifle*. ON, Canada: Fortress Pubs., 1979.

Walter, John. *Rifles of the World*. Northbrook, IL: DBI Books, 1993.

Webster, Donald B. *Military Bolt Action Rifles*. Alexandria Bay, NY and Bloomfield, ON, Canada: Museum Restoration Service, 1993.

Weidler, Franz W. *Deutscher Volkssturm: das letzte Aufgebot 1944/45*. Munchen, Germany: Herbig, 1989.

Wille, R. *Waffenlehre*. Berlin: Eisenschmidt, 1896.

Wirtgen, Rolf. *Die Sammlungen des Wehrgeschichtlichen Museums im Schloss Rastatt. 2. Handfeuerwaffen. Teil I. Die Historische-technische Entwicklung*. Koblenz, Germany; Bundesamt fur Wehrtechnik und Beschaffung, 1980.

Wright, John W., ed. *The Universal Alamanac, 1995*. Kansas City: Andrews and McMeel, 1994.

Zook, David H., Jr. *The Conduct of the Chaco War*. New York: Bookman Associates, 1960.

JOURNALS

Karabiner Collector Network

Pawlas, Karl R. *Das 13mm Tankgewehr von Mauser*. Waffen Revue, Nrn. 82 and 83.

Pawlas, Karl R. *Die Waffen des Deutschen Volkssturms*. T.1-6. Waffen Revue Nrn. 71-77.

Stegmuller, Manfred. *Cartridges of the Mauser Anti-Tank Rifle of 1918 and of the TU.F. M.G. made by M.A.N*. Cartridges, no. 342, July/August 1988.

SERIALS

Deutsches Soldaten Kalendarjahrbuch

Deutsches Waffen-Journal

Feldgrau

Gun Collectors Digest

International Arms Review

International Cartridge Collector

Kaiserzeit

Militaria

Militaria Collector

Spontoon

Waffen Revue

Zeitschrift Fuer Heereskunde

Zeitschrift Fuer Heeres- Und Uniformenkunde

Zeitschrift Fuer Historische Waffenkunde

Zeitschrift Fuer Historische Waffen- Und Kostumkunde

ADD THESE GREAT BOOKS TO YOUR LIBRARY

Standard Catalog of U.S. Military Vehicles 1940-65
by Tom Berndt
Tom Berndt gives in-depth profiles of 281 models manufactured from 1940-1965 and delivers accurate historical, technical and pricing information to you about collectible U.S. military vehicles.
Hardcover • 8-1/2 x 11 • 272 pages
400 b&w photos
MV01 • $29.95

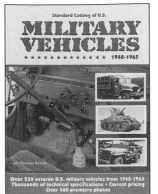

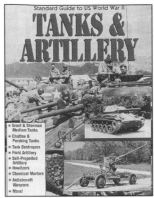

Standard Guide to U.S. World War II Tanks & Artillery
by Konrad Schreier, Jr.
Step inside World War II machines — from tanks, half-tracks and armored cars to field artillery, ammunition and antiaircraft weapons! Konrad Schreier Jr. describes the production of World War II tanks and artillery.
Softcover • 8-1/2 x 11 • 256 pages
250+ b&w photos
GT01 • $24.95

Law Enforcement Memorabilia
Price and Identification Guide
by Monty McCord
A wide-range of items are covered from miniature vehicles to clothes, patches, and restraints. You will learn how to evaluate and expand your collection with confidence. This book contains the most comprehensive collection of badges available, and is sure to set the standard for this collectible field.
Softcover • 8-1/2 x 11 • 192 pages
550 b&w photos • 16-page color section
SCLE • $19.95

Old Gunsights: A Collectors Guide, 1850 to 1965
by Nicholas Stroebel
This unique book offers an in-depth and comprehensive examination of old gunsights and the rifles they were used on from 1850 to 1965, and features 400 photos and hundreds of market prices, covering all major American manufacturers and some foreign.
Softcover • 8-1/2 x 11 • 320 pages
400 b&w photos
OLGU • $29.95

Collector's Guide to British Army Campaign Medals
by Robert W.D. Ball
Here's a complete reference that will appeal to collectors of militaria, or anyone interested in world or military history. Fascinating glimpses of the British Empire unfold in this detailed study of medals awarded to British Army troops over more than two centuries. Covers military battles and campaigns waged from 1791 through the Gulf War.
Hardcover • 8-1/2 x 11 • 160 pages
100 b&w photos • 200 color photos
AT5641 • $29.95

American Military Collectibles Price Guide
by Ron Manion
From the Civil War to the Gulf War, this first-of-its-kind price guide to American Military collectibles covers it all. Over 5,800 items from insignia and uniforms to edged weapons and medals are described in detail and accurately priced.
Softcover • 6 x 9 • 288 pages
330 b&w photos
AT5471 • $16.95

German Military Collectibles Price Guide
by Ron Manion
This comprehensive reference guide covers a full range of militaria from the Kaiser to Nazi Germany. It prices daggers, swords, side arms, medals and all insignia from the German military over the past 150 years.
Softcover • 6 x 9 • 316 pages
500 b&w photos
AT5447 • $16.95

Japanese & Other Foreign Military Collectibles Price Guide
by Ron Manion
Thousands of entries for a wide range of militaria associated with the nations of the world. Includes medals, uniforms and insignia from Japan, Vietnam, Italy, Russia, and more. Detailed descriptions with current prices.
Softcover • 6 x 9 • 248 pages
450 b&w photos
AT5439 • $16.95

For a FREE catalog or to place a credit card order
Call **800-258-0929** ☐ **Dept. GNBR**

M-F, 7 am - 8 pm • Sat, 8 am - 2 pm, CST
Krause Publications, 700 E State St, Iola, WI 54990
www.krausebooks.com
Dealers call toll-free 888-457-2873 ext 880, M-F, 8 am - 5 pm

Shipping and Handling: $3.25 1st book; $2 ea. add'l. Call for UPS rates. Foreign orders $15 per shipment plus $5.95 per book.

Sales tax: CA 7.25%, IA 6.00%, IL 6.25%, PA 6.00%, TN 8.25%, VA 4.50%, WA 8.20%, WI 5.50%.

Satisfaction Guarantee: If for any reason you are not completely satisfied with your purchase, simply return it within 14 days and receive a full refund, less shipping.

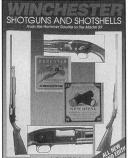

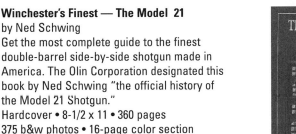

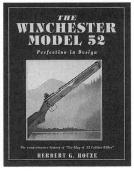
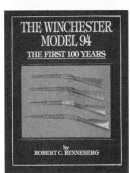